Louis Gustafson

S0-ABT-852

½ B$⊥395

PUBLIC RELATIONS:

Concepts and Practice

pp. 231 - 301

GRID SERIES IN ADVERTISING AND JOURNALISM

Consulting Editors
ARNOLD M. BARBAN, University of Illinois
DONALD W. JUGENHEIMER, University of Kansas

Barban, Jugenheimer & Young, *Advertising Media Sourcebook And Workbook*
Behrens, *Magazine Writer's Workbook*
Behrens, *Reporter's Worktext*
Burton, *Advertising Copywriting*
Burton & Miller, *Advertising Fundamentals, 2nd Edition*
Francois, *Beginning News Writing: A Programmed Text*
Francois, *Mass Media Law and Regulation*
Michman & Jugenheimer, *Strategic Advertising Decisions*
Quera, *Advertising Campaigns: Formulation And Tactics*
Rotzoll, Haefner & Sandage, *Advertising In Contemporary Society*
Simon, *Casebook In Publicity & Public Relations*
Simon, *Public Relations Management: Cases & Simulations*
Simon, *Public Relations: Concepts and Practice*

PUBLIC RELATIONS:

Concepts and Practice

Raymond Simon

Professor of Public Relations
Utica College of Syracuse University
Utica, New York

© COPYRIGHT GRID, INC. 1976
4666 Indianaola Avenue
Columbus, Ohio

ALL RIGHTS RESERVED. No part of this publication may be reproduced, stored in a retrieval system, or transmitted, in any form or by any means, electronic, mechanical, photocopying, recording or otherwise, without prior written permission of the copyright holder.

Printed in the United States.

I.S.B.N. No. 0-88244-107-8
Library of Congress Catalog Card Number 75-41599

Printing 10 9 8 7 6 5 4

*This book was edited by Jane C. Foss; stylized by Elaine Clatterbuck.
Cover design and production coordinator, Gini Baldi.*

For Melissa and Karen With Love and Affection

TABLE OF CONTENTS

PREFACE

Authors and publishers are often tempted to claim for their books a multitude of purposes to make them adaptable in more than one course in the college curriculum. No such claim is being made about this book.

This text has been written to serve one purpose: to be a useful tool for both teacher and student in the one-semester, introductory course in public relations. It is not a handbook nor a history and does not aim to set forth innumerable writing, editing, and graphic rules.

What I have tried to do is to deal *in depth* with the nature of public relations, its role in American society, the practitioners who manage the function, and the dynamics of the public relations process. It seems to me that the basic public relations course should explore in detail the essential nature and characteristics of the field, the practice, and the concept of public relations.

The book sets forth these essential parameters of the field and the practice within four major sections. Part 1 provides an overview of public relations as it relates to American society; Part 2 explains how the public relations function is managed; Part 3, the core of the book, deals in depth with the dynamics of public relations; and Part 4 is concerned with careers, ethics, and professionalism.

Although public relations is most widely known for the way it is practiced in business and industry, thousands of practitioners work in the field in government, social agencies, hospitals, colleges, and the armed forces. For this reason, this book does not restrict its scope merely to business and industry but rather to public relations in its broadest sense. In dealing with public opinion, research, planning and programming, communication and feedback, I have developed the text material as applied to all public relations practice. It's my belief that by thus dealing in depth with the basics of public relations, this text will best serve the needs of those taking and those teaching a one-semester course in public relations.

Because this book is intended as a tool for student and teacher, I have interspersed throughout the text a wide variety of mini-cases, mini-examples, mini-situations, and mini-problems. These "minis," as I've termed them, are meant to serve as practical illustrations of text material and to raise realistic questions and assignments for students to answer. They bring students face-to-face with reality, as students come to grips with examples, situations, and problems that demand their active participation in the learning and teaching experience. In coming to grips with these "minis," students are asked to utilize their verbal and writing abilities, to sharpen their perceptions and communication skills, and to form judgments and propose actions.

Likening this text-tool to a hammer and nails, the text material deals with the composition, scope, and make-up of the hammer (public relations), and the "minis" give students the opportunity to develop their skills to hammer home a wide variety of nails. The nails — or public relations cases, examples, and situations — are not perfect and the materials into which they are driven are of different compositions. Just as there are no immutable rules for using a hammer to drive a nail into a surface, so there are no immutable rules for using the text material to "solve" the mini-cases. It is my hope that the text material and the "minis" will provide a learning-teaching experience that will enable students to develop the skills, perceptions, and judgments needed to succeed in public relations practice.

I am deeply indebted and wish to express my appreciation to the following people for making this book possible: to my wife Lyn and our daughters Melissa and Karen for their patience and encouragement; Ruth Rogers, Rose Palczynski and Kim Landon for typing the manuscript; Ray Hiebert for granting permission to use some of the accreditation study guide material we co-authored for the Public Relations Society of America; Larry Baker, Don Jugenheimer, Arnold Barban, Jane Foss, and Nils Anderson for editorial review and suggestions; and those former students and practitioners who graciously granted me permission to use the raw material which made up the mini-cases, examples, situations, and problems.

Raymond Simon

Utica, New York
February, 1976

PART I
PUBLIC RELATIONS AND THE
AMERICAN SCENE

This introductory section, consisting of three chapters, provides a perspective for viewing the essential nature of public relations and its role in American society.

In order to understand public relations, one must first understand the term itself and the concept. Chapter 1 examines various definitions of public relations; differences between the term and activities that are frequently confused with the term; and questions which arise as a result of assessing alternatives posed by acceptance of the term.

The overview of public relations provided in the first chapter leads to Chapter 2 and its examination of the reasons why public relations exists in American society. Set forth in this chapter are major trends that have brought about the need for public relations and have affected the way in which public relations is practiced.

The increasing concern with the concept known as "social responsibility" and with the idea of "the public interest" is explored in depth in Chapter 3. Differing schools of thought about these two major areas and their connection with public relations practice are presented for discussion and analysis, and questions are raised to induce thought and insight about the kind of problems faced by the practitioner in everyday practice.

PUBLIC RELATIONS: AN OVERVIEW

Water, sunshine, public relations, and pornography are four widely disparate entities with one element in common when viewed by the general public. As a Supreme Court justice so cogently described pornography: "I can't define it, but I know it when I see it." Similarly, though most people can't define water, sunshine, and public relations, they believe they know it when they see it.

Using such a "know-it-when-I-see-it" guideline to pornography caused the Supreme Court more than a decade of problems in dealing with the issue of obscenity. Those who intend to deal rationally with public relations ought first to come to grips with a sound definition of the term and the concept if they hope to avoid the trap into which the Supreme Court fell in trying to cope with pornography. The "I-know-it-when-I-see-it" approach to public relations has led people to conclude that advertising and public relations are synonymous; to view public relations as an adjective or adverb instead of a noun; to see the activity solely in negative terms, and in general to draw unfounded conclusions about the concept and practice of public relations.

The problem of understanding the real nature of public relations practice is compounded by the fact that anyone can open an office and call himself or herself a public relations counselor. The problem of understanding the real nature of public relations is compounded by the fact that when the term is cited in books, magazines, and the daily press it is often used in a pejorative sense. Without bothering to explain its meaning, writers tend to use it as a code word synonymous with cover-up, deceit, propaganda, and falsehood.

The general misunderstanding about public relations has been a constant source of concern to public relations practitioners. They are fully aware that the term has been widely misused, and the concept is not clearly understood. Most public relations professionals feel there is little or nothing that can be done about the situation; an increasing number of them — as noted in the following item from the June 25, 1973, issue of *PR Reporter*, weekly public relations newsletter — are seeking a name change:

> More and more companies are discarding the term "public relations" and substituting "public affairs," "communications," "public information" or other unblemished designations for the corporate executive in charge of PR. This is largely because there is a stigma attached to "public relations," partly as the result of the term's sometimes deliberately improper use in

newspapers and magazine columns and by individuals in the news who employ the designation as a shield or a catchall term . . . or because they don't know any better.

MINI-SURVEY
PUBLIC RELATIONS AS SEEN BY YOUR PEERS

Although college students are not considered to be representative of the general population, they are usually frank and open about their views and opinions of the society in which they live. They may not always be as well informed as they profess, but their responses to questions will usually be an honest reflection of their knowledge and insight (or lack of each).

To ascertain, therefore, what kind of knowledge and insight your colleagues have of public relations, each member of the class should ask this question of seven students who are majoring in disciplines other than public relations: "How would you define public relations?"

Each member of the class should bring to the next class session a typed report of the responses given by the seven students he or she has interviewed. Do not use the names of the respondents, but do indicate respondents' sex and class. Your report should include your summation, analysis, and reaction to the responses.

After your reports have been turned in, your instructor may want to have a class discussion centered on the following questions:

1. What seems to be the general view of public relations as shown by the responses?
2. What basic themes or threads seem to run through most of the responses?
3. Do you agree or disagree with the views expressed by the majority of the responses? Why?
4. Why do you think your colleagues in other disciplines perceive public relations as they do?
5. What conclusions do you draw from this mini-survey?

Unlike Shakespeare's Juliet, some public relations practitioners seem to believe that the rose would smell sweeter if it were called by another name. Whatever we do name the process, though, we must recognize that the proper way to commence a study of public relations is to understand the term, the concept, and the activity known as public relations.

PUBLIC RELATIONS DEFINED

Two decades ago a commonly accepted definition of public relations ran something like this:

"Doing good and telling people about it."

Twenty years later, in an increasingly complex world, we have learned this definition could just as well apply to show-and-tell in the first grade. The literature of the field now bears witness to a more thoughtful analysis of the term. In considering the following definitions, keep in mind similarities and differences; do not attempt to memorize the definitions in their entirety, but rather sort out recurring ideas and phrases and come to an understanding of public relations as a *process* and *function*.

"Public relations," state Cutlip and Center in their fourth edition of *Effective Public Relations*, "is the planned effort to influence opinion through socially responsible and acceptable performance, based on mutually satisfactory two-way communication."

The above definition sees the process as a *planned effort* — leaving open to conjecture who is responsible for carrying out the activity — which utilizes two-way *communication* and *performance* to bring about the end result of *influencing opinion*. Important adjectives used to describe performance are "socially responsible and acceptable," and the implication here is that the public is the judge and jury in deciding when performance meets the standards of social responsibility and acceptability.

In its threefold definition of the term, the third edition of *Webster's New International Dictionary* described public relations as:

The promotion of rapport and goodwill between a person, firm, or institution and other persons, special publics, or the community at large through the distribution of interpretative material, the development of neighborly interchange, and the assessment of public reaction.

The degree of understanding and good will achieved between an individual, organization, or institution and the public.

The art or science of developing reciprocal understanding and goodwill; the professional staff entrusted with this task.

The author of Webster's definition of public relations visualizes first the end result sought — *the promotion of rapport and goodwill* — and sees the parties involved as being a person, firm, or institution on the one hand and various publics on the other hand. Linkage between the two groups is achieved in three ways: through the distribution of *interpretative material*, the development of *neighborly interchange* — denoting a seeming nostalgia for backyard over-the-fence conversation — and the *assessment of public reaction*. Reference to public relations as an art *or* science is indicative of widespread debate whether there is a scientific base to the activity or whether the practice is a craft. Unlike Cutlip and Center, *Webster's* makes no mention of socially responsible and acceptable performance. Both definitions are silent regarding responsibility for carrying out the public relations function within an organization.

One of the earliest definitions of public relations was developed by the *Public Relations News*, pioneer weekly public relations newsletter, and has stood the test of time as well as changes in the field. John Marston, author of *The Nature of Public Relations*, added two words — "and communication" — to the *Public Relations News* definition and they are cited in brackets in the statement below:

> Public relations is the management function which evaluates public attitudes, identifies the policies and procedures of an organization with the public interest, and executes a program of action (and communication) to earn public understanding and acceptance.

Perceptive readers will note the following about the above definition:

1. It places responsibility for the public relations function upon the shoulders of management. The term "management" is used broadly, is meant to cover all managements, not merely business managements, and applies to nonprofit as well as profit-making institutions and organizations.

2. Function and process are tied together in an orderly procedure, and the end result is a definition that provides a step-by-step analysis of public relations in action:

   Step 1: Evaluation of public attitudes

   Step 2: Identification of policies and procedures of an organization with the public interest

   Step 3: Execution of an action and communication program to bring about public understanding and acceptance

In graphic form, the public relations process described above looks like this:

Management and Policies

(Identification with public interest)

Communicating public opinion

Communicating company actions and policies

Evaluating public attitudes

Goodwill and understanding

Publics and public interest

Implicit in the definition and the chart is an approach to public relations as a continuous process. The function is carried out by evaluating public attitudes and communicating public opinion to top management. Policies and procedures are measured against these public attitudes and opinions, and when necessary these policies and procedures may well have to be changed or modified if they do not meet the public interest. Those responsible for the public relations function then communicate the organization's actions and policies to its publics to bring about goodwill and understanding.

A SUMMATION

Though they may differ in their emphasis on certain elements, the three definitions previously cited have a good deal in common. Public relations, as seen in these definitions, involves the following elements:

1. A planned effort or management function
2. The relationship between an organization and its publics
3. Evaluation of public attitudes and opinions
4. An organization's policies, procedures, and actions as they relate to said organization's publics
5. Steps taken to ensure that said policies, procedures, and actions are in the public interest and socially responsible.
6. Execution of an action and/or communication program
7. Development of rapport, goodwill, understanding, and acceptance as the chief end result sought by public relations activities

Implied in the definitions is the understanding that public relations is a dynamic, continuing *process*, but seldom the neat and orderly one described in the definitions. Those who maintain that public relations is an art and not a science point out that public relations activities and programs do not take place in the controlled situation of the laboratory. Rather, they occur in real life situations amidst constantly changing variables.

A simple example will demonstrate why the dynamics of a situation make it difficult if not impossible to bring about a cause-and-effect laboratory relationship in public relations programming. Practitioner A drafts a carefully prepared message which aims to calm public fears about a shortage in the products of A's organization. The practitioner sends the message to the media in the form of a press release. The day the release is to appear an earthquake occurs, hundreds are killed, and millions of dollars of property lost. The story of the earthquake makes page one news, and the release is lost in the back pages. Natural disasters not only bury people and property, but all other news as well.

Countless other examples abound to prove the point that the best laid (public relations) plans "gang aft a-gley," as Robert Burns noted more than 200 years ago. Within any organization internal in-fighting can often sidetrack sound public relations proposals. Although few nonlegal and nonfinancial personnel would dare to argue the merits of advice and proposals set forth by legal and financial departments, a great many nonpublic relations personnel have little hesitation to contest advice and proposals set forth by public relations departments. Numerous variables outside the purview of public relations practitioners work to scuttle and mitigate programs which are sound in concept, but which fail in execution for reasons beyond the control of the practitioners. Competition for public attention is fierce, and messages aimed at the public often get detoured down unexpected byways. Only the most skillful are able to get their story across in a form and manner to bring about the desired public understanding, goodwill, and acceptance. Achieving desired public relations skills calls for a clear understanding of the fundamental component parts which comprise the public relations process and function. Such an understanding can be brought about in two ways: by recognizing the difference between public relations and terms sometimes mistakenly associated with it, and by raising questions about some of the essential elements of the process of public relations too often taken for granted. The sections that follow will come to grips with both these areas.

TERMS CONFUSED WITH PUBLIC RELATIONS

Because it is a relatively new concept when compared with some functions that have been on the scene much longer, public relations is most often confused with *advertising; sales, marketing, and product promotion; press agentry and publicity*. Public relations, as previously defined in this chapter, at times involves each of the aforementioned areas of activity, but is more than the individual parts.

Advertising is concerned chiefly with the sale of products and/or services and involves the use of paid media space or air time. Advertising may be used in the communications phase of the public relations process, but used not to sell an organization's product, but to bring about understanding of the organization as an entity. Such advertising is most commonly called "public service" or "institutional" advertising and may be run concurrently with product advertising or by itself. Advertising, when used for public relations purposes, aims to "sell" — using the term in its most direct form — an organization; to communicate specific aspects of an organization's activities; or to deliver, intact as written, special messages that aim to bring about clear understanding by the public.

MINI-CASE
BYOIR AND THE A&P (A)

When the Great Atlantic and Pacific Tea Company (the A&P) was threatened by national legislation aimed at breaking up and divorcing the company's retail outlets from its manufacturing and distribution operations, the company turned to Carl Byoir and Associates, its public relations counsel, for assistance in meeting the governmental challenge. A wide variety of approaches were available to meet the threat to the company, but the Byoir organization decided to rely chiefly on institutional advertising.

With as much care as though they were writing a literary masterpiece, the Byoir people prepared a series of full-page institutional advertisements, each one aimed directly at the vast American public. The messages stated that government bureaucrats were trying to destroy "your" A&P; cited the A&P's long service to the buying public, and suggested that readers support the A&P by rallying to its support because to do so was in the public's interest. Cost of the advertising campaign, which ran to hundreds of thousands of dollars, was covered by replacing the usual A&P full-page product advertisements with the institutional advertisements every second week for a period of weeks. The end results were a series of endorsements of the A&P's position by a wide variety of national organizations, an outpouring of favorable letters from the general public, and the dropping of the threat to break up the company's manufacturing, distributing, and selling operations.

Whereas advertising and public relations practitioners at times find themselves in an internal organizational conflict, in the A&P antitrust case the division of responsibility was clearly established to avoid such conflict. The Byoir people, considered to be skilled in communicating institutional messages, were given responsibility for conceiving and writing the advertisements. Preparing the graphics and placement of the advertisements in the media became the responsibility of the advertising men.

MINI-CASE
BYOIR AND THE A&P (B)

Note: A helpful way to sharpen public relations perceptions is to relate with insight to examples of public relations in action. Cited in its entirety is the first full-page advertisement prepared by the Byoir organization for its client the A&P and carried in more than 1,000 daily newspapers across the United States in place of the usual full-page A&P product advertisement. Analyze and discuss the advertisement in regard to its basic theme, tone, writing style, content, editorial approach, probable reader reaction, and overall public relations effectiveness. (The ad appears on the following page.)

Do You Want Your A&P Put Out Of Business?

Last Thursday in New York, the anti-trust lawyers from Washington filed a suit to put A&P out of business.

They asked the court to order us to get rid of most of our stores and also the manufacturing facilities which supply you with A&P coffee, Ann Page products, Jane Parker baked goods, and other quality items we produce.

This would mean higher food prices for you. It would mean less food on every dinner table and fewer dollars in every pay envelope.

It would mean the end of A&P as you know it.

This poses a basic question for the American people: Do they want to continue to enjoy lower prices and better living? Or do they want to break up A&P and pay higher prices, and have lower living standards?

What do *you* want?

Why Destroy A&P?

This suit was brought under the anti-trust laws. These are good laws. They were passed about fifty years ago to prevent any company, or any group of companies, from getting a monopoly in a field and then raising prices to the public.

A&P has never done any of these things.

Nobody has ever shown that we have anything even approaching a monopoly of the food business anywhere. As every housewife knows, the retail grocery business is the most competitive in the country and we do only a small part of it.

Nobody has ever said we charged too high prices — just the opposite. This whole attack rises out of the fact that we sell good food too cheap. We would not have had any of this trouble if, instead of lowering prices, we had raised them and pocketed the difference.

Nobody has ever said that our profit rate was too high. During the past five years our net profit, after taxes, has averaged about 1¼¢ on every dollar of sales, which is less than almost any other business you can think of.

The American people have shown that they like our low-price policy by coming to our stores to do their shopping. If A&P is big, it is because the American people, by their patronage, have made it big.

Obviously, it is the theory of the anti-trust lawyers that the people have no right to patronize a company, if their patronage will make that company grow; and that any big business must be destroyed simply because it is big, and even if the public gets hurt in the process.

Do You Want Higher Prices?

There is much more involved in this case than the future of A&P. The entire American system of efficient, low-cost, low-profit distribution which we pioneered, will face destruction and the public will suffer.

A&P was the first chain store in this country. For more than ninety years we have tried to build a sound business on the simple formula the founder gave us: "Give the people the most good food you can for their money." Year after year we have tried to do a better job, make our business more efficient, and pass the savings on to the consumer in the form of lower prices.

Our efforts along these lines have led other grocers to keep their costs and profits down.

In the old days before A&P, food that cost the grocer 50¢, often sold as high as $1.00 at retail.

Today, food that costs the grocer 50¢ generally sells to the public at less than 60¢.

The methods we pioneered have been adopted not only by other grocers, but by merchants in other lines. There are today literally hundreds of chain stores, voluntary groups and individual merchants operating with the same methods and in the same pattern here under attack.

If the anti-trust lawyers succeed in destroying A&P, the way will be clear for the destruction of every other efficient large-scale distributor.

Who Will Be Hurt?

There has never been any question in our mind that it is good business and good citizenship to sell good food as cheaply as possible. As Fortune Magazine said about A&P some time ago, "It is firmly attached to the one great principle — the selling of more for less — that has made the desert bloom and the nation wax great."

We sincerely believe that we have helped the American people eat better and live better.

We believe that the hundreds of thousands of farmers and manufacturers who have voluntarily sought our business have profited by our fast, low-cost distribution of their products.

We know that our 110,000 loyal employees enjoy today, as they always have, the highest wages, shortest hours and best working conditions generally prevailing in the retail food industry; and that these men and women have found in A&P good opportunities for security and progress.

We know that thousands of businessmen — the landlords who rent us our stores, the haulers who operate our trucks, the people who supply us with goods and services — have a big stake in our operations.

Obviously, all these people will suffer if this company is put out of business.

What Shall We Do?

We admit that the interests of the owners of A&P are of little importance.

Frankly, they could make an enormous amount of money by breaking up A&P, as the anti-trust lawyers wish, and selling off the parts.

But is this what the American people want? Do they agree with the anti-trust lawyers that our food prices are too low, and that we should be put out of the picture so other grocers can charge more?

Frankly, if this were the case, we would not want to continue in business.

But we seriously doubt that this is the case. Twelve years ago, an effort was made to tax this company and other chain stores out of business. The public rallied to our support. They said they liked our quality foods and our low prices. As a result of their opposition, the tax was defeated.

Now we are faced with this new attack through the courts. We are faced with the heavy costs and all the trouble that lawsuits involve.

But we believe this attack is a threat to millions of consumers who rely on us for quality foods at low prices; to farmers who rely on us for fast, low-cost distribution of their products; and to our loyal employees.

We feel that it is our responsibility to all these people to defend, by every legitimate means, this company and the low-price policy on which it was built.

THE GREAT ATLANTIC & PACIFIC TEA COMPANY

Sales, marketing, and product promotion are concerned directly with the distribution and sale of goods and/or services. In many cases, because managements do not clearly understand the function, public relations activities and programs are expected to have a direct effect on the sale of goods/or services. This expectation, of course, does not jibe with the end result sought from public relations: goodwill, understanding, and acceptance. Further, the concept that public relations activity should and can have a *direct* result on sales — to increase sales, of course — is not only a tenuous one, but a dangerous one for the public relations practitioner to propound. Should one expect, for example, that motorists will go out of their way to buy X gasoline because the X Gasoline Company has taken action to reduce pollution? Should one expect that women will go out of their way to purchase Y deoderant products because the Y Toilertries Company has made a special effort to hire more women for managerial positions? How does one prove that a specified number of budgeted dollars devoted to curbing pollution or to employing women have led to a specified increase in sales?

None of this, however, is intended to mean that public relations has nothing to do with sales, marketing, and product promotion. On the contrary, astute use of public relations can be of invaluable assistance to all three, but most often *in an indirect manner*. As a staff function designed to be of assistance to line departments and activities, public relations can and does serve sales, marketing, and product promotion. In some organizations a major share of public relations activity is devoted to product promotion, but the essential goal in most organizations is still the development of goodwill, understanding, and acceptance. Increased sales of goods and/or services will occur, but indirectly.

Press agentry and publicity are terms that are often used synonymously, but there are differences between the two. Press agentry is chiefly concerned with gaining attention through imaginative — and often rather bizarre — stunts and events which induce media to write about or air them. Press agents have mainly been associated with show business and the entertainment field, either representing organizations associated with the field or individuals who thrive on having their celebrity status kept constantly in the public eye. The philosophy of the press agent's client was probably best summed up by the one who was reputed to say "I don't care what they print about me so long as they spell my name right."

Publicity, which might well be considered to be the more legitimate son or daughter of press agentry, involves providing information, news, and feature material about an organization or person. Publicity can be and often is linked to newsworthy events, but in a manner generally less bizarre than press agent stunts. Whereas press agents usually work as individuals, publicity men most often operate within the framework of public relations departments and counseling firms. Publicity is used as one of the tools in public relations programming and activity, but it's not unusual to find that entire programs are built on publicity. For the latter reason — that is, because some public relations programs are composed chiefly of publicity — the public frequently confuses the part with the whole and thinks of publicity as being public relations. However, important as publicity may be in the framework of some public relations programs, it should be considered an effective public relations tool, but only a tool.

MINI-CASE
THE UNSINKABLE BOAT THAT SANK

Getting the London *Times* to run on its front page a picture and caption dealing with your product is about as difficult as breaking into the Bank of England. That it can be done, even if inadvertently, was demonstrated by the case of the unsinkable boat that sank.

The publicist or press agent who was given the task of gaining publicity for a rowboat whose manufacturer claimed would not sink came up with what he considered a great stunt idea. He decided he would hire some pretty and curvaceous models, stack them so tightly into the boat they would have to stand, and let the boat move down the Thames while the press took pictures of the great event.

Came the big day. To the delight of the publicist, the press showed up in force, including the prestigious *Times* of London. Into the boat went the models, out into the Thames went the unsinkable vessel, and while cameras clicked the overloaded boat slowly sank out of sight.

The publicist had his picture all right, and it appeared in a place where pictures seldom appear: right on the front page of the London *Times*! It was taken just as the boat went under the water; it showed the group of very unhappy models trying bravely to maintain their balance in water that was just above their knees. The accompanying caption explained the situation of the unsinkable boat that sank and even included the name of the manufacturer. The press agent, like all good press agents, remained anonymous.

Questions for Discussion

1. Is there anything the publicist could have done — other than go to the rescue of the sinking models — when his carefully staged event went under?
2. What do you think was the client's reaction when he saw the *Times'* front page picture and caption the next day? If you were the publicist, what would you say to the client?
3. What is your reaction to the front page picture and caption?
4. Any lessons to be learned from the entire affair?

DON'T JUST SIT THERE, ASK QUESTIONS

This chapter, which sets the stage for the study of public relations, has included definitions that set forth various public relations verities. The most successful practitioners have reached their place in the sun not merely because of their command of skills but also because they are keen judges of people, know how to operate within organizations, and ask the right questions of situations. Unless one asks the right questions, he or she will have great difficulty coming up with the right answers. Asking questions of public relations verities and discussing the possible answers can lead to insights that will last a lifetime for those who hope to make a career in the field.

THE MANAGEMENT FUNCTION CONCEPT

As we have seen, an underlying public relations verity states that public relations is a management function, but exactly what does this mean? Does it mean that top management, the heads of organizations whether profit or nonprofit making, are responsible for carrying out the public relations function? Or does it mean that the head of the public relations department should be on a top-management level? If the former, then why have public relations personnel? If the latter, on what grounds do public relations practitioners stake their claim for being on a top-management level?

This last question demands a sound answer because in any large organization — and public relations departments and personnel are usually found only in rather large organizations — other functional areas also stake out their claim to be on a top-management level. Marketing, legal, financial, and other staff functional people raise the question: why do public relations people feel they must operate on the top-management level to carry out their responsibilities and duties? If the public relations practitioner can't supply the answer, chances are he won't find himself operating on a top-management level. He doesn't get there simply because he claims he must be there, but because he's able to come up with cogent reasons for being in a top-management position.

MINI-SITUATION
JUSTIFYING THE TOP-MANAGEMENT ROLE

Assume the time is the mid-seventies and that you head up a four-man public relations department in a metropolitan university enrolling 10,000 undergraduate and 4,000 graduate students. You have been reporting on a line level to Dr. Quakenbush, dean of administrative affairs, but he has announced he will be retiring at the end of the academic year. For some time now you have felt that you can be far more effective in your role as public relations director of the university if you were moved out from under the dean, were able to report directly to the chancellor, and were made a member of the Chancellor's Monday Group (the 12 highest officials of the university who meet every Monday morning with the chancellor). You have an appointment with the chancellor next week, and you intend to explore the possibility of a change in role and status with him.

Pre-role playing: Before assuming the role of the director of public relations, set forth what you consider to be important questions concerning the above-mentioned situation. In short, what are some facts and data which have not been cited but which you want to know before proceding?

Role-playing: Assuming you have gotten some answers to the questions you have posed about the situation, you are now to put yourself into the role of the director of public relations. Set forth and be prepared to discuss the most cogent reasons you can come up with for moving your position from under the dean, reporting directly to the chancellor, and being made a member of the Chancellor's Monday Group.

Of paramount importance in considering the public relations role within organizations are the parameters of its authority and responsibility. No matter where public relations fits into an organization it is generally a *staff* rather than a *line* function. But just what does this mean?

Briefly, management theorists state that line people are those who are concerned with the basic objectives of a company. Staff people have been described as those experts in techniques who aid the line management to do a better job of reaching an organization's objectives. One authority sees the line-staff dichotomy in terms of "activities." He states that the structure of every organization contains "central" (substitute "line") and "supporting" (substitute "staff") activities. Central activities in a manufacturing firm are described as those concerned with engineering, producing, and selling a product, while supporting activities include personnel, accounting, quality control, and public relations. Staff positions in a manufacturing firm are not involved directly with either the production or sale of the organization's products or services. Such positions do not possess command authority, but are usually classified as advisory, service, or administrative in nature.

Although a staff executive — such as a public relations vice president — has no authority over the regular line, he does have line authority over his own subordinates. Thus, in a large public relations department, the public relations vice president would have direct-line authority over everyone in his department.

Emphasizing the point, as staff people, public relations practitioners have no direct authority over line people but they are expected to assist the line people in carrying out the basic work and purposes of the organization. This assistance applies particularly to those areas of line authority that have a bearing on the organization's relationship with various publics, and obviously this can cover a considerable amount of ground. It also gives rise to some interesting questions and problems.

Take, for example, this simple statement: public relations is a staff function and as such assists the line people in carrying out the work and purposes of an organization. Who takes the initiative in involving public relations with line activities that have a bearing on an organization's relationship with its publics? Does public relations wait for line people to come to it? What if a problem develops but is not brought to the attention of public relations until it is too late to do anything except clean up the mess as well as possible? And what if public relations sees the problem developing but is rebuffed when it proffers aid and assistance? If the public relations department has no authority over line departments — and it usually does *not* have this authority — then how can public relations have its advice, counsel, and skills effectively utilized if the line departments don't want to use them? As the monarch said in *The King and I*, "'tis a puzzlement," but it's a puzzlement that has to be answered if public relations is to do its job effectively.

POLICIES, PROCEDURES, AND ACTIONS

The model public relations program postulates that after evaluating public attitudes and opinions, the public relations practitioner then checks these against organizational policies, procedures, and actions. If public attitudes and opinions are negative or hostile regarding organizational policies, procedures, and actions, four alternatives present themselves:

Alternative 1:

Public relations can utilize its skills and resources in an attempt to change or modify public attitudes and opinions.

Alternative 2:

Public relations can inform line authorities and top management about the negative or hostile public attitudes and opinions and subsequently utilize its skills and resources in an attempt to change or modify public attitudes and opinions.

Alternative 3:

Public relations can inform line authorities and top management about the negative or hostile public attitudes and opinions; suggest changes or modifications of policies, procedures, and actions so as to conform to public expectations; and subsequently utilize its skills and resources in communicating such changes or modifications to the public.

Alternative 4:

Public relations can inform line authorities and top management about the negative or hostile public attitudes and opinions; play an active role in seeking to change or modify policies, procedures, and actions so as to conform to public expectations; and subsequently utilize its skills and resources in communicating such changes or modifications to the public.

Alternative 1 is based on the concept of public relations as a communication activity whose main purpose is to communicate with an organization's publics. It assumes that words and deeds are not necessarily compatible, and that negative attitudes and opinions can be changed through the skillful use of public relations techniques without need for a corresponding change in policies, procedures, and actions. Indeed, there are on record countless case studies of public relations campaigns based on communication programs that were divorced from actual organizational practices or had but minimal relationship to actual practices. The record in regard to such campaigns actually *changing* attitudes and opinions from negative to positive is a spotty one, however.

Questions related to Alternative 1 come readily to mind. Are words more important than deeds? Are they of equal importance? Does the public buy words separated from deeds? Is not the main purpose of public relations activity to communicate to an organization's public, and are we asking too much of public relations when we ask that it do more than communicate? If there are on record "countless case studies of public relations campaigns based on communication programs divorced from actual organizational practices," then how about citing some illustrations? There should be numerous examples in the literature of the field and in current mass media, and it would be a helpful exercise for you, the reader, to cite and discuss some.

Alternative 2 is based on the assumption that public relations serves as an intelligence-gathering and communicating agency in regard to public attitudes and opinions. It postulates that the basic role of public relations is to gather intelligence and to communicate, but not to be involved with basic policies, procedures, and actions. The alternative does not intend to downgrade the importance of public relations, because it recognizes that evaluation of public attitudes and opinions and subsequent communication with the public are important duties that can best be carried out by public relations. The alternative asserts that, in carrying out these tasks of intelligence-gathering and communicating, public relations has justified its value and existence.

How valid is the above contention? Are there advantages to the practitioner in being satisfied with his intelligence-gathering and communicating role and in not becoming involved with policies, procedures, and actions? What about the disadvantages?

Alternatives 3 and 4 seem on first reading to be similar, but there is a significant difference between the two. Both assert that public relations has the responsibility to inform line authorities and management about negative or hostile public attitudes and opinions, and to communicate subsequent changes or modifications in policies, procedures, and actions. Alternative 4 proposes that public relations also has the responsibility to play an active role in seeking changes or modifications of policies, procedures, and actions so as to conform to public expectations. Alternative 3, addressing itself to the same general area, proposes that public relations has the responsibility to *suggest* changes or modifications, etc., etc.

Both alternatives thus see public relations as taking a more active role than the first two alternatives. The philosophical underpinning of Alternatives 3 and 4 is that words and deeds are inseparable. To say one thing and to be doing another, state the alternatives, is to invite public doubts about the credibility of the organization involved. Thus, in order to be credible — and hence effective — public relations must of necessity be involved in some fashion with an organization's policies, procedures, and actions. How involved forms the difference in approach between Alternatives 3 and 4.

Making a choice between the two alternatives seems to boil down to a matter of authorization, areas of responsibility, and competency. Does public relations, for example, have the authority to seek, or merely suggest, changes or modification in policies, procedures, and actions? Who is responsible for the specific policies? Is the area one in which public relations people have competency? Finally, what about jurisdiction and the natural tendency of everyone to guard his own turf?

There are no "right" or "wrong" answers to the questions posed by the four alternatives, and there may be a fifth and sixth alternative. The student who can think of further alternatives is well on his way to understanding why public relations has few eternal verities.

SOCIALLY RESPONSIBLE PERFORMANCE AND PUBLIC INTEREST

Chapter 3 of this book will deal at length with social responsibility and the public interest, but it's important at this point to consider these vital considerations briefly. There are very few instances where organizations have *openly* admitted or made it part of organizational policy to be socially irresponsible or to operate in a manner not in the public interest. However, there are numerous instances of organizations adopting and following practices not socially responsible, not acceptable to the public, and not in the public interest. Such instances pose a dilemma for the public relations practitioner because they raise serious ethical and moral problems.

The student who hopes to make a career in public relations should first realize that such problems are not the unique province of the public relations practitioner. Accountants, lawyers, comptrollers, engineers, salesmen, advertising and marketing executives, and production managers are also faced with such problems and dilemmas.

Second, such problems are not the kind to be dealt with frequently (if they were, we'd have to conclude the entire fabric of our society is rotten).

Third, and probably most important in connection with public relations practice, when problems involving social irresponsibility and nonpublic interest do arise, they are especially relevant to public relations practice for two reasons. As already noted, public relations practitioners stress the importance of the activity as a management function, and the ultimate responsibility for actions, policies, and procedures rests on management and on the public relations practitioner who aspires to counsel management. Thus, those who shoulder ultimate responsibility must also shoulder the task of resolving the problems being discussed. The second reason is that practitioners are responsible for relationships that are public, not private, and hence are responsible for the manner in which actions, policies, and procedures will be communicated (or not communicated) to various publics.

At various times in their careers public relations practitioners must face up to the resolution of organizational actions that may be socially irresponsible and not in the public interest. In such instances, do practitioners serve as the "conscience" of their organizations and fight the internal battle needed to have these actions modified or reserved? Do they merely point out possible or probable long and short-range consequences of following such actions? Do they consider themselves strictly as organizational "advocates" whose first, foremost, and perhaps only responsibility is to the organizations they serve? Do they form their judgments about their roles in terms of the magnitude and scope of the particular issue or problem being faced? Is there an imaginary line which the practitioner will not cross when dealing with issues and actions concerning social responsibility, performance, and the public interest? If the answer is affirmative, where does one draw this line and is one willing and able to handle the consequences of not crossing it?

Though many public relations practitioners may never have to deal with the issues and situations described above, the student ought to be aware of them and sensitive to their scope and resolution. For this reason they will be discussed in more detail in Chapter 3.

END RESULTS

As has been noted earlier in this chapter, most definitions of public relations stress that the end results sought from public relations activity are goodwill, understanding, and acceptance. These are laudable and sound goals and objectives, but are they sufficient? Do they provide the practitioner with the management support needed to give the function the talent, stature, and budget necessary for carrying out public relations tasks?

Many practitioners question the advisability of phrasing public relations end results in such general terms as the achievement of goodwill, understanding, and acceptance. They point out that other functions of management are more specifically phrased, and they also note that such general phrasing of end results sought makes measuring achievements almost impossible. They ask such questions as these: How does one measure goodwill, understanding, and acceptance? If such end results can't be easily measured, then why should management provide the function with needed resources?

On the other hand, other practitioners assert that public relations does not deal with measurable activities that can be tallied up as easily as the activities of other organizational functions. They stress that other organizational functions are able to control the environment in which they operate — for example, production people have control over raw materials and the manufacturing process — but public relations often has little or no control over the mass media expected to carry public relations messages. Further, they assert, to operate on the premise of such control and to promise specific end results through specific elements of the mass media would be unethical, counter-productive, and sure to bring the practice into ill repute.

The answer to these two schools of thought seems to exist some-where in the middle of the two sets of perceptives about goals and objectives. The achievement of goodwill, understanding, and acceptance is certainly a sound end result to be sought from public relations activity. Bringing about such results can lead to more sales for an organization, to more students for a college or university, to more funds for a social agency or hospital; however, such achievements will come about indirectly, and very often more direct achievements will be expected and sought from public relations activity. Working out sought-for end results is not a simple academic exercise, but one that must be handled carefully in order to justify the support needed to carry out the function.

QUESTIONS AND PROBLEMS FOR DISCUSSION

1. Cite what you consider to be key points to be covered in a definition of public relations. Explain why you would include the points you consider crucial to a sound definition.
2. Explain the essential difference between public relations and each of the following: advertising; sales, marketing and product promotion; press agentry and publicity.
3. What is meant by the statement that public relations is a management function?
4. On what grounds do public relations practitioners stake their claim for being on a top-management level?
5. What is the difference between a line and a staff function?
6. What kind of problems do public relations practitioners have with line executives in carrying out their staff function?
7. What alternatives do public relations practitioners have in dealing with situations where public attitudes and opinions are negative or hostile to organizational policies, procedures, and actions? Which of these alternatives do you consider the proper one for the public relations practitioner to follow?
8. What kind of ethical and moral problems arise for practitioners when their organizations adopt and follow practices that are not socially responsible, that are not acceptable to the public, and that are not in the public interest? How would you deal with such problems?
9. Why do many practitioners question the advisability of phrasing public relations end results in such general terms as the achievement of goodwill, understanding, and acceptance?
10. Why do other practitioners question the advisability of phrasing public relations end results in more specific terms?
11. What is your opinion about the way in which public relations end results ought to be phrased?

THE ECOLOGY OF PUBLIC RELATIONS

2

Consider for the moment some all too frequent and typical comments and statements made about public relations:

Comments and Statements	Source
Exhibit A: "Science deals with ultimate truth; public relations deals with falsehoods. Public relations is just a lot of bull served up as a fancy dish."	Observation made by a science major to a public relations major at Multi University.
Exhibit B: "I promise that if elected I'm not going to spend the taxpayers' money on publicity flacks grinding out a bunch of lies and propaganda."	Campaign remarks made by candidate for Congress.
Exhibit C: "No self-respecting newspaper would use the stuff sent to it by PR people. We don't trust public relations men because they're not interested in helping us get at the truth."	Managing editor of a large daily newspaper which is part of a group whose stock is traded on the New York Stock Exchange.
Exhibit D: "We're sick and tired of getting the run-around from the Establishment and its public relations apologists. If we don't get what we want we're going to turn the Establishment inside out."	Message from a self-styled radical group.

Faced by the above critical barrage, the public relations student is hard-pressed for a rebuttal. One way of answering is to hold a mirror up to the source of the remarks and to suggest the source consider this aspect of the reflection:

Exhibit A:
 Science may deal with ultimate truth, but in today's society even the scientific community relies on public relations tactics and skills to make its truths known. Further, both the science and public relations majors were probably drawn to Multi University through the efforts of its long-established public relations department.

Exhibit B:

There is scarcely a single political campaign today that does not utilize public relations tactics and talents. Once elected, virtually every member of congress has at least one staff member assigned to public relations tasks.

Exhibit C:

Every newspaper in America — self-respecting or not — uses material which comes from public relations sources. If you'd like to debate this point, check any issue of your daily newspaper to figure out what stories emanated in some way from public relations. Maybe the managing editor doesn't know it, but his own newspaper has either a public relations or promotion staffer on its payroll.

Exhibit D:

They may not have called it public relations, but the radical leaders in America in the early seventies were among the most skillful users of public relations techniques. They were among the most astute practitioners of the created event to draw media interest and nationwide attention from the resulting media coverage.

Forcing the critic of public relations to view his own mirror image is one way of demonstrating that he, too, uses public relations. Much more important, however, is to *recognize the inevitable role of public relations in American society*. Dan J. Forrestal, veteran practitioner, says: "Public relations, in its current concept and nomenclature, was invented simply because a wide variety of organizations couldn't afford not to have it. They recognized that merited understanding and acceptance by their principal constituencies were prerequisite for successful survival. They acknowledged the concept that performance/behavior plus communication/interpretation equals reputation. They acknowledged the notion that somewhere in this mix a need existed for specialists with specific skills . . ." (*Public Relations Journal*, March, 1974)

The recognition Forrestal speaks about demands a close look at those facets of society which have brought about the *need* for public relations and which, in turn, have created particular problems for the public relations specialist. These two elements — need and problems, cause and effect — comprise what one might call the climate for public relations in American society.

Long before the term became fashionable, Cutlip and Center linked the term "ecology" to public relations practice in answering the question: why public relations? Biologically, ecology refers to the mutual relationship between organisms and their environment. Ecology in a public relations sense relates to *those aspects of American society which have brought about the need for and the utilization of public relations* in America today and which, in turn, *have created particular problems for the practitioner*. However, before analyzing these societal aspects vis-a-vis public relations, a brief look backward and then to the present will show where public relations stood in the past and where it stands today.

A BRIEF ANALYSIS OF PAST AND PRESENT PRACTICE

Public relations was practiced prior to the present century, though on a very limited scale and chiefly in the areas of politics and government. An example was the use of public relations techniques by Sam Adams in revolutionary days, particularly the staging of the Boston Tea Party as one of our country's first created events. Another was President Andrew Jackson's utilization of the talents of Amos Kendall who served as publicist, speech writer, and counselor. A third was the use of modern campaign techniques in the McKinley-Bryan campaign of 1896.

KEY ANTECEDENTS FOR PRESENT PRACTICE

The early part of the century saw the first usage of public relations by business in response to the attacks against business by the muckrakers such as Ida Tarbell, Upton Sinclair, and others who exposed some of the more maloderous activities of big business. Most of the public relations activities by business in the period 1900 to 1914 were chiefly defensive in nature. However, one business leader — Theodore N. Vail, president of the American Telephone and Telegraph Corporation — proved to be far ahead of his time in recognizing that sound service to the public, clearly explained to the public, was the road to growth and stability for his company. His organization was one of the first to establish a public relations department — called at the time an Information Department — and to consider that the public interest and the corporation's self-interest were inseparably linked.

Operating as a "publicist" at this time was Ivy Ledbetter Lee, often called the "father of public relations." Lee formed one of the country's earliest public relations firms and also served as advisor to the Pennsylvania Railroad and the Rockefeller interests. In 1906, while representing the anthracite coal interests, Lee wrote his "Declaration of Principles" and sent it to city editors.

Ivy Lee's Declaration of Principles

This is not a secret press bureau. All our work is done in the open. We aim to supply news. This is not an advertising agency; if you think any of our matter ought properly to go to your business office, do not use it. Our matter is accurate. Further details on any subject treated will be supplied promptly, and any editor will be assisted most cheerfully in verifying directly any statement of fact. . . . In brief, our plan is, frankly and openly, on behalf of the business concerns and public institutions, to supply to the press and public of the United States prompt and accurate information concerning subjects which it is of value and interest to the public to know about. . . . I send out only matter every detail of which I am willing to assist an editor in verifying for himself. I am always at your service for the purpose of enabling you to obtain more complete information concerning any of the subjects brought forward in my copy.

Lee, of course, was not the sole practitioner of public relations at the time, and, as Dr. Ray E. Hiebert notes in *Courtier To the Crowd*

(1966), "Ivy Lee was never quite sure of the title of his profession, confessing toward the end of his life that even his children did not know what to call him." Others, spurred particularly by the highly successful use of public relations techniques in World War I by the Creel Committee On Public Information, established themselves as independent practitioners or started public relations departments within corporations and other institutions. Some of these pioneers included Edward L. Bernays, John Hill, Paul Garrett, Carl Byoir, William Baldwin, and Pendleton Dudley. By the end of World War II the term "public relations counselor" had come into current usage, and most of the practices now in use today were developed and put into motion.

THE MODERN ERA

In the past three decades — 1945 to the present — public relations has come into its own as a field of activity with recognizable practices, techniques, skills, and boundaries. Not only business and industry — the two prime users of public relations — but *every organization and institution of size has established or should establish public relations as an important staff function to assist management in carrying out its tasks*. We find public relations departments in unions, colleges and universities, social service organizations such as the United Way, religious organizations, governmental agencies, politics, and the courts. In New York City alone close to 800 public relations counseling firms are listed in the yellow pages of the telephone directory, and we find another 300 in Chicago and more than 300 in Los Angeles. Although there are no accurate figures of how many persons in the country are in the field, it has been estimated that there are somewhere between 50,000 and 60,000 public relations practitioners. Scores of colleges and universities offer sequences and majors in public relations, and more than 300 offer at least one public relations course. The Public Relations Society of America (PRSA) was first formed just after the end of World War II and has now grown to a membership of 7,000. Under the auspices of the PRSA the Public Relations Student Society of America was established in 1970, quickly grew to more than 60 chapters, and was formally incorporated into the parent body a few years later. There are three weekly newsletters (*Jack O'Dwyer's Newsletter, PR Reporter*, and the *Public Relations News*); two well-established periodicals (the monthly *Public Relations Journal* and the *Public Relations Quarterly*); a new journal of research and comment entitled *Public Relations Review*, whose first issue was published by the Foundation for Public Relations Research and Education in summer, 1975; and *A Public Relations Bibliography* by Scott Cutlip whose second edition published by the University of Wisconsin Press in 1965 contained almost 6,000 entries, and whose third edition by Robert Bishop, distributed through the University of Michigan Press, was published in 1974 and carried an additional 4,000 entries. New books about public relations have been appearing with increasing regularity each year in the past decade, and there is little doubt that public relations — whether called a field, activity, or profession — is here to stay.

MAJOR PUBLIC RELATIONS ASSOCIATIONS

Academy of Hospital Public Relations
244 E. Pearson Street
Suit 1903
Chicago, Illinois 60611
(312) 649-2294

American Association of Minority
   Consultants
c/o Charles A. Davis & Assoc.
2400 South Michigan Avenue
Chicago, Illinois 60616
(312) DA6-4140

American Jewish Public Relations
   Society
515 Park Avenue
New York, New York 10022
(212) PL2-0600

American Society for Hospital Public
   Relations Directors
840 North Lake Shore Drive
Chicago, Illinois 60611
(312) 645-9467

Association of Sports Information
   Directors
Brandeis University
Waltham, Massachusetts 02154
(617) 647-2000

Bank Marketing Association
309 West Washington Street
Chicago, Illinois 60606
(312) 782-1442

Baptist Hospital Public Relations
Church Street
Nashville, Tennessee
(615) 329-5300

Canadian Public Relations Society
88 Argyle Avenue
Ottawa K2P 1B4, Ontario
(613) 232-1222

College Sports Information Directors of
   America
Western Michigan University
Kalamazoo, Michigan 49001
(616) 383-1600

Council for Advancement and Support
   of Education
One DuPont Circle
Washington, D.C 20036
(202) 293-6360

International Public Relations
   Association
30 quai Gustave-Ador
1207 Geneva (Switzerland)

International Association of Political
   Consultants
Rue du Las 52-B-1050 Brussels
(Belgium)

Library Public Relations Council
c/o Alice Norton
Box 516
Ridgefield, Connecticut 06877
(203) 438-4064

National Communication Council for
   Human Services, Inc.
815 Second Avenue
New York, New York 10017
(212) 687-1223

National School Public Relations
   Association
1801 N. Moore Street
Arlington, Virginia 22209
(703) 528-5840

New York Airlines Public Relations
c/o Harvey Berman
National Airlines
219 E. 42nd Street
New York, New York 10017
(212) 697-8181

National Investor Relations Institute
1629 K Street, N. W.
Washington, D.C. 20036
(202) 223-4725

Public Relations Society of America
845 Third Avenue
New York, New York 10022

Publicity Club of New York
404 Park Avenue
Suite 1207
New York, New York
(212) 685-8220

Railroad Public Relations Association
American Railroads Building
Washington, D.C. 20036
(202) 293-4194

Religious Public Relations Council
475 Riverside Drive-Room 1031
New York, New York 10027
(212) 870-2200

Women Executives in Public Relations
c/o Ms. Retha Odom
Shell Oil
50W 50th Street
New York, New York 10020
(212) 262-6983

Women in Communications, Inc.
8305-A Shoal Creek Blvd.
Austin, Texas 78758
(512) 452-0119

FUNDAMENTAL TRENDS IN AMERICAN SOCIETY CAUSING THE PRACTICE OF PUBLIC RELATIONS

Public relations is here to stay because there's a felt need for it. The need is a reflection of fundamental trends in American society that have brought about the necessity of public relations. These trends have made public relations inevitable, and organizations should be and are using public relations as a management function whether they call it by that term or by other terms. In turn, these same fundamental trends have created specific problems for public relations practitioners.

To bring ecology into focus, therefore, this section will discuss and outline the nature of some of these fundamental trends to make clear why they've caused the need for public relations practice.

In a society as complex as America's, there are many major trends which have wide societal significance. Five of them, however, seem to have special pertinence for public relations practice and will therefore be discussed in some detail. They are:

1. Urbanization and suburbanization
2. Large and complex components
3. Growth in the power of public opinion and the swiftness of opinion change
4. Changes in the technology, role and impact of the mass media
5. Consumerism and environmental sensitivity

URBANIZATION AND SUBURBANIZATION

The first fundamental trend in American society that needs to be understood in considering the ecological nature of public relations is the trend towards urbanization and suburbanization. In causal terms, the ramifications of this trend cannot be overestimated.

In 1910, when there were about 92 million people in the United States, more than 54 percent of the population was classified as rural and 36 percent as urban. By 1970, our population had grown to 202 million people and a drastic shift in habitat had taken place: 73.5 percent now lived in urban areas and 26.5 percent in rural areas.

The chart below, taken from the 1974 *Statistical Abstract Of The United States*, shows the dramatic change of population in the period 1910 to 1970:

	1910	1920	1930	1940	1950	1960	1970
Urban:	46%	51%	56%	56.5%	64%	70%	73.5%
Rural:	54%	49%	44%	43.5%	36%	30%	26.5%

In their study of the American electroate (*The Real Majority*, 1970), Richard Scammon and Ben Wattenberg indicate the movement from rural to urban to suburban:

Voters By Place Of Residence, 1968

	Percent of Electorate
Central cities.............................	29.6
Suburbs......................................	35.6
Small cities, towns, farms.............	34.8

Comparing the election of 1948 with that of 1968, Scammon and Wattenberg pointed out that New York City lost a half million voters while the New York City suburbs gained 750,000; the city of Chicago lost 400,000 voters while the Chicago suburbs gained 500,000; the city of Minneapolis lost 40,000 voters while the Minneapolis suburbs gained 160,000. Considering the term "central cities" as those with populations of 50,000 or more, Scammon and Wattenberg noted that two of every three American voters live in or near (suburb) a large city, and an additional 15 percent live in cities between 10,000 and 50,000.

The opening paragraph of an article about Edward J. DeBartolo, largest developer of shopping malls in the country, brings some of the above statistics to life:

> Cruising along at 41,000 feet in the little orange-and-white Learjet . . . I look down at DeBartolo's America . . . Here, now, on DeBartolo's map, the cities shrink. Clumps of suburban sprawl spread like ground cover, stretching tendrils out across the spaces that keep Orlando from Lakeland, Lakeland from Tampa, Tampa from St. Petersburg, detouring each city as nonchalantly as ivy detours glass, twisting together on the other side and creeping on. The cities, poor lumps, retreat upon themselves, no place to go, waiting to be grown over and choked out. Across this landscape zigzags a trelliswork of straight, strong, skinny lines, the highways and expressways; and wherever these straight lines meet, at each convergence of asphalt, the face of Edward J. DeBartolo, master builder of shopping malls, takes on the bliss of Gully Jimson, the wacky artist of Joyce Cary's "The Horse's Mouth," confronting a big blank wall.
> (*New York Times Magazine*, August 12, 1973)

America, as seen by another societal analyst, consists not so much of cities retreating upon themselves, but of cities and suburbs combining together to dominate the countryside:

The yearning for a place in the country has become endemic. Some people long merely for a quiet retreat where they can lop the heads off daisies with a walking stick and discourse with acquired rusticity upon the prevalence of alfalfa thrips in the back forty. Others take a deeper plunge, hang up a sign saying "The Grange," and perhaps even invest in a cow, to discover for themselves the astonishing daintiness with which so unwieldy a creature can place her right hinder hoof in a half-filled pail of milk. But all of these bucolic pleasures are doomed to brief tenure. *The city, with its appalling advance guide of suburbs, inexorably pursues all who would flee it. And further earthly flight is hopeless. One merely encounters another city advancing upon the land from another direction* . . . From "The Talk of the Town," *New Yorker*, June 17, 1974

Whether we consider the wave of the future as city growth by itself or a combination of city-suburban satellite growth, the trend is obviously towards an urban society. What does this mean vis-a-vis public relations? Compare life in the not-so-distant past with that today (and tomorrow) and the answer becomes a bit more clear.

When most Americans lived on farms or in small isolated communities, life was relatively uncomplicated. People knew their neighbors and were somewhat independent of external forces. There was a sense of community, of belonging. There were problems, plenty of them, but one had the feeling these problems were manageable and within one's ability to solve.

Now that most of us live in cities or suburbs, life is complicated. Neighbors are often the people who moved in last week (or was it the week before?) We are almost totally dependent today on external forces for mere sustenance. There is little sense of community and a great many maladjusted people. Viewed from this perspective, the movement from rural to urban to suburban sprawl has manifold implications for public relations. In our more leisured, easy-going days the gap of understanding between organizations and their publics was as narrow as the streets of small town America. Today's gap is broad and wide.

By no means should we look upon public relations as a panacea for the better life for all of us, nor as some sort of magical cure-all for the ills or urban life. *But public relations can help bridge the gap of understanding* brought on by the ecological trend towards an urban society. Whether consciously and by plan or unconsciously in random fashion, more and more organizations are utilizing public relations as a means of gap-bridging and the building of goodwill and understanding. They're doing so because the urbanization trend has the causal effect of bringing on the felt need for public relations assistance and practice.

MINI-PROBLEM
URBANIZATION AND SUBURBANIZATION AS RELATED TO PUBLIC RELATIONS PRACTICE

When this chapter was being written the author of this text could discern existing aspects of our urban, suburban habitat which had definite implications for public relations practice. The pace of American life is so swift, however, that new aspects may already have changed the picture, and this ever-changing nature of our environment poses challenges to the practitioner.

Consider, therefore, that you work in the public relations department of the Boy Scouts of America (or the Girl Scouts of America). You have been given the assignment of exploring the *current* (at the time you are reading this text) extent of the movement from a rural to an urban to a suburban society and to set forth a position paper indicating:

1. How and in what ways the movement affects your organization's basic *programming and activities*
2. The *special public relations problems* the movement causes for your organization
3. The *public relations programming or activities* which you recommend be undertaken to solve these problems

It is expected, of course, that you will utilize a variety of resources in researching and handling this assignment.

LARGE AND COMPLEX COMPONENTS

A second fundamental trend which needs to be considered in understanding the ecological basis for public relations in American society is the fact that *the chief components of that society are both large and complex*. The Hupmobile and Stutz cars long ago vanished into such giant enterprises as General Motors, Ford, Chrysler, and American Motors. Working men and women have joined together to form the United Auto Workers, the Teamsters, and the United Steelworkers of America. Small state colleges in California and New York have become units of the massive University of California and the State University of New York. Young people may still dream about leading adult lives as individuals controlling their own destinies, but the reality belies the dream. Through large and complex organizations and components most Americans now receive their education, spend their working lives, join together for collective bargaining purposes, are provided with government services, and receive the goods and other services necessary to sustain life. Some randomly selected facts and figures — cited below — prove the pertinency of the above conclusion.

In *industry*, where large firms have taken over small firms, and conglomerates have become commonplace, the giant among giants is General Motors Corporation. In 1972 GM had 760,000 employees and its total sales amounted to 30 billion dollars; the following year its world-wide employment force rose to 811,000 and its total sales to $35,798,289,000. Lester R. Brown, a Senior Fellow at the Washington-based Overseas Development Council, used 1970 figures to compare the gross annual sales of today's large multinational corporations with the gross national products of countries. GM's total sales of 24 billion dollars were eclipsed by the gross national products of only 22 countries, and GM's total sales ranked ahead of the gross national products of such countries as Switzerland ($20 billion), Pakistan ($17 billion), South Africa ($16 billion), and 34 other countries (*Magazine of the United Nations Association*, June, 1973).

Ranging below GM in total gross sales in 1972 were Exxon ($22 billion), American Tel & Tel ($21 billion), Ford Motor Company ($20 billion), and Sears, Roebuck ($11 billion). General Electric, Mobil Oil, Chrysler, and IBM each had total sales of 10 billion dollars, and Texaco completed the top ten with 9 billion dollars.

Sales of such a nature are made possible through the combined efforts of very large numbers of employees, hence it's not surprising to find that in 1972 GM's work force of 760,000 was followed by Ford with 442,000 employees, International Tel & Tel (428,000), Sears, Roebuck (380,000), IBM (262,000), Chrysler (245,000), Westinghouse Electric (184,000), J. C. Penney (175,000), Goodyear Tire and Rubber (145,000), and Exxon (141,000).

In *labor* we find that the growth of union membership has paralleled the growth in industry. There were 9 million union members in 1940; 15 million in 1950; 18 million in 1960; and 21 million in 1970. Leading union in 1973 was the International Brotherhood of Teamsters with 2 million members, followed by the United Auto Workers with 1,400,000. Other top unions were the United Steelworkers of America (991,000), the International Brotherhood of Electrical Workers (778,000), the United Brotherhood of Carpenters (700,000), and the International Association of Machinists (627,000).

Some Side Effects

When little Peter has a backyard fight with little Paul the side effects are usually a few bruises and hurt feelings, but when Big Industry clashes with Big Labor the side effects are much more profound. Ten days into the 1970 strike against GM by the United Auto Workers, the Associated Press ran a story detailing the effects of the strike among the 39,000 firms that sell goods or services to General Motors. According to the AP, the A. O. Smith Corporation, which makes car frames and other automotive equipment, laid off 3,150 of its 5,500 employees because of the strike. An East St. Louis metals company which makes high grade slab zinc for GM's die casting operations laid off 380 of its 510 employees; some 600 men were laid off by the Grand Trunk railroad, which serves GM plants in Michigan, and Uniroyal Inc. laid off 1,100 rubber workers in Alabama. When the 349,910 employees went on strike, the hardest hit areas were Detroit with 82,180 strikers, the Flint area with

50,370, Lansing with 13,260, Buffalo with 10,600, and Chicago with 10,200. Considering the above figures, when Big Labor and Big Industry reach the point of no return, the lives of thousands of people in scores of cities across the entire country are seriously affected.

The trend towards large and complex components is found not only in industry and labor but also in many other areas of our national life. *Government* employment in the early seventies amounted to more than fourteen million with the largest share found in local government with eight million employees followed by state government with three million employees and the federal government with another three million. In *farming* there has been a steady decrease in the number of farms and a steady rise in average acreage per farm. In 1920 there were six and a half million farms with an average acreage of 147 per farm. By 1950 the number of farms had shrunk to five and a half million, and the average acreage per farm had risen to 213. By 1970 there were less than three million farms, and the average acreage per farm had grown to 383.

In *higher education* we find the same trend to large and complex component units. In 1973 there were 105,000 students enrolled in the University of California; 155,000 in the City University of New York; 143,000 in the State University of New York; 68,000 in the University of Texas and a similar number in Indiana University. At its 142nd commencement on June 6, 1974, New York University graduated 7,500 students, and on the same day the City College of New York gave diplomas to 3,687. Commenting on the higher education scene the New York *Times* reported: "Overcrowding has become routine."

The key word in that last quotation is "routine." We accept as routine the fact that large and complex organizations dominate the national scene in industry, labor, government, the military, farming, education, and all other key areas. We also accept as routine the many benefits that size and complexity brings to the average American, but large organizations cannot simply ride with the fact that they bring benefits, because these same benefits bring serious problems that affect all of us.

By their very nature large organizations become bureaucracies, and these in turn cause maladjustments and indifference. Today's highly organized society, says Professor Robert Presthus, has created what he terms "the indifferents" and he describes them this way:

> The indifferents are those who have come to terms with their environment by withdrawal and by redirection of their interests towards off-the-job satisfactions. They have also been alienated by the work itself which has often been downgraded by machine processing and assembly-line methods . . . (The indifferents) are found among the great mass of the wage and salaried employees who work in the bureaucratic situation. By a rough estimate we can say that . . . just about half the wage-earning labor force now work in big organizations. Moreover, this vast reservoir of potential indifferents is steadily increasing. (*The Organization Society*, Vintage, 1965)

Not only do we have vast numbers of indifferents in today's society, but we've got mistrustful indifferents. There is in the American charac-

30

ter a traditional, almost ingrained mistrust of size. We value competition because we know that competition is our weapon to cut large organizations down to size and to provide us with some sort of individuality and choice, some way to allow us to exercise a small amount of independence.

Thus, large organizations take pains to show that they care for the individual, and when they actually don't care the individual reacts accordingly. His and her elected representatives pass anti-trust, zoning, and anti-pollution laws; establish the Securities and Exchange Commission, the Federal Trade Commission, and the Consumer Protection Agency. Astute managements of large and complex organizations recognize our antipathy to unrestrained size, and they turn to a specialized function of management — public relations — to communicate that size can be trusted and to bring about understanding and goodwill. The causal effect of the trend towards large and complex organizations is the same as the effect of the trend towards urbanization and suburbanization: that is, it has brought about the felt need for public relations assistance and practice.

MINI-CASE
A PUBLIC RELATIONS MESSAGE FROM A LARGE AND COMPLEX ORGANIZATION

The following public relations message was presented by Union Carbide in a full-page advertisement in a national news magazine. (*Time*, June 10, 1974) Read it and answer the questions cited below the advertisement.

Imagine what life would be like without the artifacts of our civilization.

Imagine living without all the things that make our lives easier, safer, healthier and more comfortable.

It's not a very happy picture.

But it is a good way to show you what we do.

Because of all these things, there are very, very few Union Carbide doesn't have something to do with.

Some of our products have names you know well. Like Prestone II antifreeze-coolant. Glad bags. And Eveready batteries.

But most of our products you seldom hear of. Because they're used as materials to make other products.

Some are chemicals and plastics which go into the making of thousands of things we live with every day.

Like synthetic fabrics, rubber and furs. Antibiotics, paints and cosmetics. Toys, furniture, sheer stockings, bio-degradable detergents. And many more.

Some are metals or alloys. Such as the tungsten that glows in lightbulbs. Or the ferrochrome that makes stainless steel stainless.

Some are gases. Such as the oxygen

used in hospitals to save our lives. Or in factories to cut metal. Or even to propel the astronauts to the moon.

Some are gigantic electrodes for furnaces that make steel for thousands of products. Or arc carbons for motion picture projection.

And some are radioisotopes used to diagnose and treat disease.

We're a pretty big group of people — about 123,000 of us — working in over 100 countries in many different fields.

You'll find us all around you in thousands of products that make your life better today. You won't find our name on most of them.

But we're there just the same.

Questions for Discussion

1. What basic impressions do you think Union Carbide hoped to achieve on the part of readers of the above advertisement?
2. How effective do you consider the advertisement? Why?
3. What's your opinion of the slogan "Today, something we do will touch your life."?
4. Write an advertisement similar to the above, but using your own ideas.

GROWTH IN THE POWER OF PUBLIC OPINION AND SWIFTNESS OF OPINION CHANGE

A third fundamental trend in American society relates to public opinion. In a later chapter in this book public opinion will be analyzed and discussed in more detail, but our concern at the moment is with two factors: first, there has been a steady growth in the power of public opinion, and second, changes in public opinion can often be swift, sudden, and drastic.

Public opinion in America is a powerful force for the very basic reason that ours, for the most part, is an open society. There are times, of course, when a curtain hides from the general public the policies and actions of important elements of our society. During periods when we are at war, either "hot" or "cold," information is kept from the public while deliberate steps are taken to mold the public's opinion to support the nation's efforts to achieve victory. In peace time the curtain of "national security," sometimes used properly and sometimes improperly, is lowered to prevent numerous government decisions and information from reaching the public and permitting an informed public opinion. In times of negative or bad news and actions, the reaction of many business managements is to hide the news, again because of concern about public opinion.

History teaches, however, that efforts to close off information fail to survive over the long run, and sometimes even in the short run. The reach and impact of mass media is too all-embracing to permit for long the retention of negative news and information. Insiders "leak" information to the media; the press uncovers information on its own; word gets about, and public opinion begins to solidify. Once solidified, whether in a negative or positive direction, public opinion is difficult to change except through some dramatic event or action.

Astute students of the public psyche understand full well the power of public opinion in all elements of American society. Large business organizations that sell consumer products take pains to insure that products sold under their brand names achieve a deserved reputation for reliability. Why? Because about the only guide available to consumers about the worth of the product is in the reliability of the brand. Veteran senators and representatives are reelected not because of their votes on a particular bill, but because the public in their states and districts are of the opinion that they can be relied upon to serve the public's interests. Without having even the slightest knowledge of the kind of education they provide, parents send their offspring to certain institutions of higher education because general public opinion holds that they are excellent institutions. Without the slightest knowledge of the services they provide, millions of Americans support certain health foundations because general public opinion holds that they perform highly valuable services. We vote for certain candidates, buy certain products, and support certain institutions because public opinion holds them worthy of our trust and confidence. Not without reason, then, does one state that public opinion has great power in American life. Achieving favorable public opinion, maintaining it over the years, and solidifying it is the basic reason why such institutions as Harvard and Yale, such corporations as General Electric, General Motors and Ford, and such personalities as Dwight D. Eisenhower and Walter Cronkite have been held in high esteem for decades.

Yet dramatic events and actions can with sudden swiftness change and modify the public's opinion of even the most sanctified institutions and people. Marshall McLuhan makes the following point: "In the mechanical age now receding, many actions could be taken without too much concern. Slow movement insured that the reactions were delayed for considerable periods of time. Today the action and the reaction occur almost at the same time . . . As electrically contracted, the globe is no more than a village." (*Understanding Media*, McGraw-Hill, 1965)

McLuhan's "action-reaction" premise is demonstrated by numerous examples. When President Nixon ran for a second term in 1972 he won victory by carrying the electoral vote of every state in the Union except Massachusetts. Yet within a short period of time — chiefly due to Watergate, its cover-up, and subsequent reverberations — public opinion practically reversed itself. (See mini-case at the end of this section). Shortly before Thanksgiving in 1959 Arthur S. Fleming, secretary of health, education and welfare, reported at a news conference that parts of the 1958 and 1959 cranberry crop from Washington and Oregon were contaminated by a weed killer. Consumers substituted applesauce for cranberries that Thanksgiving and as a result the nation's cranberry crop, estimated to have a retail value of about forty-five million dollars, turned into a substantial loss. Negative public reaction to President Johnson's escalation of the U.S. involvement in Vietnam was the chief reason he decided not to seek reelection to the highest office in the land.

Accepting the premise that public opinion is all-powerful in American life and that dramatic events and actions can swiftly change and modify opinions, what does this mean for public relations? The answer is that there is a need for experts who have solid insights and understanding of the nature of public opinion, the manner in which it is formed, ways in which to measure it, and realistic means for anticipating its future course. Managements have turned to public relations because its successful practitioners have proved themselves to be experts in the area of public opinion. Dealing with public opinion is as essential to the public relations practitioner as the scalpel is to the surgeon, knowledge of the law to the lawyer, and mathematics to the physicist. The expertise the public relations practitioner brings to the handling of public opinion is one of his chief assets and reasons for existence.

MINI-CASE
WATERGATE, PRESIDENT NIXON AND PUBLIC OPINION

The highest level of government in the United States — that of the presidency itself — provides an illuminating case study indicating how public opinion can virtually reverse itself within the space of a year as a result of events and the reaction to them by those involved.

The break-in by a group known as the "plumbers," who were caught red-handed as they broke into the headquarters of the Democratic National Committee, took place in June, 1972. It wasn't until more than a year later, in the early stages of President Richard Nixon's second term, that the Watergate political crimes, scandal, and cover-up were brought to light by the televised Senate Watergate Committee hearings, followed by the resignations of the president's top aides, the indictments and sentencing of a score of presidential assistants and advisors, the firing of Special Prosecutor Archibald Cox and the resignation of Attorney General Elliot Richardson, and speeches by the president to explain the situation.

As it has been doing since 1930 with all American presidents, the Gallup poll posed the following trend question at periodic intervals in 1973: "Do you approve or disapprove of the way Nixon is handling his job as president?" The chart below shows the results:

	Approve	Disapprove	No Opinion
January, 1973.........	68%	25%	7%
April, 1973.............	54%	36%	10%
May, 1973..............	45%	42%	13%
July, 1973..............	40%	49%	11%
October, 1973.........	30%	57%	13%
December, 1973......	29%	60%	11%

Stated the Gallup poll in a commentary:

"Nixon's job rating has declined 39 percentage points since late January, when a survey taken immediately following the Vietnam peace settlement showed a record 68 percent expressing approval of his performance in office. This decline represents the sharpest recorded for any president since these measurements were first started during the presidency of Franklin D. Roosevelt.

"A key factor in the president's slide in popularity was Watergate. "Corruption in government" for the first time in more than two decades was, in the mind of the public, one of the most important problems facing the nation. In surveys since June, about three-fourths of the public have held the view that Nixon was, at least to some extent, involved in the scandal . . ."

> Side note: By April, 1974, President Nixon's approval-disapproval rating had virtually reversed that of January, 1973. The April, 1974 poll showed that 62 percent disapproved, 25 percent approved, and 13 percent had no opinion of the way Nixon was handling his job as president.

CHANGES IN THE TECHNOLOGY, ROLE, AND IMPACT OF THE MASS MEDIA

Legend has it that when Paul Revere wanted to arouse the Minutemen he got on his horse, rode through the countryside, and shouted at the top of his voice to arouse the sleeping citizenry. Result: a grim band of Minutemen showed up at Lexington commons. Today he would either hold a press conference or telephone the Associated Press and United Press International, the four major radio and the three major television networks; they'd put the story on the air immediately or send it over high speed teleprinters; the news would be all over America in a matter of minutes.

This exemplifies the fourth fundamental trend in American society — the changes that have taken place in the technology, role, and impact of the mass media in the United States. In two of the areas — technology and impact — the changes have been dramatic; the role played by the mass media remains virtually the same as in Paul Revere's day.

Technology

For almost two-thirds of the history of our country the major media force in society was the print media, and for a considerable period of that time, changes in the technology of the print media were of a limited nature. Newsmen wrote their stories by hand, printers set them in type by hand, and slow presses turned the stories into type and printed newspapers. The telephone and Western Union wire speeded up the reporting process; the typewriter speeded up the writing process; and the Linotype and rotary presses speeded up the printing process. Only within the last decade has dramatic technological change occurred in the print field. We have seen the development of video tape terminals and units; ultra high speed presses; and computer-run news-gathering, news storage, news editing, and printing. If there is one word to describe the technological revolution that has recently been and is still being wrought in America's newsrooms it is *speed*. Because of the nature of the printing process and because of distribution problems connected with the finished product, newspapers still lag considerably behind the electronic media in the speed race, but there's no doubt that the gap has been closed considerably within our own generation.

An example of the new technology is this excerpt from a news release describing *The New York Press*, billed as a "space age newspaper":

Heart of the newspaper's typesetting function will be two "Harris 2500" computer systems with memory discs able to receive and store copy from all sources. It includes editing and proofing terminals and video typewriters for originating copy. In addition, two optical scanners will convert regular typed copy to electronic signals, which will be communicated directly to the computers.

The Harris cathode ray tube devices will enable editors to have direct control of news copy every step of the way from the reporters' input to the final page proofs.

It works like this:

A reporter returning from an assignment will 'write' his copy on a video typewriter. He won't need copy paper, pencil, glue pot or even have to strike out mistakes.

A little larger than an ordinary typewriter, the "Harris 2500" CRT typewriter is equipped with a standard keyboard. The reporter's story is displayed on the screen in front of him as he writes it. The copy is hyphenated and justified automatically and instantly. Correcting is done by striking over a word with new characters, erasing the error from the screen as the correct character appears. It's all done in micro-seconds.

The writer can recall any of his copy to his screen to revise or rewrite prior to sending it to the computer memory bank. Editors retrieve the story on their video screens for final editing, updating, additions and headline writing. When the copy editing is completed, the news editor presses a "set it" button, and the story is set by high speed computerized phototypesetters.

The computer also holds stories which have been slugged to a specific category such as national news, financial, sports, women's page, etc., and accurately measures and reports each story's length for makeup. Proof reading is completed before type is set since the final output is seen on the video tube. Phototypesetters are not subject to the mechancial errors inherent in hot metal linecasters.

Wire service copy and stock market tables will be fed directly into the system's computer for typesetting. Revision, shortening or localizing of wire copy can be carried out on "Harris 1100" electronic editing terminals. By punching a key, editors can have copy set any width desired. If a story is set one column and the desk opts to have it run two or more columns wide, the computer rejustifies and resets the copy in micro-seconds.

(Source: Release sent by John DeNigris Associates, Inc.)

Speed, of course, is what distinguishes the newer electronic media. Radio is the fastest way of getting across a message to the largest number of people in the country, chiefly because radio deals only with sound. Within a matter of minutes the radio newsman can gather his news, telephone it into the station or network, and have it heard by millions. Television involves a team effort involving newsman and cameraman, and the latter is the one who poses the problem because his film must be delivered to the station or network before it can be transmitted. However, within a period of years we have witnessed the development of hand-held, portable cameras and the use of satellites high above the earth to bring into our living room events occuring all over the globe. In a short time there will be virtually no gap between the event, the reporting of the event, and its reception by the audience. Further, when the full potential of cable television is finally realized we will see the day when the line between print and electronic media will be erased. We will then be able to turn to channels on our television set that will carry full pages of newsprint (though probably under some fancier name).

Impact

For more than a century and a quarter the daily newspaper served as the primary source of news for the vast majority of adult Americans, but with the advent of the electronic media — especially television — there has been a significant change. The primary source of news, according to continuing trend studies conducted for the Television Information Office by the Roper polling organization, is now television, followed by the daily newspaper, radio, and magazines. The following table tells the story:

Table 2-1

Response of a national sample to the question: "Where do you usually get most of your news about what's going on in the world today — from the newspapers or radio or television or magazines or talking to people or where?"

Source of most news:	1959	1961	1964	1968	1971	1973	1974
Television	51%	52%	58%	59%	60%	64%	65%
Newspapers	57%	57%	56%	49%	48%	50%	47%
Radio	34%	34%	26%	25%	23%	21%	21%
Magazines	8%	9%	8%	7%	5%	6%	4%
People	4%	5%	5%	5%	4%	4%	4%
Don't Know or No Answer	1%	3%	3%	3%	1%	1%	—
Total mentions	154	157	153	145	140	145	142

(Source: Television Information Office)

The figures in Table 2-1 are not surprising. In 1975 more than 98 percent of American homes (69 million) had at least one television set. The CBS Evening News had an audience of 26 million, NBC Evening News an audience of 21 million, and ABC Evening News an audience of 10.5 million. The 1760 daily newspapers in that same year had a total combined daily circulation of 63 million. A total of eleven of these daily newspapers had circulations over 500,000; the circulation of the median-sized daily in most states was 12,500 and the circulation of the average-sized daily was about 36,000. In 1975 there were more than 7,000 commercial radio stations and a total of more than 400 million radio sets in use.

One has to be cautious in dealing with the above figures and with survey results such as those shown by the survey sponsored by the Television Information Office. For example, a survey sponsored in the late 1960s by a newspaper group, the Newsprint Information Committee, showed that 78 percent of a national sample said they had read a newspaper the day before the survey, 60 percent said they watched one or more television newscasts, and 55 percent said they heard one or more radio newscasts. Note that the Roper question in the television-sponsored survey refers to "what's going on in the world today," and this implies national and international news.

Except in our largest cities where television stations have large and competent staffs with a great deal of financial backing for their news-gathering efforts, local television newscasts don't come anywhere near matching the work of the local daily newspaper. By their own admission, network television commentators such as Walter Cronkite point out they barely scratch the surface with their daily half-hour news show. The newspaper remains the main source of local news and for national and international news and interpretative commentary in depth. For those millions who want the news brought into focus, the three national newsmagazines — *Time, Newsweek*, and *U.S. News and World Report* — are powerful molders of public opinion. Specialized magazines flourish because of their strong appeal and interest to special groups in the population. Ben Bagdikian, author and journalist, sums up the situation: "Even conflicting and competing surveys make clear that there has been no large-scale preemption of one medium by another, that each is used for a different set of reasons. Certain kinds of news continue to be dominant in print, other kinds in radio and television. In most kinds of news the media seem to reinforce each other — more and more people use both — rather than cancel each other out." (*The Information Machines*, Harper Colophon Books, 1971)

Further, the media monitor each other carefully and often feed on each other's output. A local daily in Peoria, for example, runs an unusual feature story. The story catches the eye of the U.P.I. bureau man in a nearby city, and he rewrites it and sends it to the U.P.I. bureau in the state capital. They put it on the national wire. Two weeks later the New York *Times* sends a reporter to Peoria, and after a day or so on the scene he writes his up-dated version of the same feature story. It runs on the front page and is also sent out to subscribers to the *New York Times News Service*. Someone on the *Today* show reads about the story, and as a result the show carries a five-minute segment the following week. Because of one local reporter's curiosity and ability with words, millions of Americans learn about a purely local feature.

Role

From its earliest beginnings in America the role of the daily newspaper has been as a supplier of news, entertainment, and opinion. Radio and television have primarily served as entertainment vehicles, but their role as suppliers of news has become increasingly important. When the unblinking eye of the television camera is focused on an unfolding event — such as happened when television carried gavel-to-gavel coverage of the Senate Watergate hearings — television's role as a molder of public opinion becomes of highly significant importance.

With the exception of the two newsmagazines *Time* and *Newsweek* — which have built their readership through skillful editing and a combination of interpretation and news — the mass media stick for the most part to straight objective reporting and separation of the news and opinion functions. But when a major story or event breaks; when the story carries implications for millions of people; and when it involves controversy and builds momentum, the usual rules go out the window. To the beleaguered organization or individual caught in the vortex of the event, the media assume the role of a thousand Paul Reveres riding about the national countryside arousing the citizenry. A few examples should suffice to establish the point: stories following the Bay of Pigs disaster in the Kennedy administration; stories following the MyLai massacre in the Johnson administration; stories about the major oil companies during the Nixon administration; and stories about automobile defects and massive recalls during any administration.

Considering, therefore, the role and effect of mass media in American society, one need not wonder why amateurs should not be entrusted with the task of dealing with the media. *With each passing year as the mass media increase in importance as purveyors of information and molders of opinion, so does it become obvious that organizations and individuals which rely on public support for their very existence turn to public relations practitioners for guidance and assistance in dealing with the media.*

CONSUMERISM AND ENVIRONMENTAL SENSITIVITY

Consumerism and environmental sensitivity — the fifth major trend in American society causing a need for public relations — have been around for a long time, but they assumed heightened significance as recently as the late sixties and early seventies. While in no way meaning to downgrade the importance of the new sensitivity to the environment, this section will deal chiefly with consumerism because of its across-the-board appeal to all segments of the population; its long history as recognized by established government agencies and by newly formed ones; the staying power and strength of broad-based national, regional, state, and local activist groups; and its obvious concern to a wide variety of organizations with direct dealing with the consumer. Further, the term "consumerism" will include concern with numerous environmental aspects of our society as well as concern for the quality and performance of goods and services.

Consumers have always been considered an important public by public relations practitioners, and especially by those whose organizations have had direct contact with consumers. When an organization's chief source of income is through sales to consumers, its relationship with customers is of key importance to profit or loss. With good reason, therefore, such organizations have long-established customer relations departments, and the public relations function has been used in establishing, maintaining, and solidifying good customer relations.

Consumerism, however, is to customer relations what this year's model cars are to the Model T. Just as it would be unwise to try to sell the Model T in today's marketplace, so is it unwise to try to sell the old customer relations platitudes in today's *consumer activist* marketplace. Commencing in the mid-sixties as virtually a one-man movement led by Ralph Nader, consumerism built up an astonishing head of steam in a few short years, and by the mid-seventies had become a force that had to be reckoned with by all major corporations. *U.S. News and World Report*, generally considered to be the most conservative of the three major newsmagazines, described the movement succinctly in a full-page ad in the July, 1975, issue of *Public Relations Journal*. Headed, "A New Breed of Activist Has Emerged in the Seventies," the ad declared in part:

> Today's corporation faces a new public interest activism. A new breed of activist has emerged in the Seventies among corporate constituencies which traditionally have looked with favor upon the business community. Skepticism is on the rise, even among shareholders. . . . Primarily middle class, today's activists bear little resemblence to those of the Sixties. Well above average in income, education and awareness, they speak out for different goals: consumer protection, automobile and airplane safety, pure food, air and water, and (most crucial) corporate accountability. Their radiating influence on the thoughts and actions of millions of others threatens to hit corporations where they live — in the profit and loss statement. . . .

Perceptive analysts of the American scene trace the swift rise of the new consumerism to a combination of factors. In part, it resulted from the general unhappiness with many forms of American life in the late sixties; the political and social activism which found voice in the massive dissent to our continuing involvement in Vietnam; and with what Arthur H. White of the Daniel Yankelovich organization called the "galloping psychology of entitlement." White summed up the essentials of this psychology in the following words:

> One of the most boat-rocking social trends in the United States is a phenomenon we have called "the galloping psychology of entitlement," and it has profound implications for the future of American business. It is the psychological process whereby a person's wants or desires become converted into a set of presumed rights.

> An American who once said "I would like to be sure of a secure retirement," now says "I have a right to a secure retirement."

A view expressed not long ago as "my job would mean more to me if I had more to say about how things are run" changes to "I have the right to take part in decisions that affect my job." From "If I could afford it, I would have the best medical care," to "I have the right to the best medical care whether I can afford it or not." From "I hope this cottage cheese is fresh," to "I have the right to know when it was made and how long it will stay fresh."

. . . The consumer movement is a special consequence of the new psychology that is having and will continue to have a profound effect on the way business and businessmen operate in this country. . . .

The consumer movement, as it exists today, has enormous strength. Its public support is massive. In our own surveys and others, an unswerving average of 80–90 percent of the public supports consumerism — virtually a consensus. Furthermore, the support is strongest in mainstream America. It is not a function of liberal politics, but cuts across ideological and class lines. The core of support is the middle and upper middle income housewife — a force to be reckoned with. Of equal significance, the consumer movement has great appeal to political leaders. They see, as we do, that it is an issue people care about...........

(from an article in the *Public Relations Journal*, October, 1973)

White's emphasis on the broad-based nature of consumerism is particularly important because it was addressed to public relations practitioners, and unfortunately many of them viewed the burgeoning consumer activist movement as being forced on Americans by the government and/or politicians.

This viewpoint was typified in an address given by a leading counselor in the mid-sixties to a group of television advertising executives and summed up in these words:

This country didn't just discover the consumer with the help of Esther Peterson or Betty Furness. We built a successful economy and an unrivaled standard of living on the philosophy that says consumer is king. I argue that business, not bureaucracy, discovered the consumer. And I say that business by and large has served him very well.

And yet business — including your business — is now being told that it can't possibly do the job without a legion of helping hands. Who wants it? Obviously not the consumer.

. . . One thing is sure. If you and I don't speak up, we can't expect others to protect us from the protectors. Even as our fellow consumers, we can be smothered by too much loving attention or drown in the overflow from bleeding hearts. . . .

The difference between White's view of the consumer movement and that of the unnamed public relations counselor cited above is clearly one of perception, but it's a difference that is highly important. White sees consumerism as "the major single cause of erosion of public confidence in business" and involving "the mainstream of American business." The counselor see consumerism as stemming chiefly from "bleeding hearts" and politicians and being directed at a few dishonest businessmen. It should be obvious that the perception one has of consumerism will affect the response to the movement.

Meanwhile, consumerism has continued to flourish through the various Nader groups; other national and state-wide consumer groups; and such agencies of the government as the Consumer Product Safety Commission, the Food and Drug Administration, the Office of Consumer Affairs, and the Agency for Consumer Advocacy.

Of special interest has been the growth of the Nader group that by the mid-seventies had become the nation's leading public interest conglomerate. As described by Susan Gross in an article in the Spring, 1975, issue of *Business and Society Review*, the first Nader organization was the Center for Study of Responsive Law and in the early days the emphasis was on exhaustive investigations and book-length reports. By 1975, however, the emphasis had shifted to litigation, lobbying, citizen organizing, and action-oriented research with most Nader programs concentrated in nine groups in Washington: the Litigation Group, Congress Watch, Health Research Group, Tax Reform Research Group, Citizen Action Group, the Center, Corporate Accountability Research Group, Public Interest Research Group, and the National Public Interest Research Group. In addition, there were almost two dozen Nader-affiliated student and citizen action state groups and other satellite groups linked to Nader through funding or personnel.

". . . Ever since the birth of PIRG in 1970," noted Ms. Gross, "Nader had been increasingly de-emphasizing Center-style massive studies in favor of hard legal and political action. Today the Nader groups rely almost exclusively on lawsuits, administrative agency actions, citizen organizing, and supportive research — while the flow of study groups has slowed to hardly a trickle, leaving the Center in the second rank of the Nader troops."

Through increased governmental and citizen action groups, consumerism by the mid-seventies was here to stay and called for the best talents that public relations could apply. Though public relations practitioners have no direct line authority in regard to consumer products and services, they do have — or should have — *insights* about a trend as persuasive as consumerism. Meeting the justified demands of consumer activists calls for the kinds of intelligence skills, sensitivity, judgment, and communication skills that public relations practitioners are supposed to have.

Some final words are in order about the heightened interest in and sensitivity to the environment. Although environmental factors do not generally have as direct and immediate an impact on the average person as consumerism factors, there is widespread concern and sensitivity about air and water pollution, waste disposal, depletion of natural resources, oil spills, and potential shoreline hazards. This concern resulted in 1970 legislation such as the National Environmental Policy Act, the Clean Air Act, and the establishment of the U.S. Environmental Protection Agency. Within five years the EPA mushroomed into the country's largest regulatory agency by 1975 with 9,000 employees, a two million dollar daily budget, and jurisdictions and responsibilities in air and water pollution, solid waste, noise, pesticides, and radiation. Direct citizen concern with the environment has been evidenced by the strong stands taken by conservation and citizen activist environment groups that fought the Alaskan pipeline project, the building of atomic power plants, and leases for off-shore drilling purposes. When such issues reach the action stage, their handling calls for public relations judgment and skills. In too many instances, however, those handling such sensitive environmental issues have called public relations professionals into play *after* rather than *before* the decisions are made.

Public relations should play the same role in regard to the environment as it does to consumerism, and one of the chief tasks and responsibilities of the practitioner should be to serve as an "early warning system" concerning public attitudes, opinions, and activities relating to environmental factors. When an organization's actions, activities, products, or services have a serious effect on the environment, advice and counsel about expected public reaction are clearly needed. No matter what the final decision, communication skills are needed. Thus, at each step in dealing with matters bearing on the environment there is an obvious need for the kinds of skills that public relations practitioners should be able to provide.

FUNDAMENTAL TRENDS IN AMERICAN SOCIETY AND THEIR EFFECT ON PUBLIC RELATIONS PRACTICE

If we want to make an analogy between the ecology of public relations and a phonograph record, then we have heard one side of the record: the causal side. That is, we have heard why certain fundamental trends in American society have brought on the need for public relations. The flip side of the same record tells us why these same trends have brought about difficult problems for public relations practitioners.

URBANIZATION AND SUBURBANIZATION

Urbanization and suburbanization have had several major effects on the practice of public relations.

On the one hand, the movement from a rural to an urban society has brought about a concentration of the population into large urban centers and has thus made it easier for practitioners to reach people through a smaller number of key mass media than if the population were spread evenly throughout the country. Various media in our largest cities reach millions of people, and it is theoretically possible to reach anywhere from ten million to sixty million people by means of a handful of carefully selected media.

On the other hand, however, these media are not simply open to the highest bidder, but are managed by experienced and sophisticated journalists careful to guard their pages and their air time from intrusion by outsiders. Veteran public relations practitioners know they must gear their messages and approaches so that they *first* meet the high demands of the media "gatekeepers," and this means a skillful meshing of one's private interests with the wider public interests serviced by the media managers.

At the same time, the move to the suburbs has brought about a further dispersion of the population and a conflict between people's allegiances. Though millions of wage earners *gain* their living from the city, they *do* their living in the suburbs. As a result, conflicts arise in regard to such areas as taxes, municipal and suburban services, and the like. The astute practitioner has to be keenly aware of the nature of one's loyalties in such conflict situations and use judgment in seeking to resolve what may often seem to be irreconcilable differences.

The trend towards urbanization and suburbanization has thus had the interesting effect of concentrating the population and at the same time spreading it out miles beyond the reaches of the inner city. The result has been a significant change in living patterns, social groupings and political affiliations, and attitudes and opinions about a wide variety of issues. All of these call for a wise understanding of the differences existing among people who live and work in our cities; people who work in the city and live in the suburbs; and people who live and work in the suburbs.

LARGE AND COMPLEX ORGANIZATIONS

Any student who attends a large university of 10,000, 20,000, or 30,000 enrollment knows what it means to exist within a large and complex organization. The perceptive student of public relations can immediately recognize the kind of problems that such an organization poses.

One of the first problems is in providing people with some sense of "belonging." A second problem is in attempting to resolve conflicts in needs and demands that inevitably arise in large and complex organizations. When the hourly worker seeks an eight percent increase, he's not really interested in learning that he can't have it because it might mean a decrease in dividends to shareholders. When customers complain about the quality of the products they buy, they're not really interested in learning that it resulted from a deliberate action by disgruntled workers. When students complain about constantly increasing tuition, they're not really interested in learning it resulted in part from a drying up of outside giving. Thus, attempting to resolve conflicts in needs and demands calls for astute and carefully designed explanations, and all too often the explanation will satisfy one constituency but not another.

A final problem facing practitioners who deal with large and complex organizations is the sheer distortion of messages that arises when communication has to move through the many layers that make up such organizations. The problem becomes particularly acute when the central headquarters and its public relations staff is in one city, and the constituency is spread out across the entire country. What seems clear-cut in an office in Chicago's Loop can become cloudy and murky in a plant community in the Deep South. The public relations staffer reporting to the chancellor on the main campus of a multi-university finds it difficult to understand what's really going on at a branch campus several hundred miles away. Maintaining contact, keeping in touch, and understanding the diverse nature, needs, wants, and desires of people existing within large and complex organizations inevitably affects public relations practice and procedures.

GROWTH IN THE POWER OF PUBLIC OPINION AND THE SWIFTNESS IN OPINION CHANGE

Public relations practitioners use primary-direct and secondary-indirect methods in dealing with the vital tasks of assaying and attempting to influence public opinion.

When public relations practice was in its infancy, practitioners relied on relatively primitive methods of measuring public opinion. Just as many small newspapers today measure public opinion by sending a reporter out to do man-woman-on-the-street interviewing, so the early practitioners conducted similar interviews with "average" people and "opinion leaders." Today, however, most practitioners recognize the need for a scientific approach to public opinion measurement and hence turn to national, regional, and state polling organizations to handle both long-range and individually-commissioned, cross-section, in-depth interview polls. These polls — described in more detail in the chapter on public opinion — are carefully designed for a variety of purposes. They're used to measure long-range trends in public attitudes and opinion, to judge consumer reaction to products and services, to ascertain general public or special public moods and attitudes, and to test an organization's reputation among the public at large or among individual publics.

There is also general recognition that a poll is able to measure public opinion only at the time it is taken. Because events and actions can swiftly change the nature of public opinion, practitioners must be cautious in their assessments and constantly alert to the sudden dips in public moods, attitudes, and opinions. This calls for constant monitoring, by means of secondary-indirect methods, of certain weathervanes of opinion change. Long before they become too obvious, changes in public opinion can be detected from trends in news stories and features, articles in national news and opinion magazines and in specialized publications, and books by men and women who have the deserved reputation for sizing up the public scene.

Through such means, practitioners treat the power of public opinion by analyzing it to provide "intelligence" data and information for the organizations they serve. They also use their other skills in attempting to influence public opinion in meeting predetermined public relations goals and objectives. These skills and techniques — described in detail in the chapters on planning, programming, and communicating — make up the core of public relations practice. They've been refined and developed because dealing with public opinion requires the highest degree of public relations competence.

CHANGES IN THE TECHNOLOGY, ROLE, AND IMPACT OF THE MASS MEDIA

Although, as noted earlier in this chapter, there have been technological breakthroughs within the mass media in the past decade, basic concepts about news have remained surprisingly constant. News can be transmitted much swifter than in the past and television has brought instant history into the living room, but the elements that make one story of national significance and another of only local interest remain the same.

Thus, the practitioner should be on top of technological changes in the mass media, but it's more important that the practitioner know when the media will be interested in a particular story or feature. Equally important, the practitioner has to be aware of changes in editorial policy, format, and personnel; to know, for example, the varying deadlines and technical imperatives of differing media; to understand how to ride the crest of the wave of mutual interest shown by all media in certain kinds of stories and events; and to be attuned to the justified criticisms leveled by the media against the amateurs who flood their offices with material that has little interest to readers and viewers.

Practitioners keep track of mass media changes by maintaining personal contact with mass media personnel and by careful reading of publications which reflect developments in the mass media. These include *Editor and Publisher, Broadcasting, Variety, More*, the *Columbia Journalism Review*, various major city and state-wide journalism reviews, *Journalism Quarterly*, the *AP* and *UPI* internal organs, *ASNE Bulletin*, the press sections of *Time* and *Newsweek*, and the numerous books about the mass media which have been published in increasing numbers in recent years. The hack keeps sending out releases en masse to hundreds of outlets which can have little interest in the material; the skilled practitioner knows the value of keying material to the needs and interests of different media and of keeping abreast of changing media developments.

CONSUMERISM AND ENVIRONMENTAL SENSITIVITY

This trend presents both an internal and external problem to the public relations practitioner. The internal problem arises because the criticisms and complaints of the consumer and those sensitive to the environment are directed at areas of organizational activities which are not directly in the control of the public relations practitioner. The practitioner does not make or produce the products or services or engage in organizational activities and actions which fail to measure up to the expectations of the consumer or the environmentalist. These are the provinces of other functions within organizations: the marketing department which distributes and sells the product through high-pressure methods;

the advertising department which extolls products far beyond normal belief; the executive who directs or countenances price-fixing, strip-mining, and carefully "washed" contributions of money to bring about large contracts. Handling and dealing with these internally produced and managed activities and factors calls for the wisdom of Solomon, the patience of Job, and the skill of Moses.

But the external problem connected with consumerism and environmental sensitivity is equally difficult and taxing. When consumer and environmental activists and/or the government target in on an organization's transgressions — or alleged transgressions — the matter becomes one of public interest and display. All too often, in such cases the practitioner is called upon to work some sleight of hand and magically disarm the dragon slayers. Unfortunately, in recent years the shafts and slings of consumer and environmental activist organizations and the government are frequently a justified reaction to products, services, and actions that do not measure up to expectations.

Thus, handling the challenges raised by consumerism and environmental sensitivity calls for ways and means of handling the dilemma posed by the internal-external demands placed on the practitioner. Some basic recommended procedures, organized by Richard A. Aszling of General Foods for PRSA chapter workshops on consumerism, suggest that the practitioner:

Be on top of developments by staying informed about legislative developments and activist actions. Know the literature and the reliable information sources

Seek to provide realistic forecasts of trends and developments

Develop effective communication upwards to boss or client and thus help him stay sensitive and to sort out fact from fancy

Be familiar with the successful programs of response to consumer pressures carried out by other companies

Advise employer or client on effective methods of responding to expressions of consumer dissatisfaction

Develop and carry out effective internal and external communication programs designed to make publics aware of steps taken on behalf of consumers

> from an article by John R. O'Connell in *Public Relations Journal*, December, 1972

By the second half of the seventies there was clear evidence that the public relations field was adjusting itself to handle the challenges of consumerism and environmental sensitivity. One piece of evidence was found in two regular columns appearing in the *Public Relations Journal*: "Environmental Update" by Edward L. Jaffee made its bow in the October, 1972, issue, and "Consumer Update" by Ms. Edie Fraser made its first appearance in the June, 1974, issue. Both columns have continued to provide readers with vital information about the consumer and environmental movement. The PRSA formed its own National Task Force on Consumerism and another National Task Force on Environment and Energy in the mid-seventies. Both groups have been active in keeping track of consumer and environmental development and in sponsoring such national meetings as The Consumer Conference and White House Briefing, held in May, 1975. Consumerism and environmental concerns have been important parts of the programs at recent PRSA national conferences; special consumer and environmental departments and sections have been set up by large national counseling organizations and industrial and business firms; and there is little doubt that the public relations field has taken steps to deal realistically with the major trends in American society evidenced by consumerism and environmental sensitivity.

MINI-CASE
MOBIL OIL RUNS AN ADVERTISEMENT

This mini-case concerns a New York *Times* article and the reaction to it three weeks later by the Mobil Oil Corporation in an advertisement by the company on the Op-Ed page of the *Times*. (The *Times* story is summarized below; students may prefer to check their library for the complete story.)

On Thursday, August 7, 1975, the New York *Times* carried a 23-paragraph story, with a Washington, August 6, dateline, written by David Burnham. The story was 26-column-inches in length and ran on an inside page under a three-column headline which read:

2,300 Scientists Petition U.S. To Cut
Construction of Nuclear Power Plants

"In a petition presented to the White House and Congress," the *Times* lead stated, "more than 2,300 scientists warned today that the dangers of nuclear power were so grave that the United States should make a 'drastic reduction' in the construction of new reactors.

"Calling for a major program of research on reactor safety, plutonium safeguards and nuclear waste disposal, the scientists said that 'the country must recognize that it now appears imprudent to move forward with a rapidly expanding nuclear power plant construction program.' "

Noting that the country has 55 operating reactors which generate about 7 to 5 percent of the nation's electricity, the story said that government planners hope there will be 830 reactors producing more than 50 percent of the country's electricity within 25 years. It pointed out that the petition was presented to the President and Congressional leaders on the 30th anniversary of the dropping of the atomic bomb on Hiroshima.

"The petition," stated the fifth paragraph of the article, "was presented by the Union of Concerned Scientists in the debate over the potential dangers of nuclear reactors as an electric power plant engineering concern — Ebasco Services, Inc. — made public a national poll it had sponsored indicating that about two-thirds of those interviewed favored the building of more reactors.''

The article quoted Dr. Henry Kendall, physics professor at M.I.T. and a founder of the Union of Concerned Scientists, as declaring the petition was significant because it destroyed the industry argument 'that no reputable scientists had doubts about the safety of reactors.'

"Among the 2,300 biologists, chemists, engineers, physicists and other scientists who signed the petition," the article noted, "were James Bryant Conant, the retired president of Harvard University; George D. Kistiakowsy, professor of chemistry, emeritus, and Victor Weisskopf, former chairman of the M.I.T. physics department, all of whom were intimately involved in the World War II effort to develop the nuclear bomb.

"Another signer was George Wald, professor of biology at Harvard and one of the nine Nobel laureates who endorsed the petition . . .

". . . To gain the signatures for its petition, the Union of Concerned Scientists sent the statement last June to 16,000 persons, most of whose names were drawn from the mailing lists of the Federation of American Scientists and the Bulletin of Atomic Scientists.

"Dr. Kendall said that the 2,300 scientists who responded represented about 20 percent of the 12,000 scientists and engineers on the two mailing lists. The physicist said this was a far better response than the 1 to 2 percent reply rate that he said mailing experts had told him to expect. The union itself has less than 100 members."

The petition, noted the article, said there are three major problems connected with the widespread use of nuclear power. The article went into detail about each of these three problems as cited in the petition. It then cited the scientists as calling for "a greatly enlarged national effort to conserve the use of energy and to develop techniques for using coal without polluting the atmosphere and for harnessing the energy of the sun, the wind, the tides and the heat of the earth's crust.''

Paragraph 16 of Burnham's story stated that a public opinion survey taken last spring by the polling firm of Louis Harris and Associates showed that 63 percent of those interviewed in a nationwide survey favored the building of more nuclear power plants while 19 percent were opposed. (This is the survey sponsored by Ebasco).

The remaining eight paragraphs of the story cited data from the survey by the Harris organization showing more people in favor of than opposed to speeding up construction of the Alaska oil pipeline; increasing efforts to produce oil shale in Western states; starting offshore drilling for oil off the Atlantic, Pacific and Gulf coasts, and allowing more strip mining of coal.

_____

The Mobil Oil Corporation advertisement — one of a series of public

relations ads the company had been running periodically in the
Times — appeared on the paper's Op-Ed page on August 28, 1975.
The headline and the copy were as follows:

The People speak.
But the message gets lost.

From time to time we have criticized Congress for its tardiness in
enacting sound national energy policy. But how can our elected representatives know the facts needed for sound legislation when the energy information they see in the press gives a misleading impression
of how Americans feel on this issue?

Consider, for example, The New York *Times* article on August 7
headlined, "2,300 Scientists Petition U.S. to Reduce Construction of
Nuclear Power plants."

The hasty reader gained the impression that a survey of the scientific
community showed scientists solidly opposed to the new plants. No
such thing. In reality, the 2,300 were those who indicated by mail
their support of a position of the Union of Concerned Scientists. And
they represented only about 20 percent of the 12,000 professionals
polled.

Was this an impressive response, even so? Far from it, says Hugh
Hoffman, who heads three opinion research organizations and is a
recognized expert in the field. "If the petition's viewpoint were
strongly held in the scientific community, a 60 percent return
wouldn't have been surprising, given the fact that these were articu-
late, concerned individuals."

The *Times* did, in the same article, report a public opinion survey
showing that 63 percent of the people *favor* building new atomic
plants, while only 19 percent are opposed and 18 percent undecided.
Among those living near existing nuclear plants, the same majority —
63 percent — favor new A-plant construction.

But that survey, unfortunately, wasn't mentioned until the fifth paragraph and supporting detail was relegated to the last part of the 23-
paragraph story. The *Times* has "balanced" the news. But had it,
really? Many readers, we suspect, never got that far down in the article.

We were sorry, too, that the *Times* did not cite — as the Washington
Post did in its story on the petition — another petition of scientists
which strongly *supported* A-plants. (Signers included 11 Nobel Prize
laureates, six of them in physics, the science most associated with
nuclear development.) In the *Post* article, a Nobel Prize laureate was
quoted as comparing opposition to nuclear power to earlier-day opposition to the advent of airplanes and railroads.

We were disappointed, too, that the *Times* chose to overlook another
recent poll, by Opinion Research Corporation, which found that 56
percent of a cross section of American engineers believe nuclear

power should receive immediate priority. Sixty-three percent of this group felt present atomic-safety regulations are basically adequate.

Why is an oil company worried about nuclear power? Obviously, because the atom can lift a great deal of the burden from oil and gas. But also because this case clearly tells why Congress and other officials aren't getting their constituents' thinking about energy. Why the message isn't getting through.

Isn't it time both sides of energy issues were presented more objectively? So that everybody can understand what's really happening, and how people really feel? So that the country can get the facts needed to formulate a sound energy program? We think so.

Mobil

© 1975 Mobil Oil Corporation

Reprinted with permission

Questions for Discussion.

1. Do you feel the criticisms of the *Times* story cited in the Mobil advertisement are justified? In expressing your conclusions, cite specifics to prove your point of view.
2. What do you perceive to be Mobil's public relations objectives in writing and running the ad in the *Times*? What's your opinion of these objectives? Do you think the advertisement will achieve these objectives?
3. What's your *personal* opinion of the ad? Your *professional* opinion?
4. Assume that you are public relations counsel to Mobil. A draft of the ad has been sent to you with this notation: "Following is a draft of an ad which we are thinking of running in the *Times* on August 28. We would appreciate your professional opinion of the ad and our intention to run it on the Op-Ed page."

Write a memorandum to the vice president of public relations of Mobil giving your reaction to the proposed ad and Mobil's intention to run it on the Op-Ed page.

QUESTIONS AND PROBLEMS FOR DISCUSSION

1. In what way does ecology, a biological term, apply to public relations?
2. Briefly identify: Theodore Vail; Ivy Lee; the PRSA.
3. Name three public relations publications.
4. Explain some of the ramifications of *each* of the following major trends in American society: (1) urbanization and suburbanization; (2) large and complex components; (3) growth in the power of public opinion and the swiftness of opinion change; (4) changes in the technology, role and impact of the mass media; and (5) consumerism and environmental sensitivity.
5. Explain several ways in which *each* of the above-mentioned major trends in American society have brought about the need for public relations.

6. Explain several ways in which *each* of the major trends has affected public relations practice.
7. When an organization's actions and policies are negative and clearly expected to draw adverse public reaction, is it wisest to communicate nothing, to wait out the resulting adverse public reaction, or to come right out and communicate the negative? Cite any example (s) to demonstrate the wisdom of your choice of action.
8. What steps would you suggest be taken by a large utility to maintain goodwill and understanding when its plan to build a nuclear power plant is vociferously opposed by conservation groups?
9. What would you suggest the public relations practitioner do when his/her organization's policies and actions are profitable to the organization but are viewed negatively by large segments of the population?
10. What would you suggest the public relations executive do when his/her management blames the executive for a loss in sales due to a nationally disseminated story over which the executive had no control?

SOCIAL RESPONSIBILITY AND THE PUBLIC INTEREST   3

Two major areas of concern to public relations practitioners have been those of social responsibility and the public interest. In recent years these areas have appeared with increasing frequency in the professional literature about the field, but two men — Edward L. Bernays and Harwood Childs — foresaw their importance in the early twenties and late thirties. In their writings both men espoused ideas which were considered innovative — as well as impractical — but time has proved them to be basic to the practice of public relations and definitely practical when considered in the long run. Looking back now, decades later, one discovers that the insights of Childs and Bernays were not merely provocative but perceptive. The two merely happened to be thirty-five to fifty years ahead of their time.

PUBLIC RELATIONS AS SEEN BY EDWARD L. BERNAYS

Author of a score of books about public relations, Edward L. Bernays had an active career of more than forty years. Starting his professional life as an admitted press agent, Bernays was the first to refer to himself subsequently as a "public relations counsel." He was also one of the first to recognize that the core of the practice is in establishing "a common meeting ground for an entity (whether a business, an individual, a government body, or a social service organization) and society."

Because public opinion is of paramount importance in a democratic society, Bernays said, the public relations practitioner must be alert to changing societal conditions and be prepared to advise modifications in policy in accordance with changes in the public point of view. As he wrote in *Crystallizing Public Opinion* (1923): "Perhaps the chief contribution of the public relations counsel to the public and to his client is his ability to understand and analyze obscure tendencies of the public mind . . . It is his capacity for crystallizing the obscure tendencies of the public mind before they have reached definite expression, which makes him so valuable."

The above statements cover but briefly the Bernays view of public relations, but they are cited specifically to indicate his awareness of the close relationship between public relations and the society in which it operates. Political scientist Harwood Childs of Princeton University amplified this relationship when he delivered a series of lectures in the late 1930s and then expanded his remarks in a book called *An Introduction to Public Opinion* (Wiley, 1940). His views, particularly when analyzed in the light of today's heightened interest in social responsibility, are worthy of careful consideration.

PUBLIC RELATIONS AS SEEN BY HARWOOD CHILDS

Disdaining what he called "the antics, stunts, tricks, and devices by which individuals and corporations often seem to obtain goodwill without actually trying to remove the real cause of ill will," Childs stated that he was not interested in the many ways to win friends and influence people. He foresaw that interest in public relations would continue and increase because, as he put it, public relations reflects one of the fundamental problems of the times. His view of the intrinsic nature of public relations is set forth here:

> Public relations may be defined as those aspects of our personal and corporate behavior which have a social rather than a purely private and personal significance.

Childs understood that public relations would gain in importance chiefly because an increasing number of private and corporate activities would have social and public significance.

"Public relations as such," he declared, "is not the presentation of a point of view, not the art of tempering mental attitudes, nor the development of cordial and profitable relations. . . . It is simply a name for activities which have a social significance.

"Our problem in each corporation or industry is to find out what these activities are, what social effects they have, and, if they are contrary to the public interest, to find ways and means for modifying them so that they will serve the public interest."

In setting forth this analysis of public relations, Childs stressed that the public relations executive is not primarily a publicist or propagandist. To meet Childs' standards the public relations executive has to be "a student of the social effects of personal and corporate conduct" and has to have a thorough understanding of society from a political, economic, cultural, and sociological point of view. Summed up therefore:

> The starting point in working out a public relations policy is a careful analysis of our personal and corporate behaviour in the light of social change generally. Without knowing the basic economic, cultural, political, and social trends of our times we cannot ascertain, much less anticipate, the public implications of what we are doing. It is the lag between social trends that gives rise to our problems, and the search for answers must be a search for the reasons why these lags exist, where they exist, and what can be done to synchronize social movement.

> The business of producing and distributing goods and services must be studied in relation to the total situation, the total environment in which we are functioning. Executives of corporations cannot afford to devote all or even the major portion of their energies solely to technological considerations. They must raise their eyes to the level of wider horizons. The public relations counsel must be something more than a publicist, a journalist or a statistician. He must be a social scientist capable of advising management regarding the environment in which it is operating.

OBSERVATIONS CONCERNING THE CHILDS THESIS

A caveat is in order before proceeding with a discussion of the thesis of public relations expounded by Harwood Childs. Most readers of this textbook will be students who hope to make a career of public relations or who hope to use it in other careers where public relations has an important bearing. Young people entering the field will not generally be given an executive position in public relations and expected to serve as elder statesmen. On the contrary, they will most likely be engaged in tasks which Childs claims are not public relations: helping with "the presentation of a point of view" and in "the development of cordial and profitable relations." In time, however, as the neophyte becomes expert in his field he will be given broader and more significant responsibilities and duties. The time to think about and to understand these broader areas is now, for tomorrow may be too late. Consider, therefore, that you were among the business leaders and professionals to whom Childs addressed himself back in the late thirties. Certain observations and questions should then come more readily to mind.

First, a question about Childs' basic premise. Do you agree or disagree with his contention that public relations is "not the presentation of a point of view, not the art of tempering mental attitudes, nor the development of cordial and profitable relations?" What arguments can be raised *against* this viewpoint? Is it possible that in his desire to underscore the importance of the societal approach to public relations Childs may have overstated his case? What do other authorities say about the issue?

Second, what does Childs mean when he says that public relations is "simply a name for activities which have a social significance?" The college edition of *Webster's New World Dictionary Of the American Language* defines the adjective "social" in many ways:

1. Of or having to do with human beings living together as a group in a situation requiring that they have dealings with one another: as, *social* consciousness, *social* reform, *social* problems
2. Living in this way: as, modern man is *social*, the family is a *social* unit
3. Of or having to do with the ranks or activities of society, especially the more exclusive or fashionable of these: as, a *social* climber, *social* notes
4. Sociable; getting along well with others, as, a *social* nature
5. Of, for or fond of friends, companionship, etc: as, a *social* club.

Which of the above, in your opinion, seems to come closest to the meaning which Childs attributes to social when he speaks of activities having social significance? What about activities having a political, economic and cultural significance? Do you think Childs meant to incorporate these three — political, economic and cultural — when he stressed only socially significant activities? How about "societal" as an adjective to describe the activities to which Childs referred?

The word "significance" also brings to mind certain key questions. When is an activity socially *significant*, when is it of moderate importance, and when is it insignificant? Childs does not answer these questions; in fact he leaves the matter up to the individual practitioner. Note, for example, that he states that "our problem" is to ascertain what activities have a social significance, to figure out what social effects they have, and to find ways and means for modifying them if they are contrary to the public interest.

Assuming that Childs' basic premise is correct, we find that he has formulated a conception of public relations which poses innumerable challenges to the competence, wisdom, and judgment of the public relations practitioner. Bernays saw these challenges clearly in 1962 when he told a New York *Times* interviewer that the task of the public relations man should be to study public opinion and social psychology and to "counsel his company on how to adjust to . . . societal forces and to enlist public support for services, products and ideas." One can scarcely counsel if one has little understanding of societal forces. Put another way: "Public relations advice, to be worth anything, must be grounded on a comprehensive knowledge of the past, of trends and relationships in the field of social change," said Childs, and his challenge to the public relations practitioner thus becomes one of being able to cope with the past, the present, and the future of our society.

That this is a tall order can be proved by the following chart and test. Listed in the left-hand column are some major organizations and institutions in American society. The second column calls for the reader to cite in brief form some *past* socially significant activities of these organizations and institutions that have posed public relations problems. The third and fourth columns call for the reader to cite in brief form some *present* and *future* socially significant activities of these organizations and institutions that have posed public relations problems. (The author has presented one example for the first two institutions in each of the three test columns, and of course his examples can be challenged. The challengers should be prepared to defend their choices.)

MINI-PROBLEM
CHILDS' THESIS PUT TO THE TEST

Organization or institution	Past socially significant activities posing PR problems	Present socially significant activities posing PR problems	Future socially significant activities posing PR problems
Airlines	Crashes in which all passengers were killed	Deafening sound of modern jets breaking the sound barrier	Air space congestion
Hospitals	Patient fear of surgery	High cost of hospital care	Impersonalization due to consolidation into large units
Private colleges			
Public colleges			
The United Way			
Labor Unions			
General Motors			
Your favorite conglomerate			
Oil companies			
The movie industry			
The Red Cross			
The American Medical Association			

Note: For each organization or institution on the left supply appropriate entries under past, present and future socially significant activities posing public relations problems for the organization or institution concerned.

Coping with the challenge of this chart may seem like an academic exercise to some, but relating to problems is a key element in public relations programming. One must first recognize public relations problems before one can hope to solve them. Such recognition comes from understanding past and noting present socially significant activities posing public relations problems and foreseeing future socially significant activities that will bring about public relations problems at some time beyond the present.

Recognition, however, is but one step in the public relations process. What to *do* about these problems is another matter. What to do is often a choice from among three alternatives: what is permissible, what is possible, and what is prohibited. Internal, rather than external, factors generally govern the choice to be made because higher authority in the management of organizations and institutions have the final word over public relations' freedom of action and activity. This is particularly true in the area known as social responsibility.

SCHOOLS OF THOUGHT CONCERNING SOCIAL RESPONSIBILITY

The concept of social responsibility is one that few people dare to challenge. It's akin to God, mother, and apple pie. It takes an agnostic to challenge the idea of God; a Philip Wylie to challenge the institution of motherhood, and a peach pie enthusiast to challenge the virtues of apple pie. Who among us are willing to stand up and say we are socially irresponsible, and what organizations and institutions are willing to contend they are not socially responsible? Everyone, it seems, is socially responsible, but in *varying degrees*. The two major views of thought concerning social responsibility have probably been best expressed by Dr. Milton Friedman and by the Committee For Economic Development.

THE FRIEDMAN VIEW

At one extreme in the debate over social responsibility — particularly as the concept applies to business — is Dr. Milton Friedman, noted professor of economics at the University of Chicago. A staunch defender of the free-enterprise, private-property system, Friedman says that those who contend that business should be concerned not "merely" with profit but also with promoting desirable social ends are "preaching pure and unadulterated socialism."

Friedman's view — set forth in a September 13, 1970, article in the *New York Times Magazine* — reminds us that corporate executives are employees of the owners of their businesses and have a direct responsibility to their employers.

"That responsibility," says Friedman, "is to conduct the business in accordance with their desires, which generally will be to make as much money as possible while conforming to the basic rules of society, both those embodied in law and those embodied in ethical custom."

Friedman observes that the corporate executive is also a person in his own right and as such he may want to devote part of his income to causes he regards as worthy. However, says Friedman, when we talk of the social responsibility of the corporate executive as a businessman we ask him to act in some way not in the interest of his employers. As one example, Friedman says that when we ask the businessman to refrain from increasing the price of his product in order to gain the social objective of preventing inflation, such a decision may not be in the best interests of the corporation. Similarly, he adds, it may be at the expense of corporate profits to ask the businessman to hire "hardcore" unemployed rather than better-qualified workers in order to gain the social objective of reducing poverty.

Professor Friedman sums up his argument in the following words:

There is one and only one social responsibility of business — to use its resources and engage in activities designed to increase its profits so long as it stays within the rules of the game, which is to say, engages in open and free competition without deception or fraud.

THE COMMITTEE FOR ECONOMIC DEVELOPMENT VIEW

Another view of social responsibility was set forth in the early seventies in a 74-page statement by the Research and Policy Committee of the Committee for Economic Development (CED), titled "Social Responsibilities of Business Corporation." Addressing itself primarily to the large, publicly owned, professionally managed corporations — though noting its remarks apply as well to smaller enterprises and to businessmen as individuals — the CED cited some negative attitudes toward business expressed by the public in nationwide public opinion polls. It concluded from these statistics that a clear majority of the public believes that corporations have not been sufficiently concerned about societal problems and that "two-thirds believe business now has a moral obligation to help other major institutions to achieve social progress, even at the expense of profitability. . . . Business is being asked to assume broader responsibilities to society than ever before and to serve a wider range of human values. Business enterprises, in effect, are being asked to contribute more to the quality of American life than just supplying quantities of goods and services."

Four basic questions raised by business in response to the above-mentioned demands, said the CED, are as follows:

1. Why should corporations become substantially involved in the improvement of the social environment?
2. How can they justify this to their stockholders?
3. How can companies reconcile substantial expenditures for social purposes with profitability?
4. What are the limitations on corporate social responsibility?

Agreeing that these are legitimate concerns, the CED said the answer to them is found in recognizing that business is a basic institution in American society and has a vital stake in the general welfare as well as in its own public acceptance.

Amplifying Harwood Childs' doctrines, the CED then set forth social responsibilities in terms of self-interest:

There is broad recognition today that corporate self-interest is inexorably involved in the well-being of the society of which business is an integral part, and from which it draws the basic requirements needed for it to function at all — capital, labor, customers. There is increasing understanding that the corporation is dependent on the goodwill of society, which can sustain or impair its existence through public pressures on government. And it has become clear that the essential resources and goodwill of society are not naturally forthcoming to corporations whenever needed, but must be worked for and developed. . . .

Indeed the corporate interest broadly defined by management can support involvement in helping to solve virtually any social problem, because people who have a good environment, education, and opportunity make better employees, customers, and neighbors for business than those who are poor, ignorant, and oppressed. It is obviously in the interest of business to enlarge its markets and to improve its work force by helping disadvantaged people to develop and employ their economic potential. Likewise, it is in the interest of business to help reduce the mounting costs of welfare, crime, disease, and waste of human potential — a good part of which business pays for.

Experience with governmental and social constraints indicates that the corporation's self-interest is best served by a sensitivity to social concerns and a willingness, within competitive limits, to take needed action ahead of confrontation. By acting on its own initiative, management preserves the flexibility needed to conduct the company's affairs in a constructive, efficient and adaptive manner.

Recognizing the cost factor in its analysis of social responsibility, the CED noted that business obviously cannot be expected to solve all the problems of society. The report pointed out that various internal constraints limit corporations in their approach to societal problems. "No company of any size can willingly incur costs that would jeopardize its competitive position and threaten its survival. While companies may well be able to absorb modest costs or undertake some social activities on a break-even basis, any substantial expenditure must be justified in terms of the benefits, tangible and intangible, that are expected to be produced."

The analysis of the two views of social responsibility cited above is obviously a truncated one. On the one hand we have Dr. Friedman's view that the business of business is just business; that management has neither the right nor the qualifications to undertake activities to improve society or to tax its constituents for these purposes, and that society's general welfare is a matter for the government, not business. On the other hand we have the CED view that it's in the self-interest of business to accept a fair measure of responsibility for improving society because "insensitivity to changing demands of society sooner or later results in public pressures for governmental intervention and regulation to require business to do what it was reluctant or unable to do voluntarily."

SOCIAL RESPONSIBILITY AND PUBLIC RELATIONS

In those organizations and institutions where the Friedman view of social responsibility prevails, the role of the public relations practitioner is a relatively simple one: assist management in maximizing profits and staying "within the rules of the game." The practitioner plays a far different — and more difficult — role in those organizations and institutions which see social responsibility through CED lenses.

Take the matter of timing, for example. Astute practitioners know that timing is often an essential ingredient. Where institutions face stiff competition the organization that reacts too swiftly to rising social pressures may find itself penalized because of the added costs involved. But failure to respond or to respond too slowly may also penalize an organization through economic penalities or a loss of reputation and sales when forced to comply with public opinion.

Being able to distinguish between temporary fads and substantive, long-lasting demands for social change poses another major problem for the public relations practitioner. The currents of public opinion run deep, and it's difficult to distinguish between ripples on the surface and the strong undertows which move beneath the surface.

In assisting organizations and institutions to deal with activities which have societal importance and consequences, the public relations practitioner faces not merely the problem of timing and evaluating the true substantive nature of the activities. His other problem is most likely to be one of *fulfilling his proper niche and role*. It is one thing to understand that public relations is involved with corporate social responsibility matters. It is quite another to make public relations effective. Effectiveness is best achieved when allowed to use its special *demonstrated* skills and talents and when the results of these skills are subsequently used by management.

MINI-ASSIGNMENT
THE CED CHECKLIST

In its 1971 report the CED said that the spectrum of business activities to improve society covered ten major fields: economic growth and efficiency; education; employment and training; civil rights and equal opportunity; urban renewal and development; pollution abatement; conservation and recreation; culture and the arts; medical care, and government. Under each were listed from five to ten activities by business aimed to assist in improving American society.

In the chart below are listed five of the areas and the activities. By use of a check mark in the appropriate column, indicate which you consider today to have been a fad of temporary nature and which you consider today to be of major importance and likely to be of importance in the future. You should be prepared to justify your decision in subsequent class discussion of the combined responses.

Field and Activity	Fad of Temporary Nature	Of Major Importance Now and in Future
EMPLOYMENT AND TRAINING		
active recruitment of the disadvantaged	_____	_____
special functional training, remedial education, and counseling.......................................	_____	_____
provision of day-care centers for children of working mothers	_____	_____
improvement of work/career opportunities.........................	_____	_____
retraining of workers affected by automation or other causes..	_____	_____
CIVIL RIGHTS AND EQUAL OPPORTUNITY		
ensuring employment and advancement opportunities for minorities	_____	_____
facilitating equality of results by continued training and other special programs....................	_____	_____
supporting and aiding the improvement of black educational facilities, and special programs for blacks and other minorities in integrated institutions..........	_____	_____

encouraging adoption of open-
housing ordinances.................
building plants and sales offices
in the ghettos ....
providing financing and managerial assistance to minority enterprises, and participating with
minorities in joint ventures ......

POLLUTION ABATEMENT

installation of modern equip-
ment.....................................
engineering new facilities for
minimum environmental effects
research and technological development.............................
cooperating with municipalities
in joint treatment facilities ....
cooperating with local, state, regional, and federal agencies in
developing improved systems of
environmental management......
developing more effective programs for recycling and reusing
disposable materials ....

URBAN RENEWAL AND DEVELOPMENT

leadership and financial support
for city and regional planning
and development.....................
building or improving low-in-
come housing.......................
building shopping centers, new
communities, new cities..........
improving transportation sys-
tems ....

MEDICAL CARE

helping plan community health
activities...............................
designing and operating low-
cost medical-care programs......
designing and running new hospitals, clinics, and extended
care facilities.........................
improving the administration
and effectiveness of medical
care.....................................

developing better systems for medical education, nurses' training	_____	_____
developing and supporting a better national system of health care	_____	_____

THE NELSON VIEW

Hale Nelson, veteran public relations counselor who was vice president of the Illinois Bell Telephone Company from 1946 to 1966, underscored this matter of role when he delivered the 1972 lecture sponsored by the Foundation For Public Relations Research and Education. Addressing himself to "The Public Problems of Business — Crucial Test Of The Seventies," Nelson said that American corporations are in serious trouble because vital data is excluded from "the decision-making mix" of the executive. The executive, in Nelson's opinion, is fully prepped by production, personnel, financial, sales and profit records and reports, but what he doesn't get is adequate *socio-political* data. Therefore, Nelson proposed that in order to regain public esteem and make corporate decision-making both responsive and responsible, organizations require:

1. A set-up to gather and deliver the socio-political data to the proper spot in the organization
2. A senior officer to process this input and to use it to advise the corporation's executive level on all basic decisions of whatever nature

Nelson's choice for his "senior officer to process" socio-political data is an officer he calls vice president-public. He suggests this officer take his place alongside the vice president-finance, vice president-law, vice president-personnel, and he feels that the domain of the new vice president should extend "to all the areas represented by the corporation's many interfaces with society." In summation, Nelson sees the public relations role in relation to social responsibility as follows:

A department, captained by a vice president-public, or similar generic title, heads up a corporate intelligence system which obtains and applies political and sociological information — processed for the business mind — to all important phases of business operations. That same input will mold the communications output, which in the new age must be marked by candor, integrity, and helpful information.

The vice president-public has just one job. That is to help the executive team reach its profit objective and at the same time live in harmony with society. He minimizes the hazards and maximizes public understanding. He does this by sensitizing the corporate nervous system from head to foot. When, despite its warning system, the corporate body receives a kick in the rear, it now feels it the same day!

THE BURSON VIEW

The Nelsonian view of the public relations role in the realm of social responsibility is a triple one of intelligence gathering, advice-giving and communication. Harold Burson, chairman of the Burson-Marsteller public relations counseling firm, visualizes an even more active role for public relations in respect to social responsibility.

"In assessing and responding to social change," Burson wrote in the *Burson-Marsteller Report* of May, 1973, "the public relations function must play a central role. It is the responsibility of the public relations professional to convince his management that there is, indeed, a ground swell of public opinion sufficiently significant to lead to social change. And it is his responsibility to participate in the policy determination that will lead to an effective response."

Burson considers that a prime function of the public relations practitioner is to act as a "mediator" between the corporation and society. In carrying out this function, says Burson, the practitioner has the following four responsibilities:

1. He serves as the sensor of social change. He perceives those rumblings at the heart of society that augur good or ill for his organization. He provides a qualitative evaluation of those movements and trends.
2. He must formulate policies that will enable the corporation to adapt to those trends. In so doing, of course, he must exercise good business judgement. At the same time, he must fulfill the role of "corporate conscience." This does not mean that a person must be a public relations professional to be sensitive. It does mean that acting the role of "corporate conscience" is not part of the job description of other executives. It *is* part of the job description of the chief public relations officer.
3. He must communicate corporate policies in two directions: internally and externally. (Burson adds here that the corporation must truly be responsive).
4. The public relations professional must serve as corporate monitor. He must constantly monitor corporate programs to make sure they match public expectations. If the programs are not

functioning or if they fall short of expectations, it is his job to agitate for new policies and programs. If he fails to do so, then he fails to live up to the requirements of his position.

OBSERVATIONS AND QUESTIONS ABOUT THE NELSON AND BURSON THESES

Analysis of the Nelson and Burson approaches indicates they are in agreement on three points regarding the role of public relations in regard to the social responsibility of organizations and institutions. Both agree that the practitioner must be sensitive to social change and transmit public demands for such change to his managements. Both agree that the public relations practitioner must be involved in decision-making regarding policies affected by the demand for social change. Both agree finally that the public relations practitioner is responsible for communicating management response.

Burson, however, carries the public relations role into the realm of policy-making when he suggests that the practitioner must *formulate* policies that will enable the corporation to adapt to social trends. He also sees the practitioner serving the role of the "corporate conscience" and "corporate monitor" who is expected to "agitate for new policies and programs" when he perceives that programs are not functioning or meeting expectations. Several questions come to mind regarding Burson's views of the practitioner as a formulator of policies, corporate conscience and monitor:

Is the public relations practitioner equipped by training, experience, and skills to deal with the formulation of an organization's policies?

Is the practitioner on a level of management where policies are formulated?

Is the organization's executive climate such that it will welcome a conscience and monitor?

Does the practitioner dare, even when he knows he's right, carry out the role of conscience, monitor, and agitator?

If the answer to the above questions is affirmative, then Burson's practitioner should expect clear sailing. If the answer is either "yes but" or "no," then the practitioner should settle for Nelson's ordained role of the public relations man in coping with corporate social responsibility.

THE PUBLIC INTEREST

As we have seen, coming to grips with corporate social responsibility is not a simple matter, but it is even more difficult to come to grips with the concept of the public interest. On the face of it, the public interest concept has the solid ring of immutable dictum and truth. Public relations practitioners continually define their activities in terms of being in the public interest, the literature of the field is replete with references to the public interest, and there exists few if any public relations experts with soul so daring that they would contend their work is *not* in the public interest.

But some disturbing questions come to mind. What is the public interest? Obviously you can't see, hear, or feel it, so how can you tell what it is? Can it be measured, weighed, and assessed? Who is to be the judge of the public interest? What if an organization's private interests and the public interest are in obvious conflict? What if an organization's policies, in order to be in the public interest, can only be modified or changed at an unbearable cost to the organization?

The following sections will examine and attempt to answer these and other questions.

MINI-QUOTE
LEAD PARAGRAPH FROM AN ARTICLE ENTITLED "WHAT IS THE PUBLIC INTEREST"

"For as long as there have been nations and wise men, the idea has persisted that at least some people, some of the time, ought to be able to rise above personal interest and work for the well-being of society as a whole. Philosophers from Plato to Rousseau to Marx conceived of this notion of harmonious disinterestedness as essential to happy statehood and citizenship alike. And even in the capitalist West — as non-Marxist philosophers came to think in terms of balanced struggles among conflicting selfishness — the idea of a definable public interest has continued to inspire good citizens, good politicians and good public-relations men. Everybody — oil barons, labor unions, churches, bureaucrats — would seem to believe that their private push-ups are only incidental to their loftier service to the common well-being, and they go to considerable effort to persuade the public to believe it too. But is there any such thing as the public interest? How can it be defined? Who if anyone serves the public interest, who only pretends to — and how can a citizen tell the difference?"

Newsweek, March 25, 1974

WHAT IS THE PUBLIC INTEREST?

The term, the public interest, is slippery, elusive, and difficult to pin down. Many have tried to do so; few have succeeded.

THE CHILDS AND GALLUP VIEW

Harwood Childs defines the public interest in these words:

It is my thesis that *the public interest, so far as the United States is concerned, is and can only be what the public, what mass opinion, says it is*. By mass opinion, I mean the collective opinions of the American people as a whole.

Childs cites data from many years of the Gallup poll to support his belief that *over reasonably long periods of time public opinion is as safe a guide to follow as the opinions of smaller and select groups*. He also cites Gallup himself as follows:

> The sampling surveys of recent years have provided much evidence concerning the wisdom of the common people. . . . And I think that the person who does examine it (the evidence) will come away believing as I do that, collectively, the American people have a remarkable high degree of common sense. These people may not be brilliant or intellectual or particularly well read, but they possess a quality of good sense which is manifested time and again in their expressions of opinion on present-day issues. . . .

Childs recognized defects in stressing the virtues of mass public opinion as a guide to public interest. In his own words:

> The competence of the masses is, of course, conditioned by the environment and by the opportunities they have to acquire information, to listen to different points of view, to discuss and express their opinions freely — and to use their reasoning powers.

Nonetheless, he said, public relations practitioners do have on hand tangible criteria for finding out what the public interest is, and he rests his case by emphasizing that "on broad questions of social, political, and economic policy the opinions of the masses seem to show a "remarkably high degree of common sense."

Let us, for the sake of argument, accept Childs' concept of the public interest as expressed in his remarks and those of George Gallup. There will still remain the difficult and expensive task of measuring mass opinion. National polling organizations, such as Gallup's, have a highly creditable record in this area of opinion measurement, but their results are fixed in time. They reveal what mass opinion was at the time opinion was measured. Further, it would be enormously costly, and often impossible, to take a measurement of the public pulse every time a public relations policy, action, or statement is to be put into effect.

LIPPMANN'S VIEW

There are also those who take direct issue with Childs and Gallup. No less an authority on public opinion than Walter Lippmann (*The Public Philosophy*, 1955) believes that in normal circumstances voters can't be expected to transcend their particular, localized, and self-regarding opinions. Lippmann adds:

> I am far from implying that the voters are not entitled to the representation of their particular opinions and interests. But their opinions and interests should be taken for what they are and for no more. They are not — as such — propositions in the public interest. . . .

The Gallup polls are reports of what people are thinking. But that a plurality of the people sampled in the poll think one way has no bearing upon whether it is sound public policy. For their opportunities of judging great issues are in the very nature of things limited, and the statistical sum of their opinions is not the final verdict on an issue. It is, rather, the beginning of the argument. In that argument their opinions need to be confronted by the views of the executive, defending and promoting the public interest. In the accommodation reached between the two views lies practical public policy.

Lippmann's references to the public interest were made in regard to political affairs, but they could just as well apply to corporate and other institutional affairs. His ideas about the public mind will be more fully discussed in a later chapter, but it is sufficient to say at this point that Lippmann felt the public is often misinformed, ill-informed, and poor judges of great issues.

Lippmann doesn't leave us dangling, however, because he provides his own analysis of what is meant by the public interest, as follows:

. . . The public interest may be presumed to be what men would choose if they saw clearly, thought rationally, acted disinterestedly and benevolently.

Stated another way, Lippmann suggests that if you want to judge whether your organization's policies, actions, or statements are in the public interest then you should view them from the vantage point of men who see things clearly, think rationally, act disinterestedly, and benevolently!

HILL'S VIEW

John W. Hill, founder of Hill & Knowlton, one of the country's largest and most respected public relations counseling firms, was so concerned about the public interest he devoted two chapters of his book, *The Making Of A Public Relations Man* (1963), to a discussion of the public interest concept. Where the public interest lies in given circumstances, said Hill, seems to be a matter of opinion and judgment. Hill surveyed fifty leaders in education, government, theology, and labor and came up with these two general answers:

1. A sizeable body of opinion exists that *no precise definition of the public interest is possible*. (One out of three responses).
2. A majority of those who said a definition was possible settled for the clause *"the greatest good for the greatest number."* However, some provided qualifications, and the essential qualification was that *the interests of the minority must be protected*.

From the thoughts about the public interest expressed by his fifty opinion leaders Hill distilled some *criteria* for determining what is in the public interest. The criteria are in the form of questions, and they seem to be sound ones to ask of policies, actions, and statements:

1. How many people will be affected?
2. How many will be harmed?
3. How many people will be benefited?
4. How significant are the effects going to be?
5. What are the probable long-range effects?

THE PUBLIC INTEREST: A SUMMING UP

John Hill's fifty opinion leaders didn't cite answers to the above-listed questions because the answers depend on the issues under consideration. Managements, however, expect answers from their public relations men and women, and this is when the going gets rough. It gets rough when an organization's private interests and the public interest conflict. It gets particularly rough in the following circumstances:

1. When an organization's private interests and the public interest conflict or collide. *An example:* A private four-year college, established twenty-five years ago in a metropolitan area of 225,000 residents, has been financially and academically successful despite having no endowment. Its revenues have come from tuition and a thriving evening division. Recently a group of community leaders — including local bankers, industrialists and the publisher of the city's only daily newspaper — has mounted a drive to get the state university to establish a four-year undergraduate college in the area. Such a college would, of course, be an economic boon to the area, but it would also pose tough competitive problems to the established private four-year college. Suggest the public relations stance of the private institution in this instance where its private interest collides with the public interest.
2. When an organization is caught in the middle between conflicting public interest. *An example:* In order to better serve a metropolitan area of one million residents, a large gas and electric utility has announced plans to build a nuclear power plant on a large lake eighty miles away in a rural area. Since the announcement, two major groups have actively come out in opposition to the proposed plant: 1) a very active conservation group which claims the plant will destroy plant and fish life in the lake; and 2) a very active citizens' group, led by responsible civic leaders, who reside in the towns bordering the lake and who are vehemently and vocally opposed to the nuclear plant. Suggest the public relations stance of the utility caught in the middle between the public interests of residents in the metropolitan area it serves and the public interests of the two groups who oppose the proposed plant.

The two examples cited above are daily duplicated in numerous ways in American society and are indicative of the difficult public relations problems organizations and institutions face when dealing with the public interest. As an instructive exercise it would be enlightening to screen last week's issues of the daily newspaper or national news magazines and cull out other examples wherein an organization's private interests and the public interest or interests ran into conflict. In such instances there are no real answers, but there have to be sound judgments and insights if public relations is to be of help to the managements it serves.

T. J. Ross, veteran public relations counselor, sized up the problem in terms of *balance* when he declared:

> In a corporation of size, decisions affecting public interest are often difficult. In striving to carry out its job with public consensus and in the public interest, the best it can achieve is what might be called *an acceptable balance of interests*. It has to deal with a number of groups, each of which seeks something for its own benefit and possibly at the expense of another group within the corporation.

> It is in these areas (balancing of interests) that one role of public relations is performed; namely, that of assisting managements in arriving at policies and practices that will be reflected favorably within the family, in the market-place, in the government, in the press and so forth. . . . The other part of our role has to do with communication. . . .

Observations about the public interest made by men like Ross, Hill, and other veteran practitioners suggest the following steps to be taken by public relations in dealing with the public interest:

1. Thoroughly study the issue and make sure you explain *why* your organization's position or proposal is in the public interest.
2. Don't use the term loosely under the assumption that your authority for it will be accepted automatically.
3. Make sure that when an action is taken or not taken it is a sound one that will be accepted as reasonable and fair under the circumstances.
4. Remember that the better informed people are, the more capable they are in judging where the public interest lies. Provide enough information so that people can judge the merits of the situation and the action.

The above guidelines, of course, are predicated on the assumption that your organization's policies, actions, and statements *are* in the public interest. When they are clearly *not* in said interest, don't try to palm them off as being so. If you are in the position to do anything about them, bring your weight to bear in modifying or changing policies, actions, and statements so that they will clearly be in the public interest and will be perceived to be so by the public.

QUESTIONS AND PROBLEMS FOR DISCUSSION

1. What does Harwood Childs consider to be the major focus and purpose of public relations?
2. What does Harwood Childs mean when he says that public relations is "simply a name for activities which have a social significance"? Do you

agree or disagree with his contention? Why?

3. If we were to grant the validity of Childs' view of public relations, what kind of problems does such a view pose for the public relations practitioner?

4. How does Dr. Milton Friedman view the social responsibility concept as it applies to business executives? Do you agree or disagree with this view? Justify your conclusion.

5. How does the Committee For Economic Development view social responsibility and self-interest? Do you agree or disagree with this view?

6. How does Hale Nelson see the public relations role in relation to social responsibility? Do you agree or disagree with his view? Why?

7. What does Harold Burson mean when he says that the prime function of the public relations practitioner is to act as a "mediator" between the corporation and society? Do you agree or disagree with his view? Why?

8. How would you define the term "the public interest"?

9. How is the term seen by Childs and Gallup? By Walter Lippmann? By John Hill?

10. What's your opinion of T. J. Ross' thought that the problem of the public interest is one of achieving "an acceptable balance of interests"?

PART II
MANAGING THE FUNCTION

Having examined public relations in broad, societal terms, it's now appropriate to focus attention on the men and women who manage the function.

Just as public relations serves as a bridge between organizations and the society in which they exist and operate, so do the practitioners serve as a bridge in this text between the societal aspects of the field and the dynamics of the public relations process. The chapter that follows — the bridge chapter in this text — deals with the two primary groups of practitioners: those working internally within organizations and those working externally in counseling firms.

After a preliminary analysis of the advantages and disadvantages of the two groups, the chapter deals in depth with the manner in which the internal practitioners and the public relations counselors operate. Spotted throughout the chapter are mini-cases designed to provide students with the opportunity to demonstrate judgments about the kind of problems involved in the management of the public relations function.

INTERNAL DEPARTMENTS AND COUNSELING FIRMS 4

Those who remember Chapter 1 will recall that public relations is generally considered a *management function*. This means that, in carrying out their job of running sizable organizations that have many publics, the managements of these organizations rely on public relations principles, talents, and techniques.

FOUR BASIC SYSTEMS

The realization is generally achieved in one of the following ways:

INTERNALLY, UNDELEGATED

Some managements utilize public relations principles without benefit of public relations talents and techniques.

In such instances *someone* in the management hierarchy keeps in mind public relations principles as the organization carries out its primary tasks. The "someone" is usually the chief operating executive of the organization. An example would be the executive director of the local Boys' Club or Girl Scouts, the manager of the town's leading department store, the president of a local business employing anywhere from 25 to 500 people.

INTERNALLY, DELEGATED TO A DEPARTMENT OR STAFF

In most sizable organizations which deal with many publics the task of utilizing public relations principles, talents, and techniques is entrusted to a *department* or *staff* — sometimes to a single person — specifically empowered to carry out the public relations function.

In such instances the public relations job is important enough and of such magnitude to justify the need for a specialized staff organized into a separate department, though sometimes integrated with another department. An example would be the public relations department of a large university or business; the public relations staff of a large hospital; the advertising/public relations department of a large industrial organization or trade association.

EXTERNALLY, DELEGATED TO A PUBLIC RELATIONS COUNSELING FIRM OR PUBLIC RELATIONS DEPARTMENT OF AN ADVERTISING AGENCY

Large organizations often assign the public relations task, by contract, to a *public relations counseling firm* or to the *public relations department of an advertising agency.*

In such instances the managements of large organizations believe that the public relations task can best be carried out by outside firms who represent a wide variety of clients and have proven expertise which may not be possible to achieve through an internal staff or department. An example would be a one-year contract signed with a public relations counseling firm to handle all or certain specific public relations tasks of a national concern whose stock is publicly owned and traded, or a similar contract made with the advertising agency that handles the concern's national advertising and is capable of carrying out specified public relations tasks.

COMBINATION OF INTERNAL-EXTERNAL

Though many large organizations have their own public relations departments, they also retain public relations counseling firms or the public relations departments of advertising agencies. Thus, we have a *combination of the internal staff or department and the outside firm* working together to achieve desired public relations results.

In such instances the managements of large organizations utilize the inside-outside arrangement. An example would be a large mid-western manufacturing concern which has its own public relations department at the concern's headquarters/plant site, but which utilizes a New York City-based counseling firm or ad agency public relations department in an adjunct capacity.

The internal, undelegated method will not be discussed in any detail because it is based on the philosophy that public relations really does not have to be managed, but can be handled as an ancillary activity of some other staff member or department or can be kept in mind as management goes about its primary tasks. This may be the only feasible or economically sound way to handle the function in small organizations, but not for sizable organizations with many publics. The other three methods require that the public relations function be *managed*, and this chapter will deal with the management of the function as carried out under the three methods.

Each of the three methods of handling the public relations function has advantages which the others either do not possess or cannot equal. Yet, given proper circumstances, what may on the surface seem to be an advantage can just as easily turn out to be a disadvantage. Consider the advantages and disadvantages of each method.

INTERNAL STAFF OR DEPARTMENT: ADVANTAGES

Authorities in the field cite the major advantages of the internal staff or department as being *knowledge of the organization, availability*, and *team membership*. Each of these, ranked in no particular order of importance, is discussed below.

KNOWLEDGE OF THE ORGANIZATION

Any competent public relations person working on the public relations staff of an organization ought to have an intimate working knowledge of the entire organization for which he or she works. This should include knowledge of the key *people, products*, and *activities* of the organization; the *"politics"* of the organization; and forthcoming and upcoming *changes* affecting people, products, and activities.

Most organizations publish nice, tidy charts which indicate where everyone belongs and the role assigned to each. But the charts often mask reality, and the astute public relations man or woman should know what really goes on. To do the job properly the practitioner ought also to have advance knowledge of important changes affecting people, products, and activities. There are three basic reasons behind this necessity of having an insider's knowledge:

1. Public relations functions at the optimum when its advice and counsel is sought *in advance*, not after the event.
2. The output of public relations staffs and departments is most effective when it accurately reflects an organization's activities and policies.
3. The public relations department ought to be the department most available to the media when it seeks information about an organization. If the department cannot provide this information or aid the media in securing it, then the media will get its information by other means.

AVAILABILITY

Though a large share of public relations activity involves such routine duties as preparing brochures and publishing periodic newsletters, reports, and magazines, every organization has moments where the unexpected demands immediate public relations action. Being on the spot at such moments is of inestimable value in providing the right kind of advice, suggesting the most effective action, and following through with the proper response.

Sometimes the situation will call only for the giving of advice, but advice given by people who are on the scene has an advantage over advice given from afar. The same applies to the action to be taken and the response to be made. The hospital with its own internal public relations department has a great advantage over one without such a department when a national figure is seriously injured and brought to its emergency room or wing. The college with its own internal public relations department has a great advantage over one without such a department when its students, faculty, or staff suddenly go out on strike. The large research complex with its own internal public relations department has a great advantage over one without such a department when an explosion takes place in one of its laboratories.

Proper timing is so often the key to successful public relations that its role cannot be over-estimated. Timing, in turn, relies on the availability of public relations personnel, and the internal public relations person has the advantage of being always available.

TEAM MEMBERSHIP

The very fact that a public relations department has been established within an organization makes the members of that department part of the management team. Most public relations functions and activities are related to other departments and their activities so the relationship should be cordial, friendly, and cooperative. As an insider who is called upon to interact almost daily with personnel in other departments, the internal public relations man or woman has many opportunities to develop a cooperative working relationship with those in other departments. The more the public relations person demonstrates his or her value and worth to the organization and particularly to other departments in the organization, the more solid becomes the relationship and the more valuable the factor of team membership.

INTERNAL STAFF OR DEPARTMENT: DISADVANTAGES

Two of the three factors which comprise the major advantages of the internal staff or department — availability and team membership — can prove to be dysfunctional in certain circumstances.

There is such a thing as being *too available*. In many organizations there is either no clear understanding of public relations or else there is a tendency to dump on the department many duties and responsibilities which do not belong in the department or which are peripheral to the department's main duties. There is no great mystery about why this happens. Public relations, by its very nature and name, involves relations with the public. Many of an organization's activities do not fall clearly within the province of any single department, but do involve the public. The organization has a public relations department; ergo, dump the matter into the lap of the public relations department.

Team membership can be as dysfunctional as availability. *Being a member of the team can cloud one's objective vision*, yet at all times the public relations practitioner needs a clear-eyed view of what's going on. When such a view indicates that one's fellow "teammate" is responsible for product flaws uncovered by an inquiring journalist, what responsibility does the public relations man have to the truth, to his organization, and to his fellow member of the team? When such a view indicates a "teammate's" clear incompetence, which in turn can lead to a loss of public confidence in the organization, it becomes difficult to expose such incompetence within the councils of the organization. The ultimate in professional frustration and dysfunction occurs when top management itself is incompetent but expects the public relations practitioner team member to present the executive to the public as highly competent and able. At such a time the practitioner would gladly trade the so-called advantage of team membership for a job on the assembly line.

MINI-CASES
AVAILABILITY AS A DISADVANTAGE

COLLEGE VERSION

An official of a small college graciously granted a local health fund-raising agency permission to have its "Walkathon For Medical Research" end on the college's campus. Unfortunately, inadequate arrangements were made to handle the reunion of parents and their offspring when more than 1,000 youngsters ended their walkathon after 5 p.m. By this time the official who had arranged the cooperative venture had gone home, but the public relations staffer who was still in her office and available became the recipient of inquiries and telephone calls from parents who couldn't find their children and children who couldn't find their parents. After all, such a state of affairs brings good will to the college, so why not have the public relations department handle it?

INDUSTRIAL VERSION

Responsibility for all fund drives carried out in the main plant of a large industrial organization is given to the personnel department at the plant. This year, however, the head of the plant has been elected president of the city's United Way organization. He is so busy running the plant he needs someone to do most of his work for the United Way (other than required personal appearances). The director of public relations for the plant is also busy with his own work, but he is assigned the president's United Way tasks. After all, being president of the United Way brings good will to the plant and the development of good will is a public relations function, isn't it?

HOSPITAL VERSION

Every year this hospital's auxiliary runs a major fashion show which draws more than 300 women and brings several thousand dollars to the hospital for needed equipment. This year's president of the auxiliary is a well-meaning matron who is totally incompetent to manage a large fashion show, but who is herself a major contributor of funds to the hospital. Though she is in the midst of writing the hospital's annual report, the director of public relations is given the job of doing the work which the auxiliary president should do. After all, such a show is a valuable way of linking the hospital with one of its major publics, and that's a public relations task, isn't it?

Question for Discussion

In each of the three cases cited above, what can and should the public relations staffer do when asked to take on the tasks and responsibilities in the case?

THE COUNSELING FIRM: ADVANTAGES

Major advantages of the public relations counseling firm (or the public relations department of an advertising agency) are seen by most authorities to be four-fold: *objectivity; wide range of experience and talents; flexibility;* and *economy*.

OBJECTIVITY

The outside public relations counselor is not a member of the inside organization or team, and this is a virtue because the counselor brings an objective view to public relations problems. The outside counselor calls the shots as he sees them, not as management thinks he *ought* to see them. He is usually retained with the expectation that he will be objective. If he tells some hard truths, gives advice and counsel which causes him to lose the account, the world doesn't come to an end as a result. (That is, unless the counseling firm has only a few accounts and this is a major one.) The outside counselor does not wear rose-colored glasses which cast a euphoric glow over every perceived problem, but bi-focals which enable a realistic, *objective* look at problems.

WIDE RANGE OF EXPERIENCE AND TALENTS

Counseling firms which have been in business for any appreciable length of time have dealt with almost every conceivable type and kind of public relations problems and situation. The longer the firm has been in business, the more its experience in handling a wide diversity of problems and situations can be taken for granted. A new problem to the client has probably been handled by the counseling firm many times in the past.

Further, the well-established counseling firms have on their roster not only account executives with wide experience but also specialists in educational, media, and financial relations; consumerism; pollution; graphics; photography, and a host of other areas. These specialists are there to serve the account executive (and the client) when the situation calls for their expertise.

FLEXIBILITY

Public relations counseling firms have great flexibility chiefly because they can move their personnel around when there is need. At any one time, as the demand requires, these firms can move staff personnel from old Account X to new Account Y or assign an account executive to take on the supervision of a new account as part of her nominal responsibilities.

Flexibility is possible because large counseling firms have a large pool of talent and personnel and a certain amount of client fluidity. Though the firms pride themselves on maintaining a long and continuing relationship with certain clients, they also have other accounts which they are either losing or are at the end of their contractual relationship. Further, when valuable account personnel find themselves temporarily without assignment they can be absorbed into one of the firm's specialized departments until new accounts come into the firm.

ECONOMY

Counseling firms are not inexpensive entitles, but they can prove to be economical in certain circumstances. For example, when an organization has a limited but definite amount of public relations work to be achieved it's more economical to utilize a counseling firm rather than to set up a permanent staff with salaries, equipment and supply needs, adjunct salaried personnel, and overhead costs. When an organization runs into a public relations problem which may last only one or two years, again the counseling firm route would be less expensive than to employ full-time staff. Finally, when an organization has certain special needs — such as the need to reach the financial community or the New York City media outlets — it's more economical to utilize a counseling firm rather than hire a financial relations expert or establish a New York City office.

THE COUNSELING FIRM: DISADVANTAGES

Advantages which counseling firms hold can prove to be dysfunctional under certain circumstances.

The outside counseling firm can generally be more objective than the internal practitioner, but it becomes difficult to maintain such objectivity when the counseling firm has had the same account and dealt with the same people for ten, twenty, or thirty years. At such times the nominal outsider virtually is looked upon as a member of the inside "team."

The larger the account, the more sizable the yearly fee, and the greater the role of a client in the counselor's roster, the more likelihood of loss of objectivity if such objectivity can lead to loss of the account. Counselors have resigned accounts when their objective advice is constantly ignored by the client. However, such account resignations become increasingly difficult and economically painful when the account is a very large one, the yearly fee is very sizable, and the account represents half of the counselor's total yearly billing.

Getting to know you — as the song went in "The King and I" — is a pleasurable experience when one is governess to the king's children. It becomes more difficult to bring about when one is outside counsel to a large and complex organization which has difficult public relations problems. Clients become very edgy in the early stages of the counselor-client relationships. They desire immediate results, but results are not usually brought about until the counselor has a close and intimate grasp of the client's organization, personnel, policies, practices, and problems. Impatience on the part of the client; the geographical distance between the client and the counselor; internal political maneuvering; innate distrust of strangers; unwillingness to give up one's turf — all these provide stumbling blocks as the counselor seeks to obtain a close and intimate grasp of the client's organization, personnel, policies, practices and problems.

MINI-CASE
GETTING TO KNOW YOU COSTS MONEY

A medium-sized Pennsylvania firm seeking to expand its market regionally retained a major New York City counseling firm at a monthly retainer fee of $5,000 plus out-of-pocket costs. The letter-of-agreement was signed after two exploratory sessions between the executive head and public relations director of the client and the president and executive vice president of the counseling firm. It was agreed that the $5,000 retainer fee would be paid monthly in advance, and out-of-pocket expenses would be billed at the end of each month in which they were incurred. Each party to the contract had the option of cancelling out by giving thirty days' notice.

On September 1, the first month of the contract, the client was billed for $5,000 and subsequently paid the bill. On September 10 he was visited by P. Brigham Broughton, an account executive whom he had briefly met at an exploratory session in New York City. Broughton made another visit on September 20, and on September 30 he sent the client a five-page program proposal.

On October 1, the second month of the contract, the client was billed for $5,000 and subsequently paid the bill. Along with the payment the client's director of public relations sent a detailed letter of response to the five-page program proposal citing serious reservations about some of the proposed ideas and projects. The client also expressed some concern because, as he put it, he hadn't seen any "action on the account," and he suggested that the account executive concentrate his activities at the moment on the handling of an upcoming trade show. On October 14 he received a reply from the counseling firm, signed by Joseph Tenney and notifying him that Broughton was being replaced on the account by Tenney but assuring him of immediate service and attention to the trade show project. A telephone call from the client brought Tenney to the client's headquarters where he spent the day getting acquainted with the client and its director of public relations.

On October 31 the client received a revised proposal from Tenney and Tenney's ideas about handling the trade show. Attached was a bill for $850 for out-of-pocket expenses for the months of September and October. The next day, of course, the client received his retainer bill of $5,000 to cover the month of November. Two days later the client notified the counseling firm it was exercising its thirty-day option and cancelling the contract.

Question for Discussion

What seems to have gone wrong here, could it have been anticipated, and what could have been done to prevent it?

Counseling firms provide Cadillac public relations service, but unfortunately most small and medium-sized organizations can only afford medium-priced cars. The most prestigious counselors are located in New York City, Chicago, and other large cities, which means they have to pay high salaries and rent and incur high overhead costs which in turn have to be reimbursed through fees which, though reasonable, are still high to many would-be clients. Though the would-be, relatively small client may not agree, he is fortunate when he is told at the outset by the large, prestigious counseling firm: "Look, you really can't afford to retain us. Why not try Firm X, they're more in your price range."

INTERNAL-EXTERNAL COMBINATION: ADVANTAGES

As has already been noted, certain advantages accrue to organizations having their own public relations departments, and there are certain other advantages to utilizing a counseling firm. It would seem logical to assume that the combination of the two would provide the best of all possible worlds.

In effect, the combination provides a balance, and when the tandem operation is working well it's hard to fault. The internal staff, for example, may be too close to the problem to be objective, but the counselor is sufficiently removed to provide objectivity. The internal public relations director may be too much a member of the "team" to be critical of a colleague when criticism is justified, but the counselor as an outsider is not so bound by organizational politics. In certain situations it may be more economical to use internal staff to handle certain public relations tasks, and in other situations more economical to use the outside counseling firm.

Another advantage of the combination system, not often mentioned because it is mainly psychological and sub-surface, is that the utilization of an outside counseling firm lends weight and substance to the internal department. When the internal director proposes a certain line of action and is backed up by a reputable counseling firm, the proposal seems to gain stature (even though it's still the same proposal).

INTERNAL-EXTERNAL COMBINATION: DISADVANTAGES

The chief disadvantage of the combination system is that it entails additional expenditures for public relations services. Two may be able to live as cheaply as one in popular mythology, but not in the world of public relations. There's no problem when management recognizes or agrees that the additional expenditures are essential and justified. There's a definite problem, though, when management is uncertain whether the additional expenditures are essential in terms of the end results. Legend has it that a newcomer to wealth thought he might want to buy a yacht so he asked J.P. Morgan how much it cost to maintain his yacht. Whereupon Morgan replied: "If you have to worry about the cost you can't afford a yacht." The same might apply to the cost of public relations counsel; if you have to worry about cost, you probably shouldn't retain outside counsel.

THE INTERNAL PUBLIC RELATIONS PRACTITIONER AND DEPARTMENT

The bulk of public relations practitioners in the United States work internally within organizations rather than in counseling firms, and the largest number of internal practitioners work for business and industrial organizations. Sizable numbers, however, are found in government, health, social service, higher education, and similar nonprofit bodies. The common denominator that binds all of them is the fact that they serve in a staff rather than a line capacity; that is, they provide advice, counsel, and public relations services to facilitate the major purpose for which the organization exists. This section will deal with the internal department's role and place in the organization, activities and functions, structure, and budgeting.

ROLE AND PLACE IN THE ORGANIZATION

A generally reliable way to ascertain the role of a particular public relations department is by noting to whom the head of the department reports. If the department head reports to top management — whether the president, executive director, or similar functionary; to the chairman of the board or board of directors; or to an executive vice president — the public relations department is a highly regarded staff function. If the public relations department head reports to someone lower down on the organization scale, the public relations department may have difficulty carrying out effectively all of its key staff functions.

MINI-CASE
VALUABLE DATA

O'Dwyer's Directory of Corporate Communications, first published in August, 1975, and described by its publisher as "the most extensive survey ever undertaken of how America's largest companies have defined, organized and staffed their public relations/communications operations," provides valuable information about the extent and role of corporate public relations departments.

Listed in the directory were 1,293 companies, and these included the 1,000 largest industrial companies as ranked by *Fortune* magazine plus the 50 largest companies ranked by *Fortune* in each of six categories: commercial banking, life insurance, diversified-financial, retailing, transporting and utilities. The Foreword of the directory made the following key points:

    . . . Companies use a wide variety of names for the PR/communications function. The most popular is "Public Relations," used by 340 companies. After this is "Communications," or "Corporate Communications" departments, used by 207. One hundred and eighteen have "Advertising/Public Relations" departments and 80 prefer the title "Public Affairs." More than a dozen other titles are in use, such as "Corporate

Relations," "Public Information" and "External Relations.
. . ."

. . . A total of 919 of the 1,293 companies listed have formal
PR/communications departments, leaving 374 with no such
departments. Many of the 374 are in basic industries such as
steel and textiles and do not have direct contact with the consumer.

. . . Four hundred and fifty-seven of the 1,293 companies report
using outside PR counsel. Of those 374 with no PR departments, 125 list outside PR counsel.

. . . Six hundred and forty four of the 919 companies with communications departments answered our query as to whom the
head of the department reports. In nearly half of the cases
(311), the reporting line is to the chairman, president and/or
chief executive officer. Fifty-two of the departments report to
advertising or marketing; 47 to a vice president of administration and 234 to other titles.

From *O'Dwyers Directory of Corporate
Communication*

Questions for Discussion

1. What's your reaction to the data citing the wide variety of
names for the PR/communications function?
2. What's your reaction to the data citing the number of companies with PR/communications departments and the number
which utilize outside public relations counsel?

The literature of the field — including this book — places great
stress on the advisability of having public relations report as directly as
possible to top management. Why? *Because the important functions of
the public relations department are of direct concern to top management and because public relations performs most effectively when in a
position to provide input into top management decisions.* Obviously,
this can best be done when the line between the head of the department
and the operating head of the organization is a direct one.

In practice, however, we find many instances where the line between public relations and top management is far from direct. Here are
some reasons why this occurs:

1. As organizations grow in size, so do organizational politics. Within large organizations there is as much jockeying for position as
there is in the first 100 yards of the Kentucky Derby.
2. As a relative newcomer to the staff field, public relations has to
compete with such veteran staff activities as legal, financial, and
personnel. The veterans have been there first, hence they occupy

choice positions and aren't too likely to open ranks for the new-comer.

3. In order to maintain their sanity, top operating executives restrict their personal contact to as few subordinates as possible. There's little room at the top of the organizational triangle.

4. Some chief executives don't seek or want public relations advice and counsel because they don't consider it important or they consider themselves to be public relations experts.

5. It takes time and *proven* expertise to gain the confidence of top management. Sometimes the opportunity to provide such proof is not given, sometimes it's given but muffed, and sometimes the practitioner is satisfied with his lower management role.

The public relations practitioner who aspires to the role of a valued staff advisor to top management doesn't overcome the above-cited obstacles by mouthing platitudes about the top management role of public relations. He or she secures that role by earning it and by providing valuable advice and service when the opportunity arises.

MINI-CASE
MONDAY MORNING POLICY GROUP

When John Champ was named director of public relations at Rawley College, the school was a medium-sized liberal arts institution with a predominantly white, middle-class student body of 2,500 students; a faculty of 135 full-time teachers; and a nonacademic staff of 35 professionals. At the time the president's top management staff consisted of the vice president of operations; the dean of the faculty; and the dean of student activities. Champ reported directly to the president, but he was not a member of the above-mentioned presidential top management group — known by some on campus as the Hatchetmen — which met every Monday morning to discuss and act on overall college plans, policies, and problems.

Champ's predecessor had devoted the major share of his time to writing news releases and photography. Though Champ wrote some stories from time to time, he assigned the major share of release writing to the news bureau manager, and he hired a student to take care of photography needs.

During his first six months on the job Champ spent half his time in his office and the rest of his time becoming personally acquainted with leaders among the faculty, student body, and staff and observing how matters were handled by the Faculty Senate, the Student Assembly, and committees of both groups.

In the following year Champ:

Assisted several senior faculty members by editing article manuscripts with which they were having trouble.

Helped the vice president of operations run a very successful regional conference on college management, and provided the vice president with guidance and direct assistance in handling statements to the press during a dispute with the maintenance staff.

Aided the dean of faculty by editing a revision of the Faculty Manual; compiling a report up-dating trends in unionization among faculty in institutions the size and nature of Rawley; writing several of the dean's speeches to alumni groups around the country.

Upon request, wrote a five-page memorandum to the dean of student activities outlining steps which could be taken to ease racial tension which occurred on campus when the college enrolled a significant number of inner city blacks. Many of Champ's recommendations were used and helped bring about better relations between black and white students.

Volunteered to take on for the president many tasks which did not fall within anyone's special area, but which had important ramifications for the college. Champ performed the major share of these tasks capably and responsibly.

A year and a half after Champ became director of public relations the president recommended, and the group concurred, that Champ be included in the Monday morning meetings of the college's top management group.

Question for Discussion

What lesson(s) might an aspiring college director of public relations learn from the above?

ACTIVITIES AND FUNCTIONS

Though the activities and functions carried out by internal public relations departments will vary — the degree of variance is most often dependent on the nature of the organization — there are certain key tasks common to most internal public relations departments. Authorities generally agree that the following represent the activities and functions considered most important:

Advice and counsel — public relations advice on organizational policies and actions which have public relations ramifications. Given to both top management and to line departments when situations and problems indicate the need for public relations input and expertise.

Publications — a wide variety of publications designed for publics considered important to the organization. These range anywhere from in-plant daily information sheets to four-color internal-external class magazines.

Promotion and publicity — news-making events and activities, press releases, press conferences, and serving as the prime source of an organization's contact with the media. Includes product, corporate, and general publicity.

Relations with publics — two-way communications with those publics deemed important to the organization. Providing public relations input and expertise in regard to an organization's actions, policies, and procedures which have public relations ramifications.

Institutional advertising — those aspects of an organization's advertising which are institutional in nature. Sometimes this is handled in coordination with the organization's advertising department, and sometimes solely by the public relations departments.

Miscellaneous — services which do not fall within the scope of any of the above, but which help provide a full range of public relations activities. This sometimes includes the handling of a speaker's bureau; visitor and tour bureau; corporate donations, scholarship, and awards program; special convocations and seminars.

Research — chiefly an intelligence-gathering activity and usually concerned with the measurement and analysis of public opinion. Useful in spotting trends, providing supporting evidence for public relations proposals and programs.

Because of variables outside the control of the public relations department there is no reliable way of gauging how restricted or how extensive will be the activities and functions of a public relations department or staff. The reasons may be *historical* ("We've always done it this way"); *personal* ("The president knows the importance of public relations and supports it fully," or vice versa); *economical* ("We're so small we can't afford a full-fledged department") or *circumstantial* ("We ran into so many problems with so many publics we needed a department large enough and expert enough to handle them").

Thus, two organizations of similar nature and size may have public relations departments whose activities and functions differ considerably. For reasons historical, personal, economical, or circumstantial departments will start out emphasizing the same activities but diverge in their approach as time goes on. This does not mean there is no rhyme nor reason to the handling of public relations activities and functions. On the contrary, it means that the handling of such activities and functions is strongly dependent on the dynamics that control every organization's history and growth. The end result sought — attainment of good will, understanding, and acceptance — will remain constant, but the ways of reaching these objectives through the utilization of public relations will vary.

MINI-CASE
A TALE OF TWO WIDGET MAKERS

The Fulmore Company and the Blasted Company (called by many of its employees as "that Blasted Company") both make widgets, have relatively similar total sales and employee forces, and are privately owned.

However, the Fulmore Company's plant is in the inner city of a large metropolis, while the Blasted Company's plant is in a small town in Iowa. Fulmore employees voted down unionization last year, but at Blasted the employees organized, won recognition for their union, and are now part of a large international union.

The public relations department at Fulmore has a director of public relations; a minority affairs manager; a press relations manager; and an internal-external publication. The public relations department at Blasted has a director of public relations, his assistant, and no publications of any kind.

Last year the Fulmore director of public relations spent a considerable portion of his time working out arrangement for a day care center and trying to convince the city council to reroute one of the city's bus lines past the plant. Blasted's director of public relations spent most of his time last year providing assistance to the personnel department in the dispute over unionization.

Question for Discussion

Why the differences between the two public relations departments, their activities, and functions?

STRUCTURE

There are no definitive guidelines for structuring an internal public relations department, though as a general rule departments are organized in such a manner as to best facilitate the carrying out of their main activities and functions. Where the department is a small one — such as in the case of a social service organization or a hospital — one or sometimes two professionals will be expected to carry out all departmental tasks. As organizations increase in size, so do internal public relations departments; major industrial organizations, for example, have departments with several hundred professional public relations staffers headed almost invariably by a vice president in charge of public relations or of public relations and advertising.

Departments which consist of more than one or two people are usually organized according to one or more of the following:

Publics — consumer relations; stockholder relations; government relations; employee relations; dealer relations; community relations; etc.

Functions — graphics; press and media relations; special events; institutional advertising; internal communications; product publicity; research.

Geography — eastern division manager; Washington office; New York City office; international.

Divisions — western division; corporate headquarters; plastics division; Texas division.

Combination — parts or all of the above, as in the case of large industrial and business organizations.

Though public relations is a staff function, the department itself is managed as though it were a line unit. Reporting to the head of the department will be a limited number of managers. Each manager in turn supervises the activities of staffers with skills and experience in the specific area for which the manager is responsible. The charts that follow exemplify a typically small, medium-sized, and large public relations department.

(1) A small public relations department

(2) A medium-sized public relations department

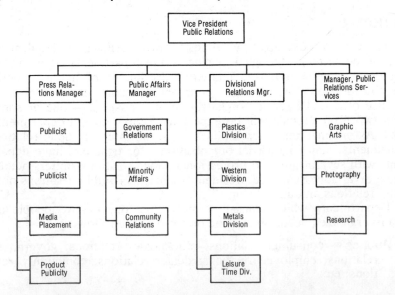

(3)   A large public relations department

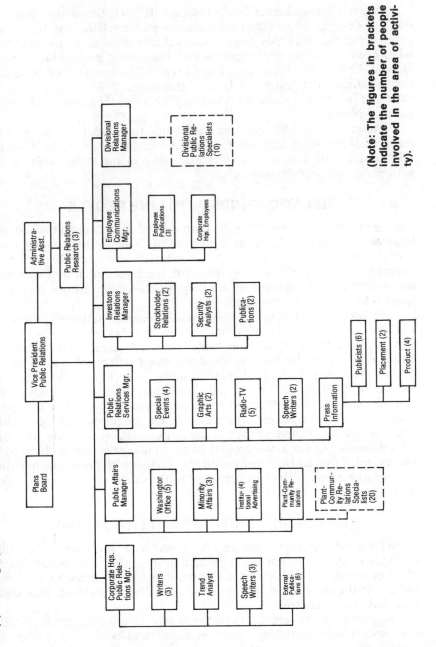

(Note: The figures in brackets indicate the number of people involved in the area of activity).

Earlier in this chapter in discussing "Knowledge of the Organization" as being an advantage to the internal public relations staffer, it was pointed out that nice tidy organization charts often mask the reality of what goes on within the organization. Dangerous medications usually include the notice: "Warning, do not keep within the reach of children." Organization charts ought to include the notice: "Warning, do not entrust this function to those who lack sensitivity to the nuances of organizational power."

The internal public relations staffer has to be acutely aware of the nuances of organizational power in two particular instances: in his or her relationship with line people; and especially in his or her relationship with plant and/or divisional people.

RELATIONSHIPS WITH LINE PEOPLE

The three charts denoting the structure of small, medium-sized, and large internal public relations departments indicate that almost every staffer reports on a direct line to someone else in the public relations department. Thus, for example, the staff specialists cited in the chart of the medium-sized department are responsible to one of the four managers who direct their activities.

However, in carrying out these public relations activities, almost all staffers have to interact with line people in other departments of the organization. In so interacting there inevitably come times when the public relations staffer and the line department staffer will not see eye to eye on the handling of a particular situation, stance, or action. How far the public relations staffer can and should go in pressing or opting for a certain public relations stance or viewpoint becomes a matter of mature judgment. Who should and will prevail when the public relations staffer and the line department staffer disagree depends on so many variables it's impossible to set down ground rules. Public relations staffers, to be successful, have to be sensitive to the nuances of power within their organizations and to the fact that they can't order line people to do anything they don't want to do.

PLANT AND/OR DIVISION RELATIONSHIPS

The public relations staffers who ought to be most sensitive to the nuances of power within an organization are those who either handle plant-community relations or division relations. A glance at the chart indicating the structure of a large public relations department provides a hint why this holds true.

According to the chart, under the public affairs manager is a staffer responsible for plant-community relations, and under this staffer are twenty plant-community relations specialists. The chart also shows there is a divisional relations manager, and under this manager are ten divisional public relations specialists. In both instances, there is a dotted line between the twenty plant-community relations specialists and the plant-community relations staffer, and a similar dotted line between the ten divisional public relations specialists and the divisional relations manager. The specialists in both instances are boxed in by dotted lines.

The English translation of this chart language means that so far as plant-community and divisional relationships are concerned this organization operates under a *decentralized system*. The dotted lines indicate that the public relations managers responsible for these two public relations staff functions *have only indirect control* over the specialists under them. The plant-community relations specialists are directly controlled by someone in the line organization of the plant-community to which they are assigned. The divisional public relations specialists are also directly controlled by someone in the line organization of the division to which they are assigned.

This arrangement can and often works well but can also lead those involved to ulcer gulch. The public relations staffer most likely to find himself in the direct line of a possible cross-fire between two superiors is the specialist. Further, the same cross-fire can take place if we reverse the situation; that is, if we have the specialist report directly to the public relations staff manager above him and indirectly to someone in the line organization for whom he or she carries out public relations task. The mini-case which follows exemplifies the dilemma.

MINI-CASE
A MATTER OF FEDERAL GUIDELINES

Joshua Mouldoon is a plant-community relations specialist working for a large national corporation which has its public relations headquarters in Boston. Mouldoon reports indirectly to Walter Cragnolin, manager of plant-community relations for the corporation, but he actually works at the Peachtree Plant of the company in a rural Georgia community. His direct supervisor there is Rip Sturgiss, director of personnel at the plant.

At the yearly meeting in corporation headquarters of all plant-community relations specialists, Mouldoon is brought up to date on recent developments in the company affecting his work. Among other things, Mouldoon and the other specialists are told by Cragnolin that the company is particularly sensitive about meeting new federal non-discrimination guidelines in hiring and promotions. Cragnolin warns the group that since the company has many federal contracts it is imperative that the federal guidelines be met. He says that the plant-community relations specialists are being involved in the compliance matter because the company recognizes that compliance will be a sensitive matter in some plant locations. Finally, he asks that the specialists send him a report in two weeks advising him what they've done since returning to their plants.

On his way back to Georgia, Mouldoon reflects on the fact that although the Peachtree Plant has 400 blacks out of a work force of 1,200, only two are in a supervisory position and 60 percent of them are in the lowest pay category. He also knows that about 40 of the black employees are college graduates.

The day after Mouldoon gets back, Sturgiss calls him into his office and asks him what he's learned at Boston that might be of some help. Mouldoon thereupon advises Sturgiss about Cragnolin's talk about federal guidelines and suggests that something ought to be done at Peachtree to meet them.

"Listen, Josh," says Sturgiss, "we're in the middle of Georgia, not in Boston, Massachusetts. Why don't you start working on that United Way report and just let me take care of the hiring and promotions, right?"

Questions for Discussion

1. What factual data or information about the people or the situation cited above would you like to have before coming to a decision about the case?

2. Assuming you now have the factual data and information you seek, what do you suggest that Mouldoon *say* in response to Sturgiss? What do you suggest he *do*? What do you suggest he say in his report to Cragnolin?

BUDGETING

Every organization, even the very smallest, utilizes a budget as a means of predetermining what its anticipated costs, income, and profit will be. Within organizations each individual department — such as the public relations department — is asked in advance of the coming fiscal year to provide a financial forecast. As the public relations department is not an income or profit center, its forecast will set forth the expenses it expects to incur in the coming year. This forecast will receive a certain number of checks and changes as it moves up the organizational ladder towards final approval. Once approved, the department's budget is expected to be adhered to carefully. The department which exceeds its approved budget mid-way through the fiscal year is going to run into considerable trouble; in fact, it could well come to a standstill.

Thus, budgeting is more than a game played on a ouija board or the future seen murkily through a clouded crystal ball. Budgeting is the financial plan which the department follows in pursuing and achieving its objectives. When objectives, plans, and programs are carefully worked out in advance, then budgeting is not a particularly difficult task. "Catch-22" becomes commonplace, however, when the unforeseen occurs, because how can one budget in advance for the unforeseen and yet how does one secure the money necessary to meet the unforeseen if one hasn't received budget approval in advance? (As will be soon demonstrated, the wily public relations executive finds answers even to this dilemma.)

In handling his department's budget the public relations executive deals with two essential costs:

Administrative costs — these are costs of salaries of the professionals, secretaries, and clerical workers plus the benefits they receive and such overhead costs as telephone, space, light, heat, office equipment, and others of a similar nature.

Program costs — these are the costs of carrying out the public relations program, and they include costs for research, publications, special events, films, press conferences and media relations in general, and others of a similar nature.

Program costs, which form the key basis for budget-making, fall within three categories: (1) carry-over or continuous programs: (2) projected or new programs; and (3) the unexpected or contingencies.

CARRY-OVER OR CONTINUOUS PROGRAMS

Unless the head of the public relations department is starting entirely from scratch, he or she has the benefit of past experience in setting up the budget for the coming fiscal year. Further, most departments have programs which are of a continuous and more or less permanent nature, and these will usually form the bulk of the department's total program for the coming year. Budgeting for these continuous programs and activities becomes a matter of projecting expected increases (or decreases in case of a dip in prices) over and above (or below) current costs.

PROJECTED OR NEW PROGRAMS

Budgeting for projected or new programs which have been approved for the coming year involves figuring out what the administrative and program costs will be. Arriving at cost figures means researching the expected expenses which will be incurred in carrying out elements of the program, and also figuring out the administrative costs. As a hedge it's also advisable to base cost figures on the "high" side in case prices go up between the time the budget is planned, approval given, and the program put into effect.

Example

Assume the department plans to institute a new external monthly publication commencing with the next fiscal year. To budget for this the department head would need to know the size and press run of the publication; paper and printing costs; and mailing costs. In addition, the department head would have to cover the costs of departmental staffers and overhead expenses. As a hedge, he would be wise to add six percent to the forementioned program costs.

THE UNEXPECTED OR CONTINGENCIES

There are three ways in which a department head can handle the troublesome budget problem of the unexpected or contingencies.

Budget for them — in short, include a specific line item in the budget to take care of the unexpected. Label this item either "contingencies" or "miscellaneous," and keep one's fingers crossed. If the line item is too large, those responsible for approving the budget will probably suggest the line figure be for an approved program item. Most budget approvers have an instinctive dislike for "miscellaneous" line figures, hence it's wise to keep the line figure within reasonable limits.

Use other line items — if management will permit the practice, the department head can use for the unexpected expenses, money which has already been approved but not expended for other line items in the budget. Some managements, recognizing that no one can reasonably be expected to predict the unexpected in advance, will permit the use of unexpended funds from other line items. The problem becomes difficult to solve when this practice is not allowed.

Ask for the funds — when the unexpected or contingencies occur the most direct way to secure money necessary to handle it is to go to management and ask for it. An understanding management knows one can't fight fires without water and one can't handle unexpected developments without money.

THE EXTERNAL PUBLIC RELATIONS COUNSELOR AND COUNSELING FIRM

The closest analogy to the public relations counselor and the public relations counseling firm is the legal counselor and the law firm. Both are retained to give counsel and advice and to provide a variety of services; one does so on public relations matters and the other on legal matters. In both fields there are small, single-member; medium-sized, multi-member; and large counseling firms. In both fields we find counsels situated all over the United States, and in both fields counsels make their living representing a variety of clients.

There are, of course, significant differences between the two. To practice law one needs to be licensed, but you don't need a license to practice public relations. Legal counseling is a much older field of activity, and one finds legal firms — generally single member entities — in even the smallest town. Public relations counselors are located chiefly in our larger cities because the bulk of their clients are not single individuals but large organizations. Further, the major share of these clients are in business and industry and as their headquarters are generally located in our large cities the public relations counselors find it advisable to locate where the clients and media are.

No one knows for certain how many public relations counseling firms there are in the country, but the most reliable estimates place the number somewhere between 1500 and 1600. This section will deal with the role and activities, structure, operating methods, and fees of firms engaged in public relations counseling.

ROLE AND ACTIVITIES

Public relations counselors fulfill the same essential role as internal public relations staffers: they provide advice, counsel, and public relations services in order to facilitate the major purpose for which the organization exists. In so doing, the counselor supplies an added dimension in that he is an outsider who may either supplement the insider's staff and work or who is retained because there is no insider staff to carry out public relations tasks.

The Counselors Section of the Public Relations Society of America, comprising more than five hundred consultant firms and individual counselors operating in all areas of the United States and internationally, describes the role of the counselor as follows:

> Public relations consultants work to assess and evaluate opinions held by one or more of the client's publics, and interpret findings to management. The consultant then assists management in formulating plans to change or improve public opinion. Public relations counsel is a partner to management, never a substitute.

> The extent and manner of such help provided by the public relations counselor will vary greatly with individual situations. In some cases, the counselor will provide both counsel and will execute a complete action program. In others, the counsel may have a more limited role.

> Public relations counsultants make their contributions to management and the success of a business endeavor by bringing seasoned experience and specialized skills to the varied tasks of communication. This contribution is strengthened by the consultant's sound judgement in business affairs and by his ability to understand and work sympathetically, constructively and objectively on the problems of the client.

> from *Public Relations and Public Relations Counseling*, the Counselors Section, Public Relations Society of America

Key words and phrases in the above statement are those which stress evaluation of public opinion, guidance and counsel in formulating plans to change or improve public opinion, providing counsel and/or executing a complete action program, bringing seasoned experience and specialized skills to the varied tasks of communication. Without denigrating the role of the internal public relations staffer — in fact, by stressing some of the same activities carried out by the internal staffer — the outside public relations counselor emphasizes his role of complementing the insider's work and provides the added attributes of the outsider.

Note how two large, international counseling firms describe their roles in the following two statements. First, here is how Hill and Knowlton describe the role of public relations counsel:

It provides objective counsel — advice uncolored by any subjective views that may exist within the business.

It provides a diversity of experience in dealing with a multitude of public relations problems.

It gives client companies access to services, facilities and various specialists in all phases of public relations. This enables the client to utilize its counsel's experienced staff for regular operations as well as for emergencies and new developments.

It gives an outside viewpoint on probable public reaction to company policies and acts.

It underwrites with its own reputation the quality and continuity of the undertaking.

> from *Hill and Knowlton Inc. Public Relations Counsel*, Hill and Knowlton, Inc.

Second, here is how Ruder & Finn, Inc., sees the role of the public relations consultant:

We see ourselves as an external public relations staff, willing to render a detached, objective opinion and speak out to management without fear of losing compensation or position. We are a group capable of assisting an internal staff in times of overload of work, of rendering professional advice in times of crisis . . . an outside force able to foresee possible pitfalls or dangers inherent in a course of action or point of view. Sometimes the function is one of cutting through the complexities and overlays of ambiguity which surrounds an issue, of encouraging reflection, of stimulating debate, of presenting the other side of a question.

Is this a franchise to cover up weaknesses and disguise deficiencies? Not at all. No real lack can be disguised for long, and it would be foolhardy for us to counsel our clients to try. Truth is always at the heart of any successful program, whether it be concerned with a product or with a cause. One of our jobs is to search out that truth and help our client to present it, cogently and directly, to those audiences which it concerns. If that sounds too facile it is nonetheless true, and perhaps not said often enough for fear of sounding glib.

> from *Looking to the Mid-70s*, Ruder & Finn, Inc.

In fulfilling their role, states the Counselors Section of the PRSA, public relations counsultants carry out the following activities:

Establishment and definition of short-range and long-range public relations goals.

Counsel and guidance to management on actions or policies which affect public relations goals.

Support of the marketing program including product or process publicity — news releases, feature articles, case studies, audio visual aids, press, radio, and television coverage.

Stockholder and financial relations — annual, quarterly or interim reports to shareholders, special releases to financial news media, assistance with the annual meeting, liaison with security analysts, investment dealers, and the professional investment community.

Employee and internal communications — company publications, information programs for employees on profits, the economics of industry, quality control, and over-all company operations.

Community relations — counsel on public relations policies at the local plant or branch office level, liaison with local news media, assistance in establishing policies of corporate giving, staging special events such as "open houses" and plant tours.

Government relations — international, federal, state, and local public relations counseling and liaison with agencies or officials whose policies influence and affect the operations of the client.

Evaluation and measurement — analysis of the effectiveness of public relations programs, application and use of budget, and attainment of identifiable objectives.

> from *Public Relations and Public Relations Counseling*, the Counselors Section, Public Relations Society of America, Inc.

Though the above list does not make the point directly, the bedrock foundation role of the public relations counsel is in *problem-solving*. Counseling firms build their reputation — and their business — on their ability to *provide counsel on problems in public relations areas and to develop programs to meet these problems*. The firms that have been most successful are the ones which have proven their ability to handle the most difficult, not the easiest, public relations problems. Illustrative of this point is the following random selection of some fairly typical situations handled by a variety of counseling firms:

1. Helping a corporation fight a takeover bid and assisting others to develop plans to avert such tender offers.
2. Mounting a successful public education campaign to defeat an anti-chain store federal tax bill.
3. Communicating management's story during an extended strike.
4. Gaining national recognition for a relatively unknown private college.
5. Guiding a company and its top management through a congressional committee hearing.

Crisis problems of the above nature don't happen every day, and counseling firms don't solve them all when they do happen. However, enough of them exist and the firms have racked up a sufficiently good problem-solving average to justify their role and function on the American public relations scene.

STRUCTURE

Counseling firms are basically organized according to (1) *the size and scope of their operations*, but their structure is also affected by (2) *the accounts they service* and by (3) the *kinds of services they emphasize*.

Items 2 and 3 are not major reasons for the structuring of counseling firms, but they occur often enough to warrant explanation. At times a counseling firm will handle a major client that requires a specific type of servicing, and if the client is retained a sufficient length of time this service department becomes a feature of the firm's operation. Given sufficient time to prove itself, the service department attracts other clients and becomes a permanent part of the firm's structure.

At one time in its past a major counseling firm had a client that needed assistance in its relationship with the world of education. This need was of sufficient scope to justify the setting up of an education department in the counseling firm. Other clients came along with need of similar assistance, and by this time the education department had proven its worth. The department today is considered one of the most valued service arms of the counseling firm.

Some counseling firms have found it advisable and profitable to concentrate on special areas of public relations competence. Rather than expand into full-service firms they prefer to maintain their limited size, capitalize on their special expertise, and prove thereby that size alone doesn't make for success. A few firms, for example, concentrate on straight counseling and very personalized service, hence keep themselves deliberately small. Others specialize in the nonprofit field or in financial or labor relations.

The major share of the counselors, however, opt for full-servicing, and the distinguishing factor among them is size. As with internal departments, these firms are divided among small, medium-sized, and large firms, size being dependent on the number of clients served.

An indication of the relative size and approximate percentage of counseling firms in each category was revealed in a survey of firms made in 1974 by Walter V. Carty, senior vice president of Hill and Knowlton. Responses from 173 or 40 percent of 445 firms surveyed showed that 61 or 35 percent of the 173 had 6 or less professionals and were termed by Carty as small; 76 or 44 percent had 7 to 25 professionals and were termed medium; and 36 or 21 percent had more than 25 professionals and were termed large. Carty's survey shows that the bulk of the firms are in the small and medium-sized categories.

Jack O'Dwyer, publisher and editor of the weekly newsletter bearing his name, compiles an annual list of the forty largest United States-based public relations operations. O'Dwyer's listing, which includes independent counseling firms and advertising agency affiliated public relations operations, ranks firms by net fee income (defined as gross fees and mark-ups minus reimbursed expenses) and includes total employees. As will be seen from O'Dwyer's 1975 listing, Hill and Knowlton topped all counseling firms and advertising department affiliates with 1974 net fee income of close to 14 million dollars and 507 employees. The O'Dwyer list also shows that twenty-four counseling firms and advertising agency affiliates had net fee income of more than one million dollars.

REPRINTED FROM THE 1975 O'DWYER'S DIRECTORY OF PUBLIC RELATIONS FIRMS

The 40 Largest U.S. PR Operations, Independent and Ad Agency Affiliated
(Based on documentation submitted to the Directory)

	1974 Net Fee Income[1]	Total Employees
1. Hill and Knowlton	$13,858,046	507
2. Burson-Marsteller*	9,575,200[2]	332
3. Carl Byoir & Assocs.	—	245
4. Ruder & Finn	6,200,000	205[3]
5. J. Walter Thompson PR (including Dialog)*	5,850,000	177
6. Infoplan International (Interpublic)*	4,000,000[4]	120
7. Harshe-Rotman & Druck	3,800,000[4]	138
8. Communications Board[5]	3,127,373	116
9. Daniel J. Edelman	3,002,392	133
10. Booke and Co.	2,714,804	81
11. Doremus & Co.*	2,634,000	88
12. Ketchum, MacLeod & Grove PR Dept.*	2,500,000[4]	90
13. Rogers & Cowan	2,379,000[6]	74
14. Manning, Selvage & Lee	2,346,268	72
15. PPR International (Young & Rubicam)*	2,000,000	125
16. The Rowland Co.	1,911,100[4]	60
17. Georgeson & Co.	1,750,000	40
18. Dickson-Basford*	1,135,000	40
19. Edward Gottlieb & Assocs.	1,200,000[6]	50
20. Dudley-Anderson-Yutzy	1,097,511	50
21. Underwood, Jordan Assocs.	1,078,000[4]	31
22. Hank Meyer Assocs.	1,033,212	25
23. Ayer Public Relations Services*	1,000,000	44
24. Albert Frank-Guenther Law*	1,000,000	38
25. Fleishman-Hillard	890,401	32
26. Bell & Stanton	880,000	34
27. Robert Marston and Assocs.	841,500	29
28. Gardner, Jones & Co.	838,000[7]	32
29. Aaron D. Cushman & Assocs.	773,041	25
30. Anthony M. Franco	725,000	24
31. The Softness Group	712,200	21
32. Darcy Communications*	685,000[4]	26
33. Grey & Davis*	605,000	20
34. Addison, Goldstein & Walsh	602,000	30
35. Woody Kepner & Assocs.	560,450	30
36. Barkin, Herman, Solochek & Paulsen	—	30

37. Fred Rosen Assocs.	550,000	20
38. Cooper & Golin	550,000[8]	25
39. Cunningham & Walsh*	550,000	25
40. Padilla and Speer	536,033	20

*Ad agency PR Dept. or partner
[1]Net fee income is for 12 months ended June 30, 1974, unless otherwise indicated
[2]Year ended Sept. 30, 1974
[3]Does not include 35 persons abroad in offices partially owned by R&F
[4]Year ended Dec. 31, 1974
[5]Includes Financial Relations Board and Public Relations Board
[6]Year ended March 31, 1974
[7]Year ended Feb. 28, 1974
[8]Year ended Jan. 31, 1974

Copyright 1975 by the J. R. O'Dwyer Company, Inc. 271 Madison Ave., NY 10016
Reprinted with permission from the 1975 *O'Dwyer's Directory of Public Relations Firms*

Though almost every counseling firm stresses its individual virtues, there is a great deal of similarity in the way firms are structured. In the small firm where there are a limited number of professionals, members of the professional staff serve as both account executives and specialists. Each member of the professional staff is expected to advise and counsel and also to handle the myriad of specialized tasks demanded by the nature of client accounts. This would include writing releases, handling press conferences and media contacts, conducting studies, writing and preparing publications, and similar tasks.

MEDIUM-SIZED AND LARGE FIRMS

As firms grow in size and take on more accounts and employees the structure of the firm takes on added dimensions. At the top of the structure will be the senior members of the firm: the chairman of the board; president; one or more senior or executive vice presidents. Each senior member of the firm takes under his wing a group of account executives, and usually these will be given vice president status after suitable service with the firm. If an account is large enough, the account executive vice president will have one or more professionals working with him on the account. In a large number of instances account executives will be handling more than one account unless an account is of sufficient substance and billing to warrant the full-time attention of one account executive.

To provide quality control and integration of talents, skills, and judgment, counseling firms add various forms of committees or boards to the above basic structure. Some firms call these a plans board, audit review committee, program review committee, or account performance review committee. Such groups provide a pooling of talents and resources which are called upon either at the onset or during a client relationship, and they serve to assist in planning and programming for the client or to measure, assess, and improve performance by those primarily responsible for the account.

Thus, the medium and large counseling firms have the senior executive and account executive tier to handle accounts, and various committees or boards to backstop the primary, front-line team. The third element in the firm's structure is provided by the specialized departments common to all medium-sized and large counseling firms. These departments are not responsible for accounts as such, but are available for use by all account supervisors as the occasion warrants. If the account executive handling Client A, for example, decides to hold a press conference he calls on the publicity department to help him plan and run it. If the account executive for Client B decides to produce a four-color brochure he calls on the graphics department for assistance. At any one time, each specialist department could be providing assistance for a wide variety and number of clients retained by the firm. How many and what kind of specialized departments the counseling firm will have varies with the firm, but Figure 4-1 exemplifies the specialized departments of three major firms.

The final structural element of the medium-sized and particularly the large firms is geographical in nature. In order to provide on-the-spot national and international service these firms either establish their own offices in major cities in the United States and abroad or work out arrangements with other U.S. and foreign counseling firms. Through such arrangements the larger firms are able to provide local, regional, national, and international service when such service is needed. Hill and Knowlton, for example, has regional, subsidiary, and affiliate offices in Los Angeles, San Francisco, Dallas, Seattle, and Chicago, and in addition has exclusive reciprocal working agreements with twenty-two public relations firms throughout the country. To serve clients abroad H & K has offices and facilities in London, Geneva, Paris, Brussels, the Hague, Milan, Rome, Frankfurt, Madrid, and Tokyo, plus affiliates in Australia, Southeast Asia, the Middle East, Latin America, Scandinavia, Austria, Greece, and other major world markets. Ruder & Finn has branches in Chicago, Washington, Dallas, Houston, Los Angeles, and San Francisco, and in addition operates a network of affiliate public relations companies in forty major areas of the country. To service its clients abroad, R & F has offices and affiliates in Toronto, London, Australia, Paris, Israel, Milan, and Tokyo. Similar national and international branch and network affiliations are in effect at Carl Byoir & Associates, Harshe-Rotman & Druck, Infoplan International, and other large counseling firms.

Figure 4-1

Some Typical Specialized Departments

Carl Byoir & Associates Inc.

General News
Radio and Television
Women's News
Magazine-Book
Business and Financial
Investor Relations
Special Projects

Hill & Knowlton, Inc.

Creative Services
  Editorial Services
  Graphic Services
Environmental and Consumer Affairs
Financial Relations
Publicity and Marketing Services
Program Research
Research and Library Services
State and Local Government Relations
Urban Affairs
Youth and Education

Ruder & Finn, Inc.

Corporate and Financial Relations
Public Affairs Communication
Environmental Affairs
TV/Film
Plus the following independent divisions:
  Research and Forecasts
  Ruder and Finn Fine Arts
  Photographic Consultants
  Intermedia
  Public Relations Production Co.
  Fujita Design

METHOD OF OPERATION

Clients who retain public relations counsel can be assured they are buying a service tailored to their measurements. In fact, public relations counseling firms operate very much like custom tailors. When you have a fine suit made to order by a custom tailor you don't go into his shop and pick your suit off the rack. Rather, you'll be greeted by the owner of the shop, have your measurements taken, shown some swatches of material, come to agreement about the kind of suit you want, come back another time or two to try on the suit while it is being made by skilled craftsmen, and finally end up with a garment that meets your objectives and is fit only for your frame.

Counseling firms work in similar fashion. Most counselors do not sell pre-packaged programs, but rather get to work tailoring a program only after the client has agreed to retain counsel. The "swatches" the client is shown are usually testimonials from other clients who have recommended the counseling firm. Most counseling firms do not sign lengthy, formal contracts with their clients but rather have relatively simple letters of agreement and, in some cases, verbal agreements. These outline the general nature of the work to be accomplished, the basic elements of the fee involved, and the stipulation that either party can terminate the contract by giving 30, 60 or 90 days' notice.

The counselor "measures" his client by conducting a careful and systematic study of the client's organization, policies, strengths and weaknesses, competitive position, needs, and problems. The account team responsible for handling the client then gets to work in the back shop setting objectives and goals and developing an overall public relations plan and budget to meet them. Some counseling firms then have the plan and budget reviewed by standing or special review committees within the organization before it is submitted to the client for approval. Once the client approves the program, the account team puts it into effect utilizing the members of the team, senior management, and the specialized departments. Further, in order to insure quality control during the contract period many firms conduct periodic account reviews or "audits" to check on account team performance, measure the program's effectiveness, and make revision when necessary.

MINI-CASE
THE BYOIR SYSTEMS APPROACH

Here is how Carl Byoir & Associates describe the way they handle a client:

"Just as successful businesses today rely on a complex and orderly organization of systems (systems of research and development, systems of finance, systems of marketing, systems of packaging, systems of management information), public relations, as we view it, must be responsive to similar discipline.

"In any area, an efficient and effective system is one in which all elements are related to each other and to stated objectives. And that characterizes the Byoir systems approach to public relations.

"In developing a comprehensive program, it is our practice to work in close, daily contact with a client in undertaking a series of methodical steps:

1. Systematic study and analysis of all elements of the company's present situation, including its management policies, relationships with various publics, organizational attributes and opportunities, competitive position, outside trends (social, political, environmental) and goals (financial, marketing, social).

2. Planning and programming of a system of specific projects and actions, related to each other and to goals determined by the preceding analysis.

3. Implementation of the program through systematic application in all communication media to achieve the stated objectives with maximum impact.

4. Regular review to measure the program's effectiveness, with revisions to meet any change of conditions or objectives.

"Many public relations programs falter because they are not based on sufficiently comprehensive and pragmatic study. They tend to scatter their efforts in all directions rather than organizing them into integrated systems of action.

"The most important result of the Byoir systems approach is: (a) to identify a company's true objectives and (b) help it achieve them by projecting a strong, clear and consistent picture of the company's activities to its various publics. Another result, though less important, is to increase the efficiency of the money spent by the company on its public relations."

from *The Byoir Way*, Carl Byoir and Associates, Inc.

Typical Systems Flow

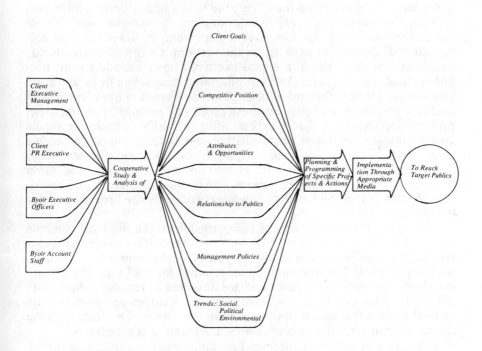

Client Goals

Client Executive Management

Competitive Position

Client PR Executive

Attributes & Opportunities

Byoir Executive Officers

Cooperative Study & Analysis of

Relationship to Publics

Byoir Account Staff

Management Policies

Trends: Social Political Environmental

Planning & Programming of Specific Projects & Actions

Implementation Through Appropriate Media

To Reach Target Publics

Reproduced with permission of Carl Byoir and Associates

FEES

In the early days of public relations counseling there was so little mention of fees in the professional literature one might have concluded that a fee was some sort of social disease not to be mentioned in polite company. In the past decade, on the other hand, there have been so many confusing articles about fees one might just as well concluded that a fee is one of the mysteries of the Far East.

Boiled down to its bare essentials, a fee is what the counselor charges the client in order to cover the *cost of servicing the client*, help pay for the counselor's *overhead*, allow a *margin for profit*, and reimburse the counselor for out-of-pocket expenses.

The above explanation is simple enough to cover the bare essentials but hardly suffices for those who want to know just what is covered. To cover *the cost of servicing the client*, the firm's billing system must provide for the salaries of everyone working on the account, and this includes reimbursement for top level management, professional, and secretarial staff time spent working on the account. *Overhead costs* include the client's share of the firm's total overhead items including rent, telephone, heat, lighting, etc. As for *profit*, most counseling firms aim for a target gross profit before taxes of 25 percent of gross billings less out-of-pocket costs. Such a 25 percent gross profit will normally produce a net profit of approximately 5 to 6 percent after provision is made for annual contribution to employee profit sharing and federal and state income taxes. Included in *out-of-pocket expenses* — which are almost always billed separately — are the cost of mimeograph, multilith, and other printing, postage, messenger service, press clippings, radio and television reports, travel, and entertainment expended by the firm in servicing the account.

There are various systems of billing the client, but the most common is to bill monthly in advance to cover an agreed-upon minimum fee or retainer for staff time, and to bill at the end of the month for all out-of-pocket expenses. The minimum fee or retainer for staff time charges are based on standard hourly rates and are designed to recover salary costs plus a factor for overhead and profit. Charges incurred in any month are applied against the agreed-upon minimum, and when the charges during the month run over the minimum they are billed at regular rates.

Though it is still most common for counseling firms to charge out-of-pocket expenses at cost, some firms now apply a percentage — usually 15 or 17.5 percent — for handling certain out-of-pocket expenses, such as printing and art work.

Where the counseling firm is retained on a continuing basis the budget is set annually and the agreement runs for a one-year period with a mutually agreed-upon termination notification period of one, two, or three months. Agreements, as noted previously, can be in the form of a formal, legal contract; a letter of agreement, or a verbal gentleman's agreement.

The following three examples are an explanation of the fee system of Carl Byoir and Associates, an explanation of the fee system of a counselor who has made a proposal for an account, and a letter of agreement covering the entire counselor-client relationship after the client has agreed to retain counselor. (Note: these are not the same counselors or clients.)

MINI-EXAMPLE
THE BYOIR FEE SYSTEM

HOW WE CHARGE

We offer two plans of payment for our services. Plan A is our basic plan utilizing a retainer fee, and we feel it provides the most satisfactory service to the majority of our clients and the best utilization of the money they wish to spend. Plan B makes our services available without retainer fee by charging for time used on a formula basis.

PLAN A

For services in the United States our clients pay us a standard annual fee which covers consultation, planning, supervision by the executive officers, overhead and profit. Contracts are written for a minimum of one year.

All direct expenses incurred in the conduct of the program are billed net to the client.

These expenses that we bill without adding commission or overhead charges include:

Salaries of the account executive and the staff assigned to the account and their payroll taxes.

Travel, telephone and telegraph, entertainment in the client's behalf, stationery, postage and supplies utilized in news releases, photography mats, printing, art work, stenographic service and all other outlays connected with publicity or promotions.

Uniform per diem or hourly charges for work performed by Byoir's special services departments, domestic regional offices and field men.

For the time and counsel of the executive officers of the Byoir organization there is no charge beyond the retainer fee except for travel and communications incident to these services.

At the time a plan of action is being worked out, an estimated annual budget for expenses is agreed upon. Expenses are then projected in advance for each month throughout the year subject to approval of the client. They are based on the activities that we recommend be carried out, and the client has the prerogative of deciding whether or not to undertake recommended projects. There is no contractual obligation on the client's part beyond the fee.

The client is billed monthly for the fee and for expenses incurred during the preceding month.

For programs conducted outside of the United States separate contracts are negotiated, fees and costs depending upon the geographical area and the nature and extent of the projects.

We make no commissions on services or materials purchased for the client's account, and there are no extra charges for overhead. Our only interest in the size of the budget is that it be adequate to implement the programs mutually agreed upon. We pride ourselves upon careful budgeting to obtain for the client the maximum result for every dollar of expense.

PLAN B

Under this plan clients pay us a monthly minimum charge on an annual basis. For actual services rendered and manpower used, we bill with a percentage markup of the actual salaries and per diem costs of employees involved. These billings are applied against the monthly minimum with any excess added on. Out-of-pocket expenses are billed as under Plan A with no markup.

Reprinted with permission

MINI-EXCERPT
A COUNSELOR EXPLAINS HIS PROPOSED FEE SYSTEM

When counselors write proposal letters — whether they be general letters outlining the counselor's competence or more specific letters outlining the proposed program — they usually end up discussing their fee. Here is how one counseling firm explained the proposed fee:

"Our fee for professional services is $48,000 annually. This covers the professional side of the budget in New York City, which would be the center of account activity.

"At this point we can only estimate the 'out-of-pocket' part of the budget for such things like publications, travel, telephone calls, photography, and so forth. We're sure we'd be well covered if you would budget $25,000–$30,000 for the year for these items. With the exception of petty cash items, disbursements from this fund would be made only with your prior approval.

"We would also like to suggest that you set aside a contingency fund of $10,000 so we could have on-the-spot support for the market-by-market program from our regional offices located in Los Angeles, Washington, Chicago, and Houston and supplemented by our Field Network in the next 25 most important cities in the country. We can use the regional office people as we need them for specific support of special promotions.

"Thus, the total cost should be in the neighborhood of $83,000–$88,000 for the year. We would want a firm one-year agreement, cancellable either way thereafter by sixty day's notice. . . ."

Questions for Discussion

1. In what way does the above fee system protect the counseling firm? The client?
2. If you were the client-to-be, what questions might you have about the above fee system?
3. If you were the conseling firm, what answers would you give to the questions?

HARSHE-ROTMAN & DRUCK INC. *PUBLIC RELATIONS*

NEW YORK   CHICAGO   LOS ANGELES   MEMPHIS   DALLAS

300 E. 44TH ST.   NEW YORK, N.Y. 10017   PHONE (212) 661-3400   TWX 710-581-5312

Date

Mr. John Doe
President
Client Corporation
000 North Michigan Avenue
Chicago, Illinois 60600

Dear Mr. Doe:

In accordance with our oral understanding, we are submitting the following
as a letter of agreement covering our relationship.

(1)   Effective (date), Client Corporation has retained Harshe-Rotman & Druck,
      Inc. as its public relations counsel.

(2)   Public relations services to be provided under terms of this agreement
      include: analysis of public relations objectives; creation, planning,
      and execution of programs designed to achieve agreed-upon objectives;
      counseling; preparation of written and other public relations materials;
      representation of Client Corporation to the public, as its agent; and
      periodically reporting on progress and achievements in a manner to be
      mutually agreed upon.

(3)   Harshe-Rotman & Druck, Inc. will be paid for its services at the annual
      rate of $_____, billable in equal monthly installments, in advance, of
      $_____.   Billing will be on the first day of each month, and payment
      will be due during that month.

(4)   The established fee is determined by the nature of the program and
      personnel necessary to implement it.   If additional service is required
      beyond that initially contemplated, we will present a budget for this
      for approval in advance.   Financial public relations work is not included
      in the fee covered in this agreement.

(5)   Services provided by Harshe-Rotman & Druck, Inc. subsidiaries
      or affiliates are not covered by this agreement unless specifically
      included and budgeted for.   At any future date such services are
      available on a special project or hourly charge basis.

WORLD-WIDE SERVICE THROUGH PR INTERNATIONAL, INC.

HARSHE-ROTMAN & DRUCK INC. *PUBLIC RELATIONS*

Mr. John Doe
Client Corporation
Date
Page Two

(6) Out-of-pocket expenses incurred specifically as part of the Client
Corporation program, which are not part of our overhead, will be
billed monthly as incurred. Expenses to be billed at our cost include
communications (telephone, teletype, telegraph, postage); transportation
and other travel expenses; restaurant and other entertainment charges
for business meetings and press conferences; fees of specialized
individuals hired for a Client Corporation project, such as models
and free lance writers; clipping services, and such other items as are
not mentioned below. In accordance with normal agency procedures, the
following expense items will be billed at our cost plus 17.65 per cent
service charge: printing, typography and artwork; photography, films,
and recordings. No major expenditures will be incurred without prior
approval. The expense budget is to be $_____for the year.

(7) Client Corporation agrees to deposit with Harshe-Rotman & Druck, Inc.
the sum of $_____to be used as a revolving credit against which
approved out-of-pocket disbursements may be paid. Client Corporation
agrees to reimburse this fund each month in the amount of such out-of-
pocket charges. Harshe-Rotman & Druck, Inc. agrees to refund promptly
to Client Corporation any unspent balance remaining therein at the
completion of this agreement or extension thereof.

(8) It is agreed that Client Corporation shall and does hereby indemnify
Harshe-Rotman & Druck, Inc. against any damages, costs, and expenses,
including reasonable attorney's fees, incurred in defending against any
action arising out of the release of materials previously cleared and
approved for and on behalf of Client Corporation, and Client Corporation
does hereby expressly hold Harshe-Rotman & Druck, Inc. harmless from
any such damages, costs, and expenses.

114

Mr. John Doe
Client Corporation
Date
Page Three

(9) At any time after the first three months of this agreement, the agreement can be cancelled by either party on 90-days advance notice in writing.

If this statement of our working relationship is agreeable, will you please sign and return one copy to us, keeping one copy for your files.

Cordially,

Harshe-Rotman & Druck Officer
Title

ACCEPTED BY:

_____
CLIENT CORPORATION

Date: _____

Reprinted with permission of Harshe-Rotman & Druck, Inc.

QUESTIONS AND PROBLEMS FOR DISCUSSION

1. Explain the four basic systems whereby the public relations function is carried out.
2. Explain some major advantages and disadvantages of having public relations handled by an internal staff or department.
3. Explain some major advantages and disadvantages of having public relations handled by a counseling firm.
4. Explain some major advantages and disadvantages of having public relations handled by a combination of an internal department and a counseling firm.
5. In what respects is it possible to ascertain the role of a particular public relations department by noting to whom the head of the department reports?
6. What are some key tasks which are common to most internal public relations departments?
7. Explain the various ways in which public relations departments are *structured*, and cite an example to illustrate each of these ways.
8. In a large organization where there is a central public relations staff and divisional public relations staff at various locations throughout the country: (1) what kinds of problems are involved when divisional public relations staffers report directly to division managers and indirectly to central public relations? (2) what kinds of problems are involved when divisional public relations staffers report indirectly to division managers and directly to central public relations?
9. Explain three ways of handling budget problems involving the unexpected or contingencies.
10. Explain the various ways in which counseling firms are organized.
11. Explain the various ways in which counseling firms charge for their services.

PART III
THE DYNAMICS OF PUBLIC RELATIONS

The dynamics of public relations concerns the process of public relations in action. Chapter 1, discussing the various definitions of public relations, pointed out that the more perceptive definitions emphasize the management function and then provide the following step-by-step analysis of public relations as an action process:

1. Evaluation of public attitudes and opinion
2. Identification of policies and procedures of an organization with the public interest
3. Execution of an action and communication program to bring about public understanding and acceptance

The management function and the relationship among public relations, social responsibility, and the public interest have been covered in preceding chapters. The aim of this section is to explain the dynamics of the public relations process by covering in detail the following key elements:

PUBLIC OPINION AND PUBLIC RELATIONS

Prerequisite to all public relations activity is an understanding of the nature of public opinion. Analyzed in detail here are the concepts of publics, attitudes morés and stereotypes, opinion formation, and some public opinion signposts.

RESEARCH AND PUBLIC RELATIONS

This chapter discusses fact-finding and the use of research, particularly research which surveys public attitudes and opinion, as the first step in the public relations process.

PLANNING AND PROGRAMMING

Though public relations in action is not always an orderly procedure, there are certain steps that should be taken in programming public relations activities. These steps are set forth to provide an *overview* of the planning and programming process.

COMMUNICATION

Communication theories and processes are explored here in some detail because of the key role they play in reaching an organization's key publics.

FEEDBACK: REPORTING, MEASUREMENT, AND EVALUATION

Feedback by means of reporting, measurement, and evaluation closes the public relations circle. This chapter explores the various ways in which the practitioner measures progress and reports the results of public relations activities.

Some words of reminder are called for at this point. Dynamics refers to forces in motion, and the public relations process is not static but continuously in action. At any one time the busy practitioner may be planning a new program while carrying out an old one and also be involved in several steps in the public relations process at the same time. To the student, however, an orderly discussion of the dynamics of public relations should be a first step in understanding the whole as well as its parts.

PUBLIC OPINION 5

How important is public opinion to public relations practice?

Socrates would probably answer that question with some questions of his own: How important are the lungs to breathing? How important are the ears to hearing? How important is the nose to smelling?

PUBLIC RELATIONS VIS-A-VIS PUBLIC OPINION

The answer to the question is self-evident. Without an understanding of the nature of public opinion and how it operates there can be no meaningful public relations practice. It's with good reason that the word "public" is an integral part of both terms; in the one case we are dealing with the *opinions* of the public and in the other we are dealing with *relations* with the public. Thus the tie that binds the two is the public, and it's the public's opinion with which the practitioner is concerned when he or she plans and carries out a public relations program. The details of the program, in turn, depend on the specific concern the practitioner has with public opinion. Is he concerned merely about the *essence* of public opinion? Does he want simply to *measure* public opinion? Does he want to *create* favorable public opinion? Does he want to *neutralize* unfavorable public opinion? These are some of the basic questions which have to be faced and answered by the practitioner.

DIFFERING PERSPECTIVES

Dealing with questions and answers to public opinion first involves recognition of the relative place of public relations as compared to other, more firmly established, fields of study, standing, and research. Public relations practitioners are relative newcomers to the study of public opinion and hence have relied on the findings of other disciplines, primarily political science, sociology, and psychology. As one goes through the literature of the three fields he discovers studies dealing with the formulation of basic theories of public opinion as well as empirical studies describing research in public opinion formulation. Some authorities have gone so far as to formulate so-called rules of public opinion, but a close analysis of these "rules" reveals that they hold true only under certain circumstances. Unfortunately, these circumstances have a disconcerting tendency to occur only once in their pristine state and are not much help.

Analysis of the theories of public opinion and the empirical studies also reveals that there is not a great deal of agreement among the political scientist, the sociologist, and the psychologist when it comes to public opinion. This is due partly to the fact that the authorities in each of the three fields approach public opinion from the unique perspective of their specialities. The political scientist is primarily concerned with public opinion in the framework of politics and governance; the sociologist's primary concern is in the framework of society; and the psychologist approaches public opinion in the framework of the individual. There is nothing wrong with each of these concerns — in fact, there's a great deal of value to be gained from them — but the fact remains that each perceives only part of the picture.

There's a final significant difference between the approach to public opinion taken by the public relations practitioner and that taken by the political scientist, the sociologist, and the psychologist. The practitioner is concerned with *practical* aspects of public opinion whereas the other three are concerned chiefly with theoretical and academic aspects. In no way should we consider theory and academic perspectives to be inferior; on the contrary, it's from them that most of what is practical in today's world is derived.

If the practitioner were dealing with tangible objects his search for answers would not be so difficult. Public opinion, however, is not a tangible object. We know that it exists, we know that it's all-powerful in a democratic society, but our problem is in defining it, measuring it, trying to influence it, and above all, understanding it. This chapter aims to examine these problematic aspects of public opinion and to relate them to the practice of public relations. As a preliminary warm-up for this examination the student should consider the questions which follow and discuss them in dialogue with his fellow classmates.

PRELIMINARY QUESTIONS ABOUT PUBLIC OPINION

1. Under what circumstances would the public relations practitioner be concerned merely about the *essence* of public opinion? About the *measurement* of public opinion? About wanting to create *favorable* public opinion? About wanting to *neturalize* unfavorable public opinion?

2. How would you rate the four public opinion goals or concerns in terms of their degree of difficulty of achievement? Justify your selections.

3. Why do you think it's so difficult to *define* public opinion? To *measure* public opinion? To *influence* public opinion? To *understand* public opinion?

4. Can you cite any organization which has little or no need to be concerned about public opinion? Justify your selection.

5. How do you think students feel about the college in which you are enrolled? How about the alumni? How about the public at large? What's the reason(s) for the similarities or differences in these views? Justify your conclusions.

6. How well do you think you are able to judge the opinions of your classmates about the kind of job the president of the United States is doing? A little experiment should give you the answer.

In advance of actual measurement, jot down on a piece of paper your assessment of the precentage of the class who you think judge the president as doing an excellent, good, fair or poor job. The instructor will now have each of you jot down your own judgment of the job the president is doing, and the total percentages will be tabulated. Now compare your prior estimate with the actual percentages.

7. In his editorials dealing with public issues the editor of a daily newspaper in a city of 125,000 invariably concluded with the remark that "rank and file Americans" or "rank and file residents" felt thus-and-thus about the particular issue. What's your reaction to this usage of public opinion?

THE PUBLIC

From Roman days to the present the phrase "vox populi" has been conjured up as a means of saying that the people have spoken. The Romans used the phrase to mean "the voice of the people," and today *the public* is used to mean anything from the entire United States population to an aldermen's ward constituency. No phrase should be used so loosely, and certainly not by public relations practitioners who claim expertise in the area of public opinion. Clarification rather than obfuscation should be the goal of those who deal with the opinions of people. The following guidelines relative to the word *public* may be of help in clarifying general misunderstandings:

"THE PUBLIC" IS A MYTH

Politicians, editorial writers, and columnists refer to the mass audience as *the public*, but they do so because necessity is the mother of invention. Plainly stated, there is no such entity as the public even though the term seems to suit the needs of those who use it indiscriminately.

Those who speak of *the public* ignore the simple fact that a public is amorphous, transitory, ever-changing, and virtually infinite in numbers. The important point to keep in mind is that there is no fixed entity called *the public*; under certain circumstances two people may constitute a public, just as thousands may constitute a public. To lump any group together under the umbrella term *the public* is to misconstrue and oversimplify the term.

THERE IS NOT ONE, BUT MANY PUBLICS

All of us, at one and the same time, belong to an almost infinite number of publics. At this very moment you may well be a Protestant, union member, Elk, youthful, a voter, football fan, bird-watcher, and a Democrat. Or you may be a Catholic, an entrepreneur, Knights of Columbus member, chess player, hunter, and a Republican. If you want to complicate matters, consider that you and your neighbor are Protestants but you are a Methodist who goes to church every Sunday and your neighbor is a Congregationalist who only attends church on Easter Sunday. First and foremost you're Methodist and Congregationalist; second, regular and irregular church-goers; and third, members of that vast body of people who call themselves Protestants.

For the sake of convenience, practitioners prefer to deal with publics in broad, general terms by referring to the employee, stockholder, customer, and community publics. Harwood Childs, however, warns against the danger of such easy generalizations. He points out that if you want to analyze a firm's actions on employees you should examine not merely broad publics but sub-publics. In seeking to predict employee reactions to company actions it's important to distinguish between employees who belong to unions and those who don't; employees who have been in the work force for decades and those who have but recently been employed; employees who hold two jobs and those who hold but one.

Further, to be successful in reaching people one must be cognizant of the fact that *the multiplicity of publics to which all of us belong can cause internal conflicts of loyalties not easy to resolve.* Examples of those who face loyalty conflicts due to multi-public membership are the professor who believes firmly in independence of mind and in professionalism and yet joins with his colleagues in a union; the young Catholic mother who is an ardent believer in feminist rights, including the right to abortion; the son of a Marine colonel who is torn between duty to country and fighting in an undeclared war which he believes is immoral. Sorting out primary loyalties for such individuals becomes a soul-wrenching experience, and should teach all of us to heed the road sign which reads: warning, publics ahead, proceed with all due caution.

That road sign should serve as a warning that the large public is always a combination of smaller publics, that individuals usually belong to different publics simultaneously, and that one of the most difficult tasks in the world is to figure out which public has an individual's loyalties when two or more of his publics are in a collision course.

ISSUES CREATE THEIR OWN PUBLICS

Though members of a public are usually not in direct physical contact with each other, there are times and circumstances when such members get together to form an audience. There are also times when a loosely organized public is activated by an issue which is of prime importance to those making up said public. At such a time, when an issue activates a public, the effectiveness of such a public as an action group becomes a matter of real concern to the public relations practitioner. Individuals who previously had an unstructured relationship to each other may join together or tie themselves to other groups with a more institutionalized structure. The result is a public which has found its voice to make its weight felt, and in such instances attention must be paid.

Issues which are perceived by members of a public to be of key importance to them are the ones which trigger a public to coalesce into an action group. Unfortunately, there is no magic means whereby the practitioner can predict with certitude that such-and-such issue will activate a hitherto nascent public to become an active public. Nor is there any magic method of predicting the degree of intensity of feelings which an issue can arouse in a particular public. The astute practitioner: (1) keeps careful watch as issues arise; (2) tries to anticipate what individuals in society are affected by them; (3) notes whether these individuals are either in an organized grouping or are in the process of becoming an organized grouping; and (4) takes steps to deal with statements or actions which he or she anticipates to be forthcoming from that particular public.

THE NATURE OF AN ORGANIZATION USUALLY DICTATES ITS PUBLICS

Probably because he didn't have to deal with the public, Thomas Carlyle was able to be rather cavalier in dismissing the public as "an old woman" — his words, not this author's — who should be left alone to "maunder and mumble." Organizations in today's society can't afford Carlyle's suggested treatment, but instead need to view their publics as Very Important People indeed. Experience provides some basic ways to size up the publics deemed to be most important.

Organizations with similar goals and purposes usually have similar publics. All colleges exist for the purpose of educating students, hence the student public is a basic college public. All appliance manufacturers exist by selling their products to consumers, hence the consumer public is a basic appliance manufacturer public. Every daily newspaper in the country exists by attracting readers and advertisers, hence the reading and advertising publics are basic publics for daily newspapers. However. . . .

The unique nature of an organization can often make its publics different from organizations which seem similar to it. Yes, it's true that all colleges exist for the purpose of educating students, but some colleges only admit women, some only admit men, some admit both men and women, some draw students from their immediate area, and some draw students from the entire country. In each case, though all colleges exist for the purpose of educating students, the college in question may have a public vastly different from the others.

There's a pecking order among publics as well as among chickens. All men and women are created equal, but some publics are much more important than others. Pin-pointing publics in order of importance is a crucial matter for the public relations practitioner, and shouldn't be handled routinely. Consider, for example, a 100-year-old, private university which has an alumni body numbering more than 100,000 and compare it with a 10-year-old, public college which has an alumni body numbering less than 5,000. Obviously, the first-named institution's alumni are a public more important to it than the alumni of the second-named institution.

Keep in mind that publics shift as organizations change. Because we live in a fast-changing world organizations are in a state of flux. Today's small private college is liable to become a part of a state university tomorrow. Today's manufacturer of widgets is liable to become a part of some vast conglomerate tomorrow. Yesterday's March of Dimes to combat infantile paralysis is today devoted to combating birth defects, and who can tell what will need combating tomorrow? As organizations change in nature and purpose, so do their publics change; an outdated list of publics is about as worthless as last year's calendar.

Beware the latent public. Keeping track of such major publics as customers, employees, and the like is generally not a difficult task. Remember, however, that there are publics within publics and many of these are hidden from view and in a latent state. As issues arise which are important to them, these latent publics begin to stir, to write letters to editors, to become organized, and to surface and cause innumerable problems if their presence is not detected beforehand and steps taken to handle them. Many a school budget has been defeated because school administrators and boards of education didn't realize until too late that a pocket of dissatisfied residents would turn out in force when the budget came up for approval. The time to treat a latent public is before, not after it becomes an overt one.

MINI-CASE
PROFILING AN ETHNIC SUB-PUBLIC

The fascinating thing about sub-publics is that they can exist virtually unknown within the larger American public, and that they often come into being in a short period of time. In the first half of the seventies a sub-public of close to 50,000 Korean immigrants settled into a two-mile stretch of Olympic Boulevard in Los Angeles, and in short order came to be known as Koreatown.

According to a *Newsweek* report by John L. Dotson Jr. (5/26/75), 200,000 Koreans settled in America after the Korean War, most of them coming between 1965–1975 and with the largest concentration in Los Angeles. By 1975, reported Dotson, there were 1,400 Korean-owned businesses in Los Angeles and these included 58 restaurants, 150 grocery stores, two hospitals, five newspapers, two radio stations, and two UHF television stations that operated on weekends.

Thus, in 1975 Koreatown represented a sizable sub-public smack in the middle of sprawling Los Angeles, yet to most Americans the mere existence of this sub-community must have been unknown until they read about it in *Newsweek*.

That sizable sub-publics of similar nature exist in every city of even medium size in America is a fact of American life. It merely takes some on-the-spot research to prove this fact, hence the following assignment:

A SUB-PUBLIC RESEARCH ASSIGNMENT

First, read John Dotson's *Newsweek* profile of Koreatown on page 10 of the March 26, 1975, issue. Second, research a similar ethnic sub-public existing within any large or medium-sized city of your choice. Third, write a 600–700 word Dotson-type profile of this sub-public.

MINI-CASE
SOME BASIC RULES FOR RELATING TO BLACKS

Concluding a four-part series dealing with public relations and the black community Frank M. Seymour, president of Seymour & Lundy Associates, Inc., of Detroit, cited eight basic rules for dealing with blacks on an individual and community level. The precepts, previously published in a Seymour & Lundy booklet called "What *Not* to Say to a Black American," were carried in a supplement to the *PR Reporter* of June 24, 1974, and are reprinted below with permission:

1. DON'T attempt to show an affinity for black people. ("One of my best friends is black.") More often than not, the best "friend" has never once been invited into the speaker's home or his social circle.

2. DON'T attempt to show an understanding of the black person's experience. ("I know exactly how you feel.") We doubt if whites know how it feels to be called "nigger," stared at, cursed and spit upon by persons whom you've never met nor harmed; to have been ridiculed and scorned as a child simply because you had "kinky hair," thick lips, or were noticeably "different" in color; to grow up with the erroneous and fallacious illusion that "your kind" is more animal than human, intellectually inferior and doomed to the most despicable conditions in a ghetto existence.

3. DON'T stereotype. ("All blacks drive big cars" or "Show me the latest dance.") It's interesting how many whites can drive through the ghetto, with dilapidated dwellings, unclothed and hungry children and notice only a big, shiny new car (which could belong to a hustler, which all societies have, or a black man who too often sweats long hours in a hot foundry to make the payments on the highest dream his country offers him) and remark: "You see, they really love to drive big cars and waste their money, so why should we listen to their complaints?"

4. DON'T misunderstand the black person's problem — "You have a chip on your shoulder." Probably so, and you can expect many more "angry young men" as today's youth, with new interest in black history, learn more and more about the black man's experience in America; as they learn that their fathers and grandfathers were not necessarily stupid and lazy, but were until recently literally barred from most professions and still are today in many trades.

5. DO be honest. Admit you may be prejudiced and, of course, you don't "know" how it feels to be black. Explain, however, that you accept the fact that blacks are people, and as such are entitled to the same rights, privileges and freedoms as any other human beings.

6. DO avoid asking how *all* blacks feel about anything! This question automatically tells the listener you consider all blacks to be alike. Remember, there are over 22 million of us in the U.S. alone, and only God knows how many in the world — a lot of room for variation.

7. DO speak to blacks in the same tone and tongue you would to anyone else. Don't try to emulate black speech or mannerisms. Blacks may perceive this as an attempt to ridicule, to "make fun," not friends.

8. DO discard the popular retort: "Maybe blacks did have it bad in the past, but things have *changed*." It is unfair to expect anyone, black or white, raised under ghetto conditions to instantly forget the mental and physical hardships of such an environment. And remember, moral behavior cannot be legislated. Change has to come from the heart.

Questions for Discussion

1. As a white (or black) student, how do you personally feel about Mr. Seymour's eight rules for relating to blacks?

2. Under what specific circumstances can you conceive of the eight rules being (or having been) of value to a public relations practitioner?

3. What rules would you (as a member of another minority group) draft for dealing with those in your group?

   NOTE: This question is addressed to those in the class who belong to other minority groups. It would be instructive to have the rest of the class give their personal reactions to the rules set forth.

NO MAN'S LAND: THE GAP BETWEEN PUBLIC AND OPINION

Lying somewhere between "public" and "opinion" is a vast no man's land made up of morés, stereotypes, and attitudes. Virtually unexplored except by the social scientists, this land is an important link between public and opinion. Anyone who hopes to understand public opinion must first understand the morés, stereotypes, and attitudes which exist between and link public and opinion.

Morés (more-rays) are *deep-rooted, customary ways of looking at and doing things in a society.* They are persistent, nonreflective, deeply ingrained, and taken for granted as being the ground rules of daily existence within a society.

Morés, which have also been termed folkways, are compelling and rigid in nature, accepted as right, true, proper, and necessary for the proper functioning of the society in which they exist. Unfortunately for the public relations practitioner, morés and folkways are largely *unwritten and are endemic to the society in which they exist.*

The student reading the above two paragraphs is undoubtedly less worried about the practitioner than about the problem of finding out about a term which describes the unwritten ways of doing things in a society. A few examples may light up the darkness.

Whistling in America is a means of indicating either contentment (e.g., while one works) or fear (e.g., while walking past a cemetery on a dark night). Whistling in Europe is a way of showing disapproval at a soccer match.

When Erskine Caldwell's "Tobacco Road" opened on Broadway New Yorkers were shocked when one of the male characters in the play strolled out of his shack, turned his back to the audience, and urinated. New Yorkers, used to the amenities of urban life, didn't realize they were observing a Deep South rural moré in action.

Circa John F. Kennedy an all-persuasive moré of American political life was that no Catholic could become president of the United States. That particular moré became extinct with Kennedy's election to the highest office in the land.

The last example illustrates two important aspects of morés. One is that morés are persistent and deeply ingrained. The second is that morés are subject to change, though the change is as slow-moving as the advance of a glacier. Because morés are so persistent and nonreflective, it is difficult to resist or try to change them. A person or organization runs grave risks when taking a stand or action which is contrary to public morés, hence the necessity to know when one is dealing with public morés or with public opinion.

The morés of Puritan America regarding sex were light years removed from general American sexual morés of today. At the same time, however, in certain sections of the country views about sex are still not far removed from those of Puritan America, and it's imperative to understand how strongly and to what degree morés govern thought and action in rural and urban America, in Appalachia, in the Northeast, and throughout the entire country.

Stereotypes are conventional labels or preconceptions which are acquired from the culture. Psychologist William Albig reminds us that stereotypes may be counterfeits of reality, but they are also psychological realities. Stereotypes, like morés, are generally unwritten ways of viewing things and people, but they can become embellished through the written word.

The concept of stereotypes was first enunciated by Walter Lipp-mann in his 1922 book, *Public Opinion*, which was reprinted in paper-back in 1960 by the Macmillan Company.

DR. KENNETH CLARK LEARNS A LESSON

In an interview on the occasion of his retirement as a teacher at City College of New York after thirty-five years at the school Dr. Kenneth B. Clark remarked:

> . . . One of my most interesting learning experiences came some time ago when I went to teach at the University of California at Berkeley for a while.

> I said I was looking forward to it because there were not too many Asian-American students at C.C.N.Y. at that time. I went out with the idea that Asian-American students would be more profound and would stimulate me with Oriental ways of think-ing.

> They were just like the students at City, with the same number of alibi students, too. It 'taught me that stereotypes, even posi-tive ones, tend to fall. I had to travel 3,000 miles to learn that. And I'm a psychologist, too!

> from an interview in the New York *Times*
> May 31, 1975

Lippmann described the world of 1922 as "out of sight, out of mind." He meant that for most Americans of that period the world was that of Sinclair Lewis's Sauk Centre, Minnesota, or of Chicago, Illinois, but certainly not that of Germany, Russia, Japan, or China. Not only was the world far removed from the average American, but the average American was too busy with his own life to pay much attention to what was going on thousands of miles away.

Lippmann further noted that there were major factors which limited access to the facts about the wider world beyond America, and he cited them as follows:

1. Artifical censorship

2. The limitations of social contact

3. The limited amount of time available in each day for paying atten-tion to public affairs

4. Distortions arising because events have to be compressed into very short messages

5. The difficulty of making a small vocabulary express a complicat-ed world

6. The fear of facing those facts which would seem to threaten the established routine of men's lives

Despite these barriers to a true understanding of the wider world, Lippmann said, the American nonetheless made for himself "a trustworthy picture inside his head of the world beyond his reach," and all too often this picture was a stereotype, or what Albig referred to as a "counterfeit of reality."

Do we still stereotype our vision of the world when today television brings the world right into our living rooms? To a disquieting extent, the answer is yes. Some examples to prove the point:

> Many Americans still see the Russians as uneducated peasants (until we learn they've put up as many satellites into the sky as we have).

> Many American manufacturers believed there was nothing like Yankee manufacturing ingenuity (until the Japanese and German auto makers entered the American market and made a huge dent in it).

> Many Americans considered American military might to be invincible (until we fought an undeclared war in Vietnam and 56,000 of us died).

The lesson is clear: we have to understand when we're dealing in stereotyped thinking and when we're being realistic. We can't afford to treat the world as though it were out of sight and out of mind, and we ought to make sure that the pictures in our head conform to reality. As communicators, we also have to understand clearly the degree and extent of stereotyped thinking in the publics we're trying to reach.

Attitudes are the *predispositions, thoughts, or feelings of people toward issues that have not yet materialized in a specific way.* Attitudes have been described as the sum-total of one's feelings, inclinations, notions, ideas, fears, and convictions about any specific topic or issue. As such, they represent a tendency to act in a particular manner. They form what Daniel Katz terms the raw material out of which public opinion develops, and hence understanding the nature of individual and group attitudes is critical to understanding the nature of public opinion.

Attitudes and opinion are so closely intertwined it's often impossible to ascertain any distinction between the two terms. It is generally agreed that, with certain exceptions, opinion is usually consistent with attitude. (One such exception, for example, would be the verbal response or opinion given by a bigoted person to a racial question; under social pressures, such a person may well state an opinion which is inconsistent with his or her attitude). Because of the close connection between attitude and opinion a fuller discussion of the roots of attitude and opinion will be held in abeyance until later in this chapter.

MINI-CASE
INFANT EUTHANASIA

An article in the *New England Journal of Medicine*, written by two doctors, reported that doctors in the special-care nursery of a teaching hospital connected with a major university had withheld treatment from forty-three deformed or seriously defective infants who were thus allowed to die.

The article summarized such deaths at the hospital over a thirty-month period, and said the action was taken only with the parents' consent. The report said the infants suffered from multiple deformities, mongolism, heart and lung defects, intestinal malformations and severe spinal cord and nervous system defects. One of the authors of the article said he believes other hospitals follow similar practices "but people are often afraid to report them."

Shortly after the journal article appeared the Associated Press transmitted a story summarizing the article, and this story ran in newspapers across the country. The daily newspaper in the city where the hospital was located followed with a story of its own reporting that disclosure "brought an avalanche of public inquiry down on the doctors who coauthored the report" and upon the hospital.

Questions for Discussion

1. Do you consider euthanasia to be a moré? Why or why not?
2. How would you judge people's attitudes towards infant euthanasia? Other forms of euthanasia? Would you make any distinctions among different publics as regards individual attitudes and opinions about euthanasia? If yes, what would these distinctions be? If no, why not?
3. If you were the director of public relations for the hospital cited in the case, what actions(s), if any, would you take? Explain your reasoning.
4. In deciding your answer to the previous question, what facts other than those already cited would you want to know? In what way would knowledge of these facts affect your response?

OPINION

Opinion is to attitude what the hand is to the arm. One is an extension of the other.

Simply defined, an opinion is *an expression of attitude*. Some authorities contend that opinion is a *verbal* expression of attitude, and although verbal means are the most common way of demonstrating expression, a person can express opinion by nonverbal means. A grimace or a gesture may often express better than words the opinion held by a person. This nonverbal method of expression must, however, be capable of being readily translated into words.

One of history's most famous examples of a nonverbal expression of attitude which showed opinion is that of Winston Churchill's "V for Victory" expression of determination and faith in England's ability to defeat Hitler Germany.

At Hamilton College in Clinton, N.Y., the students have a tradition of signifying nonverbal approval by snapping their thumb and second finger. The snap-snap of 500 undergraduates is a clear indication of favorable opinion of a speaker's remarks.

Some other modern nonverbal expressions of attitude are the clenched fist or the nose held between thumb and index finger.

Though the Hamilton College example cited above seems to indicate otherwise, *an opinion is always the opinion of a person, not a group*. In the Hamilton case, individual students used the same method of expressing their opinion and hence identified their opinions as a body. However, it's misleading to think in terms of a "group mind" because public opinion always refers to a collection of individual opinions. This point will be explained in more detail after a brief analysis of the dimensions of an opinion.

The characteristics or dimensions most commonly used to describe an opinion are *direction, intensity, stability,* and *latency*.

DIRECTION

Describing an opinion in terms of its direction means to state whether a person approves or disapproves of something. In the pioneer days of opinion measurement this approval-disapproval was indicated via a pro-con dichotomy, but as techniques of measurement became refined the simple pro-con description gave way to finer distinctions of opinion.

Simple pro-con, for-against, yes-no measurements of direction all too often conceal wide gradations of opinion. Asking a woman whether she is for or against the death penalty could easily produce statistics which are misleading. A person may be for the death penalty in certain circumstances, but not under other circumstances. A simple for-against or pro-con expression of opinion would obviously provide an insufficient measurement of the direction of opinion about the death penalty.

Scaling, which means providing a choice ranging from one extreme to the opposite extreme, is now used to set forth more accurately the direction of opinion. The opinion of an individual can be located at one of many points along a scale, and thus sets forth a better estimate of public opinion direction than was possible through the earlier pro-con method.

V. O. Key (*Public Opinion and American Democracy*, p. 11, Alfred Knopf, 1961) cites the difference between the pro-con and the scaling methods of measuring direction in the following example: "A division of people who support and oppose government ownership of industry does not provide a useful indication of the nature of public opinion on the question of government policy toward economic activity. Views on economic policy may be arranged along a scale from the extreme left to the extreme right. The opinion of an individual may be located at any one of many points along such a scale. One person may favor governmental ownership of all the means of production; another may be satisfied with a large dose of governmental regulation; still another may prefer only the most limited control of the economy; and others may wish to abolish whatever controls exist."

INTENSITY

The intensity of opinion describes the *strength of feeling* existing in that opinion. Certain issues may induce strong feelings of opinion among people while other issues may be of little importance. In dealing with people's opinions the public relations practitioner would be wise to know which issues arouse or are likely to arouse opinions of high intensity and which arouse or are likely to arouse opinions of low intensity.

Political Scientist Key suggests that we use common sense in seeking to distinguish between high and low intensity issues. This may well be too generalized a guideline for those who seek a more scientific way of prejudging the expected intensity of opinion about issues, but it makes sense to anyone who keeps abreast of social, economic and political issues in the country.

In the mid-seventies issues which aroused a high intensity of opinion were abortion; busing; foreign policy as it applied to the Mid-East and Southeast Asia; and inflation. Issues which aroused a low intensity of opinion were foreign policy as applied to Afghanistan, South America and Europe; civil rights; boxing; and physical fitness.

The same strictures apply to the measurement of intensity of opinion as apply to the measurement of the direction of opinion. Scaling, rather than the simple pro-con method of measurement, provides distinctions which ensure a more accurate assessment of opinion. Scaling indicates not merely the low and high of intensity of opinion on an issue, but gradations in between.

An example of a pro-con measurement of intensity of opinion would be a question asking a respondent if she has much or little confidence in the president. The same question, scaled, would ask the respondent if she has very much, much, some, little, or very little confidence in the president. A numerical way of measuring intensity using the same question would be to rate opinion on a scale ranging from one to seven, with one representing the lowest degree of intensity of opinion and seven the highest.

STABILITY

Whether an opinion has stability is of concern to the public relations practitioner because it indicates the degree of commitment to the issue in question. Opinions which have a high degree of stability are not easily changed. They demonstrate that the individual having that opinion has held to it for a long period of time, considers it important, and is not likely to alter it readily. Low stability or unstable opinions, on the other hand, are not important to those holding them and may readily be changed given the proper circumstances.

Public opinion polls taken over a long period of time that ask the same questions at varying intervals show that on certain issues there is a high degree of opinion stability. Over a period of many decades the majority of Americans have been consistently negative in their opinion about communism and consistently firm in their feeling that America should maintain a strong military establishment. Opinions about the job being done by the president, however, have been highly unstable, and it doesn't seem to matter who happens to be the president. According to the Gallup Poll, President Truman had an 87 percent approval rating when he became president in 1945, but by October of the next year his rating went down to 32 percent favorable. The early ratings for President Kennedy were in the low 70 percent range but they dropped to 59 percent just before his assassination. Similar highs and lows have been recorded for Presidents Eisenhower, Johnson, and Nixon.

As a general rule, there has been a high degree of stability of the opinion of Americans concerning matters which are of basic concern to them, and instability regarding personalities. Pollsters Charles Roll, Jr. and Albert H. Cantrill (*Polls*, Basic Books, 1972) report that among the American people "the overarching concerns continue to be good health, a better standard of living, peace, the achievement of aspirations for one's children, a good job, and a happy family life."

LATENCY

Latent opinion, according to V. O. Key, is "really about the only type of opinion that generates much anxiety" in the practice of politics and government. He suggests the following kinds of questions should be asked of latent opinions: "What opinion will develop about this prospective candidate? What opinions will be stirred by this legislative proposal? What opinions, anxieties and moods will be generated by this event or by that action?"

Key's questions certainly apply to policies, statements, and actions of all, not merely political, organizations and institutions. The college mulling the size of a tuition increase should ask: "What opinion will develop about this prospective increase?" The trade association advocating a fair trade law should ask: "What opinions will be stirred by this legislative proposal?" The company trying to decide whether to close a plant and move it elsewhere should ask: "What opinions, anxieties, and moods will be generated by this event or that action?"

Key suggests that in considering latent opinion we should distinguish between latent opinion of the "attentive public" and the "great inattentive public." As examples of the attentive public he cites the American Medical Association, the National Association of Manufacturers, and the AFL-CIO, and he says that over the short run the latent opinions of such groups can be anticipated because, as he puts it, "these attentive publics have their patterns of reaction that serve as bases for predictable response." The inattentive public, on the other hand, poses a much more difficult problem and situation. The problem, Key says, results from "uncertainties about whether mass attention will be mobilized or whether it will remain indifferent and uninformed."

Handling latent opinion, then, becomes a matter of predicting and sensing when public response to an issue or event will be temporary or more than just of the moment. It would be wise to view latent opinion as one might view a sleeping German shepherd dog. Because it's dormant doesn't mean it's dead; because it's sleeping doesn't mean it can't be aroused; because it seems so peaceful doesn't mean it's not powerful once aroused.

Estimating latent opinion involves the estimation of three elements: (1) *those sectors of society* — the various publics and sub-publics — *affected by an issue or event*; (2) *the nature of the event* or *issue*; and (3) *the intensity of feeling one might expect from the aroused latent opinion*. Because all three elements are interrelated, the practitioner must use thoughtful judgment in assessing and dealing with them.

The nature of the issue or event seems to be the crucial factor in trying to assess its impact on latent opinion. Some issues or events are of such a universal nature that they're bound to command a wide audience and arouse strong feelings in that audience. Others will be perceived as being of minor significance and will impact only on a small number of people. Not to be overlooked is the fact that issues and events are in competition with themselves for public attention; an issue or event that might normally be expected to arouse strong feelings among many segments of society may pass unnoticed because it takes place at the same time as a far more profound issue or event.

Is there a guideline for attempting to assess the impact of an issue, event, or statement? Key makes the following suggestion:

> An action that clearly conflicts with a widely held attitude may be expected to stir up controversy if it comes to public attention; an action patently within the limits of the firmly held norms may pass unnoticed or arouse only mild approbation. Many governmental actions attract little attention because they raise questions within the permissive limits fixed by latent opinion. The excoriation of cancer, the idealization of the American mother, and the condemnation of sin never get a politician in trouble . . . (*Public Opinion And American Democracy*, p. 266).

PUBLIC OPINION

In attempting to define public opinion the social scientists have had as much trouble as the poets and philosophers have had in attempting to define beauty. To John Keats, "Beauty is truth," and if that doesn't help he proposes that "truth is beauty" and advises us that it is all we know on earth and all we need to know. Taking the safer approach, philosopher George Santayana tells us in one breath that beauty is indescribable and he then proceeds to describe it as "a pledge of the possible conformity between the soul and nature. . . ." Kahlil Gibran conceives

of beauty as "eternity gazing at itself in a mirror." Those who seek to
capture the essence of beauty by relying on the poets and philosophers
have been given some fascinating choices: they can either find it in truth,
the indescribable, or eternity.

Though they are considered to be a more practical lot than the poets
and philosophers, the social scientists have been equally obtuse in trying
to define public opinion. Their attempts to pin down the term range from
the simple to the complex, from the tentative to the definitive, from
being so describable as to be virtually unfathomable.

This conclusion is evident from Floyd H. Allport's article in the
very first issue of the *Public Opinion Quarterly* in which he described
public opinion as follows:

> The term public opinion is given its meaning with reference
> to a multi-individual situation in which individuals are express-
> ing themselves, or can be called upon to express themselves, as
> favoring (or else disfavoring or opposing) some definite condi-
> tion, person, or proposal of widespread importance, in such a
> proportion of number, intensity, and constancy, as to give rise
> to the probability of affecting action, directly or indirectly,
> toward the object concerned.

If you're adventurous you might try playing Allport's definition on
your flugelhorn, but it won't be of much help if you try to use it to deal
with public opinion in a practical situation. Allport's definition is important, however, because it indicates his tortuous attempt to cope with the
many contingencies which involve public opinion. All too often those
defining public opinion do so from the vantage point of their special interest. Note, for example, the connection (in italics by the author) between the specialist and the definitions cited below:

> *Political scientist* V.O. Key defines public opinion as "those
> opinions held by private persons which *governments* find it pru-
> dent to heed."

> Lucien Warner, writing about *public opinion surveys*, de-
> scribes public opinion as "people's reactions to *definitely word-
> ed statements and questions under interview conditions.*"

> James Bryce, one of the earliest writers of the *government
> process*, saw public opinion as "the power exerted by any such
> view, or set of views, when *held by an apparent majority of citi-
> zens.*"

> *Sociologist* G. A. Lundberg described public opinion as
> "that opinion though it be the opinion of a *single individual* in
> which the public in question finds itself for any reason con-
> strained to acquiesce."

> *Social Psychologist* L. L. Bernard considered public opinion
> to be "any fairly uniform collective expression of *mental or
> inner behavior reactions* . . ."

Harwood Childs (*An Introduction to Public Opinion*, John Wiley & Sons, 1940) felt it necessary and important to cut through the verbiage and to eliminate the specialist's approach. His simple definition, which this author believes sufficient for the purposes of this book, states that public opinion is *"simply any collection of individual opinions designated."* Though he admits his definition is a very broad one, he believes it's applicable to public relations because both "public opinion" and "public relations" are very broad in meaning and assume validity when they relate to particular publics. Noting that an opinion is always that of a person, Childs stresses that public opinion always refers to a collection of individual opinions and hence *if we want to ascertain a given state of public opinion we have to ascertain the opinions of individuals.*

Childs is also critical of those who set forth certain principles of public opinion or who would narrow the meaning of the term to include only those collections of opinion which have a specific degree of uniformity. In his view *there are no public opinion principles which are applicable under all circumstances.*

"All principles," he notes, "hold true only under certain circumstances. Given the conditions, the principles will apply. But the conditions must be stated. This is what makes the study of public opinion and public relations so difficult. Conditions vary; publics differ; the relations between groups are always changing. Generalizations regarding human behavior and human relations are peculiarly hazardous to make." (*An Introduction to Public Opinion*, p. 46).

As for the alleged need for the existence of a degree of uniformity, Childs points out that this is a matter of investigation not an a priori condition of public opinion. As he puts it: "The degree of uniformity is a matter to be investigated, not something to be arbitrarily set up as a condition for the existence of public opinion."

Summed up, then, public opinion is a general and inclusive term. It always refers to a collection of individual opinions. It can be studied with some degree of significance when related to a particular public and to specific opinions about definite subjects. The source for the opinions of individuals and an analysis of how opinions are formed will be examined in the section that follows.

THE FORMATION OF PUBLIC OPINION

Of crucial importance to the student of public relations is not merely understanding the nature of publics, opinion, and public opinion, but also understanding how public opinion is formed. Unfortunately for those who dote on pat answers that can be highlighted by multi-colored markers, there are no pat answers to the process of opinion formation. So many factors are involved in the process of opinion formation that it is well-nigh impossible to state with certainty that this factor, that factor, or a set of factors cause opinion to develop in a certain way. At best, one can seek the answer to the quandary of opinion formation only in very broad, general terms. Stated in such terms, the two major elements in the process of opinion formation are the *person* and the *environment*.

THE PERSON

When we look at the individual we should recognize that the list of tangible and intangible attributes that can be used as factors to explain personality, attitude, and opinions are endless. Some authorities concentrate on such factors as perceptions, habits, complexes, frames of reference, and values. Other cite self-esteem, loyalties, moods, and drives. Still others cite traits such as introverts, extroverts, and inner-and-outer directed. The list of personal attributes of the individual is infinite and impossible to weigh and assess with any degree of certainty.

Though it may not be possible to weigh personal attributes accurately, their importance in the process of opinion formation cannot be denied. Our physiological, biological, and psychological traits and make-up undoubtedly play a role in the way we view issues, actions, and events. Thus they form an integral share of the mix that results in the formation of our opinions.

TWO PERSONALITIES VIEW A PRESIDENTIAL RESPONSE

A few weeks after the United States withdrew from South Vietnam in the Spring of 1975 an unarmed American freighter named the Mayaguez was seized in disputed waters in the Gulf of Siam and forced to anchor off a tiny crescent island called Tang. After briefly trying via diplomacy to secure the liberation of the ship and its crew of 39, President Ford ordered the use of force: U. S. planes blasted five Cambodian vessels out of the water; the marines boarded the Mayaguez and assaulted Tang Island; American fighter-bombers blasted an oil depot and air base on the Cambodian mainland. The crew was subsequently rescued, the Mayaguez retaken, and the event became a minor footnote of history.

However, in the first days of the operation the outcome remained uncertain and there was the possibility that the United States could again become involved militarily in Southeast Asia. Other factors aside, consider the probable initial reaction of two different personalities to the unfolding situation. Mr. Shy is an introvert, inner-directed, fearful, cautious and timid. Mr. Bold is an extrovert, outer-directed, fearless, impetuous and aggressive. Given these traits — and for the sake of argument omitting all other factors — there is little doubt that Shy's opinion of the president's action would be essentially negative and Bold's would be essentially positive.

The example cited above is a set-up situation, of course, because people don't come to their opinions solely on the basis of their personality traits. These traits come to grips with issues and events within the vortex of other factors mainly environmental in nature.

THE ENVIRONMENT

As with personality traits, there is no end of environmental factors affecting the process of opinion formation. Some are general and some specific; some are remote and some proximate; some are stable and some changeable; some are large and some small. The list includes economic, religious, and political institutions; physical, biological, and sociological factors; demographic, climatic, and topographical features; professional, peer, ethnic, and special purpose groups; the government and mass media of communication. Mind-boggling in its array and diversity, the list is of great importance because each element can play a vital role in the formation of public opinion.

The dubious reader may cast a jaundiced eye on some of the previously mentioned environmental factors, but consider the answers to the following questions.

Re climate: Would the cold climate of the frozen north cause an Eskimo to have a different opinion on certain issues than that of an Amazonian who lives in the torrid climate of the equator?

Re demography: Would a woman, age 76, have a different opinion of Social Security than a young woman, age 21?

Re profession: Would a doctor have a different view of malpractice insurance than a trial lawyer?

Re sociology: Would an inner city mother have a different view of busing than a suburban mother?

The answer to all four questions is yes, chiefly because of environmental factors influencing the people concerned. Of course, the factors have been posed here within the context of situations to which they are directly related. In most cases, however, such a connection between environmental factors, situation, and opinion formation is much more tenuous. Those factors which are significant and those which are insignificant in the formation of opinion usually cannot be sorted out.

In the early formative years of most people three environmental factors — the family, church/religion, and the school — are considered to be of paramount importance.

The *family* is the source of one's first impressions, early habits, likes, dislikes, prejudices, and goals. The family has a direct influence on the selection of childhood companions and on attitudes towards a wide variety of subjects. Because the family isolates the small child from other countervailing forces, it has a great influence on his character, motivation, personal habits, and ideals.

The *church and/or religion* begins to make its influence felt at a very early age and for many people continues throughout a lifetime. In addition to providing the basis for beliefs and opinions relative to God, life after death, salvation, and other tenets, the church and religion influence opinions about sin, sex, tolerance and intolerance, economic, social, and political matters.

The *school*, and especially the public school, commences the process of socialization which continues throughout a lifetime. Traditions, learning, and skills necessary to maintain a society are transmitted through the schools. The range of information about public policies increases in direct proportion to the amout of schooling an individual has. On economic and political matters, the school tends to reflect family and community attitudes. Observes V. O. Key: "In the largest sense the educational system is a great mechanism for *conserving* the values, the institutions, the practices of the political order, as it inculcates from the primary school even through college the memories, the unities, and the norms of the system." (*Public Opinion and American Democracy*, p. 343).

As the child becomes the youth and the youth the adult, other key environmental factors come into play and either reinforce or subvert the early influences of family, church/religion, and the school. By the manner in which they funnel information, entertainment, and opinion the media provide the means whereby the individual ascertains facts, perceives and identifies issues and problems, and becomes aware of alternative solutions. Peer, professional, and interest groups exert a modifying influence on individual opinions, and in some cases profoundly shape such opinions. Even the issue itself — the time it takes place and its setting — becomes an environmental factor influencing opinion formation. All these factors play roles in the opinion formation process. Trying to ascertain the relative importance of each factor becomes a task worthy of a Solomon, who might not even be up to handling it.

THE FORMULA APPROACH

In attempting to bring order out of the chaos of the many factors involved in the process of opinion formation, some authorities have evolved tidy formulae to describe the process. They usually imply or directly contend that opinion formation is an orderly, rational procedure with debate pro and con followed by some form of agreement or consensus.

For example, here is how one book describes the process of opinion formation:

1. A number of people recognize a situation as being problematic and decide that something ought to be done about it. They explore possible solutions and do some fact-finding.

2. Alternative proposals for solving the problem emerge, and these are discussed back and forth.

3. A policy or solution is agreed upon as best meeting the situation recognized as problematic. Agreement and a decision to promote its acceptance lead to group consciousness.

4. A program of action is undertaken, and this is pressed until the requisite action is obtained or the group becomes weary of the battle and its members turn to other projects and other groups.

Another author has a shorter version of the opinion formation process: A treatment of the dynamics of public opinion formation must concern itself with at least three major phases: (1) the rise of the issue;

(2) the discussion about the issue and proposed solutions pro and con; and (3) the arrival at consensus."

The major problem with the above-mentioned formula approaches to the opinion formation process is that they either seem to be taking place in some sort of apolitical vacuum or else they're describing how organizations supposedly debate alternative solutions to problems. Properly labelled, they may well describe "How Insiders Debate An Issue and Decide On Action To Be Taken."

But *public* opinion, which is the subject being discussed, is not arrived at so tidily, nor is the public usually privy to the discussion and the pro and con that may well take place before some organization decides on a policy or action. Further, the public is not some sort of neat entity which by some means or other goes through a series of steps to reach a decision on an issue. To visualize opinion formation as a standard pattern is to engage in a set of generalizations which can lead only to the illusion of reality but which reality itself belies. The members of publics and sub-publics may well form opinions about issues and events, but they are seldom in the position to have a direct influence or part in the actions taken by authorities and organizations. V. O. Key sums up the criticism of the tidy formula approach to the process of opinion formation in the following words:

> More is lost than is gained in understanding by the organismic view of the public. Occasionally, in relatively small communities, citizen concern and involvement over an issue may be widespread and community consideration may move in close articulation with the mechanism of authority to a decision that can realistically be said to be a decision by public opinion. At far rarer intervals great national populations may be swept by a common concern about a momentuous issue with a similar result. Yet ordinarily a decision is made not by the public but by officials after greater or a lesser consideration of the opinion of the public or parts of the public. (*Public Opinion and American Democracy*, p. 9)

In summation, the following can be said about the process of public opinion formation:

1. The factors involved in the formation of public opinion relate to the *person* and the *environment* but they are so numerous it is impossible to state which are paramount and which secondary.

2. The influence on opinion of the family, church/religion, and the school are considered to be of paramount importance in the formative years. Thereafter, other key environmental influences begin to be felt.

3. There is no pat formula to describe the process of opinion formation. The process is too full of variables; untidy rather than tidy; often irrational rather than rational.

NEWSOM'S PUBLIC OPINION SIGNPOSTS

Seekers of truth, wandering among the public opinion thickets, will be helped along the way by four signposts erected by veteran counselor Earl Newsom. (From a Newsom talk reprinted in Raymond Simon's *Perspectives in Public Relations*, University of Oklahoma Press, 1966)

Newsom notes that many carefully conceived and executed campaigns designed to "educate the public" subsequently fail because of myopia about the intended audience of these campaigns. All too often, says Newsom, the sponsor of an idea, point of view, or opinion fails to ask this simple question: "Does it clearly help toward the solution of a problem which worries those I am addressing?" If the answer is yes, the sponsor of the idea has correctly read Newsom's first signpost which is cited below.

THE IDENTIFICATION SIGNPOST

> *"People will ignore an idea, an opinion, a point of view unless they see clearly that it affects (in a positive way) their personal fears or desires, hopes or aspirations."*

Self-motivation — the id and the ego that possesses all of us — is a powerful force. "What's-in-it-for-me?" asks the recipient of a message. In too many instances the sender is too busy composing his message to consider the recipient, and there are far too many cases where the sender is so inconsiderate he sends the message "to whom it may concern." Sending messages without careful consideration of a specific audience and of the desires, hopes, and ambitions of its members is like blowing dandelion seeds into the wind.

To reach people, to influence their opinions, a first necessity is to *appeal to their personal interests*, to show them clearly that your words or actions *identify with their present and pressing problems*.

Thus, identification provides the first of Newsom's signposts. The second involves meshing actions with words.

THE ACTION SIGNPOST

> *"People do not buy ideas separated from action – either action taken or about to be taken by the sponsor of the idea, or action which people themselves can conveniently take to prove the merit of the idea."*

We tend to reject words which are divorced from actions. An organization's words and its actions must be compatible if the words are to be believed. In forming their opinions about organizations, individuals base their judgments as much on what organizations *do* as on what they say. And if what they "do" is contrary to what they say, the public will generally base its opinions on the doing rather than the saying.

Modern-day life abounds with illustrations — usually in the negative — of the action guidepost. There's the corporation which touts the free enterprise system in its advertising but which engages in price-fixing and other anti-competitive activities. There's the legislator who promises to cut down on unnecessary government spending but then votes himself a hefty salary boost. There's the United States of America which is dedicated to democratic principles but which at times provides economic and military aid to totalitarian regimes.

Eliza Doolittle spoke for the cockney in all of us when she shouted, "Show Me!" in response to a torrent of words, words, words about love. We seek to be shown by actions, not merely by words, and our opinions tend to be positive when we perceive that the actions of organizations are those which affirmatively affect our important personal interests.

Summed up, the action signpost warns that words are insufficient by themselves to engender favorable public opinion. Taken together, words and actions support themselves if they are compatible, honest, and appeal to people's self-interests.

THE FAMILIARITY AND TRUST SIGNPOST

> *"We the people buy ideas only from those we trust; we are influenced by, or adopt, only those opinions or points of view put forward by individuals or corporations or institutions in whom we have confidence."*

Simple ideas sometimes have profound meanings, and this third Newsom signpost teaches an important lesson about the formation of public opinion in the twentieth century.

The world is too much with us yet, as William Wordsworth reminded us in the eighteenth century. Wordsworth was able to retreat from his world by turning to nature, but modern men and women retreat by turning off the world. Wise in the knowledge that the world is too complex and complicated to understand, the individual today must nonetheless have opinions and judgments. Wisely or not, the individual relies on the opinions and judgments of those he trusts.

Very often these "trustees" of opinion and judgment are newspaper columnists and editorial writers, radio and television commentators, political figures, teachers, doctors and priests, rabbis and ministers. Or, on a smaller scale, the trustees may be certain key people among the many groups to which we belong. To the leaders who rise up to serve our needs, we entrust our opinions, our judgments and our decisions.

"Our every act," says Newsom, "is the voicing of a preference. We 'vote' when we pick our grocery store, our gas station, our doctor, our college, the movie we go to, the radio program to which we listen, the charities to which we send our checks."

Is our vote based on intimate knowledge of the store, the gas station, the doctor, etc? Scarcely, because we haven't the time to acquire this knowledge. We give them our vote because we've learned at some time or another to have confidence and trust in them; once we lose this trust and confidence we cast our vote elsewhere.

THE CLARITY SIGNPOST

*"The situation must be clear to us, not confusing. The
thing we observe, read, see, or hear, the thing which
produces our impressions, must be clear, not subject to
several interpretations."*

The American landscape is unfortunately littered with statements
which are obtuse, unclear, confusing, and open to varying interpretations. On the presidential level there's the press secretary's use of the
word "inoperative" to explain away his own crossed signals. On the
professional level in almost every field there's the use of jargon, circumlocution, and obfuscation in phrases which talk about:

maximization of profits
delimitation of debt
cancellations
factor analysis by means of chi
   square deviations

empirically derived taxono-
   mies
normative sanction patterns of
   causative behavior
the limited channel capacity of
   the perceptual system

Reading the above, one wonders what's happened to the English
language. Organizations can't expect others to understand them if they
can't explain their actions clearly and without equivocation. The basic
trouble seems to reside in the fact that the truth of an action or statement, simply and clearly stated, seems to be an insurmountable barrier
among organizations which are afraid to trust the people with simple,
unvarnished truths. But if we can't trust people with the truth, then we
don't deserve their support.

Newsom's fourth signpost is predicated on the premise that the action point of view being clarified is one that reflects favorably on the
organization or individual taking the action or advocating the point of
view. There are two circumstances, however, where the action or point
of view reflects unfavorably on the proponent and yet is illuminated with
such blinding clarity as to remain indelibly fixed in the public mind.

The first of these two unfortunate circumstances most often occurs
on impromptu occasions and usually results from off-the-cuff remarks or
from hasty responses to press inquiries. The thoughtless statement
which triggers unfavorable public reaction almost never occurs as a result of carefully designed and written statements because these are
usually edited with care and foresight. Rather, it's the quick response
that brings about the negative reaction, and it takes place in interviews;
at question time following press conferences; on radio and television talk
shows; and at impromptu sessions during political campaigns. There's
little the public relations specialist can do about such situations except
to brief his client or spokesman in advance or to batten down the
hatches and try to repair the damages once the winds blow.

MINI-EXAMPLE
ROMNEY'S BRAINWASHING REMARK

George Romney, former industrial leader and thrice elected governor of Michigan, was considered the front-runner for the nomination as the Republican candidate for the presidency in 1968. He had a proven record of effectiveness, was hard-driving, sincere, and above all, looked like a president. However, as Theodore H. White observed, there was a "cloying naivete about his statements and a fuzziness of international issues. (*The Making Of The President 1968*, Atheneum Publishers, 1969). Most importantly, the Vietnam war was beginning to press on the nation, and Romney's credentials as an expert in world matters were of conspicuous concern to everyone."

Appearing for the taping of a talk show after a particularly busy and hectic day, Romney was asked about his position on Vietnam, and he replied, "Well, you know when I came back from Vietnam, I just had the greatest brainwashing that anybody can get when you go over to Vietnam. Not only by the generals, but also by the diplomatic corps over there, and they do a very thorough job. And since returning from Vietnam, I've gone into the history of Vietnam. . . .And, as a result, I have changed my mind . . . in that particular. I no longer believe that it was necessary for us to get involved in South Vietnam to stop Communist aggression."

White reports that nobody on Romney's staff thought the brainwashing remark was important, but they found out differently when the line was picked up by the national media. The day after the telecast the New York *Times* ran a story on the interview with the headline: ROMNEY ASSERTS HE UNDERWENT 'BRAINWASHING' ON VIETNAM TRIP. The wire services picked up the story and it was carried on the national network TV news shows. The picture the nation received of candidate George Romney was that of an innocent. As White commented: "And no one wanted an innocent for president." Richard Nixon, not George Romney, became the Republican candidate.

Obviously, Romney's "brainwashing" statement wasn't the only reason he did not gain the Republican nomination. If the press hadn't reported it, it would have been quickly lost to view. However, the press did pick it up and there's no doubt it illuminated and pictured a presidential candidate as an innocent man subject to "brainwashing" by those more sophisticated than he.

Questions for Discussion

Shortly after Romney's statement became national news the Democratic National Chairman declared that Romney's statement had "insulted the integrity of two dedicated and honorable men," General Westmoreland and Ambassador Lodge, who had briefed Romney in Vietnam. According to White, Romney's pride was involved over the way the statement was being spread and for the next six weeks, against the advice of his staff, he continued to reply to the charge of innocence.

1. What is your opinion of the comment by the chairman of the Democratic Party?
2. What is your opinion about the advice of Romney's staff that he ignore the adverse press and other reactions to his "brainwashing" statement?

The second of the two unfortunate circumstances involving clarity occurs when remarks are stated clearly but subsequently are either wrongly reported or simply distorted. Public relations men and women are, of course, not responsible for the manner in which statements and remarks are handled by the media. However, it is their responsibility to monitor press treatment of statements and/or actions and to suggest appropriate and, hopefully, judicious response and reaction. The response, of course, may well be a decision not to respond. The decision whether to respond or not to respond becomes a matter of professional judgment, experience, and thoughtful assessment of expected public reaction.

MINI-EXAMPLE
A LITTLE CASE OF VICE VERSA

Two little words, taken literally, illustrate how a statement can be misconstrued and its meaning changed by subsequent press handling.

The two words are "vice versa," and they mean conversely. They formed the end of a remark made by Charles Wilson, former head of General Motors and a large stockholder when he was being questioned during closed hearings on his nomination as Secretary of Defense.

Wilson was asked by a senator whether he could make a decision in the interests of the United States government were there to be a situation where the decision would be extremely adverse to General Motors. His reply was: "Yes sir, I could. I cannot conceive of one because for years I thought what was good for our country was good for General Motors, and vice versa . . . ."

That particular part of his remarks which were "leaked" out of the closed hearings was reported in three ways shortly after they were made. For example, the New York *Times* cited Wilson as declaring he was "unable to conceive of such a situation because for years I thought what was good for the country was good for General Motors, and vice versa." *Time* magazine quoted Wilson as saying, "What is good for the country is good for General Motors, and what's good for General Motors is good for the country." *Newsweek* magazine quoted Wilson as saying, "Anything that's good for General Motors would

148

be good for America and anything that's good for America would be good for General Motors."

Over the years the version that became accepted by the press became the simple statement, "What's good for General Motors is good for the country," and of course this version reflects a cavalier belief in the virtues of the nation's largest corporation. The "vice versa" of his original remark made the switch possible. As the *Times* noted in its Wilson obituary, "it was the three ambiguous words, 'and vice versa,' that got him in trouble."

Whether the fault lies in the one who makes the statement or in the media handling of the statement, Newsom's clarity signpost holds true and should be a steadfast guide: the situation must be clear . . . not confusing. The more clear the situation, explanation, or statement, the less likely it will be misinterpreted. Even though we identify with our publics, even though we have their trust, and even though our words and our actions are compatible, we don't gain public approval or understanding unless we explain ourselves clearly.

MINI-CASE
THE PRESIDENT OF OTIS ELEVATOR DELIVERS A TALK

Not many weeks after the Alexander Smith Carpet Company moved its mills from Yonkers, New York, to a new location in the South, President Le Roy A. Petersen of the Otis Elevator Company delivered a talk to an invited audience of over 2,000 employees and Yonkers city officials. (The same talk was given to employees of Otis in Harrison, New Jersey).

At the time (January, 1955) Otis had been part of the industrial base of Yonkers for 101 years, had a local yearly payroll of more than ten million dollars, and was one of the community's major taxpayers. The talk was given at 9 a.m. and the setting was the Brandt Theatre in Yonkers.

President Petersen began his talk by citing the loyalty of the 2,000 Otis men and women who had received service pins the previous year for service records ranging from 25 to 55 years with the company. Stressing the fine reputation of the company in the design, manufacture, and installation of elevators and escalators, Petersen discussed the large number of competitors who had entered the field in the past decade.

"These statements," he said, "should not be interpreted as indicating that the Otis Elevator Company has ceased to be a profitable company or is on the verge of becoming an unprofitable one. On the contrary, it is anticipated that, since our income is derived from a variety of sources, including a substantial service business and extensive operations throughout the world, the annual report for 1954 will show an increase over the previous year in sales and earnings. In addition, it is believed that our backlog will assure a profitable level of operations in 1955.

"However, the Yonkers Works is primarily engaged in the manufacture of equipment for new elevators for domestic use and has relatively little to do with service or foreign operations and its performance must be judged solely by the quality and cost of the products it makes. . . .

"The Otis Elevator Company has prospered and has been a source of employment in Yonkers for more than a hundred years because it has continued to manufacture a high quality product at a cost sufficiently low to permit it to be sold with a fair profit at a competitive price.

"Unless we can continue to do this, we will cease to be a prosperous company and will also cease to be a source of employment. It is, therefore, my duty and obligation as president of this company to take such steps as may be necessary to maintain Otis quality and still reduce costs to the point where we can continue to secure the necessary volume at a profitable price."

Stating that an extensive study had been conducted to ascertain how the needed reduction in cost best be accomplished, Petersen said:

"Of particular interest to you, however, is the result of the study relating to manufacture, and this study indicated that an annual saving in manufacturing costs of several million dollars could be secured by building a single plant to replace the Yonkers and Harrison plants, and that this plant should be located in the middle west near the geographical center of our elevator market. . . .

"A further careful study has, therefore, been made which indicates that about half of the savings that are attributable to a new midwestern plant could be accomplished in our present plants, providing we secure the enthusiastic and understanding cooperation of our employees and of the city authorities.

"With the purpose of preserving as many as possible of your jobs with Otis in Yonkers and a local payroll amounting to about ten million dollars per year, we are willing and anxious to make every effort to continue the operation of the Yonkers plant providing we are able to accomplish, with a minimum delay, the reduction in cost which we believe is reasonably obtainable in this location.

"A definite decision to take such steps as are necessary to reduce costs substantially has already been made, and the only question remaining is which of the known methods will be chosen. If we are unable to bring about these reductions in cost in our present plants, we will have no choice but to transfer our manufacturing, as soon as possible, to a new midwestern plant — and will not hesitate to do so if it becomes clearly necessary. . . .

"Kindly note that our plans for reduced costs are not based upon any change in our past policy of paying all who work for Otis at least as much as is paid by other reputable and comparable companies for similar jobs, both in the form of wages and salaries and in supplementary benefits. It is still our desire to keep the Yonkers Plant not only a place in which to work, but a *good* place in which to work.

"Rather, our ability to secure reduced costs here and now is dependent upon our receiving your active cooperation in eliminating avoidable and unjustifiable expense and in reducing lost time and motion, in increasing the efficient use of existing equipment and in utilizing to the utmost the production capacity of such new equipment as we may be warranted in installing. We will welcome your suggestions.

"In seeking to accomplish our objectives, we propose, of course, to work with and through the unions which you have selected as your bargaining agents and to solicit the active cooperation of their officials. . . .

"I trust that you will clearly understand that this is not an attempt to persuade you to do anything that you do not want to do or which you do not recognize as being clearly in your own interest.

"It should be apparent that the Yonkers Works has, in effect, become a community enterprise. The Company, because of its earnest desire to retain its present organization and to continue to provide good jobs for its loyal employees, has indicated its willingness to forego some of the larger savings obtainable by other methods and to continue to operate the Yonkers Plant as long as it can afford to do so. It cannot afford to continue to operate it under present conditions — but is offering you an opportunity to help create the conditions under which we could afford to continue its operation.

"We could, of course, have decided to go ahead immediately with the building of a new central plant, basing our decision solely upon the outcome of the study which clearly showed savings sufficient to justify the investment, the cost of transfer and the loss on existing plants.

"We could, and some may say that we should, have done this without prior discussion with you. I trust that you feel, as I do, that, in fairness to you and to the City of Yonkers, this prior general discussion is desirable.

"I also trust that you realize that we are trying to help you retain your jobs with Otis and that we hope that, together, we will be successful in doing so.

"Next week, we will present to your union officials concrete proposals outlining the conditions which we consider reasonable and essential for continued future operations in Yonkers.

"We sincerely hope that these proposals will be recognized as consistent with the interest and welfare of our Yonkers employees and that agreement will be reached for their early adoption.

"We are prepared to make substantial additional investment in the Yonkers Plant, if such investment appears to be clearly justified. We will do our best to further improve our methods. We will look to the city authorities for fair treatment on taxes and for a disposition to help in all other ways consistent with the welfare of the city as a whole.

"The rest is up to you, and we hope that you will give the problem careful consideration."

The day following Mr. Petersen's talk, the New York *Times* reported it in a front-page story with the headline:

OTIS ULTIMATUM
GIVEN IN YONKERS

City Officials and Employees
Told Costs Must Be Cut or
Elevator Company Moves

The lead paragraph stated that "The Otis Elevator Company issued an ultimatum today to 2,000 employees and city offiicals. It said: 'Cooperate to cut costs or the company will move to a new plant in the Midwest.' "

After reporting the essence of Petersen's talk, the story continued:

"Members of the audience sat throughout the talk quietly. There was scattered applause when the company president walked from the wings to a mid-stage lectern. There was no interruption of his speech and no visible reaction at its conclusion. His listeners filed quickly and silently from the big theatre."

The story quoted the union representing the Yonkers plant employees as calling attention to the following points:

> 'The Otis Elevator Company has averaged over $9,400,000 net profit for the last eighty years. This represents a return of 18 percent of net worth. Most companies regard 8 percent as a high return. A few shorts months ago Mr. Petersen in reporting to the stockholders of this corporation stated that the outlook for the future was for increased business. He also reported a record for bookings.'

"The existing contract between Otis and the union," the story continued, "does not expire until next June. In 1947 the company closed its Buffalo plant, employing 1,000, and transferred operations to the Yonkers and Harrison works. The move was attributed to 'changes in the elevator industry and the plant's obsolete equipment.'

"Last month Mr. Petersen announced an extra common stock dividend of 50 cents a share. At the same time a regular quarterly dividend of 62½ cents was declared. Dividend declarations for 1954 came to $3 a share, or 25 cents a share more than in the previous year. The net income for the first nine months of 1954 was $6,689,057. For the same period in 1953 the net was $6,179,807.

"Charles Curran, Yonkers City Manager, when asked for comment on Mr. Petersen's appeal for 'fair treatment on taxes and for a disposition to help in all other ways consistent with the welfare of the city as a whole,' declared:

" 'We certainly don't want to lose Otis. We'll give them all the cooperation we can.' "

Questions for Discussion

1. *What's your judgment of Mr. Petersen's talk* — its contents, circumstances of delivery, and reported audience reaction — *as it relates to the four signposts of Earl Newsom?* That is, evaluate the speech in terms of Newsom's signposts for achieving favorable public opinion.

2. Assume that you are public relations counsel to the Otis Elevator Company. You have been shown a draft of the speech prior to its delivery and have been told when, where, how and to whom it will be given. You are asked to provide your professional advice about the speech and its projected delivery. Please do so, and justify your conclusions.

3. What questions would you ask and what kind of information about the Otis situation would you want to know about which have not been given in the case description?

4. Comment on the following release which was sent out by public relations counsel to the company:

FOR: OTIS ELEVATOR COMPANY

FROM: (Name, address, and
phone number of PR
counsel)

*NOT FOR RELEASE BEFORE 12:00 NOON
SATURDAY, JANUARY 15, 1955*

(Note: Copy which follows
was double-spaced)

At a meeting held today at the Brandt Theatre in Yonkers, New York, L. A. Petersen, President of Otis Elevator Company, told over 2,000 employees of the Otis Yonkers Works and a group of city officials that sales and earnings in 1954 were expected to exceed those of 1953 and that satisfactory operations were anticipated in 1955.

He pointed out, however, that the number of competitors had more than doubled during the last eight years to a present total of 262 and that substantial reductions in cost were necessary to retain the Company's competitive position.

Mr. Petersen stated that an extensive study had indicated that a saving of several million dollars could be secured by establishing a single midwestern plant to replace the present plants at Yonkers, New York, and Harrison, New Jersey, but that, in consideration of the hardship that would be imposed upon present employees, every effort would be made to secure a sufficient reduction in costs in the present plants to avoid the necessity for moving to a new central plant.

Mr. Petersen emphasized that the plans for reducing cost were not based upon any change in the past policy of paying all who work for Otis at least as much as is paid by other reputable and comparable companies for similar jobs, both in the form of wages and salaries and in supplementary benefits, but that such plans were based upon eliminating avoidable expense, upon improved methods and upon the efficient use of new and existing equipment.

He expressed the opinion that the success of these efforts would depend upon the cooperation received from employees and union officials.

A similar meeting was held later on today at the Otis plant in Harrison, N.J.

5. In response to a request by the author, the account executive of Otis's public relations counsel sent the above news release and a copy of Mr. Petersen's remarks. He closed by stating: "I am sure you will understand how delicate a matter this is and that it requires the utmost fairness and tact. Mr. Petersen approached the problem and the employees in this spirit."

What is your reaction to his statement?

QUESTIONS AND PROBLEMS FOR DISCUSSION

1. Why is it misleading to speak of *the public* as an entity?
2. Cite some examples — other than those mentioned in this chapter — of individuals who face loyalty conflicts due to multi-public membership.
3. Take any current issue of importance to groups of people and explain the various publics it affects.
4. List, in order of their importance, the publics which are of major concern to your college or university. In what way(s) would this list differ, if it does differ, from any other college or university you care to select for comparison?
5. Select any organization which has had a major shift in purpose and/or goals and explain how this shift has brought about a shift in its major publics.
6. Explain some current student-life morés which exist on your campus.
7. Using the next week's issues of the daily newspaper clip, paste up, and comment on five to ten examples of stereotyped thinking or writing.
8. Explain the meaning of an opinion in terms of its *direction, intensity, stability,* and *latency.*

9. What current or recent major issue of national or local concern illustrates how latent opinion became active? Explain your choice.
10. Selecting any major issue of national or local concern, explain which specific environmental factors played a vital role in the formation of public opinion concerning the issue.
11. In what respects has your family, church/religion, and education affected your attitudes and opinions about specific issues?
12. Why is the so-called formula approach to opinion formation open to criticism?
13. What examples can you cite to illustrate each of Newsom's four public opinion signposts?

RESEARCH 6

Public relations practitioners view themselves as humanists rather than scientists. Because their work is generally far removed from the precise, measured work of the physical scientists, the practitioners tend to be uncomfortable with techniques which are scientific in nature.

However, public relations practitioners certainly need — and many use — research and the scientific method as much as any scientist. This chapter aims to strip the mystique from research and show how its usage aids and abets public relations practice.

A SHORT COURSE IN RESEARCH

Professor Edward J. Robinson provides a simple definition of research when he describes it as "methods used to obtain reliable knowledge." (*Public Relations and Survey Research*, Appleton-Century-Crofts, 1969). He further points out that everyone uses reliable knowledge merely to function as human beings and that the major difference between the scientist and the nonscientist is how this reliable knowledge is achieved.

The nonscientist, says Professor Robinson, depends on his own judgment, intuition, hunches, and previous experience in attempting to solve problems. The extent of his use of reliable knowledge is personal and nontransferable. The scientist, on the other hand, makes his decisions on the basis of knowledge gained from scientific research and according to a set of rules or steps. There is no agreement about the number and kind of rules involved, but Professor Robinson cites nine steps in the scientific research process: (1) statement of the problem, (2) narrowing the problem to manageable size, (3) establishing definitions, (4) searching the literature, (5) developing hypotheses, (6) setting the study design, (7) securing data, (8) analyzing the data, and (9) interpreting and drawing conclusions about the results and reporting them.

A briefer version of the steps in research is provided by Claire Selltiz and others in *Research Methods in Social Relations* (Holt, Rhinehart, rev. ed, 1962): (1) formulation of the problem via a statement of purpose, (2) description of the study design, (3) data collection, (4) presentation of results, and (5) conclusions and recommendations.

Professor John Marston conceives of public relations research as *"planned, carefully organized, sophisticated fact finding and listening to the opinion of others"* (*The Nature of Public Relations*, McGraw-Hill, 1963). The connection between the Marston and Robinson descriptions of public relations research are apparent. Both stress the collection of data — one terming it "sophisticated fact finding" and the other "reliable knowledge" — and both stress the need to apply the scientific approach either by means of careful planning and organization or by step-by-step methods.

RESEARCH AND THE PUBLIC RELATIONS PROCESS

No matter how one approaches the public relations process, the need for research is paramount.

In Chapter 1 we described public relations as involving the evaluation of public attitudes and opinions; counseling management on policies and actions to ensure they're socially responsible and in the public interest; and executing an action and communication program to secure public understanding and acceptance. In the chapter that follows this one programming will be described as a series of steps ranging from a preliminary study to communication and evaluation. As a continuous process — no matter how it's viewed — public relations in action is circular in motion. If we were to compare the public relations process to a wheel, research is the center core with spokes to the outer rim at all key points.

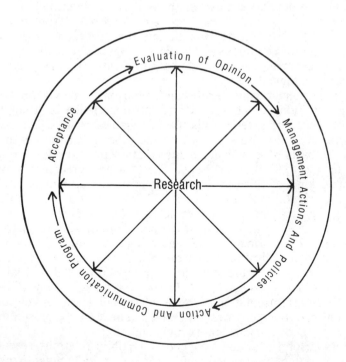

Research and public relations seen as a continuous process with research as the core with spokes to the major elements of the process

There are six major ways in which the research "spokes" support the public relations "wheel."

RESEARCH PROVIDES INPUT ABOUT PUBLIC ATTITUDES AND OPINION

Research, primarily public opinion-survey research, is the means whereby the practitioner is able to use the scientific method to ascertain public attitudes and opinions. As Professor Robinson points out, this form of research is the most prevalent type of research utilized by public relations practitioners. Surveys of attitudes and opinions may be initiated at the onset of a program, while a program is in process, or after a program has been carried out. They may be used to spot trends or for short-range, more immediate purposes. They may be self-produced by the practitioner or assigned to professional organizations which specialize in such research.

RESEARCH PROVIDES FACTUAL INPUT FOR PROGRAMMING

Ascertaining public attitudes and opinions enables the practitioner to pinpoint with some degree of accuracy the relative standing of his organization vis-a-vis its important publics and sub-publics. Given this raw material, the practitioner is then able to fashion a program designed to solidify or improve that standing.

Research also serves the valuable purpose of providing *data* useful in subsequent programming. Through library sources and a search of the literature the practitioner is able to make a preliminary study of the organization as an entity and as part of the larger body of which it is a unit. Programming undertaken without supportable data will be superficial in nature; reliable data, gathered through research, makes it meaningful.

RESEARCH SERVES AS AN "EARLY WARNING" SYSTEM

Countless hours of time, effort, and talent are wasted handling public relations problems after they arise. Research, which can serve to spot problems *before* they arise, enables the practitioner to use his time, effort, and talents to purposes more productive than solving problems which could have been prevented.

Using research to keep abreast of those developments in our society that have consequences for organizations served by public relations is crucial to effective handling of the function. Gathering information and data about such developments is similar to the role intelligence-gathering serves with the military. Such research helps spot long-range trends in society and short-range trouble spots which can develop into festering sores.

RESEARCH SERVES TO SECURE INTERNAL SUPPORT FOR THE PUBLIC RELATIONS FUNCTION

As a relative newcomer to the management of organizations, public relations often finds itself at a disadvantage when matched against legal, financial, and marketing departments. When a problem arises in which there are differences of opinion among these departments and the public relations department, the others often win out because they rely on factual data and evidence to support their point of view.

Research provides the means whereby the public relations practitioner gains support for his/her point of view by evidence secured through scientific methods. Research replaces hunch with facts and data and thereby strengthens and supports the counsel and advice put forth by the practitioner. Research is thus not merely of value because of its substantive aid, but also because of the manner in which it builds and sustains status.

RESEARCH INCREASES THE EFFECTIVENESS OF COMMUNICATION

Studies which explore the communication process provide important lessons for those practitioners who seek scientific evidence about the effectiveness of the various forms and means of communication. Such studies are reported in articles and books and are readily available to those practitioners who seek to mine this valuable resource.

Research aimed at measuring the effectiveness of communication can also be used by the practitioner himself as part of an on-going program. A limited number of practitioners have used before-and-after studies to measure the effect communication has had on various audiences, while others utilize communication research on a regular basis as part of the total public relations program.

RESEARCH LUBRICATES THE PUBLIC RELATIONS MACHINERY

All machines, including the public relations machine, need periodic lubrication. Research is often the lubricant needed to oil all parts of public relations programming: at the commencement of a program; at various intervals during the program; and after the program has come to a halt.

When there is uncertainty about public attitudes and opinions, research can be applied to find out what motivates the public. When there are doubts about steps to be taken in programming, research can be applied to resolve these doubts. When there are concerns about the effects of program activities, research can be applied to ascertain effects.

RESEARCH METHODS AND TECHNIQUES

Public relations research — as has been noted in the first section of this chapter — refers to the process or methods used for obtaining reliable knowledge. A variety of techniques are available for obtaining this knowledge, but the major ones used in public relations are considered to be the following: *compiling basic data; trend study and analysis; public opinion study and analysis.*

COMPILING BASIC DATA

As depicted in far too many movies and novels the typical public relations practitioner solves organizational problems by uncovering his trusty typewriter and dashing off a fast press release. In reality, the work done by the responsible practitioner is the result of long hours of careful research and fact-finding, just as the case presented in court by the trial lawyer is the result of similar long hours of research and preparation. Both the public relations practitioner and the trial lawyer may *seem* only to have a glib command of language, thought, and expression, but this is merely the surface appearance of the hard preparation which preceded the public presentation.

There are sound reasons for this preparatory fact-finding on the part of the practitioner. First, the public relations department should be the natural source of information about the organization. Unless the organization has a library and information department of its own — and only the largest organizations have such libraries and information departments — queries directed to the organization by the public, media, and by others in the organization will normally be referred to the public relations department. Such queries can best be answered when files of reliable material are available.

Second, no respectable and responsible public relations practitioner would dare practice his profession without recourse to authoritative facts and data. Because the practitioner's work deals with every aspect of the organization, it is the practitioner — more than anyone else — who has to be an authority about the organization. He has to know its history; key personnel; objectives; operations; products and/or services; and its role and place in the field and in society. In his dealings with publics and sub-publics, the practitioner will find daily need to call upon the resources of his fact-file of information and data. Compiling, maintaining, and keeping this fact-file up-to-date becomes one of the prerequisites of sound public relations practice.

BUILDING THE FACT-FILE

Though there are many ways one can compile, maintain, and keep a fact-file current, there are two essential elements to the process. One is to establish a library of basic reference books, and the other is to establish a basic system of compiling and maintaining data.

The public relations department's *basic library* cannot, of course, be expected to rival that of the average public or university library and will obviously be limited by available space, money, and the special needs of the organization. At a minimum, the following basic library is recommended:

Britannica Book of the Year. Encyclopedia Britannica, Chicago, Illinois (Annual update of the *Encyclopedia Britannica*)

Columbia Encyclopedia. Columbia University Press, Columbia University, New York, N.Y. (Latest Ed.)

Facts on File. Facts on File, Inc., New York, N.Y. (Weekly)

New York Times Index, New York *Times*, New York, N.Y. (Bi-Weekly)

1970 Census of Population, U.S. Government Printing Office, Washington, D.C. 1972

Official Congressional Directory. U.S. Government Printing Office, Washington, D.C. (Annual)

Statistical Abstract of the United States. U.S. Government Printing Office, Washington, D.C. (Annual)

U.S. Government Manual. U.S. Government Printing Office, Washington, D.C. (Latest Edition)

Vital Statistics of the United States. U.S. Government Printing Office, Washington, D.C. (Annual)

Who's Who in America. Marquis Co., Chicago, Illinois (Latest edition)

World Almanac and Book of Facts. Newspaper Enterprise Association, New York, N.Y. (Annual)

Webster's Third New International Dictionary of the English Language, Unabridged. C & C Merriam Co., Springfield, Mass. 1970

Whether one uses an alphabetical file or simply places material into compartments, there must be a *basic system of compiling and maintaining data*. The following alphabetical classification system should suffice to cover public relations source material for fact-file purposes:

Background material on the organization, including historical, statistical, and legal material

Biographies of key personnel in the organization

Competitor and opposition literature and data

Government agencies, committees and hearings related to the organization

Legislation: pertinent bills, laws and regulations

Organizational communications: public relations ads, press releases, feature stories, speeches, and the like

Press clippings from newspapers, magazines, and trade publications

Public opinion studies relevant to the organization

Reference materials dealing with the organization's special field

Trade association literature

Setting up the above system is a relatively simple task; much more difficult is maintaining and keeping it current. Such files tend to get out of hand quickly, but as public relations departments learn to use computers, data banks, and terminals, more sophisticated retrieval systems are being developed and put to use. When background material and data are needed in a hurry — as they usually are — there's no reason why they can't be conjured up by the push of a button. For those organizations which have far-flung, dispersed public relations operations there's even more reason for the use of terminals connected to a central data bank installation. But whether maintained by hand or by means of computers, the use of a central repository of facts and data relevant to the organization is vital for research as an aid to effective public relations.

TREND STUDY AND ANALYSIS

Carrying out the intelligence function — whether in the military, in economics, or in public relations — is a tricky, elusive, but highly necessary task. Military intelligence agents provide valuable information about the disposition and intentions of enemy forces and when these agents are right in their estimates, thousands of lives are saved but when wrong, thousands of lives are lost. Economic forecasters provide valuable information about the probable state of the economy and when the forecasters are right in their estimates, millions of dollars are saved but when wrong millions are lost. (See adjoining Mini-Case for a commentary of forecasting gone wrong.) Public relations researchers provide valuable information about the state of society and when they're right they pinpoint incipient problems before they become real problems, but when wrong the real problems become apparent all too quickly. Being right or wrong is a matter of research, vigilance, perception, and judgment.

MINI-COMMENT:
WHEN CRYSTAL BALLS CLOUD UP

As a social science discipline economics has traveled a long way since Adam Smith, and the forecasters with their expensive computers and models have been in the forefront of those economists who apply scientific research and methods to their forecasting. Despite the scientific paraphernalia at their disposal, the forecasters have found that even computerized crystal balls cloud up, as highlighted in the following *Business Week* observation:

"Economists will remember 1974 for many things: for the squeeze on energy, for the breathtaking rise in prices, and perhaps for events yet to come. But mainly they will remember 1974 as the year the forecasting blew it.

"Passing the midpoint of the year, the forecasters are scrambling to revise the projections they made so bravely last November and December. They disagree not only about the prospects for the economy in 1975 but also about the outlook for the remainder of 1974. They cannot decide whether the U.S. is going into a recession. They cannot even agree on the trend of production, income, and employment at the end of the second quarter.

"Such confusion among the experts is frustrating for businessmen and government officials who must make commitments and choose economic policies on the basis of forecasts. It is equally frustrating for the economists themselves. For a forecast, essentially, is the statement of a theory with specific values instead of abstractions. When the forecast goes seriously wrong, it suggests that something is wrong with the theory. And when all forecasts miss the mark, it suggests that the entire body of economic thinking — accumulated in the 200 years since Adam Smith laid the basis for modern theory

162

with his *Inquiry into the Wealth of Nations* — is inadequate
to describe and analyze the problems of our times.''

Business Week, June 29, 1974

Questions for Discussion

1. What aspects of economic forecasting make it such a difficult
   task to carry out with accuracy? (Note: Members of the class
   may find it advisable to seek the advice of those members of
   the faculty who teach economics.)

2. What have you learned from the answers to the above question
   which may be of value to public relations researchers?

3. Check the files of newspapers and newsmagazines of a year
   ago for examples of social, political, or economic forecasting
   and then check these forecasts as they've worked out (or not
   worked out) in actuality.

FAD, TREND, FIXTURE

The major reason why it's so difficult to track societal movements
and changes which have important public relations ramifications is that
each change is unique. Whereas the scientist in the laboratory can base
his experiments on previous findings and can control the variables, the
public relations researcher deals with changes which have few if any
precedents and has no control over the variables involved. Perceptions
and judgment are the tools available to the public relations researcher as
he observes and records societal changes and draws his conclusions.

A useful way of arranging societal changes is to visualize them as a
continuum ranging from fad to trend to fixture.

Fads flash across the national scene like meteors and then disinte-
grate and disappear. Where they come from and where they go, nobody
knows. One can merely observe and report their progress and marvel at
the pyrotechnics. For most institutions, fads usually have little importance from a public relations point of view, though a fad can be of great
importance for a limited number of organizations.

In the late fifties the hula hoop craze hit the United States,
and in a few short weeks more than twenty million units were
sold to children as stores rang up sales amounting to more than
thirty million dollars. The fad obviously had importance for a
limited number of entrepreneurs, but beyond that was just a fad
that passed into history along with the dodo-bird.

At the end of the thirties a Harvard freshman won a ten
dollar bet by swallowing a live goldfish. As fast as you could say
"gulp" collegians all across the country in the spring of 1939
were swallowing live goldfish, but by the time the term ended

students had figured out that fish taste better when cooked and another fad came to an end.

Fads abound in every generation and seem to emanate from the young and the adventurous. Examples that come quickly to mind are the yo-yo, skate board, twist, mini-skirt, short-shorts, long hair, mustaches and beards on 18-year-olds, pot, rock, and sock hops.

In the continuum from fads to fixtures there's the interim stage of the *trend*. Fads become trends when they spread out beyond their original narrow bank of innovators and are taken up by wide segments of the population. It doesn't take much perception to conclude that the hula hoop would have a limited life span and that college students would soon tire of eating goldfish. It takes an astute observer to conclude that a fad has become a trend and, most important of all, might well become a fixture of American life, manners, and customs.

MINI-CASE
PUBLIC RELATIONS EXTENDED PLANNING

Harshe-Rotman & Druck, 44-year-old international public relations counseling firm, offered in 1975 a new service called PREP, or "Public Relations Extended Planning." The service was announced by various means, including a brochure which was distributed in the fall of that year. Details of the service were spelled out in this brochure in the following description of the program:

PREP

In an era of unprecendented, monumental, and accelerating change, public relations professionals have an added and demanding dimension to their jobs: They must be able to alert the rest of their top management group of these changes before they happen or while the changes are in the early stages of development. Failure to act until changes have matured and almost run their course often can be disastrous.

Harshe-Rotman & Druck offers a new service that it has been developing for about a year, from elements that go back several years, a specialized, four-part program to help top management in public affairs planning.

Harshe-Rotman & Druck, a 44-year-old international public relations firm, developed the program to allow public relations professionals to present, in an organized and well-documented way, potential or evolving public affairs issues deserving top-level management attention.

Called PREP (an acronym for "Public Relations Extended Planning"), the program is tailored, based on specialized research, to the needs of the company or other groups, such as associations or nonprofit organizations, contracting for it.

164

The program is a four-part presentation that requires one to two days, depending upon the complexity of the group to which the presentation is being made.

Part I — A broad overview of what's gone before in areas of public opinion.
Part II — What's ahead during the next year or two that could affect the specific audience hearing the presentation.
Part III — What might happen during the next two to ten years.
Part IV — What the audience can do to accelerate or slow down potential changes.

I. The presentation begins with a review by a spokesman from National Opinion Research Center, University of Chicago, which has been conducting nationwide public opinion studies for 34 years. The NORC representative describes attitudes, especially those affecting the business community, that have changed dramatically during past years and those that have held relatively constant. While the NORC spokesman does not try to predict from past studies, he does provide a backdrop for the rest of the presentation and suggests which opinions are likely to be relatively constant and which are likely to change.

II. The next part of the presentation is made by John Naisbitt, chairman and president of Urban Research Corporation and publisher of the *Trend Report*, a specialized publication that is subscribed to by such companies as Bank of America, Xerox, General Motors, General Electric, Squibb, and Celanese. Naisbitt outlines developments that are likely to evolve during the next year or two and have a substantial impact on the group hearing the presentation.

III. Dr. John G. Keane, president of Managing Change, Inc., a company that specializes in what Keane calls "anticipatory intelligence" for major corporations, then describes developments that can affect the group two to ten years into the future.

IV. The fourth part of the presentation is by a representative of Harshe-Rotman & Druck. He describes what public relations techniques can be used to accelerate or combat evolving trends.

Presentations tailored to the group contracting for them require about $4,000 in time for a one-day presentation to a company with a relatively uncomplicated product line. Other presentations, dealing with more complicated structures, require appropriately more time for preparation. Not inexpensive, but valuable.

Top management groups that have heard elements of these presentations speak extremely highly of them. If you're interested and would like to see some of their comments, please contact one of the seven U.S. offices of Harshe-Rotman & Druck.

Reproduced by permission.

Questions for Discussion

1. What is your opinion of the PREP program as spelled out in the brochure?

2. What changes, if any, would you suggest be made in the PREP program?

3. What is your opinion of the way in which Harshe-Rotman & Druck presented the program in its PREP brochure? Cite specific elements of the brochure which you approve or disapprove.

4. Assume that you have been given the responsibility for "selling" the program. In a memorandum to A. R. Roalman, executive vice president of H-R & D, explain how you intend to merchandise PREP.

The fixture is the fad and trend become permanent. The fixture is the meteor which has flashed across the national scene, impacted, and as a meteorite is now a part of the earth's crust. One can observe the progress of a fad or trend and try to do something while it's in progress, but one can only deal with a fixture after it's firmly in place. By that time, of course, the task of dealing with it is much more difficult.

Way back when the horseless carriage first chugged into the American landscape the owners of the new-fangled machines were subjected to shouts of "Get a horse!" as they drove down the dirt roads. The shouts and the horses have long since disappeared, but just think how wise the astute research-observer would have been had he been able to predict in those early days what profound changes the automobile would bring to all aspects of American life!

Mid-way through our involvement in Vietnam groups of young people throughout the country started to protest our participation. Most Americans viewed them as radicals and unpatriotic beatniks, but the peace movement continued to gain strength; by the end of the Tet offensive it included hundreds of thousands who marched in massive protests against our continued involvement. What had started as a limited movement drew people of all ages and from all ranks in life and as a wide-based trend convinced an American president that he shouldn't seek another term in office. Again, just think how wise the astute researcher-observer would have been had he been able to predict in those early days what profound changes the early peace protesters would bring!

The public relations researcher serves an extremely valuable function as he observes those meteors of change which flash across the American landscape at periodic intervals. If his perceptions and judgment conclude they are just fads, the implications are few and of minor consequence for most organizations. If he concludes they are trends, the implications are many and can be of serious consequences for many organizations. If he concludes they are fixtures, the implications are numerous, serious, and of profound consequence to virtually all organizations. Perceptions and judgments are not inherent traits, but come through experience and study.

MINI-CASE
JUDGE BEN B. LINDSEY'S COMPANIONATE MARRIAGE

The case of Judge Ben B. Lindsey and his advocacy during the late twenties of a concept termed "companionate marriage" provides some interesting lessons about mores, fads, trends, and fixtures.

When he published his book *The Companionate Marriage* in 1927 Ben Lindsey had been a county judge for twenty-six years and the man who innovated the juvenile court in Denver, Colorado, which the *Dictionary of American Biography* termed "the best-known court of its kind in the world."

Alarmed and concerned about the sexual laxity of the time, Judge Lindsey felt that because of the mores existing at the time the result of such laxity could only result in divorce, illegitimacy, broken homes, and ruined lives. He believed that reform and an attempt to revise the mores would lead to social change, and he set forth his ideas about such reform in a series of articles in *Redbook* magazine and in the book, *The Companionate Marriage*.

In his book the judge advocated compulsory education in sexual matters, legalized birth control, and liberalization of the divorce laws to permit childless couples by mutual consent to obtain a divorce without the cost and formality of a conventional lawsuit. Neither party, he proposed, would have any financial or economic claim on the other.

As might be expected, Judge Lindsey found himself in the center of a storm of controversy that arose over his proposals. He was sharply criticized and attacked by churchmen, physicians, and laymen who, aided by some sensational news reporting, claimed that Lindsey advocated "free love," "trial marriage," and the like. The ideas Lindsey proposed in his articles and book were shot down like deer on the opening day of the season.

When Lindsey died in 1943 the New York *Times* obituary noted that Lindsey "was bitterly opposed to trial marriage which, he declared, the American people always confused with companionate marriage."

The confusion continued years after his death. Lloyd Morris, in his book *Postscript to Yesterday* (Random House, 1947), reported that Lindsey "proposed that society legalize a pre-nuptial trial period, a companionate marriage." In his book, *Contemporary America* (Harper, 1955), Harvey Wish termed Lindsey's companionate marriage "a plan that called for a preliminary trial period."

Questions for Discussion

1. What specific American morés do you perceive to be involved in the following key elements of Judge Lindsey's companionate marriage concept: compulsory education in sexual matters; legalized birth control; divorce by mutual consent for childless couples; neither party to such divorce having any financial or economic claim on the other?
2. Which of the above key elements, in your opinion, seem to have moved from the fad to the trend to the fixture stage? If some of these elements haven't moved to the fixture stage, what do you consider their prospects to be for so doing?
3. Name some organizations which, in your opinion, ought to consider public relations ramifications as regards public attitudes and opinions about these key elements. Explain what these ramifications might be.
4. What do you think would be the reaction to Judge Lindsey's book and ideas if they had been put forth today instead of in 1927? Justify your conclusions.

WAYS TO STUDY FADS, TRENDS, AND FIXTURES

In seeking to keep track of fads, trends, and fixtures in American society the public relations researcher has four basic tools at his disposal: (1) *reading*, (2) *viewing*, (3) *observation*, and (4) *survey research in the form of public opinion polling*.

MINI-CASE
TREND SPOTTING AT GENERAL MOTORS

Today's complex and changing public issues require that corporate executives be informed promptly of problems and trends that affect their operations.

At General Motors, this task is the responsibility of the public affairs section of the public relations staff, which is headed by A. V. Gagliardi, Manager of Public Affairs. With a staff of seven, and buttressed by libraries and staff in Detroit and New York, GM's public affairs section devotes its time to:

* Reading and reviewing a broad selection of newspapers, magazines and books
* Pinpointing trends emanating in academic and scientific circles
* Sponsoring and monitoring public opinion studies relating to issues that affect the auto industry
* Preparing and distributing reports and digests to GM management

The material reviewed includes well-recognized publications such as *Fortune, The Atlantic, Harper's,* the national weekly magazines and the *Harvard Business Review*. In addition, it covers ecology newsletters, technical publications, political publications, and television and radio programs that relate to the automobile industry. The more specialized material is covered by staffers with engineering and economics backgrounds.

The reports that are distributed to management vary in format. They may be a single page digest of a speech; a brief memo of an article in *Nature* magazine; or a lengthy analysis of an important book on economics. The writers strive to be concise and readable, aware that their work must compete with the many other reports the average auto executive lugs home.

Distribution of public affairs reports usually begins with the chairman and extends down to middle management.

Questions for Discussion

1. What qualifications do you think someone would need to work in GM's public affairs section?
2. What are some other publications this section might review?
3. Do you feel this activity would increase or decrease in importance in the future? Why or why not?
4. What do you perceive to be some major problems involved in the public affairs work described in the case? How would you handle them?
5. In addition to air pollution and automotive safety, what other issues do you feel GM might be following? Why?

With the exception of Item 4 — which is not generally available — the researcher's tools are at the disposal of almost anyone who cares to use them. The difference between the researcher and "almost anyone" is that the researcher uses the tools in a purposeful way: not only does he try to spot and keep track of fads, trends, and fixtures, but he seeks to make reasonable assumptions and judgments about their probable influence on public relations practice.

Reading

One of the first lessons that the public relations graduate learns when he gets his first job in the field is that the reading he's done in college is just a prelude to the reading he will have to do for the rest of his professional life. Others may read for pleasure or not read at all, but the public relations graduate reads because reading is the lifeline to a successful career.

Purposeful reading is an important research tool because the printed page reflects the facts, ideas, and opinions about the society in which we live. At a minimum this reading should include the daily newspaper (s) published in the city where one works; the nearest metropolitan newspaper of national stature; either *Newsweek* or *Time* or both; *Variety, Broadcasting, Editor and Publisher*; trade and specialized publications; and nonfiction books related to one's special field or which provide insights about important trends in American life.

The local newspaper(s) will provide timely intelligence about local affairs, but may print a minimum amount of state, national and international news. The nearest metropolitan newspaper of national stature fills out the daily intelligence diet by the volume and quality of nonlocal news it carries. Considered to be papers of national stature are the: Boston *Globe*; New York *Times*; Washington *Post*; Miami *Herald*; Chicago *Tribune*; Des Moines *Register* and *Tribune*; St. Louis *Post Dispatch*; Denver *Post*; Los Angeles *Times*. If your public relations activities concern business or industry, then the *Wall Street Journal* would also be required daily reading.

Newsweek, Time, or both not only serve to bring together into a single weekly package the loose ends of daily national and international news, but their many special sections are guides to the entire spectrum of American life.

Because the public relations practitioner is so dependent on mass media, he must be aware of what's happening with the media, and *Variety, Broadcasting* and *Editor and Publisher* serve this purpose. Trade and specialized publications are indispensible as information sources about the fields they cover.

MINI-LESSON
LETTER FROM A FORMER STUDENT

Shortly after graduating from Utica College with a degree in public relations, David D'Alessandro secured a position with a major counseling firm in New York City. Asked by his former professor to sum up his major conclusions after three months in the field, D'Alessandro wrote a long letter and spoke of reading in the following words:

The most important, and I mean *most* important, thing I have learned is to READ, READ, AND READ. I know we discussed this a few times, but I cannot over-emphasize the reading needed to stay alive in this game. I read at a minimum 25 magazines a week (trade and general) plus many other articles brought to my attention, and of course newspapers (TIMES, WALL STREET JOURNAL, and the NEWS). Surprisingly, I like the WSJ the most since it gives me the financial scene and a general news dropback. The TIMES goes a bit too far for the amount of time it takes to read and to do justice to it.

Why read? First of all, when your boss calls you in the morning and says, "Well, what do you think of page 43 in the WALL STREET JOURNAL this morning," you had better be able to say, "But there were only 42 pages in the

JOURNAL this morning. You must mean the article on air pollution on page 31." Secondly, clients expect you to keep abreast of anything remotely related to the account and then some. Third and most importantly from a personal standpoint, reading has two advantages. Creativity is the name of the game, writing is taken for granted. You are paid to come up with ideas and know how to follow through. By ideas I mean the way to get the media and your client's message to have intercourse and to maximize what you want said. If you don't know what the hell is going on in the world, how the hell can you be creative? Secondly, once you have attained this knowledge from steady reading, it is something that never can be taken away from you. You can use it wherever you go and impress people with worldliness, which is also the name of the game.

It's also not a bad idea to read up on the client's interests if they are not too way out. Don't try to be an expert, or even let him know you read up on it. At least he knows you're interested in him and the account that much. . . .

Questions for Discussion

1. At the time he wrote his letter, D'Alessandro was working on two accounts. If you were he and the two accounts were a major oil company and a data processing manufacturer, what 25 magazines (trade and general) would you read each week?

2. D'Alessandro sees a close connection between creativity and reading. As he states: "If you don't know what the hell is going on in the world, how the hell can you be creative?" Do you agree or disagree with the connection he sees between creativity and reading? Justify your conclusions.

3. As you will note, D'Alessandro suggests it's a good idea to read up on the client's interests, but he adds: "Don't try to be an expert or even let him know you read up on it." Why do you think he adds the warning, and what do you think about it?

Viewing

Motion pictures and television are not merely powerful media of communication but molders of national life styles, manners, dress, and customs. Prior to the advent of television — particularly in the twenties, thirties, and forties — motion pictures were *the* trend-setter in depicting the so-called American way of life. The fact that the movies of that period were more fantasy than reality is less to the point than the fact that they set trends in dress, style, manners, and morals.

In the fifties, television replaced motion pictures in the trend-setting department. Excluding its coverage of news and live events, the bulk of afternoon and prime-time television in 1975 was devoted to fantasy in the form of game and sit-com shows. Although neither of these can be considered reality, they set trends, and the avid TV watcher can keep up with trend changes by watching.

Whether motion pictures and television initiate or mirror trends is less important than the fact that both have enormous influence on the viewing public. Successful movies and television shows attract audiences numbering in the millions. The public relations practitioner can make movie and television viewing productive by assessing it in terms of spotting the trends depicted in each medium.

Observation

Whether the research is that carried out by the scientist in the laboratory or that followed by the public relations practitioner in real life situations, the need to observe pertinent phenomena is a paramount concern. The phenomena that the practitioner observes is the current scene. Such observation is open to everyone, of course, but most people are casual observers; the practitioner is, or should be, a purposeful observer. If he travels widely throughout the country he notes local, regional, and national aspects of American life, manners, and style. At all times he keeps in touch by recognizing that there is more to the country than the route he travels from his home or apartment to his office.

Keeping in touch becomes more difficult as the practitioner's income and status rise. In fact, the more successful he becomes the greater the distance between him and the rest of the country. Trying to observe how most Americans live is almost impossible when the observation post is a first class seat on a 707 flying at 32,000 feet between New York City and Los Angeles. Because America itself is the practitioner's laboratory, the practitioner must observe American life on the ground where it exists. From time to time he should travel by subway instead of taxi, by car instead of plane, through cities instead of around them on super highways; visit Disney World instead of London; eat at McDonalds instead of the Four Seasons; shop at Sears instead of Count Charles; go to baseball games instead of the opera; in short, mingle with and observe the majority of his countrymen on their home turf.

Observation as a research tool comes in varying degrees of difficulty. Such life-style appendages as dress, public behavior, work and play habits, and manners can be observed with the naked eye. More difficult to discern and chart are morés, private behavior, reactions to major institutions and their actions and policies, and similar covert aspects of life-styles. Impossible to discern and chart through mere observation are attitudes and opinions, and to cope with trends in these areas the practitioner turns to more sophisticated techniques. Survey research is such a technique.

PUBLIC OPINION STUDY AND ANALYSIS

Survey research in the form of public opinion surveys and polls is the most scientific and prevalent form of research used by public relations practitioners. Its techniques — particularly those developed by such national polling organizations as the Harris organization, the American Institute of Public Opinion (Gallup), Opinion Research Corporation, the Yankelovich organization, the Roper organization, and others — have been refined and honed to the point where they are universally accepted as scientifically proven ways of measuring public opinion. National organizations with large public relations departments use their own resources to carry out public opinion polls, but the more common practice is for public relations departments and counseling firms to contract for surveys with professional polling organizations.

Depending on the degree of refinement desired, public opinion polls and surveys consist of a series of steps or procedures. At a minimum these include the following: (1) *defining the purpose*; (2) *identifying the population*; (3) *selecting the research method*; (4) *selecting the sample*; (5) *constructing the questionnaire*; (6) *interviewing and processing data*; and (7) *analyzing, interpreting and reporting the data*.

DEFINING THE PURPOSE

Defining the purpose is as important and crucial a step in public opinion surveying as defining the problem is in public relations planning and programming. Taking a survey without a clear understanding of the reasons for the survey can lead to no end of trouble and can be a sheer waste of time, money and talent.

On the surface, there seems to be no problem involved in defining the purpose of a survey. After all, isn't a survey conducted to ascertain public opinion? The answer is "yes, but" with public relations becoming the "butt" when results turn out to be negative instead of positive.

All too often when managements approve the commissioning of a survey of public opinion they do so on the assumption that said opinion will be favorable. Unduly sensitive managements tend to consider negative public opinion to be a personal affront to their competence — which it sometimes is — and although they may seem to approve an impartial survey they really expect the mirror on the public opinion wall to show them to be the fairest of them all. When it doesn't, public relations is blamed for the bad image the mirror reflects.

Thus, one of the first steps to take when surveying public opinion is to find out if management really and honestly wants to ascertain public opinion or only go through the motions of a survey but really doesn't want to face up to any negative findings. Securing the answer to this question is no simple matter, but the practitioner must settle the problem of purpose — whether directly or by circumlocution — before the survey has been taken.

Assuming that management does seek honest answers, the practitioner must decide just what he wants to know about such opinion. Does he seek to find out what people *know* about his organization? Does he seek to find out what people *think* about his organization? Is he seeking public reaction to *specific organizational actions, policies and/or plans?* Does he want to measure and assess the *impact and effectiveness of the organization's public relations program* or specific aspects of said program? Is he attempting to assess *trends* in public opinion? Is he seeking to assess *probable public reaction to projected* organizational and public relations actions and programs? Each of these purposes is a valid target and goal of survey research, but each calls for a specific and special set of questions. Such questions cannot be devised unless the purpose or purposes have been clearly established in advance.

IDENTIFYING THE POPULATION

People, not animals, form the audience for public opinion surveys, but that's about the easiest distinction that can be made. *Who* forms the population becomes a matter of setting parameters and eliminating the noninvolved.

Assume your firm has been asked to conduct a survey to ascertain who will be elected alderman in Ward 10 of a city of 80,000 population. First, forget about the entire city and concentrate on Ward 10. Second, eliminate all those under 18 years of age. Third, eliminate those of voting age but not eligible to vote. Fourth, try to screen out those most likely to stay away from the polls. Those remaining form the true population for your survey.

Another example. The Calcium Chloride Institute has budgeted between $3,000 and $5,000 for a survey of attitudes and opinions about the use of calcium chloride to keep down dust on Iowa roads in the summer and to clear ice off roads during the winter. Accepting the assignment, you have an initial interview with the CCI and learn that county highway engineers and county supervisors have responsibility for highway maintenance and the purchase of appropriate highway clearance agents. Your population is not the adult population of Iowa but the county highway engineers and county supervisors.

These are two examples of problems connected with the determination of the population to be surveyed in public opinion polling. Similar problems arise in all surveys, whether you are surveying *employees* (all employees, hourly employees only, division employees, field employees only?); the *college* community (all students, full-time students only, dormitory residents, faculty, administration?); the *community* (adults only, everyone 16 years and older, opinion leaders, everyone except those in nursing homes and hospitals?); and similar general groupings of people. In each case a clear distinction must be made of the exact population to be surveyed.

SELECTING THE RESEARCH METHOD

There are a variety of ways to describe and discuss the major survey research methods available to public relations practitioners, but the simplest is to consider them as *structured* or *unstructured*.

Unstructured

The *depth interview* is the most common and widely used form of the unstructured survey and is best described as informal in nature and lasting from a half hour to an hour. The interviewer usually compiles in advance a series of "probe points," but these are not set up in the form of carefully designed and worded questions but rather as general areas to be explored with the interviewee. The basic idea of the depth interview is to explore in depth the respondent's ideas, attitudes, opinions, knowledge, and expertise on a series of subjects.

The depth interview has plus and negative factors. On the plus side is the fact that such an interview provides a more intensive reading of the respondent's mind and thinking than is possible from a structured questionnaire interview. The relatively free-wheeling atmosphere of the depth interview often brings out information, ideas, and opinions not anticipated by the researcher. Because the interviewee is not restricted by the confines of specific and carefully worded questions, the interviewee is able to express his or her intrinsic and honest thoughts, attitudes, opinions, and feelings.

On the other hand, few interviewers have the talents required for depth interviewing and such interviews are costly because of the time and talent involved. Furthermore, tabulating, codifying, assembling, analyzing, and reporting the results are extremely difficult tasks. Because such interviews are free-wheeling, long, and involved, the answers to "probe questions" are also free-wheeling, long, and involved. Yet for purposes of reporting the results, answers have to be compressed, analyzed, and put into final report form and this inevitably leads to editorial tinkering and interpretation. Finally, because of the time, talent, and cost factors already cited, depth interviews cannot economically be used for large samples or where respondents are widely dispersed. Because of these limiting factors, depth interview surveys are seldom representative of total populations but represent the views of a limited number considered to be unusually well-informed about the areas being surveyed.

MINI-EXAMPLE
EXPLORING BANK CREDIT CARD USAGE

Professors James Mullen and Michael Bishop presented a strong case for depth interviewing — they term it "clinical interviewing" — in an article they wrote for *Public Relations Quarterly*, Spring, 1975. They cite the following example to demonstrate the value of such interviewing:

One study concerned the use of bank credit cards. The organization behind the card had a number of unanswered questions concerning the acceptance, use, and nonuse of its card. Among the questions were these: (a) Who is a good prospect for a bank credit card? (b) Why do some people keep a bank card but fail to use it? (c) Is there a difference in perception of bank card credit vs. other types of credit among users? (e) Why do some people use these cards only for "big ticket" items while others use them for anything *but* such items? (f) How have various bank public communications (personal contact, letters, media advertising) been received by users and prospective users?

Such "why" and "how" questions as these have represented a prime source of difficulty for those using regular survey research. One can't be certain about what constitutes the universe when dealing with such a diversity of questions. (To include everyone who should be involved in *one* part of the study would mean that large numbers of people could be included who should *not* be involved in *other* parts). Using the clinical method, any person interviewed would contribute only to those sections of the study where his contribution is relevant.

In order to obtain answers to these questions using quantitative survey methods, it may have been necessary to draw three or four separate samples and prepare a specific questionnaire for each. Instead, the authors were able to obtain useful results with just one small sample and no questionnaire. They conducted all 75 interviews themselves (in three states, in communities of varying size, with old and young, rich and poor, black and white). They were able to stop with 75 interviews as they found they were getting little new information and were largely confirming what they had already learned.

The project cost must less than would have a series of quantitative studies, and all parties concerned were convinced that the results (while not projectable) were reliable and therefore useful. Three years after the study was completed, its conclusions are still being employed as a basis for guiding successful corporate communications.

Questions for Discussion

1. What's your opinion of the study and the authors' conclusions about its effectiveness?

2. Do you agree or disagree with the authors' contention that finding answers to the six questions would have required three to four samples and surveys using quantitative survey methods?

3. What criticism, if any, do you have about the composition of the 75 interviews?

Structured

The most common form of the structured public opinion survey utilizes a questionnaire as its basic tool. Such surveys are carried out in three major ways: by *mail*; by *telephone*; and by *personal* interviewing.

Mail surveys are most often used when the universe (or population to be surveyed) is so widely dispersed it would be very costly and time-consuming to carry out by personal interviewing. If the universe to be surveyed is not too large — for example, all public relations teachers in the United States — it could be economically feasible to survey the entire universe through the mail. However, if the population to be surveyed is a large one — for example, all high school English teachers in the United States — then a representative sample would have to be drawn and that sample surveyed through the mail.

Whether surveying an entire universe or a representative sample through the mail, there must be available a listing containing everyone in the universe. The sample would then be drawn from the list or the entire list would be used.

The most serious drawback of the mail survey is in regard to the number responding to the mailed questionnaire. First mailings of a questionnaire and return envelope sent through the mail can draw a response ranging anywhere from 20 to 40 percent; a return response rate of over 50 percent is considered to be a good response, but of course this raises serious questions about the representativeness of the responses. What about those who did not respond? In order to boost the response rate, those using mail surveys generally arrange for a second or follow-up mailing, and this can be depended upon to bring in an additional 10 to 20 percent response, but there would still be the problem of the large number not responding.

Thus, whenever possible, those using mail surveys often include demographic questions in the questionnaire, and checking responses to such questions can determine whether those responding measure up to known characteristics of the entire universe.

Telephone surveys are used in circumstances similar to those existing for mail surveys. That is, they are useful when the population to be surveyed is so widely dispersed it would be very costly and time-consuming to carry out the survey by personal interviewing. In addition, telephone surveys are useful when *time* is a crucial factor. Unlike the situation with mail surveys, the problem of nonresponses can be handled by repeated call backs until the respondent answers the telephone. The decision whether to include the entire universe or a sample of the universe is dependent on the same circumstances as exists for mail surveys. Also, the same dependence on lists — in this case, a listing of those having telephones, and having such a list available — is similar to that for mail surveys.

The most serious drawback to the telephone survey is the fact that not everybody owns a telephone and not everyone has a listed telephone. Nonownership is most prevalent among lower income families, and nonlisted telephones are most prevalent among those who feel a special need for privacy. In both cases, and particularly if the survey aims to survey general public opinion, it would be questionable whether the survey could be considered representative.

A further drawback about telephone surveys is the fact that the use of the telephone for surveying public opinion restricts the number and kind of questions that can be asked of respondents. There is a limit to the amount of time people will give to a questionnaire administered over the telephone, and there are serious problems relative to personal and involved questions.

Personal interviewing, the third form of the structured survey, is the most extensive and most commonly used form of surveying public opinion. Survey research in public relations generally means public opinion surveying by means of a questionnaire administered to a representative sample of the population or universe. Such surveying will be described and analyzed in detail in the remaining discussion of the steps in public opinion surveying.

SELECTING THE SAMPLE

Polling a sample of the population or universe rather than the entire population or universe is a basic feature of virtually all public opinion polls today, yet the concept of sampling seems to be least understood by the lay person. In their national pre-election polling and predictions the polling organizations work with samples ranging between 1500 and 2500 adults of voting age, and these numbers inevitably cause doubters to question how such minute samples — when compared to the total number of persons of voting age — can be considered representative of the entire universe of voters. The answer is found in an explanation of sampling theory, practice, and procedures.

The first important point to understand about sampling is that *the size of the sample is far less important than representativeness*. The key to proper and effective sampling is to use a system of sample selection which gives each individual in the universe an equal opportunity to be selected in the sample polled. If improperly drawn, a sample of one million cannot be considered a true indicator of the universe it supposedly represents. Properly drawn, a sample of 1500 can be considered a true indicator of the opinion of millions.

Random or Probability Sampling

To make sure that the sample polled is representative of the universe, the major polling organizations draw a random or probability sample. Such a sample means that it has been selected in such a manner that *each element* in the universe has an equal or known chance of being in the chosen sample. The term "random" should not be taken to mean that selection has been obtained willy-nilly, but rather that the sample has been obtained without bias and by a carefully designed process. Further, probability sampling enables the pollster to specify the degree by which the sample is representative of the universe. Here is an explanation by the Gallup Organization of the manner in which it designed the sample for a national survey:

> The design of the sample is that of a replicated probability sample down to the block level in the case of urban areas and to segments of townships in the case of rural areas.

> After stratifying the nation geographically and by size of community in order to insure conformity of the sample with the latest available estimates by the Census Bureau of the distribution of the adult population, about 320 different sampling locations or areas were selected on a strictly random basis. The interviewers had no choice whatsoever concerning the part of the city or county in which they conducted their interviews.

Approximately five interviews were conducted in each such randomly selected sample point. Interviewers were given maps of the area to which they were assigned, with a starting point indicated, and required to follow a specified direction. At each occupied dwelling unit, interviewers were instructed to select respondents by following a prescribed systematic method and by a male-female assignment. This procedure was followed until the assigned number of interviews was completed.

Since this sampling procedure is designed to produce a sample which approximates the adult civilian population (18 and older) living in private households in the U.S. (that is, excluding those in prisons and hospitals, hotels, religious and educational institutions, and on military reservations), the survey results can be applied to the population for the purpose of projecting percentages into number of people. The manner in which the sample is drawn also produces a sample which approximates the population of private households in the United States. Therefore, survey results can also be projected in terms of number of households when appropriate.

Reproduced by permission of The Gallup
Organization

Size Versus Representativeness

A comparison of the ill-fated *Literary Digest* straw polls of the thirties and the modern-day Gallup, Harris, and Roper national pre-election polls illustrates the matter of sample size and representativeness. In the decade preceding the 1936 presidential election the *Literary Digest* conducted its straw polls by mailing out millions of postcards ballots to persons listed in telephone directories, on lists, or who were owners of automobiles. Despite the fact that such lists numbered in the millions they did not represent the entire American electorate, and were particularly deficient in lower income representation. The *Digest's* straw poll hut came tumbling down in 1936 when it mailed out ten million postcard ballots and received a return from two million persons who marked their choices. The *Digest's* final pre-election poll showed that Landon would win by 57 percent and Roosevelt would lose with 43 percent of the popular vote. The actual vote was 62.5 percent for Roosevelt and 37.5 percent for Landon. The 19 percentage-point error was one of the largest in polling history.

By comparison, using proper representative techniques and relying on a sample of less than 1,500, the Gallup Poll predicted a 55.7 percent vote for Roosevelt and a 44 percent vote for Landon. The Gallup organization was on target in its prediction of the winner, though it erred by 6.8 percent in its predicted percentage of the vote that would go to Roosevelt. That 6.8 percent error, by the way, was the largest error in Gallup Poll predictions in the period from 1936 through 1974. Gallup has correctly predicted the winners in all but one (1948) of the elections held in the years between 1936 through 1974 and has come remarkably close to the actual vote figures with the exception of the 1948 election when Gallup, and all the other national polling organizations, failed to conclude polling close enough to election day. (The Gallup Poll record of accuracy in pre-election polling is shown in Table 6-1.)

RECORD OF GALLUP POLL ACCURACY IN NATIONAL ELECTIONS

Year	Gallup Final Survey*		Election Result*		Error on Winning Candidate or Party, Based on Major Party Vote	
	%		%		%	
1936	55.7	Roosevelt	62.5	Roosevelt	−6.8	Roosevelt
1938	54.0	Democratic	50.8	Democratic	+3.2	Democratic
1940	52.0	Roosevelt	55.0	Roosevelt	−3.0	Roosevelt
1942	52.0	Democratic	48.0	Democratic	+4.0	Democratic[1]
1944	51.5	Roosevelt	53.3[2]	Roosevelt	−1.8	Roosevelt
1946	58.0	Republican	54.3	Republican	+3.7	Republican
1948	44.5	Truman	49.9	Truman	−5.4	Truman
1950	51.0	Democratic	50.3	Democratic	+0.7	Democratic
1952	51.0	Eisenhower	55.4	Eisenhower	−4.4	Eisenhower
1954	51.5	Democratic	52.7	Democratic	−1.2	Democratic
1956	59.5	Eisenhower	57.8	Eisenhower	+1.7	Eisenhower
1958	57.0	Democratic	56.5	Democratic	+0.5	Democratic
1960	51.0	Kennedy	50.1	Kennedy	+0.9	Kennedy
1962	55.5	Democratic	52.7	Democratic	+2.8	Democratic
1964	64.0	Johnson	61.3	Johnson	+2.7	Johnson
1966	52.5	Democratic	51.9	Democratic	+0.6	Democratic
1968	43.0	Nixon	43.5	Nixon	−0.5	Nixon
1970	53.0	Democratic	54.3	Democratic	−1.3	Democratic
1972	62.0	Nixon	61.8	Nixon	+0.2	Nixon
1974	60.0	Democratic	58.9	Democratic	+1.1	Democratic

*The figure shown is the winner's percentage of the Democratic-Republican vote except in the elections of 1948 and 1968. Because the Thurmond and Wallace voters in 1948 were largely split-offs from the normally Democratic vote, they were made a part of the final Gallup Poll pre-election estimate of the division of the vote. In 1968 Wallace's candidacy was supported by such a large minority that he was clearly a major candidate, and the 1968 percents are based on the total Nixon-Humphrey-Wallace vote.

[1]Final report said Democrats would win control of the House, which they did even though the Republicans won a majority of the popular vote.

[2]Civilian vote 53.3, Roosevelt soldier vote 0.5 = 53.8 Roosevelt. Gallup final survey based on civilian vote.

Reprinted by permission of The Gallup Poll
Table 6-1

The Gallup Poll, and the other polling organizations dealing with nationwide polling, draws its sample by dividing the population into strata according to the size of the locality in which the people live. A specified number of interviews are then conducted after specific geographical areas are selected by a systematic, random basis. Those interviewed are chosen for the sample on a chance basis, and the result is the closest approximation of all characteristics of the universe being surveyed.

The same procedure can be used for *lists* provided the lists include everyone in the universe and are up to date. For example, assume we want to survey student opinion in a college with 10,000 students. If we determine to use a sample of 200, then we would first divide 200 into 10,000 and thus arrive at intervals of 50. By random selection we would chose a starting point within the first 50 on the list. If the choice falls on the 25th person, then that person would be the first to be interviewed and the next person would be the 75th on the list. The resulting 200 interviews would comprise a probability sample reflective of the key characteristics of all 10,000 students.

The list procedure can also be used in drawing a probability sample of a town or city, though in such a case we would want to deal with addresses rather than individuals. Using an up-to-date city directory we would first number every single household address, including apartments, in the city. (We do this because people move, but houses and apartments don't). If the last numbered address turns out to be 30,000 and our designated sample is 300, we would divide 300 into 30,000 to arrive at an interval of 100. Again, by random choice we would select a starting number within the first 100 addresses and then interview at intervals of 100.

Instead of using intervals and drawing every nth name from a designated list, another way to select a sample is to utilize a table of random digits. Such tables are sometimes found in the appendix of a statistics textbook; a valuable source is The Rand Corporation, *A Million Random Digits with 100,000 Normal Deviates*, the Free Press, 1955. Each page of such published tables of random digits contains a large number of random digits divided into blocks of five for the sake of convenience. The digits can be read in groups of two, three, or more to produce two, three, or more digit numbers. The starting point is selected haphazardly. Following is an excerpt from a table of 10,000 random digits:

Line No.	1–5	6–10	11–15	16–20	21–25	26–30	31–35
0	10097	32533	76520	13586	34673	54876	80959
1	37542	04805	64894	74296	24805	24037	20636
2	08422	68953	19645	09303	23209	02560	15953
3	99019	02529	09376	70715	38311	31165	88676
4	12807	99970	80157	36147	64032	36653	98951
5	66065	74717	34072	76850	36697	36170	65813
6	31060	10805	45571	82406	35303	42614	86799
7	85269	77602	02051	65692	68665	74818	73053
8	63573	32135	05325	47048	90553	57548	28468
9	73796	45753	03529	64778	35808	34282	60935

To use the above table the first necessity is to number every name (or address) on the list representing our universe. The next step is to decide on the size of the sample, and then to draw the sample from the table of random digits. As an example, assume the last number on our universe list is 2,530 and we want to draw a random probability sample of 200. We have chosen as our starting point line 2, column 3. Reading four digits across and then down, our first eight four-digit numbers are 4226, 0190, 8079, 0657, 0601, 2697, 5733, 7964. Because they're under 2530, the first numbers to be included in our sample would be 0190 (190), 0657 (657), and 0601 (601). Continuing to draw from the table, our next numbers would be 2533, 4805, 8953, 2529, 9970, and so on running down columns six, seven, eight and nine. Of the five numbers, only 2529 would be included in the sample selection because it's the only four-digit number that is lower than our 2530 limit. We would continue our selection of four-digit numbers ranging under 2530 until we had reached a total of 200, the size of our sample.

Thus, in choosing a sample from lists we can either use a procedure of selecting every nth number or make our selection by means of a table of random digits. The remaining questions about sampling concerns the way in which we can calculate the chances that our sample is representative of the universe, and this is done through the statistical concept known as "sampling error."

Sampling Size and Error

Samples are used in polling public opinion because it is usually impossible to poll the entire population, and even if it were possible, the cost would be prohibitive.

The same two reasons apply when we consider how large a sample must be to secure a truly representative reading of public opinion. Deciding on the size of the sample is a matter of achieving a balance between the cost of the survey and the degree of precision needed. The end goal is to use a sample that will produce results within *acceptable margins of error*, and it is important to understand that in dealing with probability sampling reasonably accurate findings can be achieved with surprisingly small samples.

Professional polling organizations operate on what is known as a 95-confidence level, and this means in effect that "in an infinite number of similarly designed and executed surveys the percentage results would fall within a given margin of error in 95 percent of these surveys." (*Polls* by Charles Roll, Jr., and Albert H. Cantril, Basic Books, 1972, p. 70) Thus, the Gallup Poll estimated margin of error at the 95-confidence level is three percentage points for a sample of 1,500; four percentage points for a sample of 1,000; five percentage points for a sample of 600; and six percentage points for a sample of 400. If a Gallup Poll survey of 1,500 interviews shows the president having the support of 50 percent of the population he might actually be supported by as few as 47 percent or as many as 53 percent. If the sample consisted of 400 interviews that 50 percent support could be as high as 56 percent or as low as 44 percent.

Table 6-2 shows the suggested tolerances for the Gallup Poll.

TABLE OF SUGGESTED TOLERANCES FOR THE GALLUP POLL*

The table below provides the suggested sampling tolerances for the Gallup Poll's standard sampling unit on the basis of procedures presently in use. The figures take into account the effect of the sample design upon sampling error. They show the range, plus or minus, within which results can be expected to vary with repeated samplings under exactly similar conditions.

In Percentage Points
(at 95 in 100 confidence level)*

	1500	1000	750	600	400	200	100
Percentages near 10	2	2	3	3	4	5	7
Percentages near 20	2	3	4	4	5	7	9
Percentages near 30	3	4	4	4	6	8	10
Percentages near 40	3	4	4	5	6	8	11
Percentages near 50	3	4	4	5	6	8	11
Percentages near 60	3	4	4	5	6	8	11
Percentages near 70	3	4	4	4	6	8	10
Percentages near 80	2	3	4	4	5	7	9
Percentages near 90	2	2	3	3	4	5	7

*The chances are 95 in 100 that the sampling error is not larger than the figures shown.

To use the table above, these directions should be followed. Suppose a reported percentage is 33 for a group that embraces 1500 respondents. Since 33 is nearest 30 in the table, look in row 30 under the column headed 1500. The number in the table is 3, which means that the 33 percent figure obtained in the survey is subject to a sampling error of plus or minus 3 percentage points. Another way of saying this is that very probably (95 times in 100) repeated samplings of this size would yield figures ranging between 30 and 36, with the most likely figure being the 33 percent obtained.

It should be noted that the table deals with the normal sample unit now employed by the Gallup Poll. Many surveys of this organization embrace a far greater number of persons, usually multiples of 1500 unit.

----

*Reprinted by permission of The Gallup Poll

Table 6-2

Roll and Cantril raise an important question that relates to the suggested tolerance of error shown in the preceding table. They ask: "Would it be worth nearly doubling the cost of a survey by increasing the sample size from 750 to 1,500 in order to reduce the expected sampling error from plus or minus four percentage points to plus or minus three percentage points?"

The answer would be "no" when considering most surveys carried out for public relations purposes. If our survey reveals that 60 percent of those surveyed think poorly or highly of our organization's policies and actions, it really doesn't make that much difference if the percentage were 56 percent or 64 percent. The important consideration for the practitioner is to make sure that the sample is a carefully drawn random-probability sample which is broadly representative of the universe and which has given every individual an equal opportunity of being selected. Sample size is certainly crucial when polls are used to predict election results, but not for other public opinion assessment purposes. Carefully drawn, samples as low as 200 to 400 are adequate to reveal public attitudes, opinions, and knowledge concerning organizational policies, actions, programs, and standing.

MINI-EXAMPLE
SURVEYING AMONG GHETTO HOUSEHOLDS

In its report to the Carl Byoir & Associates account executive responsible for the Children's Television Workshop account, the Daniel Yankelovich survey organization first stressed the care taken in handling survey methodology. Stated the report:

This is to report to you on the extremely encouraging and outstanding results for "Sesame Street," which we found in our recent study, conducted among ghetto households in the Bedford-Stuyvesant area of Brooklyn, New York.

Indeed, the results are so outstanding that we feel it is important to first state the methodology, sampling methods, field interviewing procedures, and validation techniques used to guarantee that these results are completely reliable and projectable.

1. *Qualifications of Respondents:* In order to qualify for the interview, a respondent had to have either children between the ages of 2 to 5 who were neither in day care or nursery schools during the day, or to care for other children of this same age group on a regular (five day a week) basis. All interviewing was done during the daytime to guarantee that the mothers or babysitters were at home during these hours and could speak from first hand knowledge. The second qualification was that there had to be at least one television set in working order in the household.

2. *The Sampling Procedures:* The sample was designed to insure maximum representation of the entire Bedford-Stuyvesant area, and minimize any bias due to either the clustering of the interviews or possible interest generated by the appearance of the interviewers in the area. A total of 40 sampling points were used. In each sampling point, an interviewer was given a starting point, and a route to follow. When it was necessary for the interviewer to return to the sample point for a second day to complete her assignment, she was given a second starting point and routing. Listing sheets were kept to account for not at home, ineligibles, and refusals.

In order to obtain the 500 completed interviews, a total of 1676 households were contacted. The results broke down as follows:

Total Contacts	1676
Completed Interviews	502
Eligible Respondents — Refused to be interviewed, language problems, etc.	42
Ineligible Respondents	
No child 2 to 5	1037
Eligible on child 2 to 5 qualification/no working television set	22
Refusals/before eligibility could be ascertained	73

Both the recovery rate and the low incidence of refusal, we believe, are exceptionally good.

3. *Field Interviewing:* All interviewing was conducted by black interviewers living within or immediately adjacent to the Bedford-Stuyvesant area. No one interviewer was assigned more than two sampling points. Almost all of the interviewers had had previous interviewing experience. Despite this, each interviewer assigned to the project was personally trained for this assignment.

4. *Validation:* Close to 100 percent validation was made of all completed interviews. Respondents were asked whether or not they had been interviewed, and the subject of the interview. In addition, direct questions were asked about the viewing of Sesame Street and the demographic characteristics of the household.

Each of the completed interviews was also carefully read and checked by the project director as a final validity check.

Reprinted with permission

Questions for Discussion

1. What do you consider to be of significance about the qualification of respondents? About the sampling procedures? About the field interviewing? About the validation?

2. Why do you think the Yankelovich organization stressed that "indeed, the results are so outstanding (etc.)"?

3. Do you think there would be special problems in polling in Bedford-Stuyvesant? If so, why and what do you feel they would be? If not, why not?

CONSTRUCTING THE QUESTIONNAIRE

The document which is the major tool used In structured random probability survey research is the questionnaire. Designing the question to be asked and arranging them in proper order requires the most careful attention on the part of the researcher. As Stanley Payne implies by the title of his book (*The Art of Asking Questions*, Princeton University Press, 1951) there is an art to asking questions, and this art will be discussed in respect to the *placement, form,* and *wording* of questions.

Placement

Unless one is willing to have the interviewing terminated early in the interview, difficult or challenging questions should not be among the first questions asked. The initial questions should be the kind that are easy for the respondent to answer. They should not challenge the respondent's intelligence or knowledge, but should be of such a nature as to put the respondent at ease. Preferred as opening questions are those which can be answered with a simple yes or no, will give the respondent confidence in himself, and are not of a sensitive or embarrassing nature.

There should be a logical arrangement of the questions, and this is best achieved by grouping them so that the conversation leads logically from one question to another. Thus, questions relating to a specific area of concern should follow one another and not be spread throughout the questionnaire. When posing general and specific questions, ask the general ones before asking the specific questions. If this is not done, the respondent is likely to answer the general questions in terms of the specific ones asked earlier. Avoid grouping sensitive questions, but rather intersperse them with neutral ones. If a question poses some long or involved alternatives, put these on cards which can be handed to the respondent. The interviewer then reads out the question and asks the respondent to make his choice from the card.

Form

There are three basic forms of questions with many varieties of each form. Only the basic forms will be described here.

Dichotomous questions are those which provide two options. Examples of dichotomous questions are those which pose a choice between yes and no, approve and disapprove, good and bad. Proper procedure is to provide also for a third response, such as don't know, no opinion, or neither. If the third possibility is not provided then the question may force respondents to make a choice which they would not really want to make.

On the positive side, dichotomous questions are simple, easy to pose, understandable to the respondent, and easy to tabulate.

On the negative side, such questions may force respondents to make a choice they do not want to make. Opinions about many subjects do not fall readily into a simple yes-no choice, but may fall in between the two extremes.

Multiple choice questions in a variety of styles provide alternatives not available in dichotomous questions. Such questions are most often phrased to provide three-four-and five-point rating scales. Examples of three-point scales: above average, average, below average; higher, the same, lower. A four-point scale would be excellent, good, fair, poor. Some five-point scales: much greater, somewhat greater, equal, somewhat less, not at all; strongly approve, approve, undecided, disapprove, strongly disapprove.

A refinement of the verbal multiple choice rating scale is the graphic rating scale in which the respondent is asked to show strength of opinion on a line of numbers. Highest approval might be a plus five, middle would be zero, and lowest would be a minus five.

The virtue of multiple choice, rating-scale questions is that they allow degrees of opinion to be expressed. On the negative side is the fact that such questions tend to be long and place a heavy burden on the respondent's remembrance of the choices.

Open end questions make up the third major form of questions. Instead of providing preconceived response choices they permit the respondent to answer the question freely and allow wide latitude for his answers. Their major virtue is that they pick up the full flavor of a response and often reflect unanticipated opinions. Their major problem is that they are hard to categorize and often have to be forced into a mold for tabulation purposes.

Wording

Though the wording of questions seems to be a simple matter, it actually requires a great deal of care and skill. The following major guidelines are suggested:

1. Use simple rather than complex words. Aim questions so they're understood by those with a tenth grade level of education.

2. Be precise and absolutely clear. Payne suggests the following six-point test of a proposed question:
    a. Does it mean what we intend?
    b. Does it have any other meanings?
    c. If so, does the context make the intended meaning clear?
    d. Does the word have more than one pronunciation?
    e. Is there any word of similar pronunciation that might be confused?
    f. Is a simpler word or phrase suggested?

3. Cover only one point at a time, not two or more in one question. Asking "Do you like the taste of wine and cheese?" assumes that everyone considers the two in combination with each other when judging their taste. It's possible for someone to like the taste of wine and dislike the taste of cheese, but the question does not permit such an answer.

4. Avoid leading questions. Any question that is likely to produce a biased answer can be considered to be a leading question. Leading questions lead to misleading answers. Unless the surveyor is deliberately trying to secure predetermined answers, he should avoid phrasing the question to bring about desired answers.

5. Make sure the question will elicit the exact information sought. Questions which are not explicit enough will often produce answers which can't be combined for data reporting. For example, asking employees to estimate how much profit their company makes can bring answers in dollar figures, percentages, and gradations ranging from "a lot" to "not much." If you want the figure to be in dollars, specify dollars in the question. Further, does the question mean "net profit" or "gross profit?" If the surveyor is not sure what he means then he can't expect the respondent to be sure.

6. Frame alternatives carefully and honestly. Provide the same number of alternatives for each side of a question. Recognize that the more alternatives, the less likely respondents will favor the extremes. Try to phrase alternatives realistically the way people think and feel about problems and issues. Do not combine issues and partisan arguments. Balance the wording of alternatives so as to avoid biasing the results.

MINI-EXAMPLE
A COMMUNICATIONS QUESTIONNAIRE

To provide his class with survey experience a college professor designed a questionnaire dealing with readership of the local daily newspaper. Following are some of the questions prepared by the professor:

1. Do you read the Gazette? Daily_____ Frequently_____
   Seldom_____ Never_____

2. Do you read any other newspapers? Yes_____ No_____
   Which ones? (1) _____ (2) _____
   How often? Daily_____ Occasionally_____ Sundays only_____

3. What part of the newspaper do you usually read first?
   Comics_____   Local news_____
   Sports_____   Front page stories_____
   Editorials_____   Advertisements_____
   Favorite columnist_____   Obituaries_____
   _____   Other_____
   What do you read next_____

4. Do you read the editorials? Daily_____ Frequently_____
   Seldom_____ Never_____

5. Are there some parts of the newspaper you never read?
   Yes_____ No_____ Which parts? (1) _____
   (2) _____ (3) _____

6. Which candidate in the current presidential campaign does your newspaper support? (Check one)
   Nixon _____   McGovern _____

188

7. Do you feel that your newspaper is giving fair news coverage to both major candidates?
Yes____ No____ Don't know____ If not, who is more favored?_____
8. Do you think the editorials deal fairly with both candidates?
Yes____ No____ Don't know____
9. Do you think the columnists deal fairly with both candidates?
Yes____ No____ Don't know____
10. Do you think both the Republican and Democratic viewpoints are presented by the editorials and columnists in your newspaper?
Yes____ No____ Don't know____ Do you approve of this?

_____

Why?_____

Questions for Discussion

1. In your opinion, which questions need rewording? Specifically, what is wrong with the questions which you think need to be reworded?
2. Rewrite the questions which the class found unacceptable.

INTERVIEWING AND PROCESSING DATA

Good interviewers are basically good listeners rather than good talkers. Interviewing requires the ability to be at ease in social situations and to be able to adapt easily to one's surroundings. Above all, interviewers must be reliable, honest, and able to work on their own. Although interviewers have to go through a preliminary training session, thereafter they work independently and hence must be trustworthy.

Professors James Mullen and Michael Bishop ("Clinical Interviewing in Public Relations Research," *Public Relations Quarterly*, Spring, 1975) consider the field work aspect of public opinion polling to be an area of real concern. They cite laziness and dishonesty as two human failings with which all organizations must do constant battle. "When just a little of either creeps into an interviewing organization," they state, "accuracy in survey research is no longer possible. Given large doses of either or both, the value of a survey is totally destroyed."

Guarding against bias or inaccuracy resulting from interviewing failures is a constant problem for polling organizations. The national ones rely on checking and supervision to weed out undesirable interviewers, but checking is difficult when interviewers are widely dispersed and work independently, as all interviewers do. Finding good supervisors is even more difficult.

Handling survey data is done chiefly through machine processing and has reached a stage that cannot be described in detail in a textbook of this nature. The major polling organizations use skilled punch card and data processing operators and machines for sorting, compiling, and storing the survey data, and this calls for a preliminary coding of responses. In small surveys this work can be done manually, but the task is a tedious one that calls for the utmost care and attention to detail in handling data and percentages.

Robinson describes the steps in preparing data for analysis:

> Translation of raw data into analyzable form requires a number of steps, some comparatively simple and others much more complex. Easiest is the straight forward tabulation of the various direct questions (age, income, and so forth) that were precoded beforehand and which require only a checkmark or a circle on the part of the interviewer. The open-ended question and the various indirect data collection techniques require more elaborate procedures. Generally these questions elicit answers that range from a few words to hundreds of words, depending upon the question and the purpose of the survey. In order to make sense out of these thousands of words, they must be analyzed and put into response categories that *reflect* the content of the answer in manageable form. This process is known as *content analysis*. Essentially, it is a technique which permits a systematic, objective, and exhaustive analysis and classification of the responses or "thought units" obtained from all of the interviewees in a given survey into response categories that sum up their replies to a certain question or series of questions. . . .

> After the raw data have been prepared for analysis (by simple tabulation or content analysis), they are generally expressed in terms of tables, which pull together all of the replies to a given question and enable the researcher to make his interpretations. . . .

----

from *Public Relations and Survey Research*, p. 97

ANALYZING, INTERPRETING, AND REPORTING DATA

If wrapping up the results of survey research were only a matter of presenting the data in tabular form, life would be relatively uncomplicated. The facts could speak for themselves. However, as Robinson warns, there is no such thing as a fact standing by itself. Raw data has to be reassembled into some form of logical order and interpreted to those for whom the survey is designed. One way to achieve such meaning is to *apply percentages* to the findings. A second is to *describe* the findings by means of adjectives and adverbs, and a third is to apply some interpretation to the findings.

Percentages are important because they widen the narrow focus of the sample figures and make them applicable to the universe. Let us say we used a sample of 100 respondents and the universe is 2,000 people. A response to a question shows that 75 out of the 100 are "very much" in favor of a particular action. Widening this finding we can say that 75 percent of the universe are "very much" in favor of the action.

Stating this same finding in descriptive words we can say that "a high proportion" or "three-quarters" or "more than seven out of ten" people favor the particular action.

Thus, by the use of percentages and descriptive words we're able to express the findings in a variety of ways and at the same time to place them in perspective. Relatively dull figures take on life through such techniques, but description and interpretation should honestly reflect the figures on which they are based. Unfortunately, managements often either expect interpretation to gloss over deficiencies or else don't want to face up to negative findings. The positive ones are always easy to handle; the negative ones can be the moment of truth for the public relations practitioner.

RESEARCH, ONLY THE BEGINNING

In concluding this chapter on research it's appropriate to cite this reminder by Professor Robinson:" . . . a research study, survey or otherwise, seldom tells the practitioner what to do." Through the use of fact-finding, trend study, and public opinion survey research, the practitioner gains valuable information for subsequent public relations programs and activities. Ways of making the most intelligent use of research findings will be explored in the chapters that follow.

MINI-EXAMPLE
REPORTING RESULTS OF AN EMPLOYEE SURVEY

To measure and evaluate employee knowledge, attitudes and opinions a large manufacturing company contracted with a professor of industrial relations to prepare a questionnaire and personally supervise the polling of employees on company time. The results were presented in a 15-page printed report which was divided into sections dealing with areas such as pay, profits, opportunity, etc., and distributed to employees. Each section contained the questions, responses in percentages, some typical comments, and an interpretation in the form of a "management comment." Following is the first section of the report dealing with pay:

> *Pay:* How do you feel your pay compares with that paid in other companies for similar type of work?
>
> Lower.................. 31%   The same.............. 52%
>   Higher.................... 16%

Employee
Comments: "Skilled experienced workers are paid too low in comparison with production workers. . . . For what we have to know, they're too low. . . . Pay isn't everything when you like the company and work. . . . I have checked with other companies and wages are higher. . . ."

Do you feel you are paid what you are worth to the company?

Much less 11%	About worth 41%
Somewhat less 43%	More than worth 2%

Employee
Comments: "If a company paid employees what they (the employees) thought they were worth, no company could stay in business today. . . . Starting wages are too low. . . . I could use some more money. . . ."

Management comment: We were most interested to see that on the vital subject of pay, more than two-thirds of you felt that you were receiving the same or higher pay than in other companies for the same work. Our policy is to try to make our pay scales higher by helping and encouraging you to operate with higher efficiency. This is the only way higher than average pay can be permanently maintained under our competitive system. We believe our pay scales as well as our efficiency are generally higher than average today, and we hope we can progressively increase them.

About half of you feel you are worth more than you are paid. That's human nature. It was once remarked that there were only two classes in society: Those who get more than they earn, and those who earn more than they get. The other fellow, naturally, is the one who gets more than he earns, while we are the folks who are earning more than we get. A certain amount of dissatisfaction on this score is healthy and necessary, for we would have no ambition if we were entirely satisfied on this point.

We have been conscientious in making periodic reviews of pay and job classifications and making adjustments wherever and whenever they seem fair. We shall continue that policy.

As the business expands, we employ more people. However, in most departments, and often in branch office, clerical and service departments, a given amount of work may be done by fewer people at higher pay — rather than by more people at lower pay. In other words, if we can find ways to increase our efficiency and productivity, we naturally open the way for advancement and higher pay.

Questions for Discussion

1. What is your opinion of the wording of the two questions about pay? If you were to change them, how would you reword them?

2. What is your opinion about the "employee comments" cited at the end of each set of results?

3. What is your opinion about the "management comment?" Discuss in terms of content, tone, length, and wording.

4. If you were to change the "management comment," how would you change it?

QUESTIONS AND PROBLEMS FOR DISCUSSION

1. How would you distinguish between scientific and nonscientific research? Would you consider public relations research to be scientific or nonscientific?
2. What is meant by the statement that "public relations in action is circular in motion?"
3. Why does the author place research at the center core in comparing the public relations process to a wheel?
4. Explain some major purposes served by public relations research.
5. What is meant by the statement that "research is . . . not merely of value because of its substantive aid, but also because of the manner in which it builds and sustains status?"
6. Name the three basic research techniques used in public relations for obtaining reliable knowledge, and briefly explain the nature of each.
7. Cite what you consider to be two current fads. Explain what public relations implications they may have for specific organizations. Why do you think they may or may not become trends and/or fixtures in American society?
8. Cite two trends which, in your judgment, will have serious implications for your college or university, and explain the nature of these implications or consequences as you see them.
9. Cite and explain some specific examples of current American life styles, manners, dress, and customs which, in your opinion, have been molded by current motion pictures and/or television.
10. What seven basic steps are the minimum ones involved in public opinion surveying?
11. Why may it be necessary at times to use indirect rather than direct methods to ascertain management's reasons for approving a public opinion survey? If circumlocution seems called for, specifically how would you go about ascertaining management's reasons?
12. List and explain some valid goals of public opinion surveying for public relations purposes.
13. What are some of the problems which arise in identifying the population of a public opinion survey?
14. Explain the major advantages and disadvantages of depth interviewing.
15. Under what circumstances would one prefer to conduct a mail and/or telephone rather than a personal interview public opinion survey?
16. What is meant by a random/probability sample, and what steps need to be taken in drawing one?
17. What is meant by the statement that "the Gallup Poll estimated margin of error at the 95-confidence level is three percentage points for a sample of 1500?"
18. What are the differences among dichotomous, multiple choice, and open end questions? What are the advantages and disadvantages of each?
19. Explain some major guidelines for wording questions, and draw up some survey questions to illustrate each guideline.
20. Why should survey data be expressed in percentages?

21. Beginning in 1959, the Television Information Office has commissioned the Roper Organization to design and conduct a survey of national public opinion towards television and other mass media. The first question in all the surveys was worded as follows:

> First, I'd like to ask you where you usually get most of your news about what's going on in the world today — from the newspapers or radio or television or magazines or talking to people or where?

Do you think the wording of the question is fair to all media or do you think it is worded in such a way as to result in responses favorable to one or more media? Explain your conclusions.

PLANNING AND PROGRAMMING

Following his sound defeat in a Republican gubernatorial primary in South Carolina, General William C. Westmoreland (Ret.) told his supporters:

> "I was an inept candidate. I'm used to a structured organization and this civilian process is so doggone nebulous . . ."

The former army chief of staff could have been talking about public relations planning and programming: much of it is really "so doggone nebulous" one might well eschew plans and programs and rely on experience and instincts (as many practitioners often do and with resultant success).

In actual practice — just as in the military — the seasoned practitioner uses both planning and instinct/experience in carrying out public relations programming. Of necessity the most detailed planning preceded the allied invasion of Normandy in World War II, but once the troops landed improvisation took over. In similar manner, the public relations practitioner can draw up the most detailed plan but improvisation takes over simply because so many ingredients necessary for successful completion of the planned program are *out of the control of the planner*. Most public relations projects involve a combination of events, people, and media, and though the practitioner has control over his own events and his own people, he certainly has no control over other events which affect his project; no control over most of the people affected by his project; and certainly no control over the mass media. Therefore, through long experience the seasoned practitioner develops a program which starts with a plan but which recognizes the inevitability of the unplanned taking place.

David Finn of Ruder & Finn notes there are two schools of thought about public relations programming:

1. *The inspirational school* which operates on the assumption that sound programming is at best a matter of keen intuition and that the practitioner is most effective when he is alert to problems that arise from day to day.

2. *The planned school* which operates on the assumption that working on the basis of a carefully chartered program is the only way to be businesslike and to enable management to know clearly what the practitioner is doing at all times.

Recognizing there is merit to both approaches, Finn feels the solution is found in a *balanced* program.

"The key to balanced service," he says, "may be program development not as a schedule of activity to be followed but rather as a thoughtful document setting forth the major direction which public relations effort should take." (*Public Relations and Management*, Reinhold Publishing Co.)

Finn is undoubtedly correct when he contends that programming involves part planning and part inspiration. The experienced chef follows a set routine in preparing a souffle but uses instinct and judgment in deciding the exact moment to take it out of the oven. The experienced practitioner follows certain routines in carrying out public relations activities but also uses instinct and judgment in deciding when the activities are half-baked or well done and in dealing with day-to-day problems that require creative thinking. Whether baking a souffle or carrying out public relations activities, one is advised to start with a plan. Three of the major advantages of public relations planning are as follows:

1. *The thinking that goes into planning helps clarify the problem(s)*. As has been emphasized several times in this book, public relations practitioners are problem-solvers, but the problems they deal with generally do not come in convenient, prepackaged shapes. Public relations problems are most often untidy and amorphous and must be clarified long before the attempt is made to solve them. The thinking that goes into planning helps induce such clarification.

2. *The plan provides a blueprint and a working schedule*. Public relations problems are more often complex rather than simple. The more complex the problem, the more the need for an operational blueprint to enable activities to proceed in an orderly and predetermined fashion. Plans will often be subjected to sudden changes, but the blueprint and working schedule serve to provide *direction* and guidance.

3. *The creation and approval of a plan prevents misunderstandings*. Public relations is such a relatively new field and management tool that there is need to ensure understanding of its essential nature and thrust. In almost all but the very smallest organizations, most plans involve rather large groups and require the cooperation and understanding of other departments. As a "support" function, public relatons itself needs internal support. Further, when approved, the plan provides the practitioner with needed authority and serves as a "document of record."

Counterbalancing the advantages of planning are some common pitfalls, and Finn cities the following three:

OVER-PROGRAMMING

Public relations people, like advertising men, often are guilty of "running it up the flagpole," which is a euphemistic way of suggesting as many ideas and projects as one can conceive to see if they'll be "saluted." The trouble with saluting is that it can turn into a mindless exercise, and the trouble with over-programming is that the plan will contain too many projects to be carried out successfully. Having projects which do not meet basic objectives is as mindless and unproductive as over-saluting.

UNDUE PROGRAM RIGIDITY

When taking a long trip it's helpful to have a detailed road map, but when you come to a detour which is not on the map it's better to obey the dictates of the detour and not the road map. When the unexpected happens — as often happens in public relations activity — it's wise to discard the plan and take care of the unexpected.

FAILURE TO PAY ATTENTION TO THE APPROVED PLAN

Because detours do show up from time to time does not mean that all road maps are obsolete. Following a planned public relations program is often as difficult as driving a car with three back seat drivers shouting "turn right," "turn left," "go back to that last crossroad." There are many back seat public relations "experts" in every organization, and the practitioner has to have sufficient faith in his own ability and judgment to disregard well-intentioned, but unwise advice from the back seat drivers.

Programming is one of the two major ways in which public relations people justify their existence, the other being the counseling function. In turn, there are basically two major types of programming: (1) daily, on-going activities carried on from year to year, and (2) special, planned projects, events, and activities meshed into a blueprint for action.

DAILY, ON-GOING ACTIVITIES CARRIED ON FROM YEAR TO YEAR

In many organizations the public relations function has become so routinized it seems to exist like the gyroscope spinning in its own orbit impervious to outside forces. This is particularly evident in those organizations where public relations is handled by one or two professionals who provide public relations advice (when asked) and also produce public relations "hardware." The latter could take the form of news releases, feature stories, some internal publications, and brochures. As the organization grows in size, or as new public relations activities are called for, additions are made to the public relations staff to handle them and in time these new activities become routinized and are carried on from year to year.

There seems to be little planning and programming in the above situation, but this does not mean the public relations function is being handled poorly. So long as the staff's activities are geared to meet specific public relations objectives and goals, the fact that formal planning and programming hasn't taken place does not automatically imply a failure on the part of the public relations staff.

Furthermore, even in large organizations where there is formal planning and programming there are always certain public relations tasks and activities which are so obviously necessary there is no need to plan for them. At some point in time someone responsible for the function had to make a decision to carry out the activity and that decision became part of the regular program of the department.

The important point about programming in this type of arrangement is that it consists chiefly of daily, on-going activities carried on from year to year, and these involve both counseling and public relations "hardware" such as releases, internal publications, etc.

SPECIAL, PLANNED PROJECTS, EVENTS, AND ACTIVITIES MESHED INTO A BLUEPRINT FOR ACTION

This second major type of public relations programming is that referred to by David Finn when he speaks of "balanced service," and is the kind of programming most often developed and followed by counseling firms.

In essence, such programming involves a series of steps or procedures. These are not institutionalized to the extent that every counseling firm always proceeds from Step A to B to C, etc., but the approach is common enough to provide a blueprint for programming. The pattern provides a logical means of handling public relations problems via the following steps:

1. Making a preliminary study
2. Defining the problems
3. Establishing objectives and goals
4. Defining the audience
5. Establishing a theme
6. Initiating action and activities: projects, tactics and timing
7. Communicating and evaluating

MAKING A PRELIMINARY STUDY

Folklore has it that the public relations practitioner is a magic medicine person with secret potions to cure organizational ills. Actual practice is far removed from this stereotyped impression. The experienced practitioner knows that it's impossible to carry out an effective public relations program without having intimate knowledge of the organization he or she represents.

When a counseling firm is retained, almost inevitably the *first action taken does not involve public relations per se*, but research concerning the organization, its environment, its policies, its people, publics, problems, and reputation. How does the counselor go about conducting such research? Very much like a veteran reporter assigned to cover an involved story. Interviews are held with key personnel within the organization and with outsiders who are most likely to have knowledge about the organization. If the client is a business or industry, then important sources of information are editors of business, trade, and financial publications; key suppliers, dealers, and customers; trade association executives; and any others who are most likely to be knowledgeable about the client. Valuable sources of print material — such as annual reports, brochures, publicity files, etc. — are also consulted. Like the investigative reporter, the counselor probes to find weaknesses and strengths, to become intimately aware of almost every conceivable facet of the client organization. The end result of the investigative reporter's probing will be an article or series of articles; the end result of the counseling firm's probing will be a written report which forms the foundation for subsequent public relations activities.

Reading the above paragraph has probably taken about a minute or two, but compiling data for a preliminary study and writing a background report can take a month to six weeks. It takes time and skill to interview key personnel and editors, conduct library research, gather facts and data about an organization's history, facilities, products, people, et cetera. Into the preliminary study goes much hard, unglamorous but extremely valuable work which, as one practitioner declares, serves three functions: (1) *it provides a logical foundation for the program*; (2) *it enables the account executive to secure a solid grounding in the client organization*; and (3) *it demonstrates to the client that the counseling firm has the proper background and experience to interpret the client to its publics*. From a substantive point of view the first function served by the preliminary study — that is, providing a logical foundation for the program — is most important. Without a logical foundation based on data and facts about the organization, a public relations program would be like a house built on hot air — supportable for a limited amount of time only.

Thus, if the preliminary study or background report is to be solid enough to support the superstructure of the public relations program, it has to be built with this superstructure constantly in mind. No two studies will, or should, be exactly alike, but at the minimum they should encompass the following elements:

1. *Facts and data about the organization* as they relate to the organization's public relationships. For example, if the organization is a business, what are its products, gross sales and net profits; employee force; customers; rank and place in its industry; dealers; suppliers; past history; future possibilities?

2. *Reputation and standing.* What do others — especially those in a position to know — think about the organization? Is it held in generally good or ill repute and why?

3. *Personnel.* What kind of management does the organization have? Who are the key people? What do they think about public relations and what is their level of sophistication about the public relations function? What's the relationship between management and its employee force?

4. *Past and present public relations practices.* What has the organization done in the past about public relations and what is it now doing? What changes ought to be made, and what seems to be the climate for acceptance of proposed changes? What should be retained and/or modified?

5. *Weaknesses.* What, if any, activities or policies of the organization are causing unfavorable opinions about the organization? Will the organization be receptive to suggested changes or modifications of these activities and policies?

6. *Strengths.* What, if any, activities or policies of the organization are causing favorable opinions about the organization, and has the organization sufficiently capitalized on these? Are there any unique or unusual activities or policies which can be emphasized in future public relations programming?

7. *Opportunities.* Is there anything about the present climate or the situation of the organization which provides opportunities for creative use of public relations?

8. *Obstacles.* Is there anything about the present climate or situation of the organization — including personnel and "politics" — which would cause obstacles to public relations programming?

9. *Conclusions and judgments.* Is the background report factually correct, will it sustain careful scrutiny and criticism, and does it convey the proper analytical and professional tone?

Each of the above elements is amplified by questions for a specific reason: no public relations textbook can provide instant answers to public relations problems. However, in going through the process of asking proper questions of a situation the practitioner finds that complex problems narrow down. The answers to the right kind of questions suggest a focus for future public relations programming, but before any programming can begin the questions have to be posed and answered.

MINI-EXERCISE
CONDUCTING A PRELIMINARY STUDY OR BACKGROUND REPORT

The class is to assume that its members work for a public relations counseling firm. At this particular point in time a most unlikely but welcome state of affairs has taken place: suddenly, new accounts have retained the firm as public relations counsel. There is an immediate need to conduct a preliminary study or background report for each of the new accounts, and each of these has to be completed four weeks from today. Therefore, to carry out this assignment your instructor — who is president of the firm — has divided the class into teams, each team to be responsible for doing a preliminary study or background report for one of the following new accounts.

(One member of each team will be designated as the group leader and he or she will divide the study work among the team members and will write the final report. As an addendum to the report, the group leader will clearly indicate who was responsible for specific sections of the report.)

Client A: The inter-fraternity and/or inter-sorority council on your campus is concerned about its (or their) public relations problems and has retained your firm to help solve them. Conduct a preliminary study and present a background report for this new client.

Client B: The public relations department of your college has been so busy handling such daily routines as writing news releases, feature stories, etc., it has never had time to develop a public relations program. Conduct a preliminary study and present a background report for this new client.

Client C: The United Way organization in your community — or in the nearest community which has a United Way organization — is concerned about its public relations problems and has retained your firm to help solve them. Conduct a preliminary study and present a background report for this new client.

Client D: The Boy Scout organization in your community — or in the nearest community which has a Boy Scout organization — is concerned about its public relations problems and has retained your firm to help solve them. Conduct a preliminary study and present a background report for this new client.

Client E: This client is the Girl Scout organization in your community (or in the nearest community which has a Girl Scout organization.) Your assignment for said organization is the same as for client D.

Other Clients: These may be assigned by your instructor to fit any special circumstances existing in the area of your institution.

DEFINING THE PROBLEMS

Practically every organization of size has public relations problems, and these range in scope and intensity from those which can be safely ignored to those which demand immediate attention lest they get out of control. The preliminary study, like a medical check-up, will uncover many problems. Many of them can either be cured by simple treatment or can be dismissed as being relatively inconsequential. Others will need action taken to check their development, and finally a number of them will be so deep-seated and dangerous as to call for surgery.

The skilled practitioner, like the skilled internist, is able to make *distinctions* about problems. Public relations problems come in all sizes and shapes. Some are internal and some are external; some are temporary and some are permanent; some are on the surface and some are deep-rooted. Recognizing, dissecting, and handling them calls for skills born out of years of experience.

"One of the greatest shortcomings of public relations programs, and of the planners who write them, is *failure* to understand the problem," states H. Zane Robbins, vice president and general manager of Burson-Marsteller. "Most public relations men and women can tell you in 25 words or less: 'The company's basic problem is . . .' But that doesn't mean they really understand the broad implications of that problem. There's a wide gap between enunciating a problem and comprehending it."

The gap that Robbins cites can be bridged by applying a four-fold approach to problems: (a) ask the right questions, (b) recognize that problem identification is largely a result of assumptions, (c) get rid of nonessentials, and (d) establish an order of priorities.

Ask the Right Questions

As in the preliminary study stage of programming, it is essential to ask the right questions about a situation. Asking the right questions doesn't necessarily mean that the right answers will be immediately forthcoming, but start with questions to come up with answers. Fools rush in with answers; wise men ask questions. Note the emphasis which the late Earl Newsom put on questions in a talk he gave at the New School for Social Research:

> (There) is an implication that we are the white-haired boys who have easy answers to everything and are responsible for all the good deeds of our clients. That isn't true, of course. The facts are much less dramatic and, I am afraid, not nearly so complimentary. This kind of thing is much nearer the truth: somebody in some department of management finds himself with a problem — or a potential problem — that cuts across the interests of large groups of people. He calls us up and says, "We would like to talk to you about this." He might also quite properly bring in the head of the company's public relations department or the officers of other departments that might also be involved. So we sit down and consider the situation. It might be, for example, a threatened strike. Primarily, of course, this is a problem of industrial relations. But it becomes a problem of public relations because not only are the employees an important part of the company's public, but in moments of tension of this kind the whole situation is apt to become a public matter.
>
> I hope you don't get the notion that we hurry into such a meeting and say, "Well, what you should do is this." Such problems are complicated and many things have to be considered besides what the public will think. How will actions that the company might take affect the industry as a whole? How do they relate to national policies as set in Washington? What do polls show about trends of public thought? What do economists have to say about the future? What is the wise thing to do about this? In those discussions our voice is no louder than our judgment, or the opinion of our client on how good we are in matters we are supposed to be good about. . . .
>
> . . . Or another kind of thing. Somebody in Washington on the floor of the House may get up and say something that is

untrue or misleading about a client corporation. A first question is, "How important is this?" Who made the statement? Why did he make it? Should we do something about it? So we're apt to get together and talk about it and present our ideas. Perhaps the president of the corporation should telephone or telegraph the Congress and ask to be heard. If so, facts have to be gotten together and help given in assembling them.

Those are problems that are apt to come up. You can't do business without stepping on the toes of people and the problem is to deal with it as best you can. . . .

Newsom's questions, it should be noted, aim to broaden one's view to extend beyond the seemingly narrow scope of the problem. Perceptive questions expose the ramifications which exist within most public relations problems and enable the practitioner to get to the real crux of a situation. Asking the right questions, in short, is where one starts to define the problem(s).

Recognize That Problem Identification is Largely a Result of Assumptions

In developing a conceptual framework to analyze the public relations function, Professor Edward J. Robinson stated that one of the key factors in isolating or identifying problems is the assumptions that the practitioner brings to the problem-solving situation (*Communication and Public Relations*, Charles E. Merrill Books). He points out that in dealing with a problem all of us make certain assumptions, even though we may not be consciously aware of doing so. These may be true or untrue, but the important thing is that *assumptions influence the way we look at the problem and then attempt to solve it*. If our assumptions are correct this can help clarify the problem, but if they are incorrect they can lead us down many a wrong path. Robinson therefore suggests that the practitioner ask himself continually:

What are my assumptions?

What have I assumed to be true (or false) in this particular situation?

What implicit assumptions have I made about the *human* element — i.e., What convenient generalization have I made about human behaviour?

The relationship that assumptions have to problem viewing is similar to the relationship that a cataract has to sight. We "see" because light rays move freely through the lens of the eye to reach the retina:

Light rays → lens → retina = clear vision

However, when the normally transparent lens of the human eye becomes clouded by a cataract, clarity of vision is lost because the rays are blocked from moving through the lens to the retina:

Light rays → cataract = loss of vision

Substitute "assumptions" for the lens of the eye. If one's assumptions are correct, then the light rays thrown on the problem will move freely through the lens of correct assumptions of the retina of possible answers to the problem:

Light rays → lens of correct assumptions → retina
= clear perceptions of the problem

However, if one's assumptions are incorrect, then the light rays thrown on the problem will be blocked by the lens of incorrect assumptions and will result in opaque perceptions of the problem:

Light rays → lens of incorrect assumptions =
cloudy perceptions of the problem

If we are to view problems with clear vision we must be vigilant about the assumptions we bring to problem-solving situations. In today's fast-moving world, it is particularly important that our assumptions about people and society are in tune with the times; in trying to cope with problems, attempts based on outdated and false assumptions are almost certain to flounder.

Eliminate Nonessentials

Problems, like grapes, tend to come in clusters and one of the difficult tasks of the practitioner is to eliminate from the custer of problems what the late Verne Burnett called "nonessentials." In his view handling public relations problems calls for a process of elimination.

> For instance, a trade group asked a public relations firm to get the general public conscious of twelve facts about an industry. All of these facts seemed important to the trade group. There was an ancient law suit, but the public would have no interest in that. There had been some involved labor negotiations several years ago. Again the public wouldn't bother to learn the details. One by one the twelve points were whittled down until there were three to which the public might pay attention. Finally the three, which were closely related, were condensed into one. Thus it was possible for the public relations worker to concentrate all efforts on explaining a single idea, with considerable success.
>
> (From a talk by Verne Burnett given to students at the New School For Social Research)

Burnett's advice to whittle down problems is echoed by most veteran public relations practitioners. They realize that the public finds it difficult, or doesn't have the interest, to grasp a mass of information too extensive or complex. Given a set of problems, the practitioner strips away the relatively unimportant ones and by a process of elimination tries to focus on those that are primary and essential. The process is simple when the major problem is obvious, but requires sound, objective

judgment when the major problem is obscured by a host of other problems. Since almost every public relations problem situation is unique,
the process of defining the key factor by stripping away nonessentials is
always a challenge, but one that must be met before further action is
taken.

Establish an Order of Priorities

Whether done by design or accidentally, the act of defining the problem will culminate in establishing an order of problem priorities, which
will lead in turn to a similar order of solution priorities.

The usual way of establishing priorities is to decide which problems
are immediate and which are long-range. Put another way, which problems should be handled today and which can be taken care of over a
period of months or years? Another method is to rank problems in order
of importance, though the end result is usually the same because of the
general assumption that immediate problems must be most important
because they must be taken care of at once while long-range problems
aren't as important because their handling can be delayed.

Such an assumption — as with many assumptions examined superfi-
cially — has to be scrutinized carefully. While it is true that practitioners tend to concentrate on immediate problems — chiefly because
practitioners can't very well ignore their existence — these are not necessarily the most important problems facing an organization. In fact, one
of the fatal flaws of many public relations programs is that they tend to
be "fire-fighting" efforts aimed at dousing the flames caused by immediate problems. Because the practitioner is so busy trying to solve immediate problems, long-range problems are ignored even though they may be
more important.

The sensible way of insuring that proper attention will be given to all
problems is to establish a realistic order of problem priorities and put it
in writing. If it's possible to rank problems, then the ranking ought to be
in terms of most important, next most important, and so on down the
line to those considered least important. If an immediate problem turns
out to be the most important problem then the practitioner has a perfect
match. However, if an immediate problem is not the most important one
but still has to be handled immediately, the practitioner must remember
that the most important problem still exists and must be treated at some
time. The practitioner may still handle the immediate problem at the
moment it faces him, but he shouldn't put the most important problem
on the back burner indefinitely.

MINI-CASE
A PROFESSIONAL SOCIETY LISTS ITS PROBLEMS

In a report to its members, the public relations chairman of a state
pharmaceutical society prefaced his proposed public relations plan
with the following statement:

"We know that the professional and economic well-being of the
pharmacist today is in serious danger.

"Our status in the eyes of the public is declining and our ability to earn profits is being eroded as results of a strong combination of negative forces . . .

Unfavorable legislation
Discount competition
Bad press
Attacks by opinion leaders
Public dissatisfaction

"These forces are gaining speed and intensity every day because of:

Lack of information about the pharmacist and the pharmacy and their role in the community

Lack of understanding by outside publics about the economics of our profession

Consumerism

Society's drug orientation

Poor practices on the part of some fellow pharmacists

Pharmaceutical industry marketing practices

Inertia on the part of our professional organizations and members

Health care trends

Medical ignorance of the general public

Political necessitites and opportunism."

Class assignment:

You are to assume that the above-mentioned analysis is grounded in fact and by documentation.

Your assignment is to rank the ten listed problems in terms of (a) their importance to the pharmaceutical society, and (b) those which can or should be handled immediately and those which can be handled over a longer period of time.

Support your rankings in a memorandum explaining the reasons for your rank listings.

ESTABLISHING OBJECTIVES AND GOALS

The act of establishing public relations objectives and goals is a logical follow-up to the problem-definition stage of programming because of the close affinity between problems and objectives. If, for example, it has been decided that an immediate major problem facing a publicly financed organization is virtual ignorance about the organization among financial analysts, then an obvious immediate public relations objective and goal would be to inform these analysts so they will recommend its stock as a good buy.

The example is illustrative of several important criteria of sound public relations objectives and goals: (a) they should be directly related to the basic objectives of the organization, (b) they should be specific rather than general, and (c) they should be set forth in order of importance and time.

Public Relations Objectives Should be Related to the Basic Objectives of the Organization

There is no utility value to public relations objectives with little relationship to the basic objectives of the organization they supposedly serve. It is, at times, very tempting to set forth a public relations goal that can be achieved through some dramatic and imaginative program activity or event, but if the goal has little relationship to the basic goals of the organization the result will be a meaningless waste of time, money, and manpower. There's little point in trying to increase applications to a prestigious law school when that school already has so many applications it can only accept 10 percent of those who apply. It makes little sense to aim your public relations efforts at establishing among citizens in Plant Community A that your firm's plant there is a strong, stable one if management has already decided to close the plant a year from now. If a public relations program is to keep in step with reality, the objectives of that program and the objectives of the organization must march to the same tune.

The previous paragraph seems to imply that it's the responsibility of public relations to keep in step with the organization of which it's a part. There are times, however, when the preliminary study and setting forth of problems show that the policies and actions of an organization, not public relations, are clearly out of step with public opinion, the public interest, and commonly accepted standards of behaviour. Knowing this to be so, does the practitioner continue to march along with his plans and programs or does he come to a parade rest?

Those who have read the earlier chapters in this book ought to know the answer to that last question. If an organization's basic policies and actions are clearly counter to the public interest and to commonly accepted standards of behaviour, it's the responsibility of the practitioner to use his influence to modify or have such policies and actions changed. In the short run it is conceivable — and it has happened — that clever use of techniques might camouflage shoddy organizational policies and practices, but in the long run they will be shown up for what they are. The time to align organizational and public relations policies, actions, and objectives with the public interest and in accordance with commonly acceptable bounds of behaviour is before, not after programming has begun.

Public Relations Objectives Should be Specific Rather Than General

Though public relations, as a general concept, aims to bring about the end result of "goodwill, understanding and acceptance," programming objectives must be stated in more specific terms if they are to be meaningful and acceptable to management. Particularly in business and industry, but also in other areas of human endeavor and activity, managements expect, demand, and receive specific inputs and goals from the various main functional areas of organizations. These are then measured against end results. The sales department doesn't project a general increase in sales, but rather a 2 percent or 5 percent or 10 percent increase. The production department doesn't project a general increase in production, but rather a 2 percent or 5 percent or 10 percent increase. The admissions director of a college doesn't project a general increase in the freshman class, but a 2 percent, 5 percent or 10 percent increase. In each instance the responsible executive is held to account if end results fail to measure up to forecasts. Public relations, though involved with factors more difficult to measure than the production and sale of products and the admission of students, should expect to be held to thorough measurements and management expectations.

Unfortunately, many public relations objectives and goals are fuzzy in conception and much too general in nature. Note, for example, the following "seven objectives of a representative gas utility," and decide which are specific and which are general:

1. To establish the company as a valuable citizen
2. To make all personnel more PR-minded
3. To offset competition
4. To cultivate and maintain good will of customers, editors and key citizens
5. To devise new ways of interpreting modern gas service to the public
6. To strengthen private management of utilities
7. To educate the public on need for adequate utility earnings

John F. Budd, Jr. of Carl Byoir and Associates cites a different kind of objectives when he discusses public relations objectives for Republic Aviation:

A 31-page program analysis and recommendations for Republic Aviation opened with five specific public relations objectives. One, "to report and reiterate the technological expansion and new capabilities of the company." Two, "to emphasize the financial soundness of the company." Three, "to find ways to dramatize the mission of the F-105." Four, "to improve impressions of corporate management and to introduce the new sales and engineering heads." Five, "to restore community confidence in the company's future."

from *An Executive's Primer On Public Relations*, Chilton Book Co.

H. Zane Robbins of Burson-Marsteller contends that objectives should not only be specific, but measurable as well. Although measurement of public relations activities and results is both difficult and expensive, Robbins feels that management is justified in expecting and demanding specificity and measurement of public relations activities. He makes his case as follows:

Here are some fairly typical public relations objectives:

> To enhance the image of the company.
> To win greater acceptance for our boll weevil extractor.
> To attract more college graduates to our training program.
> To win the favor of the professional financial community.

You can guess the sort of projects that are dreamed up to go along with goals of that type. Usually they are as ill-conceived, as fuzzy, and as poorly executed as the goals themselves.

Nowhere can good, effective opinion research be more useful than in planning the public relations program. If you're going to "enhance the image of the company" or "win greater acceptance for the boll weevil extractor" or do anything else, you must first know your starting point.

What percentage of your audience — which also must be clearly and specifically defined — has a favorable impression of the company right now? Of those who don't like the company, what influences their attitudes? What is the size of the market for boll weevil extractors? What percentage of this market do you now have? Why have you been unable to sell your product in some areas?

Research can answer those questions. Research can show you not only how your company ranks in an absolute sense, it also can show you how you rank in a relative sense — compared to similar companies in your field. Research can tell you what businessmen like or dislike about your company. Research can tell you why customers buy or don't buy your product. And research can tell you where you stand today — in numerical terms — in any market or in the opinion of any audience.

If you have that sort of benchmark, you can rewrite your objectives in a meaningful way. Instead of citing a meaningless goal such as "to enhance the image of the company," you might state it this way:

> To improve attitudes toward our company among business managers, cotton farmers and members of the professional financial community. Our objective is to increase favorable response from 12 to 25 percent in the first category, from 15 to 25 percent in the second category and from 9 to 30 percent in the third category over the next two years.

Now that is a meaningful objective. It's specific. Management can understand it. And your success in attaining those goals can be measured simply and inexpensively by followup research.

> from remarks made at a Public Relations
> Society of America seminar

Both Budd and Robbins, as noted by their remarks, agree on the need to stress specific objectives, and in Robbins' view these objectives should be aligned with numerical, percentage parameters. Most practitioners do not "lay it on the line" as directly as does Robbins, but few would argue the wisdom of being specific rather than general.

Public Relations Objectives Should be Set Forth in Order of Importance and Time.

As with problems, public relations objectives and goals should be set forth in order of their importance and the time period within which they are expected to be reached. In effect, this means setting priorities for objectives and goals.

Some objectives are so clearly important and immediate there is no question about the need to meet them at once. Others, while important, can await their solution over a longer period of time. When Whitaker and Baxter, for example, took on the assignment of handling The American Medical Association account two decades ago they defined their objectives in this manner:

The first objective was an uncompromising immediacy: to stop the Compulsory Health Insurance legislation then pending (in Congress).

The second objective, longer-range and more constructive, was to establish firm proof with the majority of the people that the American medical system not only is the finest in the world's history, but that it can meet the medical needs of the people by voluntary means and without Government control.

Depending on one's views, one might argue the merits of the issue, but no one can argue about the specific nature of the campaign's objectives. They were direct, to the point, and included both short and long-range goals. In effect, they provided the client (or management) with a timetable and a way to judge whether the program was proceding according to schedule.

Too rigid a timetable can be dangerous, however, and it's for this reason that practitioners provide for periodic review of objectives, plans, and programming. Unless one provides for flexibility in setting forth objectives and programs there will be too many instances of missed opportunities and programs outdated by unforeseen events. By all means be specific, work according to a timetable, but don't be inflexible.

DEFINING THE AUDIENCE

All public relations programs are aimed at some group or groups in our society, and therefore the audience should be precisely defined and delineated *before* a program is charted and put into effect. Usually this process is a matter of simple, logical deduction. As the practitioner goes through the process of defining an organization's essential public relations problems and objectives, the audience for the ensuing public relations programming should come into focus. Problems arise because of relationships with *people*; objectives deal with goals concerning *people*; to meet these objectives one must first zero in on the *people* to be reached.

Charting the audience can be achieved in a variety of ways. Audiences can be defined as *primary, secondary* and *tertiary*, and obviously such a delineating implies that the main effort of the program will be directed first at the primary audience and later at the secondary and tertiary audiences. Or, the audience can be divided into *internal* and *external* groups with specific programming aimed at each or both groups. Audiences are often divided into *local, regional*, and *national* groupings and again subsequent programming can be charted for each group.

As a simple example, let us assume that the Boy Scouts of America are having difficulty attracting inner city youngsters to scouting. The problem results from the fact that inner city youngsters of scouting age feel that scouting has little relationship to their lives. The objective of the public relations program is to demonstrate that modern-day scouting bears a close and direct relationship to the lives of inner city youngsters. Logical deduction tells us that a public relations program designed to attract inner city youngsters to scouting ought to be directed specifically at inner city youngsters and not at youngsters living on farms.

However, research revals that inner city youngsters have such a deep-seated suspicion of the so-called Establishment they reject the usual type of appeals stemming from the Scouting Establishment. Further research reveals that well known professional athletes are looked at with awe and respect by inner city youngsters of scouting age. These athletes might thus become the primary audience and the conduit for a public relations program aimed at attracting inner city youngsters to scouting.

Thus, though audience-projection is often a matter of simple logical deduction, circumstances may indicate that a straight line may not be the most effective way of moving from Point A to Point B. Consider, for example, the previously cited program that Whitaker and Baxter carried out for the American Medical Association. The objective, as noted, was to head off pending national health insurance legislation. Such legislation is the province of Congress, and one might well conclude therefore that the program Whitaker and Baxter devised for the AMA would have the Congress as its primary audience. Whitaker and Baxter, however, aimed their campaign not at Congress but at the general public because they felt that Congress had to be shown that the American public was against the pending legislation. In a two-week period in October the issue was taken to the public in a $1,000,000 advertising campaign which included every daily and weekly newspaper, the principal national magazines and the electronic media in the country. Thus, to get from Point A (the AMA) to Point B (the Congress) the program was routed through Point C (the general public).

No matter what system is used in focusing on the audience(s), certain questions have to be posed:

- Who are we trying to reach?
- Which publics are most important?

- Where are they?
- Who are their opinion leaders?
- What do they read, listen to and view?

When you've found the answers to the above questions you're really just out of the starting gate in the race to reach target publics. If you hope to finish in the running you now have to uncover key facts about each group on your target list, and this means listing everything you know about them or can ascertain through research. You'll need to know what kind of people they are, their relationship to your organization, what's on their minds, why they should or could be interested in your program. In effect, what you have to do is to pose some further pertinent questions about each target audience and then, through research, find the answers.

As an example, assume that you hope to reach students of marketing by producing a thirty-minute film about your company's product and have it shown by marketing teachers in their college courses. Here are some pertinent questions you might ask:

1. Do marketing teachers use films of this nature?
2. Why should a marketing teacher be interested in your film?
3. Would the film interest students of marketing?
4. Would the film be a teaching aid?
5. In what specific marketing course might the film be used?
6. Is there anything in the film which would make marketing teachers reject its use?
7. What's the best way to bring the film to the attention of marketing teachers?

Other questions undoubtedly could be asked, but the object of any list of questions is to pinpoint as exactly as possible the essential characteristics of target audiences. Doing so requires research, some careful thought, and an understanding of people and the groupings into which they divide themselves in today's society.

MINI-CASE
TARGETING THE AUDIENCE FOR COLLEGE AND HOSPITAL LINENS OF AMERICA

Spotless Laundries, a hitherto privately owned commercial laundry in Wilmington, Delaware, whose chief customers are restaurants, colleges, and hospitals in the state of Delaware, was sold one year ago to a three-member group in their early thirties.

Determined to extend the operations of the firm, the new owners went "public" in order to raise more capital and for the past six months the stock has been traded on the American Stock Exchange. With the modest amount of new capital which has been accrued, the new owners built a new plant in Bethesda, Maryland, and the two plants in Wilmington and Bethesda now service customers in the two states and in the District of Columbia.

Traditionally, the commercial laundry field has consisted mainly of firms very similar to Spotless in that their business is mostly local, and in some cases regional, and serve customers within one day's driving range of the firm's trucks. To break this pattern and with the eventual goal of becoming a truly national firm, the new owners of Spotless have aimed their efforts at capturing an increasingly larger and larger share of the lucrative college and hospital linen fields. The former is served chiefly by local commercial laundries and the latter by local commercial laundries and by laundries owned and operated by the hospitals themselves.

The new owners have set up two wholly-owned subsidiaries of Spotless — College Linens of America, Inc., and Hospital Linens of America, Inc. — and are now planning to extend their operations. As the necessary finances become available, the owners hope first to build new plants anywhere in the Northeast where there is a reasonable certitude that colleges and hospitals will make use of their services, and then to move out into other geographic areas of the country. The major selling tool of both subsidiaries is a "total systems approach" which CLA and HLA have developed and which is demonstrably able to provide interested colleges and hospitals with faster, more dependable and cheaper service than they can secure from either their own facilities or from local commercial laundries.

Your assignment at this point in time is to set forth the major target publics for a public relations program aimed at gaining the objectives cited above. You are to write a memorandum to Mrs. Melissa Gordon, president of Spotless, setting forth the *specific* target publics with a brief explanation citing the rationale for your selections.

(Note: Merely citing "colleges" as a target public does not suffice to meet the test of specificity)

ESTABLISHING A THEME

Public relations programs which involve a variety of projects — as most successful programs do — achieve a unity of purpose through the use of a basic theme or set of themes. In the continuum of public relations planning and programming a theme bears close relationship to musical and literary themes. In both music and literature a theme is the underlying tie which runs through an entire work and binds it together. In similar fashion, a theme is the underlying tie that runs through the various facets or projects in a public relations program and makes for a unified, consistent approach to public relations problems.

A theme is to public relations programming as thread is to the tailor. With thread the tailor fashions a suit; without it he's got so many swatches of cloth. With a theme the public relations practitioner fashions a campaign; without it he's got so many isolated projects. When Whitaker and Baxter were handling political campaigns in California, themes formed the basic core of all their campaigns. Before starting a campaign the husband-and-wife counseling team would work out a theme and a plan, and then with equal care they would work out another theme and plan. Both themes and plans were then matched against each other and a decision made as to which would be used in the forthcoming campaign. Every subsequent speech, poster, brochure, television and radio spot would then emphasize and develop the campaign's basic theme.

A theme can be set forth in a variety of ways. It may be expressed in the form of a summary statement or of a slogan, but its basic purpose remains that of providing unity to programming. Whatever its form, a theme should:

1. Make its point clearly
2. Be capable of being retained by those at whom it is directed
3. Be relevant and honest

The last point bears close analysis because of the glib way in which some themes are too often put into effect.

David Finn makes the case for relevancy and honesty in the following words:

> . . . It is not the slick job that does the trick, but the job that most genuinely reflects the way management feels about itself. Dapper Frank Lloyd Wright did not have a better public image than toussled Albert Einstein. Both won public respect and affection because they looked like what they were: people could feel that both of them were being honest with themselves. Above all, the way they looked was consistent with what they stood for, and this is the key to good graphic public relations.
>
> from *Public Relations and Management*, Reinhold Publishing Corporation.

Because catchy themes have eye and ear appeal there is often the temptation to employ themes whether they honestly reflect the organization that uses them. But on ethical, moral, and practical grounds irrelevant, dishonest, and meaningless themes should be avoided. Such themes may gain immediate approbation for the practitioner who creates them, but in the long run they serve no useful purpose, do little intrinsic good, and eventually backfire.

Today's public is too wise, jaded, and jaundiced to be taken in by superficial slogans and themes, and this conclusion is particularly true of those organizations whose products and services are sold to and used by the general public. If the product purchased by the average consumer proves to be shoddy or if the service rendered proves to be abysmal, no catchy theme or slogan is going to convince him to "put his trust" in that company's products or services. As Finn puts it: "A theme makes sense only when it is deeply felt by the people running the business. All of the company's publics then recognize that the idea or theme is genuine and not an artificial concoction of clever promoters."

MINI-PROBLEMS
SETTING FORTH SOME THEMES

1. Assume you have been given the assignment of setting forth two major themes which can be used as the basis for public relations programming for your college or university for the coming academic year.

   In a memorandum to your vice president for public relations explain the essence of the two themes you would propose for your institution. Do *not* use a slogan format, but explain the nature of your proposed themes in a paragraph for each.

   As a supplement to your memorandum, explain *why* you have proposed each theme. In short, justify your themes.

2. Themes can be discerned in most major advertising campaigns of national concerns and organizations. Some are astute, relevant, and honest, and some are not.

   Select and analyze one such major, current advertising campaign of a national concern or organization, and in a memorandum to your instructor explain the nature of the theme or themes you discern in the campaign; provide illustrative material from the campaign to demonstrate how these themes are used; and critique the use of said themes in terms of their effectiveness, relevancy, and honesty.

3. Select any organization with which you are familiar — it can be local, regional, or national; profit or nonprofit — and set forth two major themes which can be used as the basis for a projected public relations campaign for the coming year.

   In a memorandum to your instructor explain the essence of the two themes you would propose for the organization. Do *not* use a slogan format, but explain the nature of your proposed themes in a paragraph for each.

   As a supplement to your memorandum, explain *why* you have proposed each theme. In short, justify your themes.

INITIATING ACTION AND ACTIVITIES: PROJECTS, TACTICS AND TIMING

At the core of most successful public relations programs is an action and activity plan of strategy involving three major elements: projects, tactics, and timing. *Projects* provide the vehicle whereby public relations objectives and goals are reached; *tactics* involve the mechanics in carrying out planned projects; and *timing* is often the crucial difference between success and failure.

Projects come in all shapes and forms and are limited only by the imagination and ingenuity of the practitioners who plan, create, and carry them through to completion. One veteran public relations man sees projects as "the only convenient way in which an otherwise nebulous undertaking can be analyzed, organized, and controlled," and in his opinion the more projects clustered around a theme the better.

Some projects are of such a magnitude that a single project may comprise the entire public relations program. Into such a project would go all the talent, manpower, and resources that public relations can provide. Most often, however, programs are built around a variety of projects that overlap each other and act as a series of waves cresting towards a common shoreline goal. The analogy to waves is deliberate: at times practitioners initiate and carry through projects that demonstrate activity is taking place, but unless projects build towards a common public relations objective and goal, the practitioner is merely going through the process of making waves that go nowhere.

A project may be as simple as a normal press conference announcing a new product or may be as complex as an American vice president debating with a Soviet premier in a typical American dream house set up in a Moscow exhibit to demonstrate the virtues of the American way of life (and the products in that house). A project may be local in nature, such as an Open House initiated to have residents in a plant community learn first-hand about an industrial organization, or it may be national and involve a sixteen-city tour by a well-known personality to demonstrate to a wide geographical audience the virtues of a product. A program may consist of a major, one-day event — such as a Walk-a-Thon for a disease-fighting agency — or it may entail several major events and some minor ones spread out over a months-long campaign.

Projects and public relations program activities are not easily categorized because they exist in a wide variety of guises, and new ones are constantly being initiated by imaginative and creative practitioners. However, some projects and activities have gained such wide-spread acceptance their utilization by practitioners justifies their listing as major types. By no means should one consider that the following project and activity categories represent the only effective ones to be used in programming. The listing is chiefly a means of setting forth some major ways in which projects and activities have been used in public relations programming.

SOME MAJOR PROJECT AND ACTIVITY CATEGORIES

Following, in no particular order of importance, are some major ways in which projects and activities have been used in public relations programming:

SUPPORTING, DISPLAYING, AND/OR DRAMATIZING AN EXISTING EVENT, FACILITY, OR SITUATION

Virtually every organization, at one time or another, carries out activities or events that need public relations support, and in many instances the facilities of organizations are also the focal point of public relations activity. Some facilities, events and situations utilize public re-

PLANNING AND PROGRAMMING   217

lations support on a regular, recurring basis, others as the need arises.

For example, every local United Way organization in the country conducts a yearly fund-raising campaign aimed at raising sufficient funds to support the agencies belonging to the United Way. Usually of a month's duration, these campaigns inevitably commence with a kick-off dinner or event, are followed by periodic report meetings and luncheons, and culminate in a final victory dinner or event. Throughout the entire campaign period the UW's public relations department serves a key role in devising ways and means of supporting, dramatizing, and communicating the activities and events taking place during the campaign. Some typical projects include an opening day parade; a lighted thermometer placed on top of a large building to indicate fund-raising progress; a fireworks display to demonstrate the campaign has gone over the top; a costume ball to increase attendance on the final report night.

The United Way campaign as an existing event requiring public relations support is duplicated in many ways. Colleges and universities hold convocations, commencements, Parents' Days, and Alumni Days. Cities and department stores sponsor and run the Tournament of Roses Parade, the Thanksgiving Day Parade, the Peanut Queen Festival, and the Kutztown annual Pennsylvania Dutch Folk Festival. There's the annual Westinghouse Science Talent Search, the Sealy Golf Classic, and the American Legion Boys' State and Boys' Nation. Rockefeller Center has its outdoor skating rink, major resorts have outdoor ski slopes, and a number of large cities have a variety of gas-light, take-me-back-to-the-good-old-days areas. Each of these existing events, facilities, and situations are supported and dramatized by public relations projects and activities.

Even factories and plants — not usually considered prime areas for public relations programming — have been utilized to good public relations advantage because someone with imagination figured out that wineries and breweries could attract millions of visitors if tours of their facilities were spiked with sampling of the product at the end of the tour. Designing, establishing, managing, and promoting many of these tours has become partly or wholly a function of public relations departments. In some instances the facility tour has become so successful a drawing card that the sponsoring company has split it off from the brewery operation, broadened the scope of the attraction, and run the activity as a profit center. An example is the Busch Gardens operation of Anheuser-Busch, Inc., described in the following case.

MINI-CASE:
BUSCH GARDENS IN TAMPA, FLORIDA

The original Busch Gardens opened in Tampa, Florida, in 1959 as a fifteen-acre tropical garden, bird sanctuary, and hospitality spa next to the company's brewery, and seven years later Busch Gardens-Los Angeles was opened as a beer promotional facility next to the Van Nuys brewery of the parent Anheuser-Busch company. A third Busch Gardens was opened in Williamsburg, Virginia, in 1975 at a cost of thirty million dollars.

By 1975 the original Tampa facility was drawing two million visitors a year and had been expanded to cover 300 acres. It included a huge veldt section where more than 100 species of rare, big and wild game roam in a natural habitat; a monorail safari which brings visitors face-to-face with lions, zebras, giraffes and hundreds of other wild animals; a trans-veldt railway, patterned after African trains of the late 1800s, which tours two miles of the outer veldt and stops at a replica of Stanleyville; a half-mile barrel flue ride; a Moroccan village complex; a bird sanctuary containing 2,500 birds of some 350 species, and a 1,000-seat amphitheatre. One admission price entitled the visitor to all rides, shows, and special attractions.

No longer just a brewery tour, Busch Gardens in 1975 had become a division of the company specializing in the family entertainment business. When it opened its Williamsburg facility the company stated that it did so as the result of a corporate commitment to enter the lucrative family entertainment business on a big scale basis. Commenting on a study of U.S. theme parks the group vice president of the new division stated:

> Our study basically considered two features of themed family entertainment centers: "tangible" and "intangible." The tangibles include rides, attractions live entertainment, stores and shops. Intangibles refer to cleanliness, friendliness, and pleasant surroundings. . . . They are our strengths. In that sense, we're ahead of everyone else; we were ecologically oriented long before people became interested in environmental protection. Both parks (at Tampa and Los Angeles) are much more than a combination of plants, trees, and animals; visitors can become intimately involved with nature . . .

Questions for Discussion

1. As part of a multi-million dollar expansion program that began at Busch Gardens-Tampa in 1973 the company built a new Moroccan village entry complex consisting of an authentic assortment of small African shops, stores, eating places, and a theatre within a massive walled fortress with ramparts and Arabesque archways. Atmosphere and entertainment were provided by strolling musicians, craftsmen, and peddlers in the open air "Kasar el Kebir" entry plaza and the "Casino de fe Dala" arcade.

You are to assume that you are the publicity manager for Busch Gardens-Tampa. "Morocco" is due to be opened to the public in a few weeks. You have been assigned to draw up detailed plans for a Press Day prior to the public opening. Present your proposal in a memorandum to your instructor.

2. As its tribute to the U.S. Bicentennial, Busch Gardens, Inc., commissioned the production of "The Eagle Within," a fourteen-min-

ute, multimedia show combining motion pictures, still photography and ultrahigh fidelity sound to create a mosaic of fifteen Americans with one thing in common: they are the very best at what they do. To examplify excellence in industry, science, athletics, and art, "The Eagle Within" consisted of a series of fast-action sequences of Bob and Chris Wills, champion hang gliders; Eric Danielson, 12, one of America's brightest young skiers; Max Zylberg, master diamond cleaver; Lou Brock, base-stealer par excellence; Walter Brady, driver of the Anheuser-Busch eight-horse Clydesdale hitch; and others. After its May premier, the presentation was scheduled for continuous showing at theatres at all three Busch Gardens through the rest of 1976.

a. What's your opinion of the multimedia show as a vehicle to commemorate the Bicentennial?

b. In picking the "stars" for the fifteen sequences the film makers obviously had a wide choice of subjects. After appropriate research, select ten Americans who, in your opinion, exemplify excellence in their chosen field and would seem to be natural subjects for such a show. Only one of the ten should be a widely-known celebrity. Briefly justify each of your selections.

c. In a memorandum to your instructor, describe a project other than "The Eagle Within" which you believe would have been appropriate and of use at Busch Gardens as a salute to the Bicentennial.

3. Assume that Busch Gardens, Inc., has retained your public relations counseling firm and you are the account executive assigned to handle the account. The client has asked you to submit a memorandum describing five major public relations projects to be carried out by your firm for Busch Gardens, Inc., for the coming year.

SUPPORTING AND/OR DRAMATIZING COMMUNICATION EVENTS OR ACTIONS

There is a narrow but significant difference between existing organizational events and communication events supported and/or dramatized by public relations projects and activities. By *communication events* are meant those designed as part of public relations programming rather than those that exist as part of an organization's activities. For the most part communication events are "one-shot" affairs, although they can prove so successful and integral to an organization that they become recurring affairs and thus an integral part of an organization's activities.

Criticism has been leveled against communication events for being "manufactured" and "pseudo," and the criticism has a good deal of validity. However if the communication event serves purposes other than merely being reported by the media, the argument that it is manufactured loses a good deal of its weight and substance. Practitioners can create event after event, but unless they interest the public they will inevitably fail to bring about media coverage. The test, therefore, is not in the event but in the substance of the event.

There are innumerable ways in which communication events are meshed with public relations programs, projects and activities. Some of the more common ones are seminars, forums, competitions, special awards, surveys, educational campaigns, conferences, and convocations. The best of them pass three basic tests: (1) they meet and dovetail with fundamental objectives and goals of the organization; (2) they provide a public or publics with information, knowledge, or ideas which is in the public interest; and (3) they merit and secure media attention and coverage. This three-fold test is a difficult one to pass; only those created communication events which are the most thoughtful and imaginative pass with high marks.

MINI-EXAMPLES:
SOME CREATED COMMUNICATION EVENTS

Cited below are a variety of created communication events. Either in class discussion or in a memorandum to your instructor, rate and judge each event's public relations effectiveness by applying the three-fold test cited previously. Justify your conclusions in each instance.

1. At their first meeting in October members of the Blank College chapter of the Public Relations Student Society of America decide that their major chapter project for the year will be the staging in March of the First Southwest Collegiate Communications Conference. Planning takes up the chapter's attention for the entire academic year. Two mailings are sent out to all PRSSA chapters and to journalism and public relations schools, departments, and teachers in the southwest. Speakers and panelists at the March event include two nationally known public relations practitioners and journalists from the southwest. Attendance at the two-day conference consists chiefly of public relations students of Blank College — many of them to handle classroom assignments based on conference activities — and fourteen students from four other southwest colleges and universities. Good media coverage of conference activities is given by media in the Blank College area, and brief mention of the conference is also carried in national public relations news letters, the *Public Relations Journal*, and the PRSSA's *Forum*. The Blank College *Weekly Record*, student newspaper, runs many pre-conference stories and a long story with pictures the week after the conference.

2. By arrangement with local and state automobile clubs, an international oil company which markets its products throughout the United States conducts a cross-country automobile competition. Entries are restricted to one-owner automobiles which are at least twenty years old. Local, state and regional elimination competitions are held, and the final race consists of twenty automobiles in a race from Paramus, New Jersey, to San Francisco. All entrants have to use gasoline and oil produced by the sponsoring oil company. The

winner is feted at a dinner in Detroit addressed by the president of one of the major automobile manufacturers, and the automobile which won the race is put on permanent display in a new National Automobile Museum erected on the outskirts of Detroit. The winner is awarded the top of the line in a new model car of the winner's choice. Media coverage is excellent on all levels: local, state, regional, and national. The oil company "merchandises" the races and final winner in newspaper, magazine, radio, and television advertisements and commercials and by point-of-sales displays at its gas stations throughout the country.

3. Retained by a national association of nurserymen, a public relations counseling firm proposes two major projects for 1973:

a. Plant-A-Tree Week, to be held in August in commemoration of the sixtieth anniversary of the appearance in *Poetry* magazine of Joyce Kilmer's poem "Trees." Local nursery associations throughout the country would be provided with detailed project kits telling them (1) how to conduct a poetry contest with awards going to hitherto unpublished local poets whose poems dealing with nature are judged to best exemplify Kilmer's tribute to trees; (2) how to have the mayor of their city proclaim August 15 as Joyce Kilmer Day, and to have a ceremonious planting of a budding tree — donated by the nurserymen — by the mayor or his deputy; and (3) ways to demonstrate proper plant and shrub care on a local television show during Plant-A-Tree Week. The proposal also projects a similar set of activities on a national level to be conducted by the national nurserymen's association and subsequently publicized by the counseling firm.

b. The underwriting of a grant by the national association of nurserymen to the romantic poetry section of the Modern Language Association to support a symposium dealing with "Nature, Poetry, and Modern Man." As visualized by the counseling firm, the grant would be used to underwrite the costs of the symposium where major papers would be delivered by leading romantic nature poetry scholars. The papers would later be compiled and published in book form and the book distributed to all libraries and teachers of poetry in colleges and universities throughout the country. All costs of publication and distribution would be covered by the nurserymen's association. The only mention of the association would be a brief acknowledgment of the grant in the preface to the book. In a covering letter to the libraries and teachers receiving the book, the association would cite its sponsorship of the symposium and the group's commitment to the beauty that is inherent in nature and in poetry concerned with nature.

SUPPORTING AND/OR DRAMATIZING PRODUCTS, SALES AND SERVICES

Public relations projects and activities conceived and carried out to support an organization's products, sales, and services are so common they're often handled on a regular basis by staffers specifically assigned to this purpose. Such projects and activities are also the ones most enthusiastically supported by other functions and divisions of organizations because of the direct help they provide to these functions and divisions.

Product, sales, and service promotion comes in many forms. It can consist chiefly of press releases and feature stories sent to trade and consumer publications, newspapers, syndicates, radio, and television outlets. Sometimes it takes the form of making the product available to movie makers and television producers and subsequent viewing by millions when the film is released for distribution. Though this is a form of subliminal impact which is hard to measure, there is no doubt that some members of the movie and the television audience will be influenced by seeing the product.

Introducing a new product to the market is primarily a function of the sales department, but public relations assistance is often provided in the form of press releases, press conferences, advance showings, press showings, packaged presentations for use on morning and afternoon television shows, and a host of other devices and methods.

A common form of product promotion is to tie it up in a promotional package and take it on a tour of leading cities and markets by a personality accompanied by a public relations representative who schedules bookings and appearances and works with the media in the cities visited. Another common form is the tie-in promotion wherein the product is put to use and shown in action at some facility that draws millions of visitors. Power boats and outboard motors are an integral part of the daily shows at Cypress Gardens in Winter Haven, Florida; they may as well be X powerboats and Y outboard motors as anyone else's.

Supporting products and sales by means of public relations projects and activities is easier to achieve than supporting services, chiefly because the former lend themselves more readily to dramatization. Services are more intangible than products, hence more difficult to "package" and dramatize.

An effective way of dramatizing services is to substitute things or people for services, and to utilize these in subsequent dramatization and promotion. The United Way of America did this very effectively with public service cameos on pro football television broadcasts, utilizing a brief statement by a pro football star, showing him in action, then switching to someone who has benefitted by the services of a United Way agency, and finally combining both the star and the United Way client in a wrap-up sequence.

In a similar manner, Smokey Bear was used for many years to personalize messages about the dangers of forest fires, while Reddy Kilowat was used as the symbol for services performed by an electric utility. To show the services they render to their communities, high schools and colleges often allow their athletic fields, pools, and auditoriums to be used by community groups. In times of disasters many companies have donated supplies and manpower to help those whose homes have been devastated by floods, tornadoes, and fires. Project Hope was a service project on an international scale supported by funds, manpower, and supplies provided by American companies and industries. The white hospital ship which brought medical supplies, teachers, and treatment to other countries is a fine example of a project which serves others and at the same time brings goodwill to the sponsors.

BUILDING PROJECTS AROUND SPECIAL OCCASIONS

One day may be just like another to the average person, but not to the alert public relations practitioner who builds projects around the days that are special in American life.

Holidays are special days, and many a public relations project has been tied in to Columbus Day, Independence Day, Labor Day, Ground Hog Day, and all the other days which are spelled with a capital D. The key to a tie-in is that it be intrinsic and not foreign to the day to which it is aligned. You've got to be a near genius to carry out a public relations project that connects Grandma Brown's Beans to Columbus Day, but it just takes a little forethought and planning to tie Franco-American spaghetti to that same day. Ground Hog Day is a natural for any organization that is concerned with the weather, but not to a lumber company. The latter might better try to do something with Paul Bunyan Day.

Most of us check the calendar to see how many days are left until the weekend comes, but alert practitioners check their calendars to see what important years may be in the offing. In public relations offices throughout the land plans and projects were being fashioned in 1974 and 1975 for the all-important year 1976 when the country would be celebrating its bicentennial. If you're going to produce a special movie, book, series of publications, or other means of connecting your organization with the nation's 200th birthday, you don't start it on January 1, 1976, but a year or two earlier.

To those two certitudes — death and taxes — one can add a third meant particularly for public relations people: special days and occasions lend themselves neatly to public relations projects, but the competition is fierce because this knowledge is widely shared. To capitalize on these days and occasions the practitioner has to plan wisely in advance and be more imaginative than the competition.

MINI-PROBLEM
BUILDING PROJECTS AROUND SPECIAL OCCASIONS

1. You are to assume that it is early in 1976 and the National Football League has agreed to allocate to the Public Relations Society of America fourteen half-minute public service cameos which will be put on the air during games in the 1976–77 season.

Because these are to be public service spots, the television network is not charging air time. However, the NFL stipulates that the spots should be built around a central theme involving the nation's bicentennial.

The Board of Directors of the PRSA has raised the funds needed to cover production costs for the fourteen cameos and has assigned you tentatively total responsibility for the project. However, before giving you final approval the board requests that you prepare and send it a position paper covering the following:

A. A concise statement explaining why you perceive the NFL cameo opportunity meets basic objectives and goals of the PRSA

B. An explanation of the specific central theme which you propose to be exemplified in each of the fourteen half-minute spots

C. A brief explanation describing the nature of *each* of the fourteen cameos

D. A rough video-voice script for any one of the cameos

E. A concise statement explaining your perception of how your proposed theme and the fourteen cameos you have projected will meet the basic objectives and goals you have outlined in Item 1

2. You are to assume you are vice president for public relations of the John Hancock Life Insurance Company. A year before the nation's bicentennial you proposed to the president and the company's board of directors that your department be given the authority and funds to carry out five major projects during the bicentennial year. You have been asked to submit a memorandum covering the following:

A. The basic objectives and goals of the year-long program

B. The major publics to be reached and the theme(s) of the program

C. A description of the five major projects in sufficient length to enable the president and board to have a clear understanding of their nature

D. A statement of reasons why the company should support and carry out the program

Two reminders are in order in summing up the subject of projects in public relations programming. First, projects should be closely related to organizational and public relations objectives and goals and should not be undertaken unless this relationship is clear.

Second, projects should provide a blueprint for public relations action and indicate clearly to management the strategy of a program; the manpower and resources needed to carry out the program; and the budget and funds needed to support the activities set forth in the program's blueprint. By setting forth a series of projects the practitioner offers management a choice of options and thus if management decides — usually for financial reasons — not to authorize the entire package there should still be sufficient projects remaining to make up a viable program. It is thus to the advantage of the practitioner and the organization he represents to program via projects rather than via one single irreducible activity or event.

TACTICS

In setting forth a program composed of a series of projects the practitioner should also indicate a clear order of priorities based on a descending degree of importance. Project A, for example, should head the list because the practitioner, as the expert in public relations, considers it most important in terms of reaching objectives and goals. Last on the list should be the project considered least important.

In setting up an order and description of planned projects, more than one list may be needed. For example, a campaign may well involve actions to be taken on a national and local level, and if so there would be an order of priorities within each list of projects.

The program blueprint should also indicate the funds, talent, and mechanics necessary to carry through various projects. In dealing with the latter great care should be taken to distinguish between those which are within the control of the practitioner and those which are not. Project D, for example, may involve a sixteen-city tour by a national personality, and it is tactically within the practitioner's control to arrange contracting with the personality and setting up all the minute details of the tour. Guaranteeing that specific media will cover the event in each city and print stories about it, is *not* within the control of the practitioner and hence is tactically unwise; such a guarantee is also ethically wrong and indefensible.

TIMING

Experienced practitioners know that poor timing is the fatal flaw that can upset even the most carefully designed program and project. Many aspects of timing can be anticipated in advance, and from long experience the practitioner takes these into consideration in planning. For example, it's a well known fact that Saturday morning and afternoon newspapers are the thinnest of the week. The news "hole" for such papers is meager and therefore events scheduled for Friday evening may never be covered in the next day's newspapers. Because the early evening network news shows need sufficient lead time to process film and to match sound with film, events scheduled for late afternoon have little chance of being covered. Most of the material in Sunday newspapers have to be set in type Thursday or Friday, hence a feature submitted on Saturday stands little chance of being published in Sunday issues.

These anticipated aspects of timing deal essentially with technical aspects of the mass media, but there are others which are more directly within the purview of the practitioner. Most of these are spatial in nature in that they deal with the *spacing* of events, activities, announcements, and similar aspects of programming. It's generally not wise, for example, to schedule two major activities on the same day because they will inevitably compete with each other for public and media attention. Scheduling an event on election day is like committing public relations hari-kari; major disasters may be able to vie at such a time with the political news, but certainly not a press conference announcing the selection of a firm's new chief executive. Taking their cue from political campaign managers, astute public relations practitioners are aware of the danger of "peaking" too soon when spacing a project over a period of time, but they are also aware of the need to be on top of a situation and to take advantage of unexpected breaks.

Unfortunately for the novice, there are no hard-and-fast timing ground rules, but there is the need to be sensitive to the ebb and flow of the tides of public interest in issues and events. An organization's private project may have solid substantive value and interest, but has little chance of gaining public attention if promoted at a time when public and media receptivity is low. How does one know when public interest is high or low? Chiefly through a great deal of reading of daily newspapers and weekly news magazines, viewing network television news shows, keeping abreast of what's going on in national, state, and local community affairs, and being sensitive to the things that are of interest to those publics which are most important to an organization.

MINI-CASE:
A PROGRAM FOR COLLEGE AND HOSPITAL LINENS OF AMERICA (CHLA)

You are to assume that you are a retired public relations counselor and a long-time personal friend of Mrs. Melissa Gordon, president of Spotless Laundries. (See description of the first mini-case about Spotless at the end of the section on "Defining The Audience.")

Mrs. Gordon has written informing you that she recently had discussions with a counseling firm relative to taking on the assignment of handling public relations for CHLA. The firm, writes Mrs. Gordon, has submitted a program proposal which includes the following ten major projects, and Mrs. Gordon would be most appreciative if you would review them and let her know your reaction to them in a return letter.

1. *Case History Program:* CHLA's satisfied clients are its best press agents. We would ask you to open doors for us. Then we would go in, interview some of your customers, prepare their comments in article form, and place them for publication. Among other things, this is a very valuable way for CHLA to improve its client relations.

2. *By-liner Program:* The top executives of CHLA ought to receive a certain amount of exposure in important publications via by-lined articles. These could deal with the total CHLA service, but more likely possibilities would deal with particular aspects of the service, how it solves specific problems, etc.

3. *A Standard Logo:* Ready identification can be established for CHLA by the development of a new, distinctive, and impressive logo which can be used on everything from calling cards to signs on delivery trucks.

4. *Sales slide presentation:* Our graphics and multi-media departments will prepare an exciting slide presentation which can be used to sell CHLA to prospective customers. We would schedule this presentation for important college and hospital industry meetings, trade shows, and similar gatherings.

5. *Survey and Report:* We can put this technique to use in several ways valuable to CHLA. We would design a telephone or personal interview survey to spotlight the views of specific audiences, and then we would report the results of the survey through appropriate media. The technique lets you know what your prospects are thinking and it provides a means for spot publicity. Subject matter can range all the way from how business leaders view their community hospital problems — or college financial problems — to the way hospital purchasing agents view their linen problems. The material developed through surveys would also have many secondary uses: in subsequent articles, speeches, booklets, and sales manuals.

6. *Sales Brochures:* We would develop two of these to be used for a local and national program. They would stress the systems aspects of the service and show how it differs from the ordinary linen supply operation.

7. *Monographs:* We would contract with leading authorities to write a series of informative monographs dealing with various aspects of college and hospital management, and these would be given wide distribution throughout both fields to college and hospital executives. The monographs would be noncommercial in nature, and the only reference to CHLA would be on the cover page.

8. *Seminars:* Here is another noncommercial way of establishing CHLA as the leader in its field. We would contract with leading authorities to take part in these seminars — to be held throughout the country — and to discuss important college and hospital problem areas. The seminars would generate local publicity in print and electronic media, while national exposure would be gained by selective mailing of seminar summary remarks to a key list of important community and professional leaders.

9. *Speaking Dates:* Another useful way of gaining valuable exposure for CHLA is to have some of your executives speak before local and regional business and professional organizations. The talks would have to be broad in nature, rather than commercial and would help sell CHLA as the authority in the hospital and college fields.

> 10. *Reprints:* This is Standard Operating Procedure, but it's an excellent means of keeping your name before important individuals and groups.

COMMUNICATING AND EVALUATING

Lumped together as the final elements of planned programming are two areas of professional endeavor in which the average practitioner is both the most and the least adept.

Communication, particularly the use of the written word and knowledge of media to reach various publics, is the one skill common to most practitioners. The average practitioner may not know much about communication theories, but he is generally skilled in writing and communicating, and he uses these skills to inform, influence, and gain public understanding and acceptance.

On the other hand, evaluation of plans, programs, and public relations activities is often more noticeable by its absence than by its presence. Two of the reasons for this absence is the fact that a good many public relations activities and programs do not lend themselves to accurate evaluative measurement, and the fact that evaluation can be a proposition whose costs managements are unwilling to assume.

Because both communication and evaluation are such key factors in programming they will be discussed in full detail in chapters to come. For the moment, they stand as the final steps in the orderly consideration of planning and programming.

SUMMATION

Planning and programming is at the core of successful public relations practice, whether we're considering the internal practitioner or the counselor. Though this chapter has explored the facets of plans and programs at some length, it has admittedly merely scratched the surface. In the continuum of the practice of public relations there is a wide gap between the beginner and the experienced practitioner, and this gap is bridged chiefly by the degree of sophistication possessed by the two extremes.

Given the assignment of promoting reflectorized highway signs the beginner sends out releases and art publicizing the signs; the veteran organizes seminars and develops features dealing with highway hypnosis, well aware of the fact that reflectorized signs help alleviate this danger of highway safety. Given the assignment of changing the stereotype of a metropolitan Chamber of Commerce, the beginner produces self-serving advertisements extolling the virtues of the chamber; the veteran creates a Business Advisory Bank, manned by chamber members who provide assistance in eight problem areas to more than 400 small businessmen in one year. Where the beginner is most likely to program along a line that promotes the private interests of company or client, the veteran programs to reach that point where the line of self-interest intersects the line of public interest, and when there is no intersecting point he follows another line that will intersect.

In summation, the programs developed by veteran practitioners:

1. Mesh organizational objectives and interests with public objectives and interests

2. Have continuity, are not overtly commercial, and lead to predetermined and determinable results

3. Consist of units which have individuality but which join well with each other and can be packaged and "merchandised" to maximize audience exposure and diverse organizational interests

QUESTIONS AND PROBLEMS FOR DISCUSSION

1. What are the major advantages of public relations planning?
2. In what ways can "overprogramming" and "undue program rigidity" be pitfalls in planning and programming?
3. Cite and briefly explain the nature of the seven steps cited by the author as providing a blueprint for public relations action and programming.
4. What major functions are served by carrying out a preliminary study?
5. What are some of the major elements that should go into the study or background report?
6. Just what does the author mean when he says that experienced practitioners make distinctions about problems?
7. In what respects is problem identification largely a result of assumptions, and just how does this relate to the basic matter of defining the problem?
8. What are the various ways one might go about establishing an order of problem priorities?
9. Cite and explain some important criteria to apply to the establishment of sound public relations objectives and goals.
10. What are some of the ways to categorize the audience for public relations programs?
11. Under what circumstances might it be more feasible to reach a target audience indirectly rather than directly?
12. Explain some of the basic qualities which should be inherent in a public relations theme or themes.
13. Explain some ways in which projects are used to support and/or dramatize: (a) an existing event, facility or situation; (b) communication events or actions: (c) products, sales, and services.
14. What considerations are important to the practitioner in applying tactics and timing to public relation programming?
15. Why is it important to plan programs along a line where private interests intersect with public interests? To illustrate this principle, cite some situations where this intersection takes place.

COMMUNICATION 8

In handling the five major elements of public relations in action — assessing public opinion, researching, planning and programming, communicating, and evaluating results — public relations practitioners consider that communicating presents the fewest problems. This is not because the art of communication is quickly and easily mastered, but because it is most closely aligned to the practitioner's prior professional life experience. Starting with the pioneers who commenced the practice of public relations early in this century, practitioners traditionally have begun their professional life as journalists. The basic tool of the journalist has been the word — written in the case of the print journalist and verbal in the case of the electronic journalist — and he has used it to communicate effectively with readers, listeners, and viewers. When practitioners moved from journalism into public relations they took along their skill in communicating through the word.

Newcomers to the field of public relations discover quickly that effective communication is still the core element of successful public relations practice. A few practitioners may carry out successful practice by assessing public opinion, conductiong research, planning, and programming, but the biggest game in town is still communication. Practitioners must understand the nature of public opinion and must be able to counsel and plan programs, but unless they can communicate they don't last long in the field.

And so the practitioners communicate, often successfully and effectively. But don't ask too many of them to provide a rational, thoughtful description of the communication process, to discuss how communication works, or to explain *why* some communication will affect opinion change, some behavior change, and some will do neither. This chapter will provide some of the answers about the nature and process of communication, and at the same time will raise some questions for which there are no ready and simple answers.

THREE BASIC CONSIDERATIONS

The primary approach to communication in this chapter will be by means of a communications model, but first some observations are in order about the *purpose, form*, and *process* of communication.

PURPOSE

Idle conversation — a form of daily communication engaged in by most people — serves the purpose of passing away the time of the day, but this is not the main reason why public relations practitioners engage in communication. There's purpose behind all successful communication, and this elementary fact has to be recognized and purpose clarified *before* communication is set in motion.

The mass media, the major means of communication utilized by public relations practitioners. serve three main purposes: to *inform, influence,* and *entertain.* Harold Lasswell, who pioneered in the study of communication, placed these in a social context when he postulated that the three major social functions of communications are: (1) surveillance of the environment; (2) correlation of the different parts of society in responding to environment; and (3) transmission of the social heritage from one generation to the other. The connection between the two concepts is not difficult to make: providing information serves as a means of surveilling the environment; editorials, columns, and commentaries serve to correlate the different parts of society in responding to the environment; and it is through the various means of entertainment that the mass media help to transmit the social heritage.

Valuable as the three-fold division of purpose may be, it is not distinctive nor purposeful enough for the kind of professional communication tasks assigned to or undertaken by public relations practitioners. David K. Berlo suggests a more definitive role for communication when he proposes that the nature of the *response* to be sought from communication be its paramount purpose.

". . . All communication behavior," says Berlo, "has as its purpose, its goal, the production of a response. When we learn to phrase our purposes in terms of specific responses from those attending to our messages, we have taken the first step toward efficient and effective communication." (*The Process of Communication*. Holt, Rinehart and Winston, 1960, p. 12)

Berlo's suggestion that communicators concentrate on the response to be sought is highly relevant to public relations practitioners, and at the same time it is not necessarily antithetical to the three-fold purpose model. If one wants mainly to provide information, that's fine, but at least recognize that this is the purpose and the response to be sought. If one wants mainly to entertain, that's fine also so long as the communicator recognizes what response is to be achieved from entertainment.

In Berlo's opinion, the main purpose of communication is to influence or, as he puts it, "to affect with intent." In the following criticism that Berlo makes of numerous communication efforts is a valuable lesson for public relations practitioners:

> Too often, writers think that their job is to *write* technical reports rather than to *affect the behavior* of their readers. Television producers and theatrical directors forget that their original purpose was to affect an audience — they get too busy "putting on plays" or "filling time with programs." Teachers forget about the influence they wanted to exert on students and concentrate on "covering the material" or "filling fifty minutes a week." Presidents of civic and professional organizations forget they are trying to influence or affect their members — they are too busy "having meetings" or "completing programs." Agri-

cultural extension workers forget they are trying to affect farmers and homemakers — they get too busy "giving out information" or "reporting research."

----

from *The Process of Communication*, p. 13

Berlo could well have added that public relations practitioners often are: so busy writing and mailing out hundreds of press releases they forget that the first purpose of a release is to be accepted and used by the mass media and the second is to be read; so busy creating stunts and activities they fail to relate them to the objectives and goals of the organization; so busy "doing" they forget that behind the doing there has to be the purpose of achieving a predetermined response.

FORM

The form that communication takes is divisible in many different ways. One can consider communication as being personal or impersonal, oral or written, private or public, visual or nonvisual, internal or external, tactile or nontactile, face-to-face or interposed, indoor or outdoor, and even hot or cold. The form that a particular communication takes may be dictated by the circumstances surrounding it or may be at the control of the communicator; it may be influenced by the social controls of the society in which it takes place; and it may be dependent on technological circumstances.

Form is more than just an idle exercise in semantics or academic gamemanship, particularly when the communicator has to make a choice. If you're an Indian chief whose tribe is being surrounded by an overwhelming army force, do you send up smoke signals to bring help or do you send a warrior on a fast pony? If you're Samuel Adams, do you send a letter protesting the stamp tax or do you stage an event and dump tea into Boston harbor?

None of the above examples illustrates conventional forms of communication, but they make the point that communication can take all sorts of forms, many of them unconventional, in an attempt to "get the message through" and to persuade others. Symbols are a form of communication, as witness the use of the American flag at rallies of both the far right and the far left. Both sight and smell are forms of communication, as testified to in the summer of 1975 by the millions of New Yorkers who saw and smelled their piles of garbage when the sanitationmen left it there in protest of the wholesale dismissal of their union membership. Sound is a form of communication, as anyone who has ever attended a rock festival will clearly testify.

These varieties of form are a reminder that there's more to communication form than a speech, feature story, press release, or television appearance. Given the choice, the practitioner uses that form most appropriate to the situation and which seems most likely to bring about the desired response.

PROCESS

Communication involves process. Communication does not take place in a vacuum or void, and is not singular but pluralistic. Do not expect communication to ensue if you lock a person for weeks in an air-tight, totally dark, escape-proof, sound-proof, perfectly bare dungeon with walls three feet thick; that person will not only be unable to communicate, but will undoubtedly die. Put two people in the same dungeon and they may also die, but they will communicate.

How they will communicate depends on a wide number of variables — their ages, education, nationality, ingenuity, state of mental and physical health, dexterity, and so forth. What if one of the two is 10 years old and the other 40? What if one has a sixth-grade education and the other a Ph.D. degree? What if one is American and the other Hungarian? The human spirit being what it is, the two will overcome all barriers to communication. The barriers themselves are cited to illustrate that communication does not take place in a vacumm or void but in a situational context that affects it. The dual nature of those in the situation is a reminder that communication takes place only when there is more than one person involved. Wilbur Schramm, who has devoted a professional lifetime to the study of communication, summed up these two important aspects of communication in these words: "If there is one thing we know about human communication it is that nothing passes unchanged in the process, from person to person." (*Men, Messages and Media*, Harper and Row, 1973, p. 52)

TWO EARLY THEORIES

Some of the early scientific studies of the nature of communication were so simplistic they viewed the act of communication as a one-plus-one-equals-two phenomenon. One school of researchers postulated the *"hypodermic needle"* theory of communication in which the communicator sent his message through the mass media to bring about certain behavior on the part of the audience. News stories, radio, and television programs were likened to a hypodermic needle which took the messages sent by the communicator, stuck them in the minds of the audience, and produced desired effects.

A refinement of this theory was the *"two-step flow"* hypothesis which theorized that ideas flow from the media to opinion leaders and then from them to the less active elements of the population. The key study which led to this theory was conducted in Erie County, Ohio, in the 1940 presidential election by Paul Lazarsfeld and colleagues at the Bureau of Applied Social Research of Columbia University. Using the panel research technique, the researchers concluded that very few people reported being influenced by the media about voting but rather by personal contacts and face-to-face persuasion by opinion leaders. Another study, conducted among women in Decatur, Illinois, and reported in the book *Personal Influence* by Katz and Lazarsfeld, concluded that there are different levels and degrees of opinion leadership, that some women are opinion-forming influentials when it comes to movie-going, others when it comes to fashion, etc.

The fault with both theories is that they fail to recognize that communication is a process in which key elements are constantly interacting with each other. As Schramm puts it: ". . . The idea that something 'flows,' untransformed, from sender to receiver in human communication is a bit of intellectual baggage that is well forgotten. It is better to think of a message as a catalytic agent with little force of its own except as it can trigger forces in the person who receives it. . . ."

A CAUTIONARY NOTE

The public relations practitioner is well advised to view communication just as he or she views public relations. Both are dynamic, and neither process has a beginning, a middle, and an ending. Both public relations and communication in action are continuous, always in a state of flux with their basic elements constantly interacting with and upon each other. Life for the practitioner would be simple if it were possible to freeze the communication process and set it off in time and space, but communication cannot be frozen.

What do we mean when we say that communication is not frozen in time and space? Simply that all communication takes place in a setting, and the setting is an important factor in determining whether communication will be effective.

MINI-EXAMPLE
AN INCREASE IN THE PRICE OF GASOLINE

You are director of public relations for the Standexbil Oil Company and the time is June 26, 1965, just prior to the start of the summer vacation season. It has been decided to raise the price of your gasoline three cents a gallon at the pump. You send out a press release announcing the price increase, and it is carried by the wire services and run on the inside pages of most of the country's daily newspapers. The price goes up as scheduled, people pay it, and there is little public concern.

It is now June 26, 1975, just prior to the start of the summer vacation season. There have been several years of gasoline shortages, steep price increases by the oil exporting countries, and much national concern about the energy crisis. It has been decided to raise the price of your gasoline three cents a gallon at the pump, and this will represent an all-time high. You send out a press release announcing the price increase, and it is virtually a carbon copy of the release sent out in 1965. The story is carried by the wire services and appears on the front pages of most of the country's daily newspapers. The price goes up as scheduled and people pay it *but:* there is a public outcry; consumer advocate groups issue statements highly critical of the action; letters to the editor denounce your company and other oil companies who also raised their prices three cents a gallon; senators and representatives issue statements demanding an immediate investigation of alleged price fixing and gouging; and subsequent public opinion polls show a sharp drop in public opinion towards your company and other gasoline companies.

Questions for Discussion

1. Although the two price increases and releases announcing them were identical there were sharp differences in reception to them. Why?
2. Could the difference in reception have been anticipated?
3. What, if anything, could you as public relations director have done in 1975 to modify or mute the negative public reaction?
4. What lesson(s), if any, do you draw from this example?

Though the setting for communication is a vital factor in the whole process of communication, it was not given much consideration by the "hypodermic needle" and "two-step flow" researchers, and unfortunately most experimenters in communication continue to err in drawing conclusions from their experiments as though they had been conducted in a milieu frozen in time and space. Because people differ and because the situations in which people find themselves differ, it is not wise to draw sweeping conclusions about human communication on the basis of what tends to be a controlled environment.

This does not, however, justify the equally sweeping conclusion that human communication experiments serve no valuable purpose at all. On the contrary, they help to underscore the important fact that communication is a process and that certain key elements are involved. Therefore, in order to understand the process and to learn lessons from it, these key elements need to be identified, analyzed, and discussed. To achieve these purposes, communication scholars have developed relatively simple — perhaps deceptively simple — communication models, and it is through such a model that the process of communication will be explained in the section that follows.

The process of communication itself is not orderly and does not work in linear form. However, the model will project the elements in linear form chiefly for the purpose of an orderly discussion of communication.

A COMMUNICATION MODEL: INTRODUCTION

A simple communication model consists of four major elements: the sender or source; the message; the channel; and the receiver or recipient. If we were to project these four elements in linear form to explain the communication process our model would work out as follows:

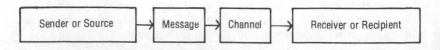

In its simplest form communication involves a source or sender whose purpose is to send a message through a channel in order to reach a receiver or recipient. Three other sub-elements, however, are usually present in the communication act and these involve *encoding, decoding,* and *feedback.*

Encoding is essentially a matter of translating the ideas of the source and giving them meaning. Usually this is performed by the motor skills possessed by the sender who uses his vocal mechanisms to produce oral words or his muscle system to produce written words or gestures. In simple communication situations the source and encoder are the same person, but the two are generally separate entities in complex communication situations in which an organization is involved. As an example, the organization may want to communicate with its union public but entrusts the encoding of the message to its public relations department.

Decoding represents the reverse of encoding and means a retranslation of a message into a form that the receiver can use. In face-to-face communication the encoder is the set of motor skills used by the source, while the set of sensory skills used by the receiver is the decoder. The source encodes by using speech or writing; the receiver decodes by using hearing or reading. In a more complex situation the functions of encoding and decoding are separable from the source and receiver functions.

Berlo reminds us that the concepts of source, encoder, decoder, and receiver should not be interpreted as being separate things, entities, or people, but as the names of behavior performed when communication takes place. Thus, one person may be both a source and a receiver and encode and decode messages. In complex communication patterns these functions would be carried out by different people. As an example to describe the communication behavior of a complex organization, Berlo cites the operation of a large-city newspaper:

> The operation of the newspaper involves a complex network of communication. The newspaper hires people whose prime job is decoding — reporters who observe one or more kinds of events in the world and relay them to the "central nervous system" of the paper, the "desk" or "slot" or central control office.
>
> When these messages are received, some decision is reached by the editorial staff. As a result of these decisions, orders are given from the control desk to produce or not produce a given message in the paper. Again, the encoding function becomes specialized. The paper employs rewrite men, proofreaders, linotype operators, pressmen, delivery boys. They are all responsible for one or another part of the encoding and channeling functions, getting the message out of the control office on to the pages of the newspaper, and thence to a different set of receivers, the reading public.

----

from *The Process of Communication*, p. 35

In the example cited above there is no direct linear line from source to message to channel to receiver, but rather a set of activities interrelated to each other, almost indivisible, and constantly in motion. Communication within this organization is also affected by the perceptions, attitudes, and beliefs of those involved in the process; by the standards and codes of the paper; and by the situation existing at the time the communication process takes place.

Among the factors involved in the dynamics of the communication process is the concept known as *feedback*. It operates at all levels, but is of particular importance at the source level. *Feedback is essentially a return flow from the message as it is received from the recipient.* Its impact and effect can be instantaneous and powerful — as in face-to-face communication — or delayed and weak — as in mass communication. When a skillful speaker addresses an audience he is constantly making use of audience feedback to judge the impact he is making. Because this feedback is instantaneous and immediate he is able to change his delivery, tone, and even the talk itself in order to adjust to the feedback he receives from the audience. Contrast this with communication by means of television where the audience is remote, removed, and out of sight. Here feedback is delayed, weak, and almost nonexistent. It's for this reason, among some others, that television shows are performed before specially assembled, live audiences, even though the real audience is somewhere out there in the remote land of the home receiver set. Feedback is what actors mean when they say there's a dynamic quality in the air when performing in the theatre as compared to the static quality when performing before the movie camera.

Feedback is highly important to public relations practitioners because it enables them to adjust, modify, or change messages in accordance with the dictates of the feedback. Practitioners can use all the skills at their command when sending a message through mass media channels, but without feedback they have no way of knowing the immediate impact these messages have on the intended recipient.

THE MODEL SUMMED UP

In very brief form we have examined the elements that must be present if communication is to take place. There has to be a *source* — one person, two people, or an organization — with some reason for engaging in communication. This source uses *encoding* to translate his or her ideas, information or thoughts, and he or she then *assigns meaning* to the ideas, information, or thoughts and puts them in the form of a *message*. The message is sent through a carrier or medium and is thereby *channeled* to a *receiver*. The receiver may be one person, two or more people, or an organization, and the receiver *decodes* the message to give it meaning. The entire communication act is a matter of process in which the key elements overlap, interact, and feed back upon each other. The process has been described in linear fashion in order to set forth the key elements, but the process is not linear and not static but dynamic. Keeping these important points in mind, it's appropriate now to explore each of the communication elements in more detail.

THE COMMUNICATION MODEL DISSECTED

The purpose of this section is to examine each of the four major elements of our communication model from the viewpoint of possible maximum effectiveness. As hi-fi enthusiasts know, the quality of sound produced by the system is at its maximum level when there is no interference anywhere within the system. Similarly, the quality of communication produced by a communication system is at its maximum level when there is no interference anywhere within the system. To produce maximum efficiency-level communication, therefore, one must dissect the communication model and explore the *factors within the four major elements that lead to maximum communication effectiveness*.

SOURCE-SENDER

The most common role played by the public relations practitioner within the communication act or system is as the source or sender of messages. As discussed earlier in this book the practitioner is also a listener and an assessor of public opinion, but his success or failure is most often based on the way in which he communicates. A score of factors are involved in this aspect of public relations practice, but four major ones concern the communicator's degree of *empathy, credibility, situational acuity*, and *communication skills*.

EMPATHY

According to the dictionary, *empathy* is the "imaginative projection of one's own consciousness into another being," and in the communication act the other being is the intended receiver. Naive communicators send their messages "to whom it may concern" and hope they will reach someone. When the owner of a pleasure boat finds his boat is sinking he sends out a "may day" call, hoping to reach someone. When my younger daughter was three years old and inadvertently crawled under her covers and found herself stuck at the end of the bed, she howled "help, *somebody, somebody* help."

In contrast, the skilled communicator composes messages with a specific audience in mind, and when sent out these messages are directed to the specified audience. Wireless operators on large ocean vessels keep in constant touch with other ships, and if trouble occurs they know exactly where these ships are. If my younger daughter, now age 8, gets into trouble today and needs help she doesn't yell for "somebody" but for her mom or dad.

The wise communicator, therefore, develops a keen sense of empathy regarding his intended receiver or audience. He recognizes that everyone exists within a variety of systems, among which are the system of self or personality; the cultural system of ideas, beliefs, values, and symbols; and the social system of human relationships and social structures and organizations. Each of these has an important influence on the receiver's view of the world, his role and the role of others in the communication process, his reaction to messages, his use or nonuse of various channels, and so forth.

Developing a keen sense of empathy with the intended audience is difficult enough when both the source and the receiver are face-to-face and of the same social, cultural, economic, educational, and political milieu, but it becomes doubly difficult where the sender and the audience are from different milieus. The best that can be done in such cases is to develop an a priori understanding and sensitivity of the audience and its social, cultural, economic, educational and political norms, modes of behavior, and ways of looking at and doing things.

Some communicators are very good at developing empathy, others very poor. The best ones, in effect, try to step out of their own skins and into those of the audience they're trying to reach. They view communication situations not from their point of view, but from that of the audience. They are as much concerned about how a message will be perceived and received as how it is worded, written, and sent. The poor ones are either uncaring, insensitive, or oblivious to the audience they're trying to reach. They write from their point of view — or that of the organizations they represent — and are more concerned with the form of their words than they are of their impact.

MINI-EXAMPLES
WOMEN IN THE WORLD OF BUSINESS

In an article entitled "A Woman Is Not a Girl and Other Lessons in Corporate Speech," Patricia Hogan projects the following five scenes as a means of learning businessmen's attitudes towards women:

SCENE ONE: A planning meeting. Ten men are seated around a large, circular conference table. One of the men leading the meeting has forgotten to bring a crucial document. Discovering this, he says, "I'll have my girl bring it right over." Five minutes later, a woman who appears to be in her early forties knocks on the door, excuses herself for the interruption, and hands the man the document.

SCENE TWO: Mr. Z calls Sally Jones, one of the firm's account executives, into his office to congratulate her on landing an account the company has been pursuing for years.

"Sally, you did a first-rate job on that Mercer account," he says. "You really surprised everyone. Don't get me wrong — it's not that we didn't think you could do the job. It's just . . . well, how did you manage to get old Mercer to sign? Never mind, we won't go into that," he says with a wink.

Later, Mr. Z sees Ms. Jones in the executive dining room, approaches her table, and again congratulates her. "Bet you guys don't know what a terrific little saleswoman we have here," he says to the men lunching with Ms. Jones.

By the day's end, Mr. Z has commended Ms. Jones five times on her achievement.

SCENE THREE: Six men and a lone woman attend a luncheon. The table conversation turns to capital gains, product diversification, and a new Management Information System (MIS) that will facilitate financial reporting for the large multinational corporation for which they work.

Halfway through the lunch, one of the men leans over and whispers to the woman, "Are we boring you?"

SCENE FOUR: A group of executives meet to discuss a merger. During the course of the discussion, one of the male vice presidents says, "This is going to be a bitch to pull off." He immediately turns to the two women present and apologizes for the five-letter word.

SCENE FIVE: A male manager has recently transferred to head a new department. On the third day of his new assignment, he emerges from his office and asks a female standing near the Xerox machine to make four copies of a report and to get him a cup of coffee. The woman introduces herself; she is one of the production managers who report to him.

Reprinted with permission from *Business and Society Review*, Summer, 1975.

Questions for Discussion

1. According to Ms. Hogan, "the men in these five situations

have violated certain basic communication rules.'' What do you consider to be the violations in the five scenes?

2. Ms. Hogan's basic premise about the five scenes is that they demonstrate "the sexism inherent in daily conversation" in the business world. Do you agree or disagree?

3. In what respects would you say that the businessmen have shown themselves to be nonempathetic to the women in the scenes?

4. Ms. Hogan contends that in order to approach communicating with women in the proper manner, there has to be de-sexing of the spoken and written language; modification of behavior and attitudinal change, and elimination of sexist stereotyping. What current examples can you cite of sexism in the spoken and written word; sexist-oriented behavior and attitudes?

CREDIBILITY

Source *credibility*, like empathy, is a key factor in establishing effective communication because of its connection with the receiver or recipient. By source credibility we mean the degree of faith and trust that the receiver has in the sender of a message, and the effect that this trust has on the receiver.

Psychological studies of opinion change conducted by Hovland, Janis and Kelley of Yale University (*Communication and Persuasion*, Yale University Press, 1953), drew the following basic conclusions about source credibility:

1. When a person is perceived to have definite intentions to persuade others, it is likely he will be viewed as having something to gain and therefore less likely to be trusted.

2. The very same presentation tends to be judged more favorably when made by a communicator of high credibility than one of low credibility.

3. When dealing with issues and problems of a highly technical nature, an individual will be especially susceptible to influence by persons who are perceived to be experts.

The above broad conclusions about source credibility were drawn chiefly from experimental studies with small groups of people under controlled conditions. In addition, they leave unanswered many questions about variations in source credibility as a factor in communication effectiveness — for example, how about an expert who does not inspire trust? — but they do underscore the fact that source credibility is an important factor in persuasive communication.

The implications for public relations practitioners are manifold because the research indicates that *cues about a communicator's intentions, expertness, and trustworthiness significantly affect the way in which communication will be received*. There is great practical value in knowing that people are likely to distrust communication when they perceive it stems from a source that has much to gain from the communication. There is similar practical value in knowing that communication from a high credibility source is more effective than one from a low credibility source, and that it is wise to use an expert when dealing with communication technical in nature.

MINI-EXAMPLE
A STATEMENT OF CONCERN

For several years, at an appropriate time and without indicating he was testing a hypothesis, the author has submitted the following quotation to groups of people and then asked the members to indicate their opinion of the statement in a space below it provided for remarks:

. . . But all agree, and there can be no question whatever, that some remedy must be found, and quickly found, for the misery and wretchedness which press so heavily at this moment on the large majority of the very poor.

. . . By degrees it has come to pass that working men have been given over, isolated and defenseless, to the callousness of employers and the greed of unrestrained competition.

. . . And to this must be added the custom of working by contract and the concentration of so many branches of trade in the hands of a few individuals, so that a small number of the very rich men have been able to lay upon the masses of the poor yoke little better than slavery itself.

Each time the above statement was distributed and opinions asked of it, the group surveyed — unknown to its members — was divided in half. At the top of the statement above given to half the members was the notation: "The following statement was printed recently as an editorial in the official publication of the Socialist Workers Party of America." At the top of the statement above given to the rest of the members was the notation: "The following statements are taken from encyclical by Pope Leo XIII in 1891."

In short, the statement remained the same; the only difference was the attribution to sources.

Questions for Discussion

1. What effect, if any, do you think the two differing notations as to the source of the statement would have on receiver reaction to it?

2. What connection do you think might exist between the statement, source credibility and probable receiver reaction when we consider the receiver's religion? Economic status? Social status? Job or profession? Educational level?

3. What conclusions do you draw from this example about source credibility?

4. First, for those who are curious, the statement is from the encyclicals of Pope Leo XIII in 1891. Second, you might care to try the experiment on a group of colleagues not in this class. Simply duplicate the statement and on the half the copies use the notation from the Pope and on the other half the notation from the SWPA.

It's not surprising that the scientific research of communication sources has documented the effectiveness of high credibility and expert sources and the ineffectiveness of communication from sources perceived as having an axe to grind. In the early days of the republic when life was relatively simple but communication difficult, people learned to accept communication from sources they considered reliable. Even though the level of education has risen, there has been such an explosion of knowledge and information, so many complex issues and activities taking place and being disseminated by so many different means and methods that people have found it impossible to deal with them personally. In trying to cope with the flood of messages, people turn to sources they can trust: a favorite columnist; commentators; political leaders who seem honest and forthright; the local bartender, mailman, and friends who have proven to be sagacious and wise.

Some Examples

The use of source credibility to enhance the effectiveness of communication has long been recognized in advertising, politics, and public relations practice — though not always wisely utilized. Television commercials feature nationally and internationally acclaimed personalities to promote products. When congressmen of the same political party as the president are up for reelection they find it useful to have him make a fast stopover during the campaign or they send out photos showing them in serious conversation in the Oval office. Colonel Sanders is made to seem like a father figure as he hovers in the background of commercials for a fast-food chain; Grandma Brown seems to give her personal blessing to every can of baked beans; Mickey Mouse and his friends are stamped on almost every product sold at two vast family entertainment centers in Florida and California. The communication message is clearly the same; you can put your trust in our products because they're endorsed by the Colonel, Grandma Brown, and Mickey Mouse. The fact that the products are the end result of vast, highly organized commercial organizations recedes conveniently into the background.

There is more to source credibility, however, than simply centering communication messages around personalities who inspire trust and confidence. What is sometimes forgotten is that there has to be some relevancy between the source and the product or institution being extolled. Many people will readily identify the famous baseball player seen in a supermarket scene selling the virtues of a coffee maker, but just as many will wonder about the connection between pounding a baseball and making coffee. Having a famous sports announcer appear in auto commercials during big league baseball game telecasts is a neat juxtaposition of commercial and sports, but one wonders what makes him an expert on automobiles. The credible becomes incredible when relevancy is missing.

Public relations practitioners seeking to maintain source credibility in large organizations operate on levels far above those of television commercials. There's the inner-managerial level within their own organizations wherein the practitioners seek to establish responsible officials as reliable and trustworthy sources of information. There's the outer-media level wherein their relationships with the mass media the practitioners seek to establish themselves as reliable and trustworthy sources of information. Between these two levels, however, there is a level not often discussed openly that causes no end of problems.

For want of a better word, let's call this level the *buffer-zone, the no-man's land in which public relations practitioners so often find themselves in trying to establish and maintain source credibility*. Managements make mistakes, but don't like to admit them. Managements have to close plants and lay off employees, but don't like to admit it. But reporters learn about these things, and they inquire. Such inquiries are directed at the public relations practitioner or they come in to management which in turn directs them at the practitioner. That's when the public relations person lands in the buffer zone.

Even children no longer believe the old chestnut about George Washington and the cherry tree, so it comes as no surprise that people lie from time to time. However, if public relations practitioners find themselves lying, obfuscating, and being disingenuous as a matter of routine, they'd better forget about establishing source credibility.

Source credibility, in summation, is so valuable a factor in the process of communication it requires careful cultivation and deserves the hard fight practitioners must put up in the buffer zone between their managements and the media and the public.

SITUATIONAL ACUITY

Although not a term commonly used in public relations circles, *situational acuity* plays an important role in determining the effectiveness of practitioners as a communication source. Given a communication situation, Practitioner A will suggest action along a certain set of lines, Practitioner B along another set of lines, and Practitioner C no action at all. It's hardly likely that all three proposals will result in the same degree of effectiveness, and hence the practitioner whose keenness of judgment about the situation — situational acuity — will be the one whose proposed action or inaction will bring about the most effective communication results.

The need for situational acuity arises in all instances where people interact with each other, but it has particular relevance in the communication process. *How* the source sizes up a communication situation will determine in large degree what he or she does about it and the results. It could be an internal communication matter involving employees; an external one involving a community public; a media matter involving an inquiry from a newspaper reporter; or any matter in which communication is involved and which forms such an important aspect of daily public relations practice.

One might well raise these questions: Why stress the need for public relations practitioners to have situational acuity? Do not other management personnel need the same sense of keenness about situations? The answer is that the need is greater for the public relations practitioner because his activities and communications involve the entire organization and affect all of its publics. As the source for most of the communication emanating from an organization to its many publics, the practitioner has the heavy responsibility of ensuring most effective communication. *Sizing up the situation — the milieu — within which communication takes place* thus becomes a matter of real concern and great importance.

Unfortunately, there are no simple ground rules — no ten easy steps — for achieving situational acuity. Public relations situations involving communication seldom duplicate themselves, and people, organizations, and times change. The men and women who run today's large businesses, colleges and universities, and the armed forces are a different breed from those who ran them thirty and forty years ago. The men and women who work on assembly lines or punch buttons in plants, who attend colleges and universities, and who serve in the armed forces are a different breed also. Today's factory and plant are a far cry from factories and plants of thirty and forty years ago, as are colleges, universities and military installations. The situation, in short, has changed and the communicator has to be keenly aware of the change and its implications.

The source has to be aware also that changes in communication situations occur not only on large but also on small scales, yet there is still the same need to be keenly tuned in to situational nuances. When your candidate for senator promises during the campaign he will conduct himself with total candor if elected, does he mean the same thing one year later when an enterprising reporter calls and says he has information about illegal contributions made to the now-elected senator? When your firm's earnings have declined appreciably and there's a dispute between you and the finance vice president about the degree of candor in reporting it in the annual report, what does the president mean and what do you do when he suggests the two of you "work it out" so no one will look too bad?

Can one develop situational acuity to make for a more effective communication source? Experience, of course, is an answer, but one doesn't have to drown in order to handle a drowning situation. The wiser course is to learn from near-drowning experiences. The following mini-case should serve as a learning lesson for those who want to develop acuity about communication situations.

MINI-CASE
TO BE OR NOT TO BE . . . INTERVIEWED

You are 27 years old and the coordinator of external publicity of a profitable division of a large industrial corporation. The division sells information services rather than a hard product, and its customers are other business firms. The time is January, 1976, and your salary is $18,500.

Head of the communication department to which you belong is a director whose background has been chiefly in advertising. Reporting to him are two managers, one of whom is your immediate superior.

Your division has recently had a change of presidents, switching from an outgoing, affable, publicity-conscious chief executive to a more reserved president whose background is technical and who is very wary of the press. One of the new president's first moves is to schedule a meeting with the director and the two managers of the communication department, but due to an unavoidable conflict in his schedule the manager to whom you report is unable to make the meeting. He is to be gone a week, and the director agrees that you can substitute for him at the briefing which is scheduled a week from today.

Before leaving, your superior calls you into his office to warn you that the new president does not believe in interviews with the press "particularly because the post-Watergate glorification of investigative reporting has even filtered down into the ranks of the business and trade press." He further says: "In no circumstances say that interviews with him are necessary or desirable because his philosophy is that he won't grant interviews."

These remarks disturb you because your job is to get favorable publicity for the division. Both of you are aware that you were given a relatively free hand to arrange interviews with the previous president and the record shows that the ones you scheduled resulted in excellent coverage by the trade and business press. However, because your superior was obviously in a rush to take off on his trip you didn't press the point.

A half hour before the scheduled morning briefing with the president — and as a result of a good deal of spade work on your part over the past previous weeks — your contact on a leading national business publication calls to inform you that he has been assigned to handle a cover story the two of you had been discussing. The story will deal in depth with the information service field, and as your division is a leader in the field the writer would like to interview your new president. You tell him you will see what you can do, and it is agreed you will call back that afternoon.

Because the call came in just prior to the meeting you have no time to discuss it with the director of the communication department. You are well aware, though, that he reports directly to the president and has remarked more than once that whoever signs his paycheck is entitled to deal with the press in any manner he chooses.

When your turn comes to make your presentation you do a very good job, and you know it's good because the new president nods warmly at its conclusions and says something like "very impressive" to the director of the communication department. The president then turns to you and says: "What do you think of my policy against personal interviews?"

Questions for Discussion

1. What would you say in response to the president's question? Do not generalize, but state exactly what you would say. (The instructor may want to set up a role-playing situation here).

2. Explain *why* you would respond in the manner you have answered the president. In short, how do you see the situation as it relates to you; to you and your immediate superior; to you and the department director; to you and the president?

3. What questions might you want to raise about the situation which may, in your opinion, have a bearing on your response? Given the answers to these questions, in what way might they change the nature of your response to the president's question?

COMMUNICATION SKILLS

Communication skills are the string which wraps up the package of the three other factors — empathy, credibility, and situational acuity — which produce source effectiveness. Even though the source is empathetic and credible and has keen judgment in sizing up situations, he will be ineffective if unable to communicate thoughts, ideas, and information with a high degree of competence and skill.

The skills of the communicator are those of speaking and writing, and they're put to use every working day of the communicator's professional life. Surveys of public relations practitioners repeatedly demonstrate that their most common activities involve some form of speaking or writing: writing speeches or giving talks; writing releases and feature stories; composing memoranda, reports, and statements; conferring with management and editors. Such skills are chiefly encoding skills, but in carrying out the communication process the source also decodes, and here the practitioner puts to use the skills of listening and reading.

Entire books have been devoted to exploring the four communication skills of speaking, writing, listening, and reading, and their importance to the source is self-evident. As sources of information, public relations practitioners stake their professional careers on mastering each and all of the skills needed to make communication effective.

MESSAGES

One way to deal with the message stage of a communication model is to treat it from the standpoint of the semanticist, anthropologist, or social scientist. In doing so we would consider factors such as learning, abstraction, extensional and intensional meanings, social reinforcement, referents, language acquisition, and a score of other epistemological features, all of which might well make for confusion rather than elucidation on the part of the readers of this book. The English language translation of that last sentence is that it's the author's opinion there are some simple, key points about message effectiveness which can be presented without resorting to complicated language. This is not to gainsay the value of the semanticist's approach to the study of language — on the contrary, such an approach can have a high degree of significance for the public relations practitioner — but simply to point out that it's not within the purview of this book.

Further, there's need to stress that there are no immutable laws about messages, and it must be emphasized that messages do not have a life of their own. They exist within the context of the communication process, and the process itself can change the meaning and effect of a message.

KEY CONSIDERATIONS FOR ACHIEVING MESSAGE EFFECTIVENESS

Given these cautionary observations, there are certain key aspects to messages as they apply to public relations communication situations. Both research studies and practical experience have shown that if certain key considerations are kept in mind, practitioners will increase the possibility of communication effectiveness by obeying the dictates of these message considerations. Their presentation shall be listed and discussed in no particular order of importance but in terms of their relevance to public relations situations.

To Be Effective, a Message Must Reach Its Intended Audience

Three astute observers of the public relations scene — Earl Newsom, Edward Robinson, and Gerhard Wiebe — arrive at the same conclusion about the need for "message reach," though each phrases his ideas in a different way.

In setting forth his four public opinion signposts — described in the chapter on public opinion — Newsom prefaced his conclusions with the observation that people don't stand still to be educated. The average person, he reminds us, is preoccupied with everyday problems and personal matters which take up most of that person's waking hours and many of the hours when he or she should be sleeping. Trying to catch the attention of this average person are thousands of individuals and organizations who want to "educate" him or her about their particular area of interest. Newsom concludes that it's little wonder, therefore, that the average person, preoccupied with personal problems, not only won't stand still to be "educated" but in sheer self-preservation because of the countless educational messages beamed at him will tune himself or herself out.

Wiebe, former dean at Boston University's School of Public Communication, postulates the "gyroscopic phenomenon" to explain the public's reluctance to be educated. Like the gyroscope, says Wiebe, people spin within their own orbits and resist outside forces. He makes his point in the following perceptive paragraph:

> If you accept this image of the public, you will necessarily reject an image that has been around too long and that dies hard — the image of the public as a bunch of nice, leisurely, receptive people who will absorb your message if you just use short simple sentences and good pictures. It isn't that simple. It is more the rule than the exception that a public relations message must be so contrived that it penetrates a field of resistance, a resistance generally characterized by a massive disinterest in your company's concerns, and an avid preoccupation with what we have called the sustaining of people's own systems of dynamic equilibrium.
>
> --
> from *Perspectives in Public Relations*, p. 141

Robinson adds another dimension to the problem of catching audience attention, and he phrases it in terms of *nonmotivation* on the part of the audience to messages beamed at them. He describes the problem of audience nonmotivation by asking the following questions:

> Who cares if the company our . . . public relations practitioner represents has been a good corporate citizen and has done its share in trying to solve a particular community problem?

> Who cares if such-and-such nonprofit health group is making progress in finding a cure for some disease that very few persons know anything about in the first place?

> Who cares if some small liberal arts college has drastically revised its educational standards and is providing good solid liberal arts education for a certain number of students, but is now in critical financial straits?

Is there an answer to the problem of audience preoccupation, disinterest, and nonmotivation? Robinson suggests you must make sure your message is available to the audience — that is, select a medium that reaches the intended audience — and you must anticipate and counteract the numerous competing factors that may intervene between source and recipient. Of course, having done this still doesn't solve the problem of audience preoccupation, disinterest, and nonmotivation, but recognizing the problem is the important first step: it forces the communicator into the realization that the audience is not breathlessly waiting for those words of wisdom which will "educate" it to his or her point of view.

The Impact of a Message Depends on How it Identifies With the Interests of the Intended Audience

Two common faults made by communicators are associated with the concept of interest-identification. One fault is to misunderstand or fail to understand the interests of the intended audience, and the other is to confuse the communicator's interests with those of the intended audience. Both failures lessen the impact of messages, and in many instances make them totally ineffective.

Identifying with the interests of the intended audience can best be achieved through *empathy, observation,* and *perception*. Fortunately for the astute communicator, these are not inherited traits but traits which can be learned, developed, and refined. In many cases the matter of interest-identification is mainly one of being careful not to operate under assumptions which are not warranted by reality.

Being careful not to confuse the communicator's interests with those of the intended audience is most often a case of being honest with one's assessment of a communication situation. It's all too easy, for example, to conclude that the audience will be interested in what we have to communicate simply because we want them to be, so we engage in a little game of self-deception in hopes our interests will somehow coincide when we honestly know they don't.

Professor Robinson provides a valid reminder about audience-interests when he notes that reactions to messages are interwoven with the drives and needs of their recipients. "A message," he points out, "must arouse certain needs in a potential recipient and indicate how these needs can be satisfied." It's also his opinion that public relations communicators tend to rely too strongly on delivering information and not strongly enough on satisfying personal needs and motivations.

Unfortunately, such reminders too often fall on deaf ears because failures to follow audience interests and needs are strewn all over the communication landscape, as indicated by the following mini-examples:

MINI-EXAMPLES
FAILURES TO IDENTIFY WITH AUDIENCE INTERESTS

In the summer of 1975 the nation was in the midst of a period of severe recession coupled with serious inflation. More than seven million people were unemployed, and people were concerned about jobs, taxes, the high cost of living, rising crime rates, and the ever-increasing cost of gasoline. At such a time, when these were the main concerns of most Americans:

1. Local school boards presented their communities with record-high budgets which gave little evidence of innovative ways of cutting costs. The local boards were mainly interested in having their proposed budgets approved, but when given the chance to vote on the budgets the public turned them down in record-breaking numbers.

2. Private colleges, faced with decreasing enrollments and rising

costs, continued to raise tuitions at a constantly increasing rate. The colleges were mainly interested in attracting more students in order to stave off budget deficits, but in all but the most prestigous schools, enrollments dropped as middle-income Americans found themselves being priced out of the private college market.

3. Major oil companies, just before July 4, announced a three-cent-a-gallon increase in gasoline prices. The companies contended the increase had nothing to do with the fact that people would be doing more travelling during the summer months, but the public concluded that the timing was so coincidental as to prove that the companies couldn't care less about the public's interests.

4. The president of the United States presented to Congress an energy plan which embodied even higher prices for gasoline in 1975 and ensuing years. He said his program was the best way to cut down on gasoline consumption and would serve as an incentive to the oil companies to drill for new oil. Many people, and congressmen, said the program would hit hardest those who had trouble enough coping with inflation, and they also wanted to know why the oil companies had to be provided with incentives to do what they were supposed to be doing at a time when they were reaping record high profits without incentives.

Questions for Discussion

1. In what ways do each of the above examples illustrate a lessening of message impact due either to misunderstanding of audience interests or a failure to mesh audience interests with communicator interests?

2. If you were the communicators involved in the four cases, in what ways might you have handled the situations?

3. Cite some current examples which either demonstrate: (a) message impact because of astute audience-communicator identification of interests or, (b) poor message impact because of weak audience-communicator identification of interests.

Messages Should Relate to Common Experience and Meaning

This precept, like the first two already cited, stresses the vital need to tie the source to the receiver of messages and emphasizes that *common experience serves as a unifying force between sender and receiver.* When this common experience is expressed in words and terms shared and understood by the source there's even more reason to expect that communication will be well received.

There are, of course, problems connected with the common experience precept. Very often there are no common experiences that have been shared by source and receiver, and there are many times when messages are expressed in words and terms that have lost meaning or are irrelevant to the receiver. Some communicators, however, seem to go out of their way to avoid common experience by beaming messages that are either cute or far-fetched and which might relieve life's daily tedium but do little to bring about desired communication effects.

The world of the television commercial continues to serve up intriguing examples of messages which violate sound communication precepts. They bring us white knights who ride through our kitchen waving magic cleansing potions; charming ladies who discuss their intimate underarm and "feminine hygiene" problems in the middle of cocktail gatherings; smiling gasoline attendants who not only gas up our cars but are willing to spend precious minutes discussing shock absorbers, mileage tips, oil treatment cues, and tire rotation principles.

There's one small problem with all these scenes; they have little relationship to reality. White knights don't ride through kitchens, and even if they did they'd seem very much out of place in the kitchens of the millions of blacks who have the same cleaning problems as the rest of us. The last thing in the world that charming ladies discuss at cocktail parties are deodorants. Gasoline station attendants not only do not smile very much, but if we are to judge from the growing number of self-service pumps they haven't even the time to gas up our autos, no less discuss all those other problems the commercials indicate they're so willing to talk about.

Thus, one of the first lessons for the communicator is to avoid stressing and creating uncommon experiences in fashioning messages. The second is to seek out, stress, and communicate common experiences in words and terms that have meaning and relevance to the recipient. And the third is to find ways to uncover common experiences when they don't seem to exist.

The last point requires some careful thought and a dash of creativity. When polling organizations conduct surveys in Watts or Harlem they make sure their pollsters are blacks and not whites. When colleges send representatives to College Days, they don't send the oldest members of the admission staff but those who have most recently been graduated. Although relatively small sums are collected from house-to-house canvassing, local social and health organizations continue to utilize such neighborhood canvassing because they know it brings better understanding of their activities because the canvasser and those canvassed share common experiences and talk the same language.

These examples all show the use of selectivity by large organizations in choosing the sources to put across their messages, and the common denominator in such selectivity is common experience with the recipients. The precept operates on all levels. If you want to reach the scientific community, you utilize by-lined articles by scientists within your organization because they share the same experience and use the same language as the readers of the publications in which their articles appear. If you want to have a new journalism textbook adopted for classroom use you seek endorsements from leading journalism professors. The wise communicator, in short, selects those representatives who have most in common with and talk the same language as the intended audience. Although he wasn't an expert in economics, politics, science, or the arts, Hal Boyle proved to be the Associated Press's most durable and popular columnist for more than two decades because he had the knack of writing about life's daily comedies and tragedies in a way that touched the average reader. His desk at the AP was a marvel of total disorganization and he was about as urbane as a backwoodsman, but what he wrote was read with joy and pleasure because he understood what interested people, and what interested people interested him. He would undoubtedly snort at the term, but he was a communicator in the truest sense of the word.

Messages Should be Tailor-Made for the Situation, Time, Place, and Audience

Elsewhere in this text it has been pointed out that tailor-made suits have a distinct advantage over mass-produced suits because they fit better. They also cost more because of the time and skills involved, and of course this has to be taken into consideration, particularly if you're operating on a limited budget.

There is no doubt, however, that given the time, talent, and money necessary to cover their cost and other production aspects, tailor-made messages have a distinct advantage over other messages. Because they're crafted with care they indicate to the receiver that "this message is meant for you."

Innumerable examples can be cited to illustrate the principle of the tailor-made message. One doesn't address a street gang as one would a gathering of bank officials. Yelling "fire" in the middle of a noisy city street won't have the same effect as yelling "fire" in a crowded and hushed theater. When a father is concerned about an impending layoff he doesn't react kindly to a request for a new car, though he might listen if you hit him up just after his ten dollar bet paid off at 30 to 1 in the fourth race.

> If you care to go back that far — and who does? — you might recall the kind of messages you sent out when you were between the ages of five and eight and wanted an ice cream bar on a hot summer day.
>
> At the age of five you simply asked for an ice cream bar and if you got it, fine; if not, a few tears. At the age of six you just didn't ask for an ice cream bar, but you demanded it and as this became a test of wills you more than likely didn't get it. At the age of seven you not only demanded an ice cream bar but you pointed out quite clearly that you were the only kid on the street who wasn't allowed to have an ice cream bar. At the age of eight you began playing off your father against your mother, and if that didn't work you went out and bought the bar yourself with money from your piggy bank.

What you were doing was applying the tailor-made principle by changing your message to fit the situation, time, and audience and at the same time using feedback and peer group pressures as a wedge. The only variable remaining constant was the place, though of course that could have been a factor had you been at home one year, on vacation the next, etc.

The same principle applies in the adult world. At one period or another, a message might be tailored to fit a situation with the other three variables remaining constant. Or, it might be tailored to fit both a situation and an audience, with the other two variables remaining constant. Here are some examples:

It is August 1 and you have announced you will be a candidate for reelection in the November mayoralty election and will run on your record of having maintained full employment in your city. On August 30 the largest plant in the city announces it is closing down effective next week. The time, place, and the audience has remained constant, but the situation now calls for a new message to be beamed at the electorate.

It is August 30, same city. You are director of public relations for the firm which owns the plant which will be closed down next week. This is but one of thirty such plants in the country, and it is obsolete and hence the decision to move its operations to a more modern installation. The firm's profits are at an all-time high and the firm is in excellent shape in all respects. The story announcing the closing will be shaped one way as released locally; another way as released in the city to which the operation will be moved; and another way as released to national trade and business publications. Thus, the situation and time remain constant, but the place and audience differ and thus will require different message treatments.

Tailoring a message should not be construed with telling one story to one audience and an entirely different story to another, for this would be akin to selling one piece of goods to one customer and a cheaper piece of goods to another and charging both the same price. You can alter the fit, but you should be sure that the basic material of the message is the same.

CHANNELS

In the communication process a channel is a *passageway, pathway, or means* by which a message passes from source to receiver. Used in this way, it's clear that a communication channel can be a smoke signal; the voice in face-to-face situations; radio, television, newspaper, magazines, and books in communication by means of the mass media. It is also possible to categorize channels in terms of whether they are *interpersonal* or *mediated* (face-to-face versus a telephone conference call); *personal* or *impersonal* (a meeting of 10 people versus an outdoor gathering of 50,000 addressed by means of loud speakers); *assembled* or *non-*

assembled (the same outdoor gathering versus a television audience of millions watching and listening to a political speech in their homes). Although in each instance the forms set forth above seem to be in contrast to each other, they should not be thought of as being opposed to each other or mutually exclusive. As Schramm points out, ". . . distinctions and boundaries are much less clear than that. Most campaigns aimed at teaching or persuading try to combine media and personal channels so that one will reinforce and supplement the other. Political campaigners use all the media but still arrange door-to-door visits and public meetings. Family planning, agricultural, and health campaigns maintain field staffs but support them with all the media they can afford." (*Men, Messages & Media*, p. 120)

The majority of communication situations involving public relations practitioners call for channels or message vehicles that are impersonal and/or mediated. This does not mean that they are more effective than other forms of channels — on the contrary, they are often less effective — but simply that the communication situation makes it impossible to use other channels. *Modern society is structured to make it an impossibility to deal with receivers or recipients of messages on a face-to-face, personal, direct basis*. For this reason the professional communicator has to rely on channels that are impersonal, indirect, and usually nonassembled.

This means in turn that there will be some intervening mediating mechanism, force, or organization occupying the channel between source and receiver. Even when the group to whom we are addressing our messages is assembled in one place, the group may be so large that the intervening, mediating mechanism has to be some method of voice amplification. When the group is out of sight the intervening, mediating mechanism or force could be in the control of the public relations practitioner — such as in the case of an internal publication, annual report, or annual meeting — or it could be out of the practitioner's control.

The channels to be considered in the discussion that follows are those that are out of the control of the practitioner but are nonetheless of the most importance and significance in the process of reaching mass audiences. These channels are the four mass media: *newspapers, radio, television,* and *magazines*. These mass media channels will be analyzed in terms of the following five questions raised by Berlo:

1. What is available?
2. Which channels are received by the most people?
3. Which channels have the greatest impact?
4. Which channels are most adaptable to the source's purpose?
5. Which channels are most adaptable to the content of the message?

KEY CONSIDERATIONS ABOUT CHANNELS

In taking up these five questions we will deal mainly with newspapers, radio, television, and magazines because they are the mass media that reach people on a systematic, regular basis and are most often used by public relations practitioners as message channels. Books and films — especially the sponsored film — are important and valuable channels for public relations messages, but they are not used as frequently as the four media on a regular basis by practitioners, and in addition the sponsored book and film is within the control of the practitioner and hence outside the parameters of this analysis.

What is Available?

For the most part when communication scholars analyze the communication process and discuss the mass media they do not dwell at length on the subject of availability. Presumably this is a nonacademic matter, but for the public relations practitioner the subject of availability is highly relevant. To what avail — other than that of making the practitioner wiser — is knowledge and understanding of the mass media channels if these media are unavailable? Obviously, availability embodies very practical considerations for the public relations practitioner.

A quick, knee-jerk reaction to the question of mass media availability might be, why of course they're available, accessible, ready for use. But are they really, and to what degree? Even the beginner knows that if you want to promote Product X or Idea Y you just can't wave a magic wand and find your story on the AP or UPI wire, the front page of the Chicago *Tribune*, or a prime time television show. Something stands between the wish and the fulfillment, and that something is most easily described by the term known as "the gatekeeper."

The mass media gatekeeper has been described in a variety of ways. The fact that the mass media are highly organized and complex means that the organization itself serves as a gatekeeper and therefore the practitioner has to understand how the media operate if he or she is to get past the gatekeeper.

> In studying the flow of Associated Press news from agency home offices to four Wisconsin non-metropolitan daily newspapers, Scott Cutlip reported that an estimated 100,000 to 125,000 words of news copy comes into the AP every news cycle. From this copy the AP editors select and send out about 238 items totaling about 57,000 words. The Wisconsin AP editors cull out and transmit 77 items totaling 13,352 words to non-metropolitan Wisconsin dailies. From this state wire, four typical Wisconsin dailies select and use about 74 items totaling 12,848 words.
>
> ---
> from "Content and Flow of AP News,"
> *Journalism Quarterly*, 31, 1954, 434–446

The above example is but one illustration of the way in which the organizational facets of the mass media — in this case concerning the wire services and the newspapers they serve — operate as a gatekeeper. Similar organizational facets serve as controls on radio, television, and magazines, and they all emphasize the fact that the complex nature of the mass media makes them difficult to penetrate.

By definition a gatekeeper means that a person is involved in guarding the mass media gates against intrusion by outsiders, and this person is found at numerous stages in the process of transmitting information, ideas, opinions, and entertainment by means of the mass media. Some typical gatekeepers are the person who selects the guests who appear on popular late evening TV shows; the section editor of a business publication and the editor of a trade publication; the disc jockey on local radio shows; wire service editors on state and national levels; assignment editors on network news organizations and on daily newspapers; the copy desk editor on all dailies.

Each of these goes through a process of *selection* and *elimination* in choosing from the "glut of occurrences" those items which, in the opinion of the gatekeeper, deserve to win out in the competition for attention. In the final analysis, therefore, it's comforting to know that the mass media are available to the public relations practitioner, but it's more important to know that at the same time the gatekeeper is constantly on guard to permit entry only to those messages which deserve to reach the mass audience. What the practitioner wants and desires is important, but more important is to understand the wants, desires, and interests of the gatekeepers because they only open the gates when these are met. Gatekeepers make their selection on the basis of maximum appeal to the audience served by their medium, and thus the most important factor in eventual use of material is the gatekeepers' perception of what will most interest their audience.

Which Channels are Received by the Most People?

In order to understand the nature of the mass media audience it's important to understand the complexities of the mass media system, and this can best be done by setting forth pertinent data about the four media. As of 1975 here is the American mass media picture in terms of newspapers, television, radio and magazines:

Newspapers. A total of 1,760 daily newspapers with combined daily circulation of more than 63 million. Half of the dailies with circulation of less than 10,000. About 125 dailies with circulations of 100,000 or more. The median-sized daily in most states: 12,500.

Between 9,500 and 10,000 weeklies serving small communities and suburbs. A few with circulations of 6,000, placing them in the ranks of small dailies in terms of circulation.

With the exception of the large metropolitan dailies, the average daily newspaper receives its state, national, and international news from either the Associated Press or the United Press International and its columns and features from syndicates or from the AP or UPI.

Television. A total of 953 television stations, 711 of which are commercial and 242 noncommercial. Of the 711 commercial stations, 513 are VHF and 198 UHF.

The three major networks — NBC, CBS, and ABC — each own and operate five VHF stations, the maximum allowed by law. Affiliates: NBC, 216; CBS, 197, and ABC, 185. Between 80 to 90 percent of programming on the affiliates is from the networks. State, national, and international news on average station stems from either AP, UPI, or national news departments of the networks.

Approximately 98 percent of the 69 million American homes have television sets. National television audience on any one day is between 75 and 80 million people. Average estimated audience for a prime-time show: 21 million people.

Radio. More than 7,800 radio stations; about 4,400 AM and 3,300 FM stations. Four major national radio networks — Mutual Broadcasting System (MBS), CBS, NBC, and ABC — and scores of regional networks, including a relatively new National Black Network with 73 AM and FM affiliates. Largest by far of the networks is MBS with 652 affiliates, three times that of nearest network rival; by a large majority most radio stations are unaffiliated.

With more than 400 million sets in use, radio virtually blankets the country with more than three sets for every two people. Radio sets are in 99 percent of American homes, in more than 75 million automobiles, and in more than 10 million public places.

Magazines. Somewhere between 8,000 and 9,500 weekly, monthly, and quarterly magazines and journals. Among these are 2,500 business and trade, 600 general circulation, 1,500 religious, and 800 agricultural publications.

Dominating the field in terms of circulation: *Readers Digest* with a combined domestic and foreign circulation of more than 28 million, followed by *TV Guide* with circulation of 15 million. *Time* leads the newsmagazines with weekly circulation of over 4 million followed by *Newsweek* and *US News and World Report*. Vast majority of magazines are written for and appeal to special audiences.

The figures cited above should be read and analyzed with care. One way to analyze the data is to look at it from the standpoint of total numbers and size. There are almost twice as many daily newspapers as television stations, and five times as many weeklies and radio stations as daily newspapers. However, the national television audience on any one day is between 75 and 80 million while the combined circulation of all daily newspapers is just over 63 million. Both audience totals for these two media do not reach the total audience for radio, but are vastly greater than the audience for magazines.

Another way of looking at the mass media audience is to note the audience for single units within each medium. For example, the combined circulation of all *Reader's Digest* editions is more than 28 million and the audience for a prime-time television show numbers 21 million. This compares with the 4 million circulation of *Time*, the largest circulation news magazine, and the 2 million circulation of the New York *News*, the largest daily newspaper circulation in the country.

A final way of looking at the mass media audience is to recognize that it's an overlapping audience. Though there are millions of people who only look at television and who do not read a daily newspaper or magazine, there are more millions who not only view television, but also listen to radio and read a daily newspaper and magazines.

Thus, the public relations practitioner must not only know data relating to the number of radio and television sets, stations and networks; the number of daily and weekly newspapers and magazines; the nature of affiliations; and the audience for each media; but he must also analyze the *specifics about the data as they relate to the organization he represents*. The data, in summation, have meaning only insofar as they are carefully applied to the practitioner's public relations needs and problems.

Which Channels Have the Greatest Impact?

Study after study has demonstrated the pervasive role of the mass media in American life. They show that:

Eight out of ten adults read one or more daily newspapers on the average weekday and spend an average of 35 minutes a day on them.

On any weekday evening, 75 million Americans are likely to be watching television. The average home set is in use more than 6 hours a day and individual viewing is now close to 3 hours a day.

The approximately 40 percent of Americans who read magazines regularly spend an average of 33 minutes a day on them.

The one-third of Americans who read books regularly spend an average of 47 minutes a day on them.

The audience for radio is far greater than that for any other single medium of mass communication.

There is no doubt about the profound impact that mass media make on public information, knowledge, culture, and patterns of living. There is considerable speculation, however, about the extent of *specific effects* resulting *from exposure to specific media*. On occasion, it has been possible to prove the spectacular effect that exposure to a specific medium has had on people, but these instances are few and far between.

MINI-EXAMPLE:
"THE INVASION FROM MARS" BROADCAST

The evening of October 30, 1938, Orson Welles and his CBS radio theatre group dramatized an imaginary invasion from Mars. The hour-long drama was prefaced by the announcement that the show was a dramatization of a novel by H. G. Wells. The show itself consisted of extremely realistic bulletins and newscasts, interspersed with music, flashes from the "scene," interviews with "experts," the police, and eye-witnesses.

The reaction was panic on the part of thousands of listeners and others who were contacted by listeners. Thousands of people called the police and agencies of the federal government; other thousands warned their friends; and still other thousands took direct action by packing up their family and belongings and driving away from the Eastern seaboard where the invasion from Mars was supposedly taking place.

Questions for Discussion

1. The radio dramatization of an imaginary invasion from Mars had an immediate, obvious and direct effect on thousands of people. To what extent do you think this was due to the time at which it took place?
2. Do you think a radio broadcast of a similar nature could have the same effect today? What about a similar television broadcast? Justify your conclusions.

Few of the effects of the mass media are as direct and sharp as those resulting from "The Invasion from Mars" radio broadcast. For the most part, the effects of the mass media are cumulative, long-term and hard to isolate. There is more or less general agreement that the mass media:

1. *Do not ordinarily have a direct effect on audiences but rather operate through a variety of mediating factors and influences.*
2. *Basically reinforce rather than convert.* Thus, most studies show that exposure to mass media campaigns solidify the attitudes and opinions of their audience but do not generally change attitudes and opinions.
3. *Serve to confer status.* The mass media focus attention on people and organizations, and they also tend to "feed on" each other. Hitherto relatively unknown people and organizations suddenly become known throughout the country because they catch the attention of the mass media and are featured in newspaper stories, on talk shows, and in magazine articles.
4. *Provide the source with credibility.* Because they're considered to be impartial and nonpartisan, mass media messages are deemed to be more credible than those stemming directly from a public relations source.

Answering the question as to which of the mass media has the greatest impact is difficult if not impossible because of multi-media exposure to the media by the public. We do know radio provides the *swiftest* means of information dissemination; that television provides the *most dramatic* coverage of events; that newspapers and magazines provide the most *in-depth* dissemination of news and information; and that all of them combined provide our basic view of the American scene and Lippmann's world which is "ought of sight, out of mind." As Schramm sums up mass media effects:

> We can be confident . . . that the mass media do have a significant effect on the organization of our leisure time and a significant effect on what we know, and when and in what detail

we know it. The effect on knowledge is sufficiently important to cause some troubled thoughts about what appears in the media and how what appears is determined. We have good reason to believe, also, that under certain conditions . . . the media can have a direct effect on social behavior and that under certain conditions they may function to inhibit social change. . . .

Men, Messages & Media p. 262

Which Channels are Most Adaptable to the Source's Purpose and to the Content of the Message?

The two questions relating to channels are so closely related they are being taken up as a unit rather than individually. The key word is "adaptable" and it correctly implies that each medium has certain characteristics that make it more suitable than the others for specific purposes. All too often practitioners utilize a particular channel — most of the time it's the newspaper — because they're more at home in that channel's milieu. But the newspaper may not be the best medium for the source's purpose or for the content of the message, hence the question reminds us that there's a need for purposeful rather than random communication.

Marshall McLuhan, the Canadian sage who was much in vogue in the sixties, cryptically maintained that "the medium is the message." If he is taken literally he means that the nature of the medium itself, irrespective of the contents of the message, is what makes the difference in the communication process. Another way of stating McLuhan's thesis is that form is more important than substance.

Though McLuhan presents us with an intriguing view of the media and though there is validity to his contention about the unique importance of the nature of the media, his thesis is all too embracing and sweeping to be accepted at face value. The nature of the medium does affect communication, but so do the nature of the source, message, channel, and receiver. A more fruitful line of inquiry in regard to the question about the media and their adaptability to the source's purpose and the content of the message is to consider the question in terms of the three essential roles of media: to inform, influence, and entertain.

If the purpose of the source is to *inform*, one has to rate print media as being more adaptable than the electronic media for the transmission of *detailed* information. It is true that radio and television may be the first to inform us of events, actions, and activities, but the information they provide is admittedly sketchy and superficial. As a nationally known, highly respected television commentator has observed, the entire contents of a half-hour network news show would take up only one part of the front page of the New York *Times*. Furthermore, as to content of the message, the more complex and specialized the information, the more adaptable it is to newspapers and magazines.

Thus, if the source wants to get across information quickly and swiftly and is not dealing with detailed and involved material, the electronic media would best suit the source's purpose. However, if the source is dealing with information not easily digested at a glance or a first hearing, newspapers and magazines would be more suitable both for the source's purpose and for the contents of the message.

If the purpose of the source and the message contents are meant to *influence*, we are faced with a situation where no one medium has a singular advantage over all the others. Radio and television have the advantage of *immediacy* in terms of influencing people, but there is no evidence to support the view that this influence has long-range, carry-over effects. Television's unique ability to take its audience right into the middle of an event or activity with both sight and sound provides that medium with vivid impact value, but again there is no evidence to support the view that this influence has long-range, carry-over effects. Highly respected print media — particularly columnists with large followings and publications that influence others through their editorials and investigative reporting — have immediate and also carry-over impact when their ideas and thoughts are picked up by others. But again, there is no conclusive proof of their long-range effects.

Equally important in the context of the relationship among source purpose, message content, and adaptability is the problem of *entry* and *control*. The three network evening news shows reach an audience of between forty and forty-five million homes, but getting past the gatekeepers on these shows is a very difficult task. Getting past newspaper and magazine gatekeepers is also difficult, but not as difficult as with television because the total "news hole" is larger on print media. Of course, control of the material is always in the hands of the media except in the case of paid advertising.

Because it is paid for and its composition is in the hands of the practitioner, public relations advertising surmounts both the entry and control problem and has been used often by practitioners by way of the print media. Such advertisements can be targeted to specific publics and later "merchandised" to other audiences for maximum exposure. There have been instances where they've had considerable impact — two that come to mind are the Byoir advertisements in behalf of the A&P and the Whitaker & Baxter advertisements in behalf of the AMA — but there has been no proof about the effects of the vast bulk of such public relations advertising.

If the purpose of the source and the message contents are meant to *entertain*, there is no doubt that television is the prime medium. People receive a good deal of their information about the world and are influenced in many respects by what they view on television, but the major strength of the medium is in its ability to entertain. Further, if we consider entertainment in the broadest sense we find that television also has the ability to meet Lasswell's concept of the media as transmitters of culture and the social fabric. Through its combination of sound and picture, television brings us the world of dance, music, drama, manners, dress, living patterns, and the many other aspects of our national life. Print media entertain and transmit culture through features, comics, essays, columns, and long articles, but they come in a poor second to television — and one might say, even a second to radio in terms of popular music — when it comes to entertainment.

Summing up, in considering adaptability of the various media to the source's purpose and message content, the practitioner has to understand and recognize the major assets and deficits created by the nature of the individual medium. In most instances, this will result in the use of all media by the practitioner, but with careful attention to the specific reasons for communication by the source.

RECEIVER-RECIPIENT

Just as Banquo's ghost hovered in the background to haunt Shakespeare's Macbeth, so does the receiver-recipient hover in the background of the communication process to haunt the source. As has been noted, the receiver is all-important, although all too often he is neglected or given insufficient thought by the source-sender when messages are conceived and transmitted.

> Big league pitchers don't simply throw baseballs to big league batters and hope their good old fast ball or change-up will smack in the strike zone. They study the line-up before the game, picking out the weak and the strong hitters and planning their general pitching strategy. When they face the batter they take note of the particular situation existing when the batter comes to plate; study his stance; try to figure out what the batter knows about the pitcher's delivery and whether he's a sucker for a fast ball, curve, or knuckle ball. Then, after an exchange of signals with the catcher and some tugging at his cap, the pitcher slams one over.

Public relations practitioners would do well to emulate successful big league pitchers. This calls for a careful study of the receiver from many different angles and perspectives, the most important of which are the *receiver's knowledge, communication skills, predispositions and group membership*, what Schramm has termed the *"fraction of selection,"* and *opinion leaders*.

THE RECEIVER'S KNOWLEDGE

In considering the receiver's knowledge we are thinking of two forms of knowledge: general knowledge and knowledge about the source.

General knowledge provides a clue about the receiver's ability to absorb information or ideas transmitted by the source. For the most part, communicators err when they operate on the assumption that the average person is well informed simply because he's bombarded on all sides with information from a wide variety of sources. Despite the advanced stage of media in the United States, the widespread ownership of radio and television sets, the millions who read newspapers and magazines, the fact remains that only a fraction of information and ideas get through the invisible net that people seem to cast about themselves.

Study after study has proven that people are ignorant about such elementary facts as the name of their congressman and senators, vice presidential candidates, the secretary of state, etc. Little wonder, therefore, that even after repeated exposure to mass media identification messages millions of people don't know whether it's Goodrich or Goodyear that sponsors those blimps; whether it's Westinghouse or General Electric in whom you can put your trust; and whether it's Vantage or True that has the lowest nicotine and tar content. If there's so little knowledge about high officials and oft-repeated slogans — and there is — then a wise course is to assume that most people have less knowledge about your organization than you think they have. Better yet, rather than draw assumptions conduct a study to ascertain for certain the degree of knowledge held by the publics you're trying to reach. Readership studies provide tangible evidence of reader knowledge as well as opinions about employee publications, and public opinion surveys provide similar input about public knowledge and opinions about organizations.

THE RECEIVER'S COMMUNICATION SKILLS

Communication skills are important factors for the source, but they are equally as important for the receiver although they involve a different set of skills. When dealing with the receiver's communication skills we are concerned mainly with the skills of reading, listening, and viewing (and tangentially with the skills of writing and speaking as they relate to feedback). When we're writing for an employee public we need to know the *decoding skill levels* existing within that public, and we should be cognizant of the probability that a management audience will be more highly educated than an hourly employee audience and hence can understand and absorb a higher level of language, expression, and thought.

Similarly, in dealing with the television audience we should recognize that the decoding level of the audience at 7:30 p.m. will differ from that of the audience at 11:30 p.m., not merely in terms of educational levels but also in terms of sophistication and insight.

In short, there's need to understand there are different decoding communication skill levels that operate within, as well as between and among, media audiences. With some exceptions, one shouldn't expect to find the same decoding communication skills among readers of the median-sized daily newspaper of 12,500 circulation and among the readers of the New York *Times;* among the vast radio audience and the readers of *Scientific American;* among readers of the *Reader's Digest* and readers of the *Atlantic*. Preparing communications for these disparate audiences entails recognizing the varying decoding communication skill levels existing within each audience and then tailoring messages to match these levels.

AUDIENCE PREDISPOSITIONS AND GROUP MEMBERSHIP

Within every audience there exist certain *predispositions* that govern the way in which members of the audience will react to messages. In part these predispositions are individual in nature and tied to an individual's basic personality, early upbringing, and education. To a great extent — as noted by the Yale psychologists Hovland, Janis and Kelley — these predispositions result from conformity tendencies induced by group membership. They are based on the individual's perception of the behavior expected of him by the group to which he belongs and often govern the manner in which he will react to messages from the source. Hovland states the point this way:

> An analysis of the influence of groups upon the attitudes of their members is of obvious importance to the general problem of changing opinions through communications. Communicators often use these social incentives to facilitate acceptance of the opinion they advocate. For instance, community leaders frequently assert that group approval will follow upon the adoption of their recommendation or that disapproval will be the consequence of failure to accept it. On the other hand, a specific recommendation may encounter resistance because a group provides strong incentives for holding original opinions. Certain methods of persuasion entail lowering the importance of the incentives delivered by the group . . . or increasing the incentive value of competing groups.
>
> --
>
> from *Communication and Persuasion*, p. 134

The concept of group membership affecting reception of messages is a reaffirmation of the point made earlier in this chapter about the modification of the old "hypodermic needle" theory. That theory, as may be recalled, postulated that each individual is directly needled by the message sent through the media. Everyone is part of a network of family, occupational, and social groupings and these influence an individual's opinions and reactions to messages. How an individual is affected by messages transmitted by the source is shaped in large part by the groups to which the individual is attached.

Thus, when the statement is made that public relations practitioners should be applied social scientists, this means that practitioners have to understand and be sensitive both to individual predispositions and to group membership because of the important role they play in the reception to messages. Members of the mass audience may be annonymous to the communicator but they are not inert. Rather, they are part of an active social environment, and it's the wise communicator who acknowledges, understands, and keeps that environment in mind when he fashions and transmits messages.

SCHRAMM'S "FRACTION OF SELECTION" HYPOTHESIS

As a rule-of-thumb way of explaining the chance of an individual selecting any given communication, Wilbur Schramm devised an interesting formula which he calls the "fraction of selection" hypothesis. His formula is stated as follows (in *Men, Messages & Media*, p. 107):

$$\frac{\text{Promise of reward}}{\text{Effort required}} = \text{Probability of selection}$$

The promise of reward, as Schramm sees it, refers chiefly to the content of messages and the likelihood that they will satisfy needs as felt at any given time. The effort required refers to the availability of media and the ease of using a particular medium.

Thus, notes Schramm, people select an easily available television show rather than entertainment which they have to go out of their homes to see or hear. In short, there is little effort required of the recipient in choosing television entertainment over other forms. At the same time, perhaps from past experience from viewing a particular show, the recipient seeks out those shows which have rewarded him in the past.

"Over the years," says Schramm, "a person tends to seek the kinds of communication that have rewarded him in the past — his favorite television programs, a built-in expectation of reward developed from looking in certain places. Beyond that, he tends, other things being equal, to select the cues of information which are close at hand and easy to find in the glut of communication."

Schramm is well aware that his fraction of selection approach is a generalized one because he warns that at some time and in some situations, some information is so important a person will go to almost any effort to secure it. As an example, he notes that we may be willing to spend years studying to get a Ph.D. even though the easier path is to be satisfied with an undergraduate degree.

OPINION LEADERS

The role that opinion leaders play in the communication process has been studied chiefly by sociologists and political scientists and has resulted in field studies carried out in both small towns and cities. These studies have assayed the manner in which political decisions are made and influenced by opinion leaders; the manner in which decisions on selected issues have filtered down from small groups of influentials to the mass public; the manner in which influentials use the mass and specialized media to influence their information-input patterns and in turn influence selected publics; and similar patterns of selectivity, leadership and influence by key persons. From the many studies which have focused on selected field situations have come some generalized concepts of opinion leadership as they apply to the communication process. These are summarized briefly below:

Opinion leaders and the people they influence are often very much alike and typically belong to the same primary groups.

What this concept means is that we not only find so-called elite opinion leaders, but we find opinion leaders operating within groups and subgroups. There is seldom a group of leaders who influence everyone in all groups on all issues, but rather leaders who influence — to name some examples — union members, political clubs, social organizations, ethnic groups, educational bodies, and so forth. The problem for the practitioner is in ascertaining who are the opinion leaders in each group considered important to the communicator. If this can be done, then the communicator can key messages to these leaders in the expectation that the leaders in turn will transmit them to a wider sub-public.

Opinion leaders are more exposed than others to contact with the outside world by means of the mass media.

A study relating to the use of hybrid seed corn showed that it took fourteen years to gain widespread adoption of the new seed corn by farmers. The study showed there were five stages to adoption: awareness, interest, evaluation, trial, and adoption. The leaders in adoption — those who first demonstrated awareness — were the most widely read. However, one should not automatically assume there is a simple two-step flow from media to opinion leaders to followers. Opinion leaders rely on *many* sources for their information and ideas, and they are also influenced by others whom they consider to be leaders.

Opinion leaders utilize a variety of media and means in relating their groups to relevant parts of society.

The study carried out in Decatur, Illinois, and reported in the book *Personal Influence* by Katz and Lazarsfeld, showed that large city newspapers served to relate fashions to the fashion leaders. A study of doctors showed that out-of-town meetings were important sources of information about new medical ideas. The hybrid seed corn study showed that contact with the city and with farm bureaus of agricultural colleges were important for the farm innovators. Thus, general media, meetings, colleges, specialized media, and a wide variety of sources are used by opinion leaders in gaining information and ideas.

In summation, opinion leaders are important as they relate to the receiver in the communication process, but once again we must remember that we are talking about a process in which an almost limitless number of factors are involved. Being aware of these factors and their roles in the process is only the first step in achieving real understanding of the complex nature of communication between and among people.

As a means of summing up some of the major points stressed in this chapter the following mini-case about a British intelligence operation is presented for analysis and discussion.

MINI-CASE
A LESSON IN INTELLIGENCE OPERATIONS

In his book, *The Man Who Never Was,* Ewen Montague tells how British Intelligence used a dead man to pull off an intelligence coup in World War II prior to the invasion of Italy. They took an unknown dead man; provided him with a complete life history and identity as a major in the Royal Marines; packed him in ice; shipped him off on a submarine after planting a letter and some documents on him;

dumped him into the sea in the dead of night near Huelva on the southwest coast of Spain. These elaborate procedures were followed to give the impression that the "officer" had gone down in a plane crash and washed up on shore in an area where the British knew a German intelligence person was operating. The hope was that the Germans would be fooled into believing that the Allies did not intend to invade Sicily (which they did) and would draw away their troops and vessels. In describing the "vital document" which was the means by which he hoped to fool the Germans, Montague cited the problem as follows:

> If the German General Staff was to be persuaded, in face of all probabilities, to bank on our next target being somewhere other than Sicily, it would have to have before it a document which was passing between officers who *must* know what our real plans were, who could not possibly be mistaken and who could not themselves be the victims of a cover plan. If the operation was to be worthwhile, I had to have a document written by someone, and to someone, whom the Germans knew — and whom they knew to be "right in the know."

> So I put up the proposal that General Sir Archibald Nye, the Vice-Chief of the Imperial General Staff, should write the letter and that he should write it to General Alexander (who command-ed an army in Tunesia, under General Eisenhower) at 18th Army Group Headquarters. . . . The letter should be what we junior officers called "the old boy type" . . . and the sort of friendly letter which can give information and explanations that can't be put into an official communication. That sort of letter, and that sort of letter only, could convey convincingly to the Germans the indication that our next target was not Sicily, and yet could be found in the possession of an officer and not in a bag full of the usual documents going from home to our army abroad.

> I was aiming high, and I had to. I expected something of an explo-sion, and I got it. For many of even the most able and efficient people failed to appreciate what was wanted for this sort of job; for to realize that needed a particular sort of approach and a pecu-liar sort of mind that could look at the same puzzle from several different angles at the same time.

> You are a British Intelligence Officer; you have an opposite number in the enemy Intelligence, say in Berlin; and above him is the German Operational Command. What you, a Briton with a British background, think can be deduced from a document does not matter. It is what *your opposite number*, with his German knowledge and background, will think that matters — what con-struction *he* will put on the document. Therefore, if you want *him* to think such-and-such a thing, you must give him something which will make *him* (and not *you*) think it. But he may be suspi-cious and want confirmation; you must think what inquiries will *he* make (not what inquiries *you* would make) and give him the

answers to those inquiries so as to satisfy him. In other words, you must remember that a German does not think and react as an Englishman does, and you must put yourself into his mind. . . .

----

from Ewen Montague, *The Man Who Never Was*, Lippincott, 1954, p. 43

Questions for Discussion

1. In what specific respect does the above case and excerpt illustrate and exemplify some of the major key points made about communication in this chapter?

2. What lessons does the case teach you about the communication process?

3. Can you cite any personal communication experiences or observations of your own to illustrate the same points?

QUESTIONS AND PROBLEMS FOR DISCUSSION

1. Of what relevance to public relations practitioners is David K. Berlo's suggestion that communicators concentrate on the response to be sought through communication?
2. Name and explain some of the forms that communication can take.
3. What does the author mean when he states: "Communication does not take place in a vacuum or void, and it is not singular but pluralistic?"
4. Explain the "hypodermic needle" and the "two-step flow" theories of communication. What are some criticisms that can be leveled against both theories?
5. Explain what is meant by encoding, decoding, and feedback, and cite some examples to illustrate each.
6. Exactly how does source-receiver empathy serve to bring about effective communication?
7. What is meant by "source credibility" and how does it operate?
8. What does the author mean when he states that practitioners often find themselves in a buffer zone or no-man's land between management and recipients when trying to establish and maintain source credibility?
9. Exactly how does situational acuity serve the source in bringing about effective communication?
10. What are the chief communication encoding skills needed by the source?
11. Explain the connection among Newsom's idea that people don't stand still to be educated, Wiebe's concept of the gyroscopic phenomenon, and Robinson's thought about nonmotivation as each of these applies to reaching audiences with messages.
12. Cite some examples to show how interest-identification with an audience improves the impact of messages.
13. What are some of the problems faced by the source in trying to relate messages to common experience and meaning between source and receiver?
14. Cite some examples to show how messages have been tailor-made for the situation, time, place and/or audience.
15. Explain or illustrate the difference between channels which are: interpersonal or mediated; personal or impersonal; assembled or nonassembled.

16. What is meant by "the gatekeeper" in communication through mass media channels? Why is the gatekeeper important to the communicator?
17. Cite some data to illustrate the extent of the mass media picture in terms of newspapers, television, radio and magazines.
18. Cite some data to illustrate the pervasive role of the mass media in American life as they impact on the audience of mass media.
19. What does Marshall McLuhan mean when he says that "the medium is the message"? What criticism can be made of this concept?
20. In rating the various mass media in terms of their adaptability to the source's purpose and to message content, how would you rate each medium as it relates to providing information? To influencing the receiver? To providing entertainment?
21. In what way is communication effectiveness influenced by the receiver's knowledge? By the receiver's communication skills? By the receiver's predispositions and group membership?
22. Explain Schramm's "fraction of selection" hypothesis as a way of judging the chance that an individual will select any given communication.
23. Explain some key concepts about opinion leaders and the way they influence the reception of messages.

FEEDBACK: REPORTING, MEASUREMENT, AND EVALUATION

9

As a general rule, most human and organizational activities and performance are subject to measurement, reporting, and evaluation. Competitive athletes and teams are measured by their ratio of wins to losses. Salesmen are measured and evaluated on the basis of their sales records. Students are measured by grades; professors by student evaluations; deans by presidents; and presidents by boards of trustees.

Reporting is even more commonplace than measurement and evaluation. The professor reports student achievement by turning in grades at the end of the term. The salesman sends back weekly sales reports to the home office. The corporation mails quarterly and annual reports to its stockholders and holds an annual meeting. From kindergarten throughout his or her entire working life the individual is the subject of reporting, measurement, and evaluation.

Many and varied are the forms which such reports, measurements and evaluations take. Some are formal, some informal; some are quantitative, some qualitative. Some are intuitive and personal; some are highly organized and impersonal.

The public relations field bears witness to the plethora and variety of forms used for reports, measurements, and evaluations, and this chapter will deal with them in orderly fashion. Because reporting is more prevalent than the other two, it will be discussed first.

REPORTING

Reports are the means whereby the practitioner details public relations activities, actions, and results achieved over a specified period of time. The report is another way of stating: this is what we have accomplished. It can be a series of brief statements; it can be pegged to previously stated goals and objectives (in which case it provides a form of measurement); and it can include work that remains to be done.

The report is an excellent way of stating accomplishment in quantitative terms. It can state, for example, how many releases were prepared and mailed out; sum up the column inches of copy resulting from use of the releases by the print media and the minutes of air time resulting from use of the releases by the electronic media; cite the circulation and audience of the media where the material appeared.

The report enables management to keep tabs on the public relations function and the people responsible for carrying out that function. It provides valuable input and serves to provide the intelligence data needed for managerial decisions relating to public relations activities. When presented regularly and in accordance with predetermined patterns, it enables comparisons to be made over a period of time.

On the other hand, the report is generally a poor way of stating accomplishment in qualitative terms. Reports seldom deal with the *quality* of the work accomplished or with the *results* of such accomplishment. To mention, for example, that a specific release was carried by the Associated Press or by the United Press International is one thing. To sum up the number of newspapers that actually printed the story is a more difficult matter, and to draw definite conclusions about the *impact* of such coverage is an almost impossible task.

For example, consider the following extracts from a monthly public relations report:

1. Gave two talks to Rotary and Kiwanis in _____.
2. Release on taurine eliminate carried by the _____ Gazette, the _____ Observer, and the _____ Daily Press.
3. Taurine eliminate brochure delivered by the printer and mailed to our A-B-C lists.

It's possible to add up the number of people who heard the talks, the circulation of the three papers which carried the taurine eliminate story, and the number of people who received the brochure. What *effect* the talks, news stories, and the brochures had is open to conjecture.

FORMS OF REPORTS

Reporting of public relations results is done both informally and formally.

INFORMAL REPORTING

A good share of the reporting of public relations activities is done through informal means, at irregular intervals, and as part of the normal operations of an organization. One should not assume, however, that informal reporting has little or no value. On the contrary, such reporting can be of more value than the formal type of reporting since it is carried out without much advance warning.

Large counseling firms with a sizable number of account executives operating under the supervision of a small number of executive vice presidents are frequent users of informal reporting. The author spent an entire working day sitting in the office of an executive of such a firm noting what transpired. A good share of that executive's day was spent going over the status of various accounts with the account executives responsible for activities on behalf of the clients. In effect, what the executive was doing was to touch base with the account men under his jurisdiction, asking questions about what had been done, what was being done, and what was planned for the future.

Similar informal reporting is also carried out in the public relations departments of organizations. Where the department is actually a single public relations person, he or she keeps in touch informally with the executive to whom he or she is responsible. Where the department is of some size, the head of the department follows the same procedure used by the counseling firm executive by touching base informally with those in the department who are responsible for various public relations activities.

Time — or the lack of time — is one of the main reasons executives rely on informal reporting as a means of checking on the work of those under them. Formal systems of reporting which require meetings and conferences take up sizable chunks of valuable time, both on the part of the executive and those reporting to him. An informal accounting takes no more time than is required for a short inter-office call or visit. The following comment made to the author by the head of a large public relations department emphasizes the problem of time:

> One reason for abandoning it (a formal audit) was that I have been too busy. . . . Now, as best I can, I follow what each staff member is doing, note areas of improvement, and from time to time broaden a discussion on a specific phase of work into a general review, with my criticisms and suggestions. A less formal approach, but more successful too.

FORMAL REPORTING

There are four major ways in which public relations results are formally reported: *memoranda and reports* provided at regular intervals; *plans board, group, and committee* meetings; *briefings and presentations*; and *year-end annual reports*.

Memoranda and Reports

Probably the most common form of reporting by formal means is through the use of memoranda and reports submitted at periodic intervals, and these can range from the simple to the elaborate. Depending on the circumstances, such memoranda and reports are provided weekly, semi-monthly, or monthly and portray a picture of account activity as described *by the person responsible for the activity*. (For this reason, one seldom finds failure writ large in said reports).

The most common form of such reports is a simple listing of activities in the period covered by the report. No attempt is made to cite activities in order of importance, nor does the report state the degree of difficulty and time involved in carrying out the activity. A stark recital of factual reporting, the memorandum or report simply sets forth work accomplished, partly accomplished, and/or still to be put into motion. In most cases the report or memorandum is a single copy sent to a superior; where circumstances warrant it, copies are sent to others.

In counseling firms account executives often send a monthly activity report to the client with a copy to the executive vice president supervising the account executive. In addition, counseling firms often require that account executives, particularly those handling several accounts, send reports to their superiors in the firm summarizing activity on all the accounts being handled.

MINI-EXAMPLE
A BI-MONTHLY REPORT TO MANAGEMENT

Every two months Benay Leff, director of community relations for the Psychiatric Institute of Washington, D.C., sends a memorandum to her superior at the Institute. Following is her report for March and April, 1975:

MEMORANDUM

To: Allan Weissburg

From: Benay Leff

Date: May 22, 1975

Subject: Activity Report of the Community Relations Office for March and April, 1975

- Completed all production work on new PI nursing recruitment brochure — blue line received May 21; brochure will be ready approximately June 1.

- Arranged the following speaking engagements, radio and TV appearances:
  - Jeanne Mitchler-Fiks spoke at Catholic University;
  - National Town Meeting — WETA/FM radio — 3 PI staff members;
  - Dr. Fram on WRC-TV (Channel 4) news feature;
  - Clare Foundraine on "Everywoman."

- Coordinated publicity and tours for Black Nurse Recruitment Day, Tuesday, March 4.

- Prepared and distributed letters notifying students' parents of Developmental School change to foundation status.

- Served as member of Afro-American Day Planning Committee; coordinated publicity and arranged for hostesses; wrote memoranda of appreciation to kitchen staff and hostesses.

- Served as member of the D.C. Mental Health Association Planning Committee for May 15 Annual Meeting Day; attended approximately six meetings; designed, prepared, and arranged for printing of advance promotional flyer and program and did other publicity work.

- Met with Tineke Haase, *Montgomery County Journal* reporter, to discuss PI programs and services for article to appear in the *Journal*.

- Met with Rev. Duke Lundeen to discuss Augustana Mental Health Center PR efforts and relationship to other PI services.

- Made initial contact with Dr. Elizabeth Schoenberg for appearance at April's Combined Clinical Conference.
- Met with the Park Manager of Glen Echo Park to discuss their programs for children and adults; explored potential relationships with PI's Personal Resource Center.
- Initiated new monthly coffee social in March; assumed responsibility for coordinating on regular basis.
- Met with Helen Burr, PI Gerontology Consultant, to plan and design Gerontological Consultation Service brochure.
- Met with Bart Kraff, Allan Weissburg, and Kaja Brent to discuss PR impact of PI admission policies.
- Designed and arranged for printing of the Admission's Office "Aftercare Planning Form."
- Met with representatives of Mailtech to compare costs and services with current bulk mailing fees incurred by PI.
- Arranged for reprinting of Children's Unit family information guide and for the printing of five PI staff members' business cards.

In addition to the aforementioned activities, the Community Relations staff maintained its publication of the BULLETIN, completed several questionnaires, responded to innumerable inquiries regarding PI's programs, attended regular staff meetings, and answered routine correspondence.

Reprinted with permission

Questions for Discussion

1. What's your opinion of the report format, wording, and contents?
2. What does the report tell you about the work assigned, assumed and/or delegated to Ms. Leff and carried out by her?
3. Rearrange the list of activities cited in the report to reflect what you consider to be those "Most Important," "Of Average Importance," and "Least Important." Be prepared to *justify* your rearrangement.

A variation of the report which contains a straight listing of activities is one which lists accomplishments under appropriate headings. In this way the report details work done with media, for example, or with community groups, executives, and the like. Another breakdown commonly used groups activities under the title of projects. Another method is to cite predetermined objectives and match results to the objectives. (Such a method provides the means for a comparison between objectives and results and thus sets forth the raw materials for evaluation.)

Computers have been put to good use by practitioners to provide the data for the reporting of public relations results, though chiefly where a large amount of publicity is being generated. A common practice in the past, and one which is still relied upon today, is to take clippings as they come in from the clip services, paste them neatly in bound books or reproduce them in a variety of fancy print form, and send them along to management. At annual meetings of trade associations or large organizations there are often several large standing panels on which are pasted large amounts of press clippings. The obvious conclusion is that the public relations department or counseling firm has been busy and productive, the releases have resulted in loads of press clippings, and somewhere "out there" people have been influenced.

The computer has modernized this "bushel basket" method of measurement of results, channelized and systematized the reporting, and made it possible to draw comparisons between periods. Here is how one large counseling firm describes its use of the computer for measurement purposes:

> One of the programs we have computerized produces between 500 and 1000 clippings a month. These clippings and their blood brothers — reports of TV and radio broadcasts — are the raw material which the computer absorbs, studies, tabulates and analyzes. They cover a variety of publicity — from photos and captions in newspapers, to straight news stories and editorials in newspapers. There is also a substantial volume of multi-page articles in trade and technical publications, as well as reports, indicating TV and radio broadcasts.

> Without the computer, counting and measurement of publicity circulation would have to be done by hand. And as all of us know, that can be quite an expensive proposition. Here's how the computer does it. As the clippings come in, a girl glances at them one by one — but she doesn't need to read them. She simply sorts them into envelopes or boxes such as a postal clerk sorts the mail. . . . Every two months these envelopes are delivered to the computer service company. There they are measured, and the column inches plus the circulation figures of the particular publication are fed into the computer, to join with similar inputs accumulated earlier during the year. A punch of the button, and out comes the readout. These show for each type of story — for the particular two-month period as well as cumulative to date in the year — the number of clips received, their length, and the total circulation of the publication in which they appeared. These figures are further broken down into type of publications — daily newspaper, weekly paper, general magazines, trade and technical magazines, etc. . . .

The counseling firm executive who wrote that statement remarked that computers are used "in the area of compiling and evaluating publicity results." There is no doubt about the effectiveness of the computer in *compiling* publicity results, but pertinent questions can be raised about the *evaluation* of such results. Computer printouts showing the number of clips, column inches, and publications certainly do sum up where the stories appeared, but they leave unanswered questions about *actual readership, impact,* and *effectiveness*.

Plans Board, Group, and Committee Meetings

Operating on the premise that several heads are better than one, many counseling firms and public relations departments — especially the larger ones — utilize plans board, group, and committee meetings for the purpose of reporting public relations activities. Such meetings serve other purposes — they are particularly valuable for exchanging ideas for programming — but one of their major purposes and the one discussed here is to bring all concerned up to date on what is happening.

In the majority of cases those attending report meetings will have a common interest or central administrative tie that binds them together. In attendance at any such meeting might be the operating heads of the various units that make up the central public relations department of a company, or the account executives who report to an executive vice president in a counseling firm, or all professional staff members of a public relations departmental unit or of a service unit in a counseling firm.

Achieving full attendance at report meetings poses more problems for counseling firms than for internal public relations departments. Client demands take precedence over report meetings of counseling firms, and such demands often mean that the counseling staffer cannot attend a scheduled meeting because duty calls for him to be elsewhere. Obviously, serving the client is more important than reporting about the client.

Briefings and Presentations

Where there seems to be a felt need for formal reporting of public relations activities, counseling firms and internal departments rely on briefings and presentations. The chief public relations officer of Client X may request that the counseling firm make a presentation as part of an annual meeting or conference of the chief executives of the client organization. Where no counseling firm is involved, the public relations department may be called upon to brief the firm's chief executives or make a presentation about public relations activities.

Annual sessions of this kind are tightly organized affairs which deal with the most important facets of corporate and organizational life. Public relations is just one small part of the corporate entity and is usually given a proportionately small amount of the available time. Because they will be in the spotlight for a brief amount of time, public relations executives wisely prepare their presentations with great care. Knowing that an oral presentation may be quickly forgotten they use such devices as slides, large charts and graphs, transparencies, and film. In some instances a presentation has been made in the form of a specially commissioned film, although it's wise to keep in mind that there's such a thing as over-kill; money-conscious corporate executives may question whether a film showing the results of public relations activity is worth the expenditure of corporate monies for what is generally a one-shot showing. One way of forestalling or countering this criticism is to be prepared with a plan to use the film not only at the annual meeting or conference but subsequently at other suitable and appropriate affairs. Thus, in effect, the filmed presentation can be likened to a "premiere" with other showings scheduled later.

Year-end and Annual Reports

The annual report, which is often the responsibility of the public relations department, is basically the means by which the corporation sums up its financial affairs. Prepared in coordination with the financial department, the annual report consists of financial tables, charts, and descriptive material. In recent years the report has been expanded to include four-color printing and art work as well as brief reports about all activities of a company. Public relations, as an important staff function, sometimes reports its activities in the annual report along with those of other functional areas of the company.

Some public relations departments prepare and print their own individual annual report to sum up the year's activity. This is particularly true where the department is a large one engaged in a wide variety of tasks and assignments. As with the use of a specially-commissioned film presentation, one has to use judgment in deciding how much money to spend on a report showing the results of spending money for public relations activities.

INFORMAL AND FORMAL REPORTING SUMMED UP

As this section has demonstrated, there are numerous ways of reporting public relations activities and all of them serve the useful purpose of informing management what public relations personnel are doing. Compiling reports takes time, and it can be argued that time might be more usefully spent carrying out rather than reporting activities. However, the management that is ignorant of the activities of its public relations people and department may have little respect for the function. Reporting thus not merely serves to keep management informed but builds support for the function and the activities carried out by the practitioner responsible for the function.

MINI-CASE
ANNUAL REPORT OF THE AMERICAN TRUCKING ASSOCIATIONS

The American Trucking Associations, Inc., the national organization of the trucking industry, is a federation of state trucking associations with a Washington, D.C., headquarters staff of several hundred employees headed by a president selected by the ATA's Executive Committee. Each year the ATA headquarters office prepares and publishes an Annual Report which summarizes activities for the year and is addressed primarily to the ATA Executive Committee composed of more than 100 trucking company executives. According to Gary LaBella, ATA press assistant, the report is also distributed to hundreds of other people in the industry and to the media. Following is the section of the 1974 ATA Annual Report describing the activities of the Public Relations Department:

The energy shortage and the resultant strikes and slow-downs by independent truck owners and drivers multiplied the problems, as well as the opportunities, for the ATA Public Relations Department during 1974.

While the trucking industry, as represented by ATA, was not a participant in the strikes and slow-downs, nevertheless, the news media focused attention on ATA, resulting in more numerous contacts with press relations staff, as well as specialists throughout the organization.

During 1974, the Press Relations Section of the Public Relations Department was brought up to its current authorized strength and developed the most active campaign of contacts with the media in the history of the department.

This fully-staffed operation issued more than 400 news releases this past year and prepared many special articles and features, on request, for newspapers, magazines and industry publications.

Special attention was given to furnishing material to state associations, including feature articles on driving safety and other topics for re-issuing from their own association headquarters.

The press section also developed a special manual on improved press relations for the specific use of state trucking associations.

As a special project, a 16-page industry background insert, run as an advertisement, and developed through the ATA Foundation and one of its members, was mailed with a letter from the press section to the editor of every daily newspaper in the United States. This mailing also offered the services of the press relations staff and precipitated requests for additional information on some of the topics covered in the 16-page insert.

A special kit of material for the news media on National Transportation Week was prepared and distributed, with press relations members conducting the major part of the operation.

Other members of the Public Relations Department staff also participated in the promotion of National Transportation Week-1974, and a kit of promotional ideas as well as news releases, speeches and radio copy was provided to the trucking industry. Indications point to wide use of this material.

This project won for ATA a special award for its work in promoting National Transportation Week by Traffic Clubs International during its annual convention in September in Phoenix, Arizona.

The 1974 Driver of the Year program was a signal success. The Public Relations Department arranged for the Driver of the Year and his wife to be presented with his trophy by Mrs. Richard Nixon in ceremonies at the White House. This and other Driver of the Year activities received wide press coverage including nearly 10 minutes on the full NBC television network during the popular "Today" program. This nationwide exposure occurred at the height of the strike by independent drivers and did much to present the organized industry's position in a favorable setting, and to offset unfavorable publicity.

Cargo theft and hijacking also attracted PR interest. As the attention of government officials, the public and the news media to this problem increased, the Public Relations Department in cooperation with the Trucking Industry Committee on Theft and Hijacking (TICOTH) — in a project funded by a member of the ATA Foundation — produced two motion pictures dealing with cargo protection. One film, directed to trucking industry and law enforcement audiences only, had its premier this spring in Washington before an impressive audience of government and law enforcement officials, as well as the Washington press corps. A second film, designed for public audiences, shows what the industry is doing to reduce cargo theft, and the role the public can play in discouraging the selling and buying of stolen goods.

The Officer Pressley "Safety Circus," sponsored by ATA, completed a most successful year during the 1973–1974 school year and now has begun a tour of the Southeastern, Southern and Southwestern states for the current school year.

Mail received from state highway and safety officials, law enforcement officers, and educators, as well as the audiences of young people, proves the solid public relations benefit of this safety program. In addition, in every city and town, Safety Circus, Officer Pressley, and the trucking industry received much press attention as well as television and radio exposure which more than offsets the cost of operating such a project. Millions of young people have been taught their earliest lesson in safety through the courtesy of the American trucking industry and the various state associations which help sponsor the show.

The Public Relations Department gave increased emphasis to the ATA National Truck Roadeo — held this year in Minneapolis — and with good result. In addition, one of ATA's regular advertisements in *U.S. News & World Report* was devoted to the truck Roadeo winners and the industry's safety programs as a follow-thru to Roadeo activity.

More than 600 tape-recorded radio interviews and more than 100 TV news films were distributed from Minneapolis during the Roadeo. Also, some 50 "live" newscasts were made direct to radio stations via telephone circuits.

Photographs from the Roadeo were sent to newsrooms across the nation via wirephoto, while local working press and trade press covered the event from press facilities provided and set up by ATA. . . .

In the field of radio public service, ATA has continued to send sets of tape-recorded public-service messages to approximately 4,000 radio stations. A steady response from stations indicates good usage. Many stations notify ATA of the equivalent advertising value of these trucking industry messages.

As a follow-up to this activity, and as part of the Public Relations Department's expanded services to state trucking associations, the department has issued scripts for public service announcements to state associations for distribution on their own letterheads to stations within their state.

Motion pictures, available through the ATA Public Relations Department, play an important part as one of the public relations tools put to use on behalf of the trucking industry.

During the past year there were more than 1,500 film showings to a total audience of nearly 11 million. There were 619 telecasts of ATA-sponsored films, and 887 showings to special audiences as well as trucking industry groups.

The Public Relations Department also added a new service in 1974 — the furnishing of "stock" artwork of trucks to trucking industry communicators, editors, and state associations. This new art service has been well received and will be continued and expanded.

Since the trucking industry is so dependent upon public understanding for its operations, advertising placed by ATA during the past year centered on the themes of safety and essentiality.

In its drive for increased productivity through weight or size increases, the industry has continually reminded influential segments of the public that it operates in a safe and efficient manner over the highways shared with motorists. The ATA advertising program has emphasized this vital factor.

By the end of the calendar year, ATA will have received some 35 million advertising exposures in the pages of *U.S. News & World Report, Newsweek* and *Atlantic* magazines. With a combined circulation of almost six million, these particular magazines were selected to carry our story after extensive evaluation to provide a national audience of business leaders and other individuals active in civic and community affairs — those vitally concerned with the transportation problems and needs of the nation. . . .

During the past year, a great amount of career literature was mailed out as a follow-up to career promotions carried out by members of the ATA Foundation.

Nearly 15,000 requests for a new career booklet were received and the majority of other requests to the Department were for vocational guidance materials. . . . More than one million publications were distributed during 1974 with more than 680,000 going to schools, for both students and teachers, and more than 387,000 going to the trucking industry and the general public. It is important to note that all of ATA's educational material is sent out only upon request.

There were in excess of 37,000 requests from teachers during 1974 and 36,000 from students and young people. This included nearly 6,000 individual requests from boys who wanted information on the Boy Scout Merit Badge on trucking. There were another 7,000 requests from trucking companies.

One of the major objectives of ATA's public relations program has been to explain and demonstrate that trucks pay for the roads they use and are not subsidized.

The ATA truck tax signs help promote this concept. In 1974, the truck tax sign project was reorganized and new signs were sold to carriers to place on the back of trailers. More than 10,000 such signs were distributed to motor fleets during the past year and the program will receive active promotion in the year ahead.

Telling the story of the American trucking industry to so many audiences on a continual basis, while at the same time responding to constant challenges, is fulfilling and rewarding for ATA's public relations professionals.

Reprinted with permission

Questions for Discussion

1. What's your opinion of the report format, tone, wording, and contents?

2. What does the report tell you about the work assigned, assumed and/or delegated to the Public Relations Department and carried out by its members?

3. Cite instances in the report whereby the Public Relations Department not merely reports but tries to provide a means of evaluating activities.

4. After citing the distribution of public-service messages to radio stations, the report states: "Many stations notify ATA of the equivalent advertising value of these trucking industry messages." What's your reaction to this statement?

5. As mentioned in the preface to the case, the report is distributed to ATA executives and others within the trucking industry and also to the media. What problems, if any, does this pose for those preparing the report? Can you cite specific instances in the report where this problem is apparent?

MEASUREMENT AND EVALUATION

Methods used to demonstrate and/or prove the *effectiveness* of public relations personnel and activities are what is meant by measurement and evaluation. The difference between *reporting* public relations activities and results and *measuring* and *evaluating* public relations activities and results is qualitative rather than quantitative. One measures and evaluates to assess the quality and value of public relations counsel, actions and activities, and this inevitably means that some *standards* are being used in the process of measurement and evaluation. These standards may be implied or they may be stated in explicit terms. They may be set forth to stand on their own or they may be compared with others. Standards are yardsticks, and whether implied or explicit they form the means of judging effectiveness.

Having accepted the public relations function as a legitmate and needed aspect of organizations — profit or nonprofit entities — the managements of these organizations want to know the *value* accruing from public relations counsel and actions. Burns W. Roper of the Roper research organization sums up management's value-oriented view as follows:

> There is a degree of skepticism on the part of managements who are users of public relations — even managements that employ large public relations departments of their own and outside public relations counsel as well. As a concept, modern management is aware of the value of public relations — or at least they are not sure enough that it is valueless to ignore public relations activities. At the same time, doubts are frequently voiced as to whether or not a particular public relations campaign is really working, as to whether or not the sponsoring organization is getting results.
>
> This skepticism is natural, because public relations operates in the field of ideas, attitudes and men's minds. There are no laboratory tests that will measure whether a public relations campaign works or does not work. You can't put a campaign in a test tube. But management nevertheless wants concrete proof of the value of public relations, just as it wants concrete proof of its other activities.
>
> (from "Can We Measure Results?," *Public Relations Journal*, April, 1958, p. 3)

How does management secure concrete proof of the value of activities other than public relations? In some cases, very easily; in other cases, the task is difficult. Almost all *line* areas of organizations — that is, those which are engaged in producing the product or service — are measured and evaluated against a set of standards. If the organization is one that manufactures and sells automobiles, the manufacturing department is measured and evaluated on the basis of the number, cost, and quality of the cars produced in a given period; in similar fashion, the sales department is measured and evaluated on the basis of the number of cars sold in a given period. Obviously, measuring the number and cost of cars produced is easier than measuring the quality of cars, but nonetheless number, cost, and quality are all measured and evaluated. If the number, cost, and quality do not measure up to predetermined quotas and standards, management takes action to bring about desired results. Processes and procedures may be changed; personnel may be shifted around, demoted or moved out.

But, say public relations practitioners, we are *staff* people who counsel, advise, and initiate actions and activities designed to assist the line and we can't be measured as easily as line people. True, but other staff functions are also measured and evaluated. The legal department, for example, takes cases to court and these are either won or lost. If the box score shows two cases won and ten cases lost, you can be sure that changes will be effected in the legal department. The financial department sets up tax shelters and systems of financial reporting, and if the box score shows that the Internal Revenue Service has disallowed ten and allowed two or that the Securities and Exchange Commission has successfully levied sizable fines, you can be sure that changes will be effected in the financial department.

There is validity to the argument that the activities and counsel of staff personnel can't be measured as easily as those of line personnel, and certainly public relations practitioners are also correct in claiming that their activities are more difficult to measure and evaluate than those of other staff functions. As Roper rightly points out, public relations operates along lines that are extremely difficult to measure and evaluate, and in addition public relations campaigns are not like laboratory experiments. One might very easily design and carry out two public relations campaigns along identical lines, but with dissimilar results because of circumstances beyond the control of the practitioner. It's with good reason that Roper, whose professional life has been devoted to survey research, concludes that "measuring public relations effectiveness with research techniques is only slightly easier than measuring a gaseous body with a rubber band."

Difficult as measurement and evaluation may be, nonetheless the attempt should be made whenever it's possible to do so. The function that can prove its effectiveness is the function that will be most valued by management. The function that can't be measured or evaluated is most likely to be cut back or dispensed with when there is a need to cut costs. For its own sake and also because measurement and evaluation are important elements in the dynamics of the process, public relations must make best use of the measurement and evaluative tools at its disposal. Such tools and methods are discussed, described, and analyzed in the sections that follow.

TOOLS AND METHODS OF MEASUREMENT AND EVALUATION

The tools and methods used in measuring and evaluating public relations counsel, actions, and activities range from the primitive to the sophisticated with various way stations in between these two extremes. In all cases where public relations is being evaluated certain value judgments are made, and these are made by people. Thus, the fact that a value judgment is based on a relatively primitive method — for example, a judgment made through personal observation rather than by means of a computer printout — does not imply that the evaluation or judgment is faulty. In the end, evaluation depends as much on the perception and wisdom of the judge as it does on the tools and methods available to him and used by him in forming judgments. For this reason, the listing of tools and methods described and discussed below are presented in no particular order of intrinsic value and importance.

PERSONAL OBSERVATION AND REACTION

Judgment of public relations performance based on personal observation and reaction by a superior is one of the most common, albeit primitive, methods used in evaluating public relations effectiveness. At all levels in all types of organizations public relations personnel and their performance are judged and evaluated by those to whom they report.

Kal Druck of Harshe-Rotman & Druck describes one level of evaluation as being *intuitive judgment*, and if we follow the dictionary definition of intuitive he means judgment made without the conscious use of reasoning. Thus, the public relations practitioner proposes an activity and management's intuitive response is "this is a good thing to do," or the practitioner takes actions and carries out an activity and management's response is "that was well done." Pinning one's professional hopes on such intuitive judgments entails a good deal of reliance on faith and charity, and where these cease to be forthcoming management's reaction could very well be "this is not a good thing to do," or "that was not well done."

Faith, hope, and charity being practiced more in the breach than in the observance these days, practitioners wisely provide their managements with tangible evidence of their performance and, as has already been noted, such evidence most often takes the form of reporting practices that have previously been discussed. Management, of course, can form its judgment by personally observing and reacting to *discernible* activity or results ensuing from public relations programming. Thus, if one aspect of the public relations program of an internationally known department store is the staging of an imaginative parade on Thanksgiving Day, the executives of that store need only observe that parade in progress to form some judgment about its effectiveness.

MATCHING OBJECTIVES AND RESULTS

As has been noted in the chapter dealing with planning and programming, public relations activity without a clearly designed purpose is not uncommon. Clearly, however, setting objectives is vital to successful programming. Even a generalized set of objectives is better than none at all, though objectives presented in *specific* terms are the most meaningful because they provide direction and also lend themselves to accurate measurement and evaluation.

When the specific terms set forth by objectives relate to actions, activities, or media coverage there is little problem in measuring and evaluating results. Thus, if a program's stated objective is to set up 1,000 "coffee houses" in order to increase the use and consumption of coffee by young people, it's not difficult to count the number of such houses established over a period of time and even to measure coffee consumption by those frequenting such establishments. If a program's stated objective is to write and place a series of feature stories about such coffee houses in at least 1,000 daily newspapers, reaching x number of people, it's not difficult to count and measure newspaper pick-up and circulation.

Much more difficult, however, is to set forth objectives in terms of specific attitudes and opinions changed or modified as a result of public relations programming. Here we are not dealing with actions or activities which are tangible things or objects, but rather with intangibles relating to points of view, frames of reference, mind-sets, and other aspects of attitude and opinion. Little wonder, then, that objectives relating to men's minds are not often couched in specific terms and not too often measured and evaluated when a program has ended and results are in.

If it's any consolation to public relations practitioners, their advertising brethren do not fare much better. Steuart Henderson Britt, nationally known professor of marketing and advertising, analyzed "proofs of success" for 135 campaigns by 40 advertising agencies and he concluded that almost none of the agencies really knew, or even could know, whether or not their campaigns were successful. ("Are So-called Successful Advertising Campaigns Really Successful?," *Journal of Advertising Research*, Vol. 9, No. 2) Britt reported that 99 percent of the agencies did not state campaign objectives in quantifiable terms; most of the agencies did not prove or demonstrate the success of the campaigns that they themselves had publicly stated were successes. Concluded Britt:

> Advertising of a product or service must prove its success as advertising by *setting specific objectives*. Such general statements of objectives as "introduce the product to the market," "raise sales," and "maintain brand share" are not objectives for advertising. Instead, they are the objectives of the entire marketing program. And even when considered as marketing goals, such statements still are too general and broad to be used to determine the extent of a plan's success or failure.

> Advertising goals should indicate (1) what basic message is to be delivered, (2) to what audience (3) with what intended effect, and (4) what specific criteria are going to be used to measure the success of the campaign.

> When the advertising campaign is over, the advertiser can best judge the results by comparing them with the intended results, as expressed in the campaign objective. Only when he knows what he is intending to do can he know when and if he has accomplished it.

If we are dealing with a public relations campaign, we can justifiably substitute public relations for advertising in Britt's above-mentioned conclusion. And if we do we will find that items one and two relating to goals — indication of the message and audience — will usually be covered in public relations programming, but items three and four relating to intended effect and criteria to be measured will most often be noticably absent.

Within profit-making organizations — and recently also within non-profit institutions — the concept and process known as *management by objectives* has been applied to public relations departments and managers as well as to the other functional areas. The process is basically a method whereby an executive and each major subordinate manager under him work out together the identification of common goals and a clear definition of the subordinate's major area of responsibility in terms of results expected of him, and then use these measures as guides for operating the unit and evaluating the work of the subordinate and the unit.

The important elements of the process are joint agreement between superior and subordinate about goals that are agreed upon in advance. At the end of a time period the subordinate's performance and that of his unit are reviewed and evaluated, usually by joint participation of superior and subordinate in the review and evaluation process. If necessary, during the specified time period adjustments are made and inappropriate goals are discarded. If there are gaps between goals and performance or results when the final mutual review is made, then steps are taken to ascertain what might be done to overcome the problems.

The major advantage of the management by objectives process is that it involves mutual commitment to goals and objectives, a clear charting of objectives, mutual review of results and evaluation. In effect, the process provides a map or chart to be followed in setting forth objectives, an order of priorities, and a method of review and evaluation. It can be used very effectively where objectives and activities to achieve them lend themselves to measurement and evaluation; it's difficult — as it is under almost all other systems — to use the management by objectives chart process as a means of measuring and evaluating programs and activities expected to lead to changes in attitudes and opinions.

An example of a management by objectives chart used in nonprofit public relations is set forth in the following mini-case.

MINI-CASE

A MANAGEMENT BY OBJECTIVES CHART USED BY A UNITED WAY ORGANIZATION

There are a variety of forms which can be used in charting objectives, action plans, and results achieved by means of the management by objectives process. In applying the process to the public relations department, the United Way of the Greater Utica Area (Utica, N.Y.) set up the following flow-chart to cover the first six-month period; as will be noted, "Results Achieved" and "Rating" has not yet been completed. (Note: A total of ten objectives were listed but only seven are cited here.)

PR WORK-PLAN
-1-

UNITED WAY OF THE GREATER UTICA AREA, INC.
MANAGEMENT BY OBJECTIVE WORKSHEET
First six months-1975

Objective	Priority of Objective	Action Plans To Achieve Objecitves	Results Achieved	Rating
Produce Annual Report/Annual Meeting Program for Thursday, Feb. 6	1	Develop slide series and accompanying script to be narrated by _____. Presentation will double as the annual report and will include a review of significant 1974 activities. Other agenda items are recognition of retiring officers and directors and election of new officers. A list of all employee groups cited will also be prepared and distributed at the meeting.		
Prepare, mail 1974 United Way Communications Report and packet by Jan. 24	2	Write report, select materials to accompany it, package and mail.		
Publish Rainbowgram on at least an every-other month basis in 1975	1	Gather information, write, print, mail. Each issue will highlight a specific area of activity. For example, the Jan. Rainbowgram will feature an explanation of the United		

...where changes are needed, select printing process, publish. Include service statistics by employer.

Objective	Priority	Action Plan
Agency Services by April 1		
Develop and distribute an Editor's kit for all weeklies and all in-plant publications by July 1	2	Prepare general news stories and photos relating to UW services, '75 campaign, etc. Include repro artwork of UW logo and theme. Distribute kits to appropriate editiors. Continually update media list adding in particular all union publications.
Have 1975 Campaign brochure ready for printers by July 1	1	Create, design, write copy, take photographs, and deliver to printer.
By June 1, recruit and organize manpower for both the Publicity and Campaign Activities sub-committees; and develop a written workplan for both groups	1	Work with Public Relations Chairman in selecting and asking local communication professionals to serve on the respective committees. Devise an outline of projects and action plans for each subcommittee, based on items recommended as priorities by the PR Director and PR Chairman. Submit workplan for appropriate committees for additional input and subsequent initiation.

Priority of Objective:
1. Primary
2. Secondary
3. Least-important

Rating of Accomplishment:
4. Consistently exceeds job requirements
3. Fully satisfactory — meets all job requirements
2. Satisfactory-some improvement needed.
1. Unsatisfactory.

Questions for Discussions

1. What is your opinion of the five-item flow chart devised by the Greater Utica Area United Way? Cite any problems you feel may occur in utilizing and implementing the chart.

2. What is your opinion about each of the seven objectives, the priority of objectives rating given to each, and the action plans devised to achieve the objectives?

3. Can you suggest any ways to modify or improve the chart? Justify your suggestions.

PUBLIC OPINION SURVEYS AND PANELS

Survey research in the form of public opinion surveys and survey panels is the major method used in gathering empirical evidence to measure and evaluate public relations performance.

Public opinion surveys are utilized in two ways: either by means of a single survey taken at the end of a campaign or after a specified period of time, or by means of a before-and-after set of surveys. In both instances use is made of the survey techniques described in the chapter on public opinion: objectives of the survey and the universe are set forth; a random probability sample is drawn; a questionnaire is designed and administered; data is collected, and a report is written and delivered to management. The major objective of public opinion surveys used in evaluation is to ascertain measurable results stemming from public relations performance and/or programs in regard to people's knowledge, attitudes, and opinions. The single survey makes no attempt to measure attitudes, opinions, and knowledge in advance of programming, but does so after the program has been carried out for a period of time.

Company Y, a leading manufacturer of chemicals, has scores of plants throughout the country. One such plant, the Zulch Plant, is located on the banks of a heavily polluted river in the mid-West. In the late 1960s and early 1970s pollution of this river became so bad that citizens formed an anti-pollution committee that campaigned for clean-up of the river. Media supported the drive with numerous editorial campaigns, and one of the chief targets was the Zulch Plant.

Called in by the plant management to give counsel and advice and to propose action was the central public relations department of Company Y. An independent outside agency was retained to conduct a study of the river's pollution, and its results showed that the Zulch Plant was but a minor contributor to the pollution. By means of meetings with concerned citizens and opinion leaders, a press conference announcing the results of the study of the river's sources of pollution, and other measures the public relations department told the story which exculpated the Zulch Plant.

A public opinion survey conducted shortly thereafter showed that 88 percent of those surveyed considered the river to be dangerously polluted; 58 percent knew who were the main polluters; and 63 percent felt that the Zulch Plant went to much trouble and expense to avoid polluting the river. In almost all respects, the Zulch Plant was given high marks and considered in favorable terms by the respondents.

Thus, by the use of public opinion survey the public relations department of Company Y was able to cite favorable survey results to measure the effectiveness of its campaign. Instead of merely reporting counsel given and action taken and then concluding that the program had been a success, the public relations department went directly to the public concerned, measured its knowledge and opinions, and cited results of the survey to prove effectiveness.

There is one single, but important flaw to the above illustration. Because no survey of public knowledge and opinion had been taken *before* the program was instituted it was impossible to show that the program had changed lack of knowledge to knowledge and/or had changed unfavorable attitudes and opinions to favorable ones.

The *before-and-after survey* technique is a means of correcting the flaw cited in the above-mentioned case. As its name implies, this technique consists of two public opinion surveys, one taken *before* a campaign or program has been instituted and one taken *after* it has run for a period of time or has been concluded. The technique thus enables the practitioner to show numerical and percentage changes in public knowledge, attitude, and opinion taking place before and after public relations action and activities had been instituted, thereby enabling the practitioner to cite more reliable effectiveness proof than could be cited by means of the single public opinion survey.

The before-and-after survey technique is not often used in actual practice for several reasons. For one thing, it is expensive. Most managements are unwilling to incur expensive obligations for the sake of measuring effectiveness, but would rather put their money into actual programming. Another reason is that public opinion surveying requires a special expertise not generally found in public relations departments or counseling firms. A third reason is that the circumstances about many public relations programs do not lend themselves to precise before-and-after measurement and evaluation because there are too many variables involved. A fourth reason is that when dealing with a large universe, those surveyed before and after will inevitably be different samples of the universe and even though these will be probability samples they are really different groups of people. A fifth and final reason is that before-and-after surveys could be the "moment of truth" for the practitioner by revealing that his carefully prepared and executed campaign produced either no change in public opinion or a change along negative lines, and certainly no one relishes that prospect.

MINI-CASE
THE CINCINNATI UNITED NATIONS CAMPAIGN

Although students seem to find that anything that took place more than five years ago is outdated, the educational campaign conducted in Cincinnati in 1947 and the surveys associated with it remain a classic case of before-and-after measurement and evaluation. It is classic chiefly because it has seldom been duplicated in the years since.

What was involved here was an information campaign designed to make Cincinnati residents better informed about the United Nations and world affairs. What makes the case of interest and importance to public relations students and practitioners is that sufficient funds were provided through a grant to carry out independent before-and-after surveys to determine the effectiveness of the six-month campaign.

The "before" survey consisted of interviews in September with a random/probability sample of 745 persons; the "after" survey consisted of interviews in March with a random/probability sample of 758 persons, 592 of whom had been interviewed in September. (The last 20 percent of the original sample either refused to be interviewed a second time or could not be located).

Between the two surveys a massive educational campaign was conducted in Cincinnati to make its residents more intelligently informed about world affairs and about the United Nations. A total of 14,000 children in the Weekday Church Schools held a World Community Day program; training courses were given to 150 leaders in the Cincinnati Council of Church Women; close to 13,000 people were reached through programs on world understanding put on by the Parent-Teachers Association; UN literature was given to every school child; radio stations and newspapers aired and printed UN news and information during the entire six-month period; and a total of 60,000 pieces of literature were distributed, 2,800 clubs reached by speakers, and hundreds of documentary film presentations were made. The slogan, "Peace Begins with the United Nations, the United Nations Begins with You," was shown everywhere and repeated in every conceivable manner.

The effectiveness of this massive informational campaign was measured by the results obtained by the two surveys, and they showed relatively few changes in public knowledge and attitude. A total of 65 percent in September and 66 percent in March were of the opinion the United States should take an active part in world affairs rather than keep out of them; 76 percent in September and 73 percent in March were of the opinion that the United States should join with other nations to establish an international police force to maintain world peace. In September 30 percent could not tell the main purpose of the United Nations, and by March the number had dropped to 28 percent. In September 55 percent knew that one job of the UN was to see that all people get equal rights and 50 percent knew another UN job was to improve health conditions everywhere; by March the comparable figures were 60 percent and 55 percent respectively. By March people blamed or praised the UN for the very things they had blamed or praised it earlier and by virtually unchanged percentages.

Questions for Discussion

1. What is your opinion of the before-and-after design of the surveys as a means of measuring the campaign's effectiveness?

2. What is your reaction to the survey results? Can you cite reasons why there was so little change in public knowledge and opinion after such an extensive educational campaign?

3. After consulting appropriate sources to ascertain the nature of international and UN relationships between September–March, 1947, explain the connection you see between these relationships and the survey results.

The *survey panel* is used in measuring public relations effectiveness because it doesn't have the disadvantages of the single public opinion survey or of the large cross-section samples used in before-and-after surveys. The panel is a sample of the same people interviewed more than once over a period of time. It is usually much smaller than the samples used in general cross-section public opinion surveys. Care is taken to ensure that the panel remains constant when the group is used to measure knowledge, attitudes, and opinions before and after a campaign has been instituted. Because the panel is small, its use as a measuring device is far less expensive than the larger cross-section sample. When the panel remains relatively constant it's possible to secure realistic measurement of campaign results as they affect the same group of people.

On the other hand, the survey panel poses another set of problems. When the panel is small — and most are small when compared to the larger samples used in normal cross-section surveys — any diminution of panel members changes the basic nature of the sample used before the campaign and the sample surveyed after the campaign. When the survey sample is as large as that used in normal cross-section samples there is an inevitable mortality that occurs in any population over even a brief period of time. Second, the smaller the survey panel the more likely it will not be truly representative of the universe. Finally, because most panelists become aware that they are being used for measurement purposes they become unduly conscious of their role and thus cannot be considered typical of the universe from which they were drawn. Despite these drawbacks, the survey panel offers the practitioner a relatively inexpensive, reliable, and simple means of measuring program effectiveness when used properly and with awareness of its methodological pitfalls.

INTERNAL AND EXTERNAL AUDITS

The process of auditing, which is most commonly identified with the field of accounting, has been used increasingly in recent years in public relations. The accounting audit entails an examination of records and accounts to check their accuracy. The public relations audit is most often used not so much to check accuracy but to check and improve the effectiveness of programs.

The *internal audit* takes the form of evaluation by one's peers and/or superiors within a public relations department or within a public relations counseling firm. The focus is usually on three areas summed up by three questions: what have you been doing and with what results; what are your problems; and what do you plan to do?

Sometimes the internal audit is a one-on-one evaluation of a staffer by his or her superior, but most often it's an evaluation by a "team" or committee selected for the sole purpose of conducting the evaluation. When the evaluation is completed, the team or committee is disbanded. Departmental audit teams are generally made up of the public relations department head and two or three middle-level or section heads. An audit of the account executive within a counseling firm is generally handled by a team composed of an executive vice president who does not directly supervise the account executive and two or three other account executives.

When a staffer or account executive is being audited, he or she is inevitably given advance notice and, in many cases, is requested to prepare an advance-audit memorandum summarizing account or program activity, problems, and future plans. This enables the audit team to focus on specifics and has the added advantage of pushing the auditee into self-analysis. The audit itself is most often informal in nature, provides the auditee with valuable inputs from colleagues and superiors, and gives the auditors insights into account activities and programs they knew little about prior to the audit.

There are certain practical and psychological negative aspects to internal audits. An audit takes time, and time is precious in departments and counseling firms. Within departments public relations staffers have their own functional problems and committee meetings to attend, and the same applies to counseling firm account executives and supervisors. Those whose perceptions and judgments are excellent for audit team purposes are usually using these perceptions and judgments to handle accounts and important departmental tasks, and hence they cannot be called upon too often for an audit. Obviously, this problem can be taken care of by spreading auditing assignments, but not in small departments or in small counseling firms.

The psychological barrier can be a serious one because relatively few creative people react with equanimity to criticism, and there is a tendency for an auditee to be defensive. Thus, the audit team must use a good deal of tact as well as judgment when an audit is being conducted.

The practical and psychological problems involved in internal public relations audits are summed up succinctly in the following excerpt of a letter sent to the author by the head of a large public relations department:

> There are two reasons why we abandoned the audit: I have been too busy, and the method was not successful — psychologically.

> Had I time, we could probably remedy the latter defect and resume the audit. The method was to sit down regularly with each section head and one of his staff peers for a discussion of his work. Objectives were re-examined, progress was discussed, and suggestion made for improvement. The difficulty with this procedure was that the co-auditor frequently did not have sufficient background for his task, and some section heads were defensive in their reaction. . . .

The author had the opportunity to spend several weeks one summer at Hill & Knowlton where account audits are conducted regularly within the firm. At H & K audit teams are called into being from within the organization, each team usually being unique and existing for the purpose of one audit. After the team has been selected, the account executive whose account is being audited prepares a memorandum describing the main aspects, objectives, plans, and programs of the account. Distribution of the memorandum is made to the team, following which the account executive and members of his staff (where there is a staff) meet with the team to discuss the items in the memorandum and to be critiqued by the auditors.

The author's interviews with various H & K people indicate that the audit brings out new ideas that can be put to valuable use. At the same time, those on the audit team gain from the process because they get insights about accounts unfamiliar to them. The chief executives of the firm do not sit in on audits, but they receive every audit correspondence and thus the system not only brings about an evaluation of program effectiveness but also provides better all-agency service to clients. A more or less typical H & K pre-audit memorandum is described in the case that follows.

MINI-EXAMPLE
AN INTERNAL AUDIT MEMORANDUM

Preparatory to an internal account audit at Hill & Knowlton, the account executive responsible for Account X wrote and disseminated the following pre-audit review memorandum which was sent to those on the audit team:

Background

The client manufactures a wide variety of products (see attached list) which are sold through independent wholesalers. The account was relatively dormant until a new president was installed and the client switched from a fee-plus-staff time basis to a monthly minimum that provides a specific service for every dollar spent.

PR Objectives

H & K's main efforts are focused on getting maximum exposure in all media for those products and brand names of the client listed under Item A on the attached list. The company's internal p.r. staff also is helped to service routine financial news. The management and its public relations department were advised on strategy to fight off possible tender offers a few years ago. . . .

Problems

The overriding concern is to give the client satisfactory performance and results without pricing ourselves out of the market. Staff charges for creative talent are expensive compared to the salaries paid the internal publicity department which is located in a non-metropolitan area. Another complication is that H & K's system of hourly charges does not make it practical to assign a writer permanently to develop ideas and news outlets for the client's products. We do not specialize in the area represented by these products and the publicity department would need to gear up to placing articles in trade magazines important to the account.

A serious situation within the company is the lack of liaison between public relations and advertising and sales promotion. This impedes sales promotion from capitalizing on later publicity placements to dealer organizations.

The new president of the company has been avoiding interviews with financial and business publications until he has established, as he says, a track record, an obstacle which may be surmounted as he gains confidence in his position.

Recommendations

Since the client's internal public relations staff is fairly competent, H & K charges can be kept within reasonable bounds by feeding his people ideas which they can proceed to develop. Such suggestions can be given more impact by uncovering new outlets for product publicity previously unexplored by the client. We can also bring the client to the attention of influential groups and audiences he is not now reaching.

A fertile, untapped field for the client is the real estate section in local newspapers. The product publicity managers are greatly impressed by circulation figures tabulated and analyzed by PR Data. These figures, in turn, are presented enthusiastically to the Division managers who underwrite the public relations program. Anything that can be done to boost the circulation totals will fortify our position.

This suggestion can be expedited by getting two or three other H & K clients with related interests to participate in a monthly clip sheet directed to special editors and sections of newspapers. Done properly, the project would go far beyond a mat sheet beamed only to weeklies and small dailies.

The client's conservative approach to publicity must be changed by generating stories with popular appeal. Pollution is a subject that is in the news, and as the client's products effectively reduce pollution this can be brought to the public's attention in a variety of ways. Service features can be developed pointing up areas where use of the client's products can be most advantageous, and publicity can also be developed to demonstrate unusual product applications. TV can be exploited profitably by developing a traveling show for interview programs, with a company representative demonstrating the various ways in which client products are useful to the consumer.

Reprinted with permission of Hill & Knowlton

Questions for Discussion

1. What is your opinion of the tone, format, and contents of the above pre-audit memorandum?

2. What questions would you ask about the problems cited in the memo? At this point, without knowing the answers, what advice — if any — would you give to help solve the problems?

3. What is your opinion of the recommendations cited in the memorandum?

4. If you were on the audit team, what points in the memorandum would you want to explore further?

5. If you were the H & K executive to whom the writer of the memorandum reports, in what ways has the memorandum influenced your evaluation of the writer?

The *external audit* differs from the internal audit in one obvious, major way: it is conducted by those outside of the organization being audited. In some cases the organization may contract with an outside expert or a panel to come in and conduct a one or three-day audit of practices, procedures, and programs and to make recommendations for improving effectiveness. More common, however, is the comprehensive audit service now being offered by an increasing number of public relations counseling firms.

In many respects the external audit is similar to the preliminary study undertaken by counseling firms when they first take on a new account. Through research, interviews, and analysis a thorough study is made of the organization's goals, publics, products and services, public relations objectives, short and long range plans, etc. The major difference between the preliminary study and the external audit is that in the former case the counseling firm usually carries out its analysis prior to establishing and carrying out a public relations program; in the latter case the analysis is usually made of an existing public relations program and is therefore an analysis and measure of the public relations effectiveness of the program. Most external audits go beyond measuring effectiveness and provide suggestions and/or a blueprint for future public relations activity. The audit is considered here chiefly as a tool for measuring public relations effectiveness.

The axiom that "you get what you pay for" applies to the external audit as well as to the purchase of most products and services. An audit may be completed in five or six weeks or it may take six months; it can deal with only one aspect of a public relations program or it can encompass the entire program; it can be carried out entirely by the counseling firm's own staff or the firm may call in national research organizations. Properly handled, the external audit is an effective means of practical research that provides management with another tool to measure public relations efforts.

MINI-CASE
SOME REFLECTIONS ABOUT EVALUATION

In its mid-sixties *EXECUTIVE REPORT*, "Inside Public Relations," Prentice-Hall quoted Charles Prout, at that time director of public affairs for Mead Johnson & Company, as stating:

> The great deficiency of public relations as it is practiced today is the lack of means of measuring the effectiveness of its efforts. . . . We are still forced to rely too much on subjective judgments — which are neither totally reliable for our own guidance nor readily communicable to others for their evaluation of our efforts.

> It is my belief that the public relations profession will reach full maturity and full productivity only when it devises adequate measurement techniques which can weigh costs against results in a meaningful balance sheet which both practitioners and management can read clearly.

> We deal in public attitudes rather than in things. We're concerned with the subtle question of what people believe. This involves two very basic problems from the standpoint of measurement: (1) What people believe is not as easily quantified as what they buy or how fast they can insert a rivet in the side of an assembly line component and (2) changing people's beliefs is a lengthy and delicate process which often is not defined with a clearly marked beginning and end.

> . . . The essential challenge here remains: How do we in public relations equate the value of these services with dollars and cents? How do we know for our own planning that 'X' dollars is a good investment in a particular public relations program, but 'Y' dollars is too much? And how do we let others know that same thing?

Questions for Discussion

1. What is your opinion about Prout's conclusions about "subjective judgment" as a means of measuring effectiveness?

2. Do you consider any of the methods for measuring and evaluating public relations effectiveness which have been described in this chapter as an answer to the need for the adequate measuring techniques mentioned in Prout's second paragraph?

3. Do you see any conflict between the ideas expressed in Prout's third and fourth paragraphs? If your answer is affirmative, ex-

plain the nature of the conflict. If your answer is no, explain why you think there is no conflict.

4. Assume that you are on Prout's staff and that he has advised you that his superior in the management structure of Mead Johnson & Co. has posed to him the three questions cited in the last paragraph. Prout has asked you to send him a memorandum which suggests answers to the three questions. Write the memorandum.

QUESTIONS AND PROBLEMS FOR DISCUSSION

1. According to the author, *reporting* public relations activities and performance is more commonplace than measuring and evaluating activities and performance. Why do you think this is so?
2. In what ways is the report of public relations activities and performance of value to management?
3. Why is the report considered a "poor way of stating accomplishment in qualitative terms"?
4. The author says that lack of time is one of the main reasons why public relations executives rely on informal rather than formal reporting as a means of checking on the work of those under them. Is this a justifiable reason?
5. Cite and explain the essential nature of the three major forms of formal reporting used in public relations.
6. What are the major advantages and disadvantages of these forms of formal reporting?
7. According to the author, the computer is now being used to report publicity results, but it leaves unanswered questions about actual readership, impact, and effectiveness. Do you think the computer might well be used for these purposes? If the answer is yes, *how* do you think this might be done? If the answer is no, why do you think it can't be done?
8. To what extent do you consider management justified in asking for concrete proof of public relations effectiveness?
9. To what extent do you consider public relations practitioners justified in contending that such concrete proof is impossible to present?
10. Why may it be advantageous or disadvantageous for the practitioner to rely on the intuitive judgment of management in evaluating his or her performance?
11. What kind of problems can be anticipated when trying to match specific objectives with specific results?
12. What are the major reasons why before-and-after public opinion surveys are not used too often in public relations practice?
13. What are the main advantages and disadvantages about using the survey panel as a means of measuring public relations effectiveness?
14. What are the main advantages and drawbacks to the internal public relations audit? The external audit?

PART IV
PERSPECTIVES AND
PROSPECTIVES

This final section and chapter deal primarily with views: the view of the prospective public relations practitioner, currently a student, who would like to know what kind of education he or she needs to get into the field and the view of the veteran practitioners who look inside themselves and at their practices.

The view of the outsider seeking to become an insider is basically practical in nature. The outsider raises questions about the kind of education he or she should pursue and the kind of activities to be engaged in so as to complement formal education. The outsider also questions ways in which to secure the all-important first-entry position and the type of work to be expected in that first job.

The view of the insider, the veteran, is colored by both practical and philosophical overtones and is focused on ethical and moral questions. As in every field, the veteran finds conflicts between personal values and organizational-societal values, and these are highlighted by considerations dealing with professionalism.

Whether viewed by the outsider or the insider, the issues raised in this chapter end ultimately in discussion of those ethical, moral and practical questions and answers which are raised in every field and calling. They deserve careful attention, and it is hoped they achieve this attention on the part of those who use this text.

PUBLIC RELATIONS   10
CAREERS: PREPARATION
AND PROFESSIONALISM

This final chapter approaches the subject of public relations careers from two directions: *preparation* for a career in public relations, and the *professional* manner in which those in the field carry out the public relations function. Among the topics to be discussed will be education for a public relations career, suggested extra-curricular activities, salary and other expectations, the search for the first job, daily work routines, personal and professional ethics and codes, the debate over licensing, the future as seen through a crystal ball. Within each of these areas there are as many questions as answers, and it is hoped that the chapter will provide a sufficient amount of both to be helpful to students who intend to take an active part in public relations practice.

PREPARING FOR A PUBLIC RELATIONS CAREER

As noted in the preface, this book's major purpose is to provide an effective teaching tool in the introductory course in public relations. The purpose therefore indicates the author's belief that a college education including course work in public relations is an effective and sound way in which young people can prepare themselves for a career in the field of public relations. This is not meant to contend that such a college education is *the* only way in which to prepare for a public relations career, and studies have shown that the vast number of practitioners now in the field did not study public relations while in college. This is not surprising inasmuch as public relations curricula and degree programs are relatively new phenomena on the American educational scene; although one or two courses in public relations were first taught in colleges in the early twenties, it's only been in the last two decades that the proliferation of courses and degree programs has taken place. Thus, the public relations veterans of today are mainly college-educated, but their college work did not include public relations courses. Most of these veterans entered the public relations field through either journalism, advertising, marketing, or that catch-all called "happenstance."

For the past two decades as graduates of public relations degree programs have sought their first public relations jobs they've run into the same road blocks that faced journalism school graduates trying to enter the newspaper field a few decades earlier. Managing editors who had entered the newspaper field as copy boys and who had never themselves gone to college couldn't understand how a college education could possibly prepare one for a journalism career. The idea that such an education would also include work in journalism was considered even more outlandish, but this tunnel-vision view gradually gave way to a broader understanding as the world became more complex and the need for college-educated newspapermen and women became more obvious. In similar fashion, now that public relations degree programs have become more established and graduates of such programs have proved their value and become established in the field, there is growing recognition of the worth, value, and capability of these public relations graduates.

EDUCATION FOR PUBLIC RELATIONS

Students using this book will probably be taking a public relations course that either is required in a degree program, is required or an elective in a public relations or other sequence within a journalism degree program, or is an elective course within some other degree program or sequence. The educational "home" for such a course — and for other courses in public relations — is shown by Table 10-1 and Table 10-2 in a study conducted by Dr. Ray Eldon Hiebert for the Foundation for Public Relations Research and Education:

Table 10-1

Number of Colleges and Universities Offering Public Relations Instruction.

	1964	1970
Degree Programs in Public Relations		
Doctoral Degrees	0	0
Master's Degrees	5	7
Bachelor's Degrees	14	7
Special Sequences in Public Relations		
Doctoral Level	0	8
Master's Level	12	28
Bachelor's Level	29	75
Elective Courses in Public Relations		
Two or More Courses Available	37	46
At Least One Course Available	200	172
Total Number of Programs in Public Relations	297	343
Total Number of Schools Offering Programs	280	303

Table 10-2

Placement of Public Relations in Academic Structure

Universities offering sequences or degrees in public relations:

	1964		1970	
	schools	percent	schools	percent
Within a liberal arts sequence	17	39.5	48	53.9
Within a professional school	24	56.0	33	37.0
Combination of the two	2	4.5	8	9.1
Total	43	100.0	89	100.0

All universities offering courses in public relations:

Within a liberal arts structure	72	53.0	73	51.4
Within a professional school..........	54	40.0	41	28.8
Combination of the two	7	5.0	23	16.2
Junior College	3	2.0	4	2.8
Other......................................			1	.8
Total......................................	136	100.0	142	100.0

from "Trends in Public Relations Education 1964–70"

Dr. Hiebert notes that public relations instruction is now offered in institutions of higher learning in 47 states and the District of Columbia, with California leading the way with 27 colleges or universities, New York with 25, Ohio with 21, Pennsylvania with 13, and Illinois with 11. The tables show that the total number of institutions offering degree or special sequences in public relations has more than doubled from 1964 to 1970 (43 to 89). Although the total number of degree programs has declined from 1964 to 1970, the number of special sequences in public relations within other degree programs has almost tripled.

Public relations and journalism educators hold similar views when considering the relationship of required public relations and journalism courses to the total number of courses and hours needed for graduation. With few exceptions, schools offering public relations degrees or sequences require from 20 to 30 percent of total course work in public relations and/or journalism and the remainder in electives in other disciplines. The problem facing students is in deciding what courses will round out their college education.

SUGGESTED ELECTIVES

There is no end to the number and kind of elective courses that well-intentioned practitioners suggest students take to prepare for a career in public relations. These range anywhere from the generalized statement "get a liberal arts education" to lists of courses that add up to as many as 201 credit hours. The usual practice in giving advice is to recommend courses which the practitioner has found useful in his or her own career, but the problem for the student is that no two careers will ever really duplicate each other. The wiser approach, it seems, is to consider as electives those courses that will most likely be of value no matter what special area of public relations is pursued, plus courses that may prove valuable for special purposes.

First, as to general courses, there seems to be agreement that courses in the social sciences — sociology, psychology, anthropology, political science, history, and economics — are sound fundamental courses to be taken. Courses in literature, the humantities, speech, and some of the fundamental areas of business administration — such as accounting, finance, organization, management, and marketing — are also considered wise educational investments. If available, students should take as many writing courses as possible.

Second, if the student knows in advance the area of public relations in which he or she hopes to pursue a career, it's advisable to take courses most closely related to the designated specialty. Thus, if you intend to handle public relations work in the social or health agency areas, take courses in the social work and health disciplines in your institution. If you hope to make your public relations career in education, take some education courses as electives. If you intend to seek public relations work in business or industry, the obvious choice of electives would be in the business area.

Third, be flexible enough to recognize that today's interest may be temporary and that you may start your career in one area of public relations and then move into another. For this reason it's wise to become as broadly educated as possible within the boundaries of your college's curriculum requirements.

Summed up, a sensible college education "package" for those intending to pursue a public relations career would include 20 to 30 percent of course work in public relations and journalism, and the remainder in electives in a broad range of disciplines and in a limited concentration within one discipline. The graduate of such a program should have knowledge of basic public relations principles and practices; a modicum of public relations and journalism skills; and a liberalizing, mind-broadening education.

A RECOMMENDED CURRICULUM

In a report issued in mid-1975, the Commission on Public Relations Education (group composed of three PRSA members and four educators from the Public Relations Division of the Association for Education in Journalism) recommended an undergraduate public relations curriculum of three major groupings of courses. The report pictured the curriculum as made up of a series of three concentric circles: "The smallest, central circle would enclose those subjects specifically concerned with public relations practice. The second circle, somewhat larger, would encompass related subjects in the general field of communications. The third and largest circle would represent the general liberal arts and humanities background expected of all students. Additionally, one might envision a satellite or 'moon,' outside the largest circle, representing a secondary area of concentration for the student (a 'minor,' so to speak) representative of some special area of public relations practice. Thus, the 'minor' might be in the field of business administration for the student who plans to enter corporate public relations; or it might be in the field of public administration for the student who plans to enter government public relations, etc. . . ."

1. GENERAL EDUCATION COURSES

The report recommended there be at least four semesters of *English* (writing and literature); introductory courses in the *social sciences*; a "sprinkling" of courses in the *humanities*; one or two introductory courses in the *natural sciences*; at least one *foreign language* or *area studies* courses; a course in *statistics*; and a course in *organizational structure and behavior*.

2. COMMUNICATION STUDIES

This part of the program would encompass the following areas: *theory and process of communication; news reporting and writing; copy editing;* and *graphics of communication*.

Suggested are one or more of the following types of courses: *advertising principles and practice; media law and ethics; feature writing; introduction to survey research*; and *communication media analysis*.

3. PUBLIC RELATIONS CORE COURSES

Recommended as *an absolute minimum: introduction to public relations; publicity media and campaigns; public relations case problems; internship or practicum*.

4. ELECTIVES

One or more of the following electives: *management communications; propaganda and public opinion;* and *magazine editing*.

5. "SATELLITE" STUDIES

Students interested in a "minor" or secondary area of emphasis should take at least two courses in a field related to their special area of public relations interest.

---

from *RECOMMENDED CURRICULUM*, a report of the Commission on Public Relations Education, a study co-sponsored by the Public Relations Division of the Association for Education in Journalism and the Public Relations Society of America, August 5, 1975

SUGGESTED EXTRA-CURRICULAR ACTIVITIES

There are several reasons for suggesting that the undergraduate's four years of course work be accompanied by a reasonable degree of involvement in extra-curricular activities. Properly selected, such activities provide the closest approximation to "on-the-job" training and experience available in a college setting. They enable the graduate to present to prospective employers not merely a record of academic but also practical experience. Finally, they're a testing ground for ascertaining personal abilities, weaknesses, and strengths.

The college newspaper, whether a daily or weekly, is highly recommended as the best extra-curricular activity for the kind of experience most closely aligned to public relations work. Students who work on a college newspaper will not only improve their reporting and writing skills, but will also gain valuable experience working with and managing others. The college newspaper also enables students to compile a sampling of stories and features that can be useful in demonstrating their competence when seeking a first position in the field.

Other valuable extra-curricular activities include work at the campus radio or television station, participation in student government, and — if available on campus — a role in the local unit of the Public Relations Student Society of America. The last-named group, first organized in 1968, now has more than 1,000 members in chapters on more than 60 campuses and sponsors both regional meetings and a national conference usually held in conjunction with the annual conference of the parent Public Relations Society of America. The special pre-associate membership category of the PRSA, available at a greatly reduced membership fee for graduates who have been PRSSA members, is a quick and simple entry into the parent body.

In following the dictates of an academic program or sequence in public relations and the extra-curricular options open at the average college or university, the student should keep in mind the kind of skills generally considered important for success in the field. The PRSA sums up these needed skills and attributes in the following terms:

> Because public relations involves many kinds of tasks, many different qualifications are needed. Probably the "ideal," or at least popularly conceived, public relations man or woman is the highly articulate and imaginative individual with more than a little salesmanship in his or her make-up.
>
> On the other hand, many public relations executives stress judgment as the most important single qualification that the worker must posses. Public relations practitioners are "counselors," and their services are often sought out when an organization is in trouble. Hence skill in practical action, based on reflective analysis, is an important part of the equipment of the able public relations worker. In addition he (and she) should have:
>
> - Imagination, which is an important attribute for coping with new problems and commanding the attention of others.
> - Verbalizing skills, which underlie competence in writing and speaking — combined with training in these arts.
> - Extroverted traits, sufficient to make possible successful frequent face-to-face contacts with other individuals and groups.
> - Sensitivity to other people. To profess a liking for people will not help a candidate get a job. However, both diplomacy and a more than ordinary ability to place oneself in the shoes of another is important in public relations work.
> - Organizing and planning skill, leadership and administrative ability. As with many other occupations, managerial skills are

invaluable assets for successfully climbing the public relations career ladder.

----

from *An Occupational Guide to Public Relations*, PRSA

GETTING THE FIRST JOB

The recession that began in 1974 and saw total United States unemployment rise to more than seven million came as a rude shock to college graduates who had been accustomed to easy entry into the job market. In previous years the job market had been wide open, but suddenly the picture changed drastically for would-be teachers, engineers, business trainees, journalists, and others. The public relations function was affected just as other functions, and this has meant that graduates seeking an entry position in the public relations field need patience, diligence, and a carefully designed search plan in order to uncover that first all-important job.

The reason why graduates need to follow a carefully designed *search* plan is that, with some few exceptions, college placement offices are not regular stops for recruiters with public relations job offers. In this respect, the public relations and the journalism graduate have had to face the same problem of going out after the first job rather than finding the first job coming to campus. Entry positions are out there and at salary ranges equivalent to those offered in such fields as accounting and similar high-demand areas, but they tend to be awarded to those who are best prepared and who seek them out. Although there are many roads leading to success in securing the first job in public relations, the following route has proven to be a sound one to travel:

1. *Prepare a portfolio* that can be easily scanned and that will provide evidence of your work and abilities. Include in it news and feature stories you've written; brochures and flyers you've produced; research and other assignments you've completed in various courses. The portfolio need not be fancy but should be well organized, easy to carry to interviews, and self-explanatory.

2. *Prepare and have printed a resume*, one page long, which will include personal, educational, extra-curricular, and work experience data. This material should be organized under the four appropriate headings. If there's room on the page, include the names and addresses of two to three references. Otherwise state that references will be supplied upon request.

   There is no single "right" form for the resume, but the resume cited after Item 6 indicates the basic form to use and should suffice as an example. Note particularly that the resume does not use complete sentences and avoids the use of the first person singular.

A final note: This is the resume of a recent graduate. Once a job record has been achieved, work experience will move to the fore on the resume and education will move into the background. After several years of work and professional experience, the applicant's major strength will be his or her previous positions and responsibilities.

3. *Compile a list* of organizations where job openings might exist. If you intend to write directly to the person heading the public relations function, the best single source of names and addresses is the annual *Register* of the Public Relations Society of America, which lists the more than 7,000 members of the society. Each member receives a copy of the Register and it may be possible to borrow a copy from a PRSA member who is nearby. Appropriate lists can be compiled by referring to the annual membership directories published by groups such as the American Hospital Association, the United Ways of America, the Boy and Girl Scouts of America, the Council for the Advancement of Education (college public relations and fund-raising directors), etc.

4. *Prepare a brief cover letter* individually typed and sent out with each resume mailed. Concentrate your mailing to organizations within a 200 to 300 mile radius of your location. Even though they may be interested in your application, organizations will not set up a personal interview if you're in New York and the position is in Los Angeles.

5. *Try to establish contact* and arrange for a personal interview with professionals in areas where there are a large number of public relations people. Even though the person who interviews you may not have a position available, he or she may know of openings elsewhere or may be able to direct you to someone who will in turn direct you to an opening.

6. *Do not get too easily discouraged.* Finding the right kind of position can easily take months of search, so explore all possibilities by reading the classified section of metropolitan papers, *Editor and Publisher*, the *Public Relations Journal*, and similar sources and by sending out letters and resumes and arranging for personal interviews. If a media job opens up, by all means consider it seriously because it will provide you with the kind of experience still considered invaluable by practitioners who themselves moved into the public relations field through this route.

A SAMPLE RESUME

ROBERT VINCENT RYAN

Box 154, South Hall
Utica College
Utica, New York 13502
Telephone: (315) 792-3296

698 Windsor Road
Uniondale, New York 11553
Telephone: (516) IV-1-1285

PERSONAL DATA

Date of Birth: 4/1/53
Height: 5'11"
Weight: 180 lbs.

Marital Status: Single
Military Status: 1-H

EDUCATION

Utica College of Syracuse University, Utica, New York 13502
Degree: Bachelor of Arts, May 1975
Dual Major in Journalism and Public Relations
Overall Grade Point Average: 3.2 of 4.0
Average in Major: 3.4 of 4.0

Courses Taken in Major: Newswriting, Reporting, Introduction to Mass Communications, Introduction to Public Relations, Reporting on Public Affairs, Graphics, Editing, Writing and Announcing for Radio/Television, Publicity, Magazine Article Writing, Cases and Problems in Public Relations, Teacher's Assistant, Independent Study

HONORS

Tau Mu Epsilon, National Honorary Public Relations Society
Student Speaker, First Utica College Convocation
Regents Scholarship

Interviewer, Telephone Conference Call Program with Reuven Frank, former president of NBC NEWS and executive producer of WEEK-END; Osborn Elliot, editor of NEWSWEEK; Jack O'Dwyer of O'DWYER'S NEWSLETTER; Skip Weiner, editor of WRITER'S DIGEST; and Babette Ashby, articles editor of FAMILY CIRCLE

ACTIVITIES

Utica College Press Club
Public Relations Student Society of America
Utica College Student Newspaper, TANGERINE
DORMWEEK, Utica College Weekly Dormitory Newspaper, Founder and Editor

EMPLOYMENT (All part-time while attending college)

1/75 to 5/75 Utica College of Syracuse University, Utica, New York 13502
Resident Living Advisor, in charge of the 300 students in South Dormitory
Dean of Students: Richard Caulk

1/75 to 5/75 Journalism Fieldwork: Course includes moderating four public service radio shows for WRUN in Utica and free-

lancing to the local daily and weekly newspapers
Supervisor: John Behrens, Professor of Journalism, Utica College

5/74 to 12/74 Rome Air Development Center, Griffiss Air Force Base, New York, 13440
Writer — Office of Information
Information Officer: Capt. Juventino R. Garcia, USAF

8/72 to 1/75 Utica College of Syracuse University, Utica, New York 13502
Resident Assistant, in charge of one floor of students in South Dormitory
Dean of Students: Richard Caulk

5/73 to 5/74 The Student Press in America Archives
Utica College, Utica, New York 13502
Editorial Assistant
Curator: Prof. John Behrens

REFERENCES

Raymond Simon, Chairman, Business Administration Division
Utica College
Utica, New York 13502

John Caponera, Writer/Editor
Office of Information
Northern Communications Area
Griffiss Air Force Base, New York 13440

John C. Behrens, Professor of Journalism Studies
Utica College
Utica, New York 13502

SALARY AND OTHER EXPECTATIONS

Any discussion of salary levels for the first job in public relations has to be red-flagged by the notation that spiraling inflation has made figures outdated almost as soon as they're reported. Thus, in mid-1972 Dr. Frederick H. Teahan, education director of the PRSA, reported that a study of a sample of pre-associate (newly graduated) members of the society showed that their starting salaries ranged from $6,000 to $14,000 with the median salary at $7,500 and the average at $8,823. By mid-1975, when the author surveyed his school's May public relations graduates, he found that their salaries ranged from $8,600 to $11,300 with the median salary at $9,300 and the average at $9,800.

Several general observations can be made about entry salaries. First, they have consistently ranged between $1,000 and $3,000 above those of graduates who have taken newspaper jobs. Second, the highest starting salaries in public relations have been in business, industry, and counseling while the lowest have been in the social and health agency and hospital fields. Third, women's salaries have lagged behind men's salaries, though this gap is constantly being narrowed in public relations as in all fields.

As to expectations, all indications point to a continuance of two of the above three trends. The bulk of entry positions in the newspaper field continue to be on small town and small city dailies while the bulk of entry positions in public relations are in large organizations situated in metropolitan areas; thus, salary levels of beginning newspaper positions will continue to be lower than those of beginning public relations positions. Entry-level public relations jobs in business, industry, and counseling will continue to offer higher salaries than similar entry-level public relations positions in other areas. However, because of governmental, legal, and activist pressures the gap between women's and men's entry salary levels in public relations, as in all fields, will become a thing of the past and will be covered over and deservedly buried.

DAILY WORK ROUTINES

Entry-level jobs in public relations tend to be involved with writing rather than with counseling for the simple reason that there are many writing but few counseling tasks that can be assigned to a relative newcomer to the field. Furthermore, the very act of counseling calls for the degree of maturity and experience that comes with age and time spent in the field. The young graduate may aspire to doling out sage advice, but he's generally not going to be asked nor paid for it until he or she gets a little older, a little wiser, and a bit more experienced.

We thus find the Public Relations Society of America describing "The Day" of the newcomer to the field in the following words:

> The junior employee will answer calls for information from the press and the public, work on invitation lists and details for a press conference, escort visitors and clients, help research and write brochures, deliver releases to editorial offices, work up contact and distribution lists, scan newspapers and journals, paste scrap books of clippings, brief his superiors on forthcoming meetings, help write reports, speeches, presentations, articles and letters research case histories, help produce displays and other audio-visual materials, do copy reading, select photographs for publication, arrange and guide plant tours, perform liaison jobs with advertising and other departments, arrange for holiday or other remembrances, conduct surveys, and tabulate questionnaires, work with lettershops and printers. The telephone, the typewriter, the mimeograph and addressograph machines, telegraph, postal and other message services are communication tools that are familiar features of the public relation man's (and woman's) work environment.
>
> --
>
> from An *Occupational Guide to Public Relations*, PRSA

On their first jobs graduates obviously won't be doing all things set forth by the PRSA occupational guide, but rather can be expected to do any one of them at some time or another. Much depends on the nature of the organization for which one works. In large organizations, public relations functions and activities tend to be compartmentalized; the beginner may well find himself or herself spending the work week writing for the employee publication or perhaps writing news releases, but not doing both. In small organizations, public relations functions or activities tend to be shared by a smaller number of professionals, and there is the opportunity to get involved in a variety of tasks. Finally, where the public relations function is the sole responsibility of one professional, this person will have to be versatile enough to handle graphics, write releases and features, deliver talks, hold press conferences, deal with printers, and counsel. Thus, although salary scales in social and health agencies and in hospitals are lower than in business and industry, the responsibilities assigned to the beginner tend to be greater and provide the opportunity to develop a wider range of skills and talents than is possible in large organizations with large public relations departments.

MINI-CASE
A DAY IN THE LIFE OF THREE PUBLIC RELATIONS PRACTITIONERS

At the request of the author of this textbook, three former students who had been in the field from four to six years selected an arbitrary date and recorded their work routine for that day. At that time in their professional careers the three were Mrs. Linda Schmidt, director of public relations for the United Way of Broome County, Binghamton, N.Y.; James Leach, director of the news bureau, the State University of New York College at Plattsburgh, N.Y.; and Robert O'Gara, manager of public relations, the Koppers Company, Pittsburgh, Pa. Following are the "logs" they compiled and transmitted, along with a few explanatory remarks:

LINDA SCHMIDT
Director of Public Relations
United Way of Broome County

Friday, August 24

8:30 a.m.... Arrived in office. Scanned morning newspaper.

8:45.......... Typed rough draft of minutes from last PR Committee meeting; minutes will be duplicated and sent to volunteer committee. (Prefer typewriter, rather than dictaphone, to transcribe notes and draft letters for secretary)

9:30.......... Went out to pick up metal printing plate I had a rush order on; plate will be used for in-house printing of campaign bulletins on small offset.

10:00.......... Read mail; checked bills for campaign supplies; wrote notes to two volunteers asking for comments on draft letters I had prepared.

10:15.......... Coffee with rest of staff.

10:40.......... Telephone calls:

> . . . checked on a permit we need to hang a banner over a downtown street for campaign, wrote letter to state for permit approval.

> . . . talked to member agency staffer who called to ask my help in getting publicity for the enrollment of their 10,000th member.

> . . . talked with a volunteer sub-committee chairman on plans for campaign Kickoff.

11:20.......... Talkative rep from local firm dropped in to chat. Couldn't be rude to him, as his firm provided some volunteer service designing our campaign information brochure.

Noon .... Called to set up appointment with TV station film editor for later in the afternoon. Conferred with secretary on pending work.

12:20.......... Lunch.

1:10.......... Telephone calls:

> . . . talked to several volunteers who are handling distribution of 1,000 posters advertising campaign Kickoff.

> . . . talked with PR Committee vice-chairman about plans for showing campaign film on Cable TV in fall.

> . . . called assistant city editor of newspaper to see if he'd be interested in a photo-feature on the agency's 10,000th member. He said "yes" and I followed up with agency. Called TV news director to see if he'd be interested in same. He said "yes." Also set up appointment with him for next week to discuss the possibility of a fall TV show on United Way.

> . . . made several other calls, but couldn't reach anyone.

3:30.......... Read recent committee reports from budgeting and planning division of United Way.

3:45.......... Went to TV station to preview a print of film we had shot; called film lab to give the go-ahead on making final prints.

4:30.......... Talked to newly-hired United Way staff member to orient him on my functions and PR committee operations.

5:40.......... Left to go home.

Excerpt from cover letter: "It was kind of interesting to see the log when I finished it (yes, it's completely honest). It was surprising how much time I spent making phone calls, for instance! All in all, it seems to be a fairly "average" day — there are some that last till 8 or 9 p.m., but some that finish at 5 on the dot. And, there are some more hectic, and others that drag by . . .''

JAMES LEACH
Director of the News Bureau
State University of New York College at Plattsburgh

Thursday, September 6

8:30 a.m.... Arrived at office, drank a cup of coffee while reviewing the morning mail and scanning the local newspaper for items of interest to the College.

9:00.......... As a service to the principal of the campus school, rewrote an article on the school lunch program.

9:30.......... Edited an article from the State University's central public relations office to accent Plattsburgh's participation in a coalition of state colleges which is joining a computerized network that provides information in the social sciences.

9:45.......... Discussed with the assistant to the president for public relations (my boss) what he feels has been a recent series of negative publicity stories appearing in the local newspaper.

10:00.......... Responding to a memorandum I sent him, a local TV newscaster showed up for an interview I arranged for him with the director of a new psychological services clinic on campus. Introduced him to the clinic director, briefed him on the scope and scale of the clinic operations, and then left for an 11:30 meeting.

11:30.......... Attended first office staff meeting of the new academic year, held during luncheon at a local club. Our five-member staff discussed college problems and pending office projects. In my area, this includes a community attitude survey, the first issue of the quarterly newsletter, the first issue of the weekly news bulletin, production of a campus guide and fact book, and the impact of a story released in anticipation of the opening day of school.

1:45.......... Reviewed newspaper clippings from the past four months to select those which will be reproduced and mailed to 20 key people on the College Council and administrative staff.

2:30.......... Researched, verified and wrote items for the first academic year issue of the campus weekly news bulletin.

4:45.......... Instructed a publications assistant in the preparation of the weekly news bulletin for distribution the following day.

5:00.......... Interviewed the director of the college community orchestra about his first rehearsal of the year.

5:15.......... Left for home.

ROBERT O'GARA
Manager of Public Relations
Koppers Company, Inc.

Thursday, September 13

8:00 a.m.... Reviewed and edited two product publicity feature stories done by staff member.

8:30.......... Informal coffee session with advertising manager to discuss future publicity campaign.

9:00.......... Morning mail . . . penciled notes for routine inquiries. Put aside two letters for formal replies, skimmed *Wall Street Journal* and *Industry Week*.

9:30.......... Dictation: four letters, three memos.

10:00.......... Inquiry from *Wall Street Journal* on capital spending. Set up phone interview with comptroller.

10:15.......... General reading: *Wall Street Journal, Business Week, Newsweek*, articles from *Conference Board Record* and *Business & Society Review*.

11:00.......... Annual Report meeting with vice president, public relations and advertising, and manager, investor relations. Discussed format and copy.

11:45.......... Luncheon with United Fund representative. Discussion of campaign.

1:30.......... Phone contact local press to arrange feature story on United Fund.

1:45.......... Wrote Annual Report outline.

2:30.......... Discussion with vice president/marketing on interview with *Business Week*, other activities.

3:00.......... Meeting with manager/architectural promotion and supervisor/product information. Subject: How to publicize regional architects' seminars in major cities.

3:30.......... Informal discussion with staff member on product publicity stories edited early in day . . . discussed placement, timing, writing, etc.

4:00.......... Informal discussion with supervisor/product information on his upcoming trip plans to cover product case histories.

4:30.......... Prepared rough draft of release announcing new order for Environmental Systems.

5:30.......... Left for home.

Excerpt from cover letter: "The log is not really a good indication of an 'average' day's activity because most days are really quite different. There seems to be a tendency to get involved in projects which may take a considerable amount of time, and to do this on a fairly sporadic basis. As an example — I am probably spending half of my time right now working on the United Fund. After October 30, I won't even think about the United Fund until next September. Another example: If we are working on a major story with the *Wall Street Journal* or *Business Week*, this could conceivably tie up a full week of time with little opportunity to do other things . . . Another very important consideration is that a good manager owes a certain amount of time to the people who work for him. With two brand new people in our department I spend a lot of time, on an informal basis, supervising their work. Time spent this way will hopefully save the public relations manager from putting out fires six months from now . . ."

Questions for Discussion

1. What similarities do you perceive in the daily activities of the three practitioners? What do you consider to be significant differences? What conclusions do you draw about these perceived similarities and differences?

2. How would you summarize the major areas of activities of the three? What kind of specific skills and attributes would you consider necessary to carry out these activities most effectively?

3. What is your reaction to the remarks made by Mrs. Schmidt and Mr. O'Gara?

4. Did these descriptions of daily activities measure up to your expectations of what you might be doing four to six years after graduation? Explain.

PERSONAL ETHICS AND STANDARDS

Writing the final sections of this book has not been an easy task. The subject of ethics is a very personal one, and the last thing in the world the author wants to do is to impose his standards on others. However, the author knows from two and a half decades of teaching public relations that many students have serious reservations about the public relations field because of ethical questions, and these questions deserve a full airing and should be faced squarely and honestly. It's the author's hope that the approach he has taken to the subject will allow for a free and open discussion.

AN OVERVIEW

To be meaningful, any discussion of ethics requires an understanding of the term itself. When we talk about ethics, we don't mean only acting within the requirements of the law. To obey the dictates of the law is necessary, but not sufficient, because ethical behavior and actions *transcend* the law. Furthermore, the law is impersonal and clear — or at least, relatively clear — whereas ethics is unclear, generally murky, and usually highly personal. This should be quickly evident as we come to grips with the term.

The dictionary definition serves as a reasonable guide when it describes professional ethics as *"conforming to professional standards of conduct."* Thus, when we talk about ethical behavior in public relations we mean responsible professional behavior as applied to both group standards and individual morals.

Frank Wylie, director of U.S. automotive sales public relations for the Chrysler Corporation, adds another dimension to the professional standards concept when he says that ethics includes a *concern for others*. "The ethical person," he declares, "acts and communicates in ways which express a concern for others. Acting in a concerned manner is the first part of the job. The second part is communicating that action."

Admittedly, ethics by the dictionary definition seems to allow one's imagination almost full rein in galloping down the road towards a public relations Valhalla guided only by "professional standards of conduct" and a "concern for others." However, there *are* certain accepted standards of conduct followed by public relations professionals, and it shouldn't be difficult to know when one's actions show a concern for others and when they are strictly hedonistic. One might, of course, deal with ethics by setting forth a detailed set of rules of acceptable behavior, but such an impossible task would be fore-doomed to failure. Therefore, although the boundaries of ethics set forth by the concepts of conformity to professional standards of conduct and concern for others are admittedly broad, hopefully they are sufficient to serve as a guide for meaningful dialogue within the areas that follow.

ETHICAL PROBLEMS EXIST IN ALL FIELDS

For a variety of reasons public relations students seem to need assurance that ethical dilemmas are not the unique province of public relations practitioners, and perhaps this is the place to provide such assurance.

In no field or profession is there a magical Land of Oz somewhere over the rainbow where its practitioners live the ethical pure life undisturbed by questions of right and wrong. Doctors, lawyers, Indian chiefs, dentists, jurists, and outright thieves, all face ethical dilemmas in which their personal ideas of right and wrong may clash with the practical demands of their working lives. In some fields and professions this clash is weak and in others strong, but it is nonetheless all-embracing, occurring wherever men and women practice their craft, profession, and calling.

To explore ways in which lay people could analyze the ethical problems they meet in their occupations, the Department of the Church and Economic Life of the National Council of Churches sponsored a project in which people in six different fields met over a period of time to discuss ethical decision-making in their areas. Here are some conclusions cited by observers who attended the meetings of four of the groups:

BANKERS

After a year of monthly meetings it can be affirmed that bankers are profoundly concerned over the conflict between their business role and their personal ethical standards as derived from their roots in church and family training. Not a session of the group was without reference to this dilemma and in some of the sessions it received attention exceeding even the practical aspects of banking.

BUILDING CONTRACTORS

There seemed to be a consensus that for them the responsible position was somewhere in between complete cynicism and ideal or absolute integrity. There was a frank recognition that so long as we continue to live in a world that is involved in corruption and sin it is not possible entirely to avoid participation in evil; if one intends to stay in the construction business then one must on occasion do things that violate one's own standard of ethics. At all costs the tension must be maintained between what one's standard of honesty and integrity demand and what is possible and necessary in a particular given situation.

PERSONNEL MEN (AND WOMEN)

There is a strong tendency within economic organizations to "translate" questions of ethics into questions of expediency. This tendency was apparent throughout the discussions. . . . It should be emphasized that there is nothing wrong in itself with expediency. Every organization with a certain purpose (even a religious one) will have to think of what is expedient for this purpose and what is not. But expediency is not ethics. It should also be stressed that ethics need not always be in conflict with expediency. Reasonable men will always hope for a modus vivendi between the two . . .

PUBLIC RELATIONS PRACTITIONERS

Ethical issues are no less complex in the public relations field than elsewhere. It is easy to speak in absolute terms about truth, for example, but there is no simple "rule of

thumb" canon which will be universally helpful to a counselor involved in the day-to-day practice of his craft.

---

from *On-The-Job Ethics*, edited by
Cameron P. Hall, The National Council
of the Churches of Christ in the U.S.A.,
1963

Thus bankers, building contractors, personnel men and women, and
public relations practitioners face ethical problems of varying degrees of
magnitude and frequency. If, as Spinoza notes, it is a comfort to the
unhappy to have companions in misery, then the ethical purist might
take comfort in knowing there are countless like him in fields other than
public relations. The realist seeks ways in which he can best come to
terms with the kinds of situations that may face him in life. This can best
be achieved by first considering ethics from a personal point of view.

PERSONAL STANDARDS

Codes of ethics set forth certain standards that members of groups
are expected to follow in their professional lives, yet ethical behavior
still remains personal in the sense that every individual — whether consciously or unconsciously — is responsible for his own actions. A journalism professor sums up the personal nature of ethics in the following
words:

Ethics is truly a personal matter, personal in the sense that it
arises from a personal *concern* for one's conduct. It is also personal in the sense that one's conduct is self-directed and self-en-
forced; the person voluntarily follows a code of conduct because
he feels it is the thing to do . . . It might be said that a person's
ethics is: (1) personal, (2) directive or predictive, and (3) rational. It is personal in the sense discussed above; it is predictive in
that it serves as a guide for conduct and indicates pretty well
what one can be expected to do in a certain situation, and it is
rational in that *reason* dictates its acceptance.

John C. Merrill in *Media, Messages and
Men* by Merrill and Lowestein, p. 246,
McKay, 1971

The idea of a personal ethical threshold has been advanced by
various writers concerned about ethics, and the concept is worth serious
consideration. David Finn applies the threshold concept to companies
when he says that "each company has its own threshold of what it is
comfortable in doing from an ethical standpoint." He further notes that
each of us also has — or should have — our own individual threshold.
As he puts it: ". . . Each of us has a breaking point beyond which we
would not go because it would make us too uncomfortable, too con-

science stricken. And this is our point of no compromise." ("Struggle for Ethics in Public Relations," *Harvard Business Review*, Jan–Feb., 1959)

Finn also suggests that public relations when functioning well, acts as "the anvil against which management's moral problems can be hammered." However, this assumption presumes that: (1) public relations personnel have a set of ethical standards, (2) are willing to put them to the test when circumstances call for it, and (3) managements are receptive to ethical testing by their public relations subordinates.

There is certainly no unanimity among practitioners about Finn's moral anvil concept. John Cook, a Phoenix, Arizona, counselor contends that the corporate conscience role is both pretentious and illogical. In terming such a role a myth, Cook declares:

> . . . There is no more in the makeup, background, training or experience of the average PR practitioner to qualify him to establish or monitor morality than there is in the makeup, background, training or experience of, for example, the engineering or sales vice president or the corporate legal counsel. Corporate social and moral responsibility is an expression of management policies and actions: PR isn't the corporate conscience, but the conveyor, interpreter and advocate of whatever conscience the corporation has . . .

> from "PR Without the BS," *Public Relations Quarterly*, Spring, 1974

Students may properly point out that they are not at the point of life when an ethical threshold has practical professional relevance, and certainly they are not now in a position to act as any kind of an anvil or conscience for hammering out managements' moral problems. However, the best time to develop an awareness of and sensitivity to ethical and moral dilemmas is when one has the option of open discussion without the need to worry about the hard realities of decision and actions. Thus, the student may start this process by debating this proposition: "With whose thesis — Finn's or Cook's — do you agree, and why?

TWO SPECIFIC AREAS OF PERSONAL CONCERN

The broad question of the practitioner's role vis-a-vis ethical and moral dilemmas can be narrowed by consideration of specific areas of personal concern.

ADVOCACY

The question of advocacy is a question of role, and it's succinctly phrased in these terms: To whom is the public relations practitioner responsible? There is virtual unanimous practitioner agreement that the primary responsibility of the practitioner is to employer or client. Admittedly, public relations practitioners are advocates.

However, just what is the extent of advocacy? To what degree is advocacy justified when the course of action that practitioners are supposed to advocate is contrary to personal convictions? And what should practitioners do when the course of action they are advocating is *not* in the public interest?

The dilemma that advocacy poses became apparent in the previously mentioned discussion among public relations practitioners who participated in the sessions sponsored by the National Council of Churches in the sixties. Here are some of the comments revealing the range of opinion about advocacy and personal convictions, and they provide appropriate raw material for student analysis and discussion:

> "The professional public relations man's job is to serve as a mouthpiece for the client, regardless of his personal views."

> "One should decline jobs that run counter to one's personal views."

> "Ethical considerations are usually not so sharply drawn that a clean choice of staying vs. quitting is posed."

> "I can work with clients holding opinions or variance with my own *as long* as these don't affect my particular task with the client. If they do it becomes an ethical issue."

> "If you have done everything possible in an effort to change the client's opinion on a certain issue and you have been unsuccessful, there may come a point at which you *have* to get out."

----

from *On the Job Ethics*

The above comments related primarily to the conflict that results when advocacy clashes with personal beliefs. But advocacy, as already noted, can also clash with public interest. The problem here is more complicated. Everyone knows, or should know, what his or her personal beliefs are, but there is widespread disagreement about what constitutes the public interest (As noted in Chapter 3). There are very few instances where an action or activity will clearly be contrary to the interests of *all* people. The more common circumstance is one where the action or activity will be contrary to the interests of one group of people, but in the interests of another group of people. The practitioner, in effect, likens his role to that of the lawyer, and like the lawyer is an admitted special pleader for one side and not for both defense and plaintiff. However, actual situations turn his seemingly simple proposition into difficult questions, as noted below:

> What should the practitioner do when it is clear that the cause, action, or activity he is supposed to advocate is absolutely contrary to the interests of the broad spectrum of the people and only in the interests of the narrow group he represents?

> Is the "court of public opinion" the same as the "court of law" in that everyone and every organization is entitled to representa-

tion by an advocate?

What should the practitioner do when the cause, action, or organization he represents starts out to be in the public interest but then changes in ways that are not in the public interest?

Two previously cited practitioners — Cook and Wylie — summarize differing views of advocacy in the following words, cited here for your analysis and reaction:

Cook: "PR should provide its specialized input as to how various publics are likely to respond to a potential policy, statement or action. *But the PR man has as much to do with morality as a lawyer does with justice; counsel's role is to represent and advocate.* And just as the responsibility for seeing that justice is done resides in the judge and jury, responsibility for corporate morality resides in the board of directors, top management and, ultimately, the law of the land."

'from "PR Without the BS."

Wylie: "In public relations you serve as an advocate. If you are good at it, you are a dual-advocate: representing the public to your management, and the management to your public. I suggest . . . insist . . . that you should be extremely careful in your choice of clients and of the concepts which you advocate."

----

from a talk over the Educational Telephone Network, University of Wisconsin, Jan. 6, 1975.

TRUTH AND CREDIBILITY

It is most common for moralists and theologians to deal with truth in absolute terms — thou shalt not lie; thou shalt not steal — and it is not difficult to agree with these admonitions about moral and ethical conduct and behavior. Virtually no one, in any field or profession, would disagree with such standards, and this includes public relations practitioners. However, the problems connected with the dissemination of truth — or falsehoods — do not generally concern outright lies and falsehoods, but rather with *degrees* of truths, the *setting or circumstance* in which communication exists, and the factor known as *credibility*.

Telling outright untruths, issuing false statements, and lying can be quickly taken care of by concluding that such actions are unethical, immoral, and unwise. Watergate and its subsequent massive cover-up is a perfect example of the precept that lies and falsehoods lead to jail sentences in courts of law and to universal public condemnation in the court of public opinion. Ironically, Watergate was attributed in part to the machinations of public relations personnel and practices when in reality the leading figures in the Watergate cover-up were lawyers, former advertising executives, and government leaders. Watergate is also a prime example proving a basic premise cited throughout this book: actions speak louder than words, and when actions are taken to insure private interests at the clear expense of the broader public interest, they will eventually backfire and be seen for what they are.

Thus, from both an ethical and practical point of view, it's unwise and wrong to lie, to communicate untruths and falsehoods. If your college's year-end budget shows a deficit, you don't report a surplus. If your social agency falls short of its fund-raising goal, you don't report the goal was reached. If your company recalls thousands of one of this year's models, you don't say no recall has been made.

But you are still an advocate and, as Wylie indicates, you may be a dual advocate. Often, within your own organization, you will find yourself arguing for dissemination of information when others will be arguing for silence. You will find yourself urging a course of action and frank communication that others may not want to take. You may win some of these internal arguments and you may lose some, but ultimately you will be the person who presents your organization's face to the outside world of publics.

In being an advocate, no one really expects you to tell only the whole truth and nothing but the whole truth because so very few people do this except under oath in a court of law. Even journalists, who look with jaundiced eye on public relations pronouncements and who are presumably dedicated to telling the whole truth, seldom, if ever, get at or reveal the whole truth. Although public relations practitioners should not tell outright lies and untruths, they do try to put their best foot forward. While reporting that your college has had a deficit, you may want to point out that it represents only one-tenth of one percent of the total budget and is the first deficit in the 100-year-old history of the institution. While reporting your agency fell short of its goal by $100,000, you may want to point out that your area has had the highest unemployment rate of the past ten years and that the total sum raised this year exceeded last year's sum by $50,000. While reporting that your company has recalled one of this year's models, you may want to point out that the full cost of such a recall is being borne by the company.

At all times, you should keep in mind that credibility is your stock in trade, takes years to build, can be lost in a moment, and once lost is hard to regain. You want to put year best foot forward, but there are times and circumstances when nothing positive can be said. You are not a miracle worker who can turn red into bright blue, a deficit into a surplus, and a Watergate cover-up into some minor burglary. As Wylie puts it: "The foundation of communication is credibility. If we wish to be heard, we must first be believable. We gain such public credibility by our actions, and secondly by our words."

SUMMATION

A summation of the various major ethical and moral considerations discussed in this section leads to the following conclusions:

1. Those who practice their craft in all fields and professions are faced at one time or another with ethical and moral dilemmas involving their personal convictions and beliefs.
2. In order to deal effectively and rationally with such dilemmas it seems wise for individuals to be aware of and sensitive to such conflicts and to have their own ethical thresholds.
3. Public relations practitioners have to be especially attuned to the need for ethical thresholds because they are advocates and are most often called upon to represent the face their organizations present to the outside world.
4. For most of their professional life public relations practitioners will be dealing with activities and actions in which there may be little concern or connection with ethical and moral values.
5. There are, however, certain "gray areas," as David Finn terms them, "in which one person feels comfortable about telling certain kinds of untruths or engaging in certain kinds of moderately deceitful practices, while another person feels entirely different about it . . ."
6. Therefore, to deal with these gray areas, it seems wise to be clear in our own minds about that point beyond which we will are unwilling or unable to go and where we will not compromise.
7. Finally, keep constantly in mind that credibility underscores all effective communication. It is difficult to attain, more difficult to sustain, and once lost hard to regain.

MINI-CASE
PRACTITIONERS DISCUSS AN ETHICAL SITUATION

To sharpen perceptions about ethical problems, staff members at Ruder and Finn met in a series of seminars with a group of theologians and philosophers to pursue the question of ethics and public relations. Following is one of the cases discussed, the question asked, and Finn's summary of the points of view expressed by the practitioners and scholars.

THE CASE

Company A decided to build an image of one of its major products as being purer than its competitors'. This was actually so. However, advertising claims of purity had been used and abused so heavily in the past by other companies that it decided to undertake a public relations program to get the story across. Accordingly, a complicated scheme was invented involving the development of an "independent" research report that was to provide the basis for newspaper and magazine articles.

The trouble was that the research was engineered; in fact, it was not even to be paid for unless the publicity appeared in print. To ensure the success of the project, the man who arranged all this had some editors on his payroll as consultants for the research, thus almost guaranteeing eventual publication. It was a neat scheme — effective for the company and profitable for researcher, editor, and middleman.

THE QUESTION

Is this a responsible method of communicating the image of purity to the public?

SUMMARY OF DISCUSSION REPORTED BY FINN

In support of the argument was the fact that the image was accurate; the product was a pure one. The public was not being deceived. It was being told the truth. And there was nothing specifically "wrong" with the plan. No one was being bribed to do something he should not do. The research was being done by qualified scientists.

Against the plan was the fact that it short-circuited the usual checks and balances which protect the public against deception. Normally, if the product was touted as being pure, the public could have the claim checked by truly independent editors, who would publish it only if it seemed valid to them. But if the cooperation of these two intermediaries could be secured by special payments, then the way would be clear to present false images to the public . . .

In our discussion, the temptation to endorse the plan was very strong, since there was very little doubt that it would accomplish legitimate public relations objectives . . . One of the scholarly consultants at our seminar paraphrased Plato to point out that if we make the choice to live in this world where each person primarily looks out for this own gain, we have to be prepared to find some form of deception everywhere . . .

And yet, after a great deal of analysis, the risk of possible exposure of the whole scheme emerged as the most important consideration of all . . . Our conclusion was that if research could be conducted on a truly independent basis — and there was no reason to feel it could not — there would be no danger whatsoever, and results would be just as effective . . . Everybody who participated in the seminar discussion of this case history felt that the conclusion was based upon practical considerations (that is, to avoid risk of exposure), rather than upon ethical considerations . . .

----

from "Struggle for Ethics in Public Relations"

Questions for Discussion

1. Do you consider the research project plan described in the case to be a responsible and ethical method of communicating

the image of purity to the public? Why or why not?

2. What is your opinion of the "pro" arguments reported by Finn?

3. What is your opinion of the "anti" arguments reported by Finn?

4. What is your opinion about the conclusion arrived at by the seminar participants?

5. Finn reports that one of the scholarly consultants participating in a series of seminars suggested as a "piece of litmus paper" that one should never do anything he or she would not want to see published in tomorrow morning's newspaper. What's your opinion of this suggestion as a test of ethical behavior?

PROFESSIONAL ETHICS AND CODES

The two-sided coin that passes for legal tender in the land of ethical standards bears the likeness of self on one side and represents the personal, self-imposed code of ethical behavior governing the individual. The other side of the same coin carries the imprimatur of the craft, field, or profession within which the individual operates and represents the impersonal, written, and unwritten codes governing those working in the craft, field, or profession. We have already examined the personal side of the ethical coin; it's time now to examine the back side of the same coin.

AN OVERVIEW

There has been considerable discussion over the years as to whether public relations is a profession, craft, calling, or trade. In the generally accepted sense of the term it's difficult to sustain the argument that public relations is a profession because it fails to meet all of the standards by which recognized professions — such as law and medicine — are judged. Both law and medicine, for example, require licensing preceded by specified education, examination, and experience, whereas anyone can enter the practice of public relations without meeting such prescribed standards.

On the other hand, public relations practitioners meet many of the other standards by which one judges whether a field is a profession. Education for public relations is now widespread; practitioners engage in a constant exchange of information by means of their journals, newsletters, institutes, and professional organizations; those in the field restrain their use of self-promotion; practitioners provide a good deal of service in the public welfare; and there is a serious concern with ethics and standards.

On balance, therefore, in weighing the pros and cons relative to the generally recognized hallmarks or professions, one would have to conclude that public relations is not a profession but that many of its practitioners are professional and that most of them follow and adhere to many of the benchmarks by which a profession is recognized by the public.

THE PRSA CODE

One of the benchmarks that denote a profession or professionalism is a written code of professional standards governing those within the field. The American Bar Association "Code of Professional Responsibility and Canons of Judicial Ethics" contains nine canons covering a lawyer's responsibilities and actions. A lawyer found guilty of misconduct can be dropped from ABA membership, and in addition a state appellate court can exercise final disciplinary authority by suspending a lawyer from the practice of law for a length of time and even disbar him or her.

Public relations practitioners are not licensed nor are their activities and practices under state control. Only 7,000 of the approximately 36,000 to 50,000 public relations practitioners are members of the Public Relations Society of America — the largest organization of public relations professionals — but the PRSA has a strong code of professional standards and rules of procedure for professional grievances very similar to the ABA.

The document, which embodies ethical standards of behavior for PRSA members, is the 17-point Code of Professional Standards for the Practice of Public Relations. This code was adopted in 1959 by the PRSA Board of Directors, ratified by the 1960 PRSA Assembly, and amended in 1963. (The code and the official interpretation of Points 6, 13, and 14 are listed at the end of the chapter).

As with many codes, the PRSA code contains some clauses that embody pious generalizations and others designed mainly to protect some members from intrusion by others. Its basic strength is found in clauses that prohibit undisclosed or "false fronts," the intentional dissemination of false or misleading information, practices that tend to corrupt the integrity of channels of public communication, and fees contingent upon or measured by the achievement of specified results.

Point 6 of the code, which prohibits a member from engaging in any practice that tends to corrupt the integrity of the channels of public communication, is particularly important because it covers a key area of public relations practice in which there is a good deal of ambiguity. To clarify this ambiguity the Society provided the previously mentioned "official interpretation" spelling out in more detail the kind of practices, involving the mass media, that are prohibited. These include payment to secure preferential or guaranteed news or editorial coverage, undisclosed retainers to media employees to serve the private purposes of a member, providing vacation trips to media representatives where no news assignments are involved, and similar dubious arrangements between journalists and practitioners.

The fact that such specific prohibitions have been spelled out in some detail indicates that there have been instances of arrangements between media representatives and practitioners that involve unethical behavior, and also indicates that it takes two partners to dance the unethical tango. Thus, in every instance where a member might provide a vacation trip where no news assignment is involved there's a journalist willing to take that trip. The Society, of course, can control only the unethical behavior of its members, but journalists who criticize public relations practitioners might well consider that where there's a giver there's also a taker.

Enforcement machinery for the PRSA code is in the hands of ten district judicial panels with power to hear complaints relative to violations of the code. In 1962 the Society established a Grievance Board with responsibility for investigating instances where no individual complaint is made but where there are indications that the code may have been violated. James E. McKee, Jr., a former chairman of the Grievance Board, explains the enforcement system in these words:

> Stated simply, panels act as courts of law. A member may complain about another member and accuse him of a breach of the Code before a panel. The Grievance Board, on the other hand, performs the dual role of the grand jury and prosecutor. Where no complaint is lodged by a member, but where PRSA or the public may be harmed by non-conforming actions of another member, the Grievance Board must investigate the case and, if it finds good reason for prosecution, bring the accused before a panel.
>
> . . . When a case is brought before a panel, the Grievance Board and its attorney — acting for the PRSA — conduct the prosecution. The accused member, of course, is the defendant or respondent. The panel as a group sits in judgment in the role of a court . . . After the close of the hearing the panel submits a report to the Board of Directors of the PRSA in which it recommends disciplinary action or exoneration . . .
>
> There are six forms of discipline: 'To warn, admonish or reprimand, or to censure, suspend or expel.' The Board in its discretion may give notice to the membership in case of warning, admonishment or reprimand; it must give notice to the membership in case of censure, suspension or expulsion. Of course, where there is an acquittal, the matter is closed and no notice ever goes to anyone. Thus, in cases of acquittal, or where the Board gives no notice to the membership in cases of warning, admonishment or reprimand, only the defendant is notified of the final decision.

----

from "The PRSA Grievance Board," by James E. McKee, Jr., *Public Relations Journal*, June, 1971

Membership in the Society is on an individual basis. Only the practitioner, not his firm or organization, can be a member of the Society, and thus the code relates only to the conduct of the individual member and not to the firm or organization with which he or she is affiliated. Furthermore, though the ultimate form of discipline is expulsion from the Society, this has no bearing on the practitioner's ability to continue to practice.

LICENSING AND OTHER ALTERNATIVES

As has been already noted, public relations practitioners are not licensed, but the idea of licensing — or some alternative close to it — has been a live issue of debate among the professionals as far back as 1953 when Edward L. Bernays proposed that practitioners be licensed. Various study commissions and members of the PRSA have presented reports and White Papers on licensing, and the Society's legislative body went on record in 1967 and 1972 as being opposed to licensing on practical, professional, and philosophical grounds. As might be expected in considering so volatile and important a step, there are as many arguments against as there are in favor of licensing, and there is no discernible or clear consensus for or against licensing on the part of the practitioners.

Arguments for Licensing

Those who favor the licensing of public relations practitioners usually cite the following arguments to support their views:

1. Licensing is a key and indispensible ingredient of a profession.
2. Licensing would safeguard the public and the competent practitioners against the charlatans and incompetents.
3. A grandfather clause would protect those now practicing in the field.
4. If those now in the field do not regulate themselves, then outside agencies — usually the government — will take on this task.
5. Licensing will ensure that only qualified people will be permitted to practice and will thereby raise the entire level of the field and the view held of it by the public.
6. The PRSA is only able to control and police its own membership whereas licensing would enable society to police all who claim to be public relations professionals.

Arguments against Licensing

Those who are against the licensing of public relations practitioners usually cite the following arguments to support their views:

1. Because of the difficulty in defining public relations it would be difficult to fashion a meaningful law.
2. Licensing poses serious constitutional questions relating to freedom of speech and press and would probably be in violation of the First Amendment.
3. Licensing does not automatically guarantee that the public will view the activity licensed as a profession, and one finds charlatans and incompetents in fields that are now licensed.
4. If, as is most likely, licensing would be by states, then what about reciprocity and differing state laws?

5. Licensing will inevitably mean control by outside agencies, and no one knows where that can lead.
6. Malpractice can be controlled by such existing laws as those relating to libel, fraud, dishonesty, misrepresentation, and breach of contract.

Since licensing is usually sought by the group to be regulated and inasmuch as there has been no real groundswell of practitioner sentiment for licensing, there has been much talk but little action in the direction of licensing. Alternatives to licensing, however, are brought forth from time to time, and one such alternative is the *creation of an independent body composed of practitioners and representatives of the public*. Jack O'Dwyer presented this alternative in a commentary in his newsletter in 1974 in the following manner:

> The PR industry is lagging far behind the news media and the advertising industry in responding to new standards of accountability that the public is imposing on all institutions.
>
> In other words, you can now make a complaint about an individual reporter, or coverage of a story by a magazine, newspaper or TV station, and have that complaint considered by a panel whose members are not just from the media. A public hearing may be held on your complaint.
>
> Or, you can criticize an ad, and find your criticism and a reply described in a monthly bulletin that is sent to the press. The panel that considers your complaint will have members of the public on it.
>
> But if your criticism involves PR, or something that a PR man has said or done, your only recourse in the industry is Public Relations Society of America. It is almost certain that your complaint will lead to no publicized action on the part of PRSA. Its grievance committee has a remarkable record — not a single negative word uttered about a PRSA member in ten years . . .
>
> Distinguished members of the PR field should form a bonda fide grievance panel that will also include representatives of the public.

> ---
> from *Jack O'Dwyer's Newsletter*, May 15, 1974

O'Dwyer didn't specify the panel that he says considers complaints about the mass media, though he may have been referring to the National News Council, which had been recently activated for the purpose of hearing complaints about certain disseminators of national news. Nor did he mention that some of our most distinguished national news organizations refused to recognize or cooperate with the National News Council. However, his suggestion about a similar body for the public relations field was echoed in the spring of 1975 by Neil A. Lavick in an article in the *Public Relations Quarterly*.

In calling for the establishment of a national public relations council Lavick described it as similar in nature, scope, and function to the press councils which have had established track records in countries such as Great Britain and Sweden. As he explained his proposal:

The council's purposes would include maintaining the character of the public relations practice in accordance with the highest professional and commercial standards, keeping under review developments likely to lead to abrogations of those standards, considering complaints about the conduct of PR practitioners and that of organizations relating to their public relations, and dealing with complaints in a systematic, orderly manner.

A group of concerned citizens and practitioners or a public interest group could draw up a constitution and select members to sit on the initial council . . . Councils would be established locally, statewide, regionally, or nationally. . . .

A grievance committee would screen complaints, which would have to be in writing . . . If no accord were reached, the grievance committee would investigate and hear the case. . . .

Neither the grievance committee nor the council would have punitive or enforcement powers, other than those of admonition, moral suasion, and public opinion. All decisions of the committee and council would be presented to the media for dissemination to the general public . . .

----

from "Public Relations Council: An Alternative to Licensing?" by Neil A. Lavick, *Public Relations Quarterly*, Spring, 1975

As its alternative to licensing, The Institute of Public Relations — recognized as the sole professional body for the public relations profession in the United Kingdom and composed of 3,500 members in 1975 — suggested the formation of what it termed a "Public Relations Registration Council." In a Memorandum to a Royal Commission on Standards of Conduct in Public Life, the British practitioner group said it was concerned about the activities of individuals who call themselves public relations persons but who are not members of the Institute and hence not subject to its code of conduct and disciplinary procedures. Noting that any individual — however unqualified or unscrupulous — could claim to practice public relations the Institute recommended the *establishment of a statutory register* and described it as follows:

An initial statute would set up a Public Relations Registration Council establishing and maintaining a register of practitioners, together with an educational board to recommend appropriate qualifications, and an admission committee. The normal route to registration could be by membership of the Institute of Public Relations, which has already established standards and discipline. The Institute would have a continuing role both in the composition of the Council and as the representative body for individual practitioners. No doubt the statute would provide for membership of the Council also to include nominees of the Public Relations Consultants' Association and of the Government.

After a stated interval, during which registration would be voluntary, a further statute would prohibit the practice of public relations as a profession by anyone not on the register.

----

from a *Memorandum to the Royal Commission on Standards of Conduct in Public Life*, The Institute of Public Relations, London, England, July 28, 1975

IN SUMMATION: A FEW FINAL WORDS

Whether or not licensing or its alternatives — a grievance panel or a statutory register — becomes a reality, the fact remains that the actions and activities of all those who practice public relations — and this includes non-PRSA as well as PRSA members — ultimately decides the kind of reputation the field will have in the mind of the public. For this reason, as they come to the end of this text, students seeking a career in public relations should recognize that the public view of the public relations field will depend on their personal role and conduct as future professionals. How they handle this role and how they conduct themselves poses a personal challenge to all individuals who practice public relations. This challenge was clearly set forth by an executive who was named in 1974 to *Time* magazine's list of 200 emerging leaders in America. Here, in an article he wrote for the *Public Relations Journal*, is the way Luther Hodges, Jr., chairman of the board of the North Carolina National Bank of Charlotte, N.C., delineated the nature of the role-and-conduct choice for the practitioner and the future of his and her calling:

Let's consider the qualities I look for in a public relations executive. And I must note for the females that my use of the masculine simply refers to all.

I'll begin by describing what the public relations professional is not. He is not a yes man.

If the boss says newspapers are no damn good, the yes man agrees. If the boss says to tell the reporter "no comment," he does so without question or argument. If the boss says let's stonewall it, he does just so . . .

The fate of the yes man is as inevitable as it is painful. Although the boss may think he's the greatest guy in the world for awhile, he's going to lose his internal credibility because he never really states his own opinion — and he's talking to a man who dotes on strong opinions and does not think highly of people who fail to offer them . . .

Nor does the good professional take the other extreme of dis-
agreeing with everything and everybody all the time. The type of
person who does this is the one who forgets that his salary is
being paid by the company he works for — and not the local
newspaper or television station. He forgets that he is hired, after
all, as an advocate for a given business, industry, government
agency or whatever . . .

The really good professional stands somewhere between these
extremes. He realizes that his function is not to run the company, but to provide input to those who do run the company, so
that they can base policy decisions on public relations factors in
addition to all other factors. In this role he often must play the
devil's advocate — and he should.

He has the ability and the knowledge to tell management in advance what the predicted public reaction to a given action or
policy decision will be. He has the ability and knowledge to
make positive suggestions about how to change these actions or
decisions, if necessary; and above all he has the self-confidence
to argue convincingly for his beliefs.

At the same time, this public relations professional is pragmatic
enough to realize that management decisions are based on many
inputs — not just his own — and that his total wishes may not
always be reflected in the final decision. He then has the duty of
supporting that decision — and helping implement it, or, in fact,
of resigning from the company if the decision is one that seriously violates his professional ethics and standards of conduct.

----

from "The New Challenge for Public Relations," by Luther Hodges, Jr., *Public
Relations Journal*, August, 1975

PUBLIC RELATIONS SOCIETY OF AMERICA

DECLARATION OF PRINCIPLES

Members of the Public Relations Society of America acknowledge and
publicly declare that the public relations profession in serving the legitimate interests of clients or employers is dedicated fundamentally to the
goals of better mutual understanding and cooperation among the diverse
individuals, groups, institutions and elements of our modern society.
In the performance of this mission, we pledge ourselves:

1. To conduct ourselves both privately and professionally in accord
   with the public welfare.
2. To be guided in all our activities by the generally accepted standards of truth, accuracy, fair dealing and good taste.
3. To support efforts designed to increase the proficiency of the profession by encouraging the continuous development of sound

training and resourceful education in the practice of public relations.

4. To adhere faithfully to provisions of the duly adopted Code of Professional Standards for the Practice of Public Relations, a copy of which is in the possession of every member.

CODE OF PROFESSIONAL STANDARDS FOR THE PRACTICE OF PUBLIC RELATIONS

This Code of Professional Standards for the Practice of Public Relations is adopted by the Public Relations Society of America to promote and maintain high standards of public service and conduct among its members in order that membership in the Society may be deemed a badge of ethical conduct; that Public Relations justly may be regarded as a profession; that the public may have increasing confidence in its integrity; and that the practice of Public Relations may best serve the public interest.

1. A member has a general duty of fair dealing towards his clients or employers, past and present, his fellow members and the general public.
2. A member shall conduct his professional life in accord with the public welfare.
3. A member has the affirmative duty of adhering to generally accepted standards of accuracy, truth and good taste.
4. A member shall not represent conflicting or competing interests without the express consent of those concerned, given after a full disclosure of the facts; nor shall he place himself in a position where his interest is or may be in confict with his duty to his client, employer, another member or the public, without a full disclosure of such interests to all concerned.
5. A member shall safeguard the confidences of both present and former clients or employers and shall not accept retainers or employment which may involve the disclosure or use of these confidences to the disadvantage or prejudice of such clients or employers.
6. A member shall not engage in any practice which tends to corrupt the integrity of channels of public communication.
7. A member shall not intentionally disseminate false or misleading information and is obligated to use ordinary care to avoid dissemination of false or misleading information.
8. A member shall be prepared to identify to the public the source of any communication for which he is responsible, including the name of the client or employer on whose behalf the communication is made.
9. A member shall not make use of any individual or organization purporting to serve or represent some announced cause, or purporting to be independent or unbiased, but actually serving an undisclosed special or private interest of a member or his client or his employer.

10. A member shall not intentionally injure the professional reputation or practice of another member. However, if a member has evidence that another member has been guilty of unethical, illegal or unfair practices, including practices in violation of this Code, he should present the information to the proper authorities of the Society for action in accordance with the procedure set forth in Article XIII of the Bylaws.
11. A member shall not employ methods tending to be derogatory of another member's client or employer or of the products, business or services of such client or employer.
12. In performing services for a client or employer a member shall not accept fees, commissions or any other valuable consideration in connection with those services from anyone other than his client or employer without the express consent of his client or employer, given after a full disclosure of the facts.
13. A member shall not propose to a prospective client or employer that the amount of his fee or other compensation be contingent on or measured by the achievement of specified results; nor shall he enter into any fee agreement to the same effect.
14. A member shall not encroach upon the professional employment of another member. Where there are two engagements, both must be assured that there is no conflict between them.
15. A member shall, as soon as possible, sever his relations with any organization when he knows or should know that his continued employment would require him to conduct himself contrary to the principles of this Code.
16. A member called as a witness in a proceeding for the enforcement of this Code shall be bound to appear unless, for sufficient reason, he shall be excused by the panel hearing the same.
17. A member shall co-operate with fellow members in upholding and enforcing this Code.

OFFICIAL INTERPRETATIONS OF THE CODE

The following interpretations of Code paragraphs 6, 13 and 14 were adopted by the PRSA Board of Directors on November 6, 1966, and became effective that date.

Interpretation of Code Paragraph 6 which reads, "A member shall not engage in any practice which tends to corrupt the integrity of the channels of public communication."

1. Practices prohibited by this Code paragraph are those which tend to place representatives of media under obligation to the member or his company or his client, such as —
    (a) any form of payment or compensation to a media representative in order to obtain, and in exchange for which, preferential or guaranteed news or editorial coverage in the medium is promised, implied or delivered.
    (b) any retainer of a media employee which involves the use of his position as a media employee for the private purposes of

the member or his client or employer where the circumstances of such retainer are not fully disclosed to and accepted by the media employer.

(c) an agreement between a member and a media employee when such agreement includes a provision that the media employee will secure preferential or guaranteed coverage in the medium for the member, his firm or his client, or utilization by a member of such an agreement between his employer, his firm or his client and a media employee.

(d) providing vacation trips to media representatives where no news assignment is involved.

(e) any attempt by a member to lead his employer or client to believe that a member has obtained independent coverage for the employer or client in a medium over which the member has financial or editorial influence or control.

(f) the use by a member of an investment made by the member, his firm or his client in a medium to obtain preferential or guaranteed coverage in the medium.

(g) the use by a member of a loan of money made to a medium by the member, his firm or his client to obtain preferential or guaranteed coverage in the medium.

2. This Code paragraph does not prohibit entertaining media representatives at meals, cocktails or press parties, nor does it prohibit the bona fide press junket where media representatives are given an opportunity for on-the-spot viewing of a news event or product or service in which the media representative has a legitimate news interest, provided that independence of action is left to the media representative.

3. This Code paragraph does not prohibit the gift or loan of sample products or services to media representatives whose assignments indicate an interest in such products or services, if the sample products or services are manufactured, sold or rendered by the member's company or client and the sampling is a reasonable method of demonstrating the product or service.

4. This Code paragraph does not prohibit the giving of souvenirs or holiday gifts of nominal value as goodwill gestures to media representatives.

Interpretation of Code Pargraph 13 which reads, "A member shall not propose to a prospective client or employer that the amount of his fee or other compensation be contingent on or measured by the achievement of specified results; nor shall he enter into any fee agreement to the same effect."

1. This Code paragraph means that a member may take into consideration the following factors in determining compensation for his services:

(a) the experience, judgment and skills required to handle the matter properly.

(b) the characteristics and difficulty of the problems involved.

    (c) the time and labor required.

    (d) the effect on the member's employment by other clients or potential clients.

    (e) the customary or prevailing compensation for similar services.

    (f) the values involved in the matter and the benefits resulting to the client or employer from the services.

    (g) the duration and character of the employment, whether casual or for a continuing period.

    (h) the equipment or personnel investment required in order to perform the function.

2. This Code paragraph prohibits a member from entering into any agreement whereby the member's rate of compensation is determined or continued by the amount of newspaper or magazine lineage obtained for the member's company or client. This applies equally to radio and television coverage, or any form of exposure to a client's message. It applies further to any contingency fee based on increase in sales volume, increase in profit margins, increase in stock value or the attainment of specified political or legislative results. (See also paragraph 9, "Official Interpretation of the Code as it applies to Financial Public Relations.")

3. This Code paragraph means that a member may guarantee to produce certain materials, such as films, feature articles, scripts, news releases, etc., and promise that these will be of high quality or specific type; but any guarantee that such materials, once produced, shall achieve a specified minimum use by media outlets, in other than paid time or space, and failing which use the fee or compensation will be reduced, is a practice prohibited by this Code paragraph.

Interpretation of Code Paragraph 14 which reads, "A member shall not encroach upon the professional employment of another member. Where there are two engagements, both must be assured that there is no conflict between them."

1. This Code paragraph is not designed to curb the freedom of a member to seek employment or business for his counseling firm by all approved and legitimate means. However, it is interpreted to mean that a member shall not invade or infringe upon the counselor-client or employee-employer relationship of another member.

2. A member would not violate this Code paragraph by —

    (a) sending copies of his resume and examples of his work to protential employers even if the employers currently employ members of the Society.

    (b) advertising his or his firm's qualifications in any publication he deems suitable.

    (c) mailing copies of advertisements, circulars or booklets describing his or his firm's services, or copies of speeches or articles to potential clients, provided any such mailing is not one of solicitation and provided the mailing contains no derogatory comment about another member.

(d) furnishing, upon specific request, factual information about his firm, its principals, personnel and types of services rendered, including names of clients, provided such information contains no proposals to a client of another member.

3. This Code paragraph prohibits a member from seeking individual professional employment by deprecating the character, ability or performance of another member.

4. This Code paragraph requires that a counselor member —

(a) before soliciting a prospective client, make all reasonable attempts to determine whether the prospective client has an existing relationship with another counselor member who would be replaced, and, if so, make no contact until the incumbent has been notified that his replacement is being considered or that the employment of the incumbent has been terminated.

(b) after making an initial contact with a prospective client and subsequently learning that a counselor member-client relationship exists of which he was unaware, shall at that point make no further overtures nor conduct any negotiations with the prospective client until the incumbent has been notified that his replacement is being considered or that the employment of the incumbent has been terminated.

5. Where a member is solicited by a prospective client to take over the functions currently performed by another member, he shall decline to consider the offer until the incumbent member has been advised that a replacement of his services is being considered. Upon specific request, the member may provide information of a factual nature about his firm and its services but shall make no proposals to the client of another member until he has determined that the incumbent has been notified of a possible change.

6. Where a member is solicited by a prospective client to perform functions separate from those currently performed for the same client by another member, it is the responsibility of the solicited member to determine that the incumbent member has been informed, since both must be assured that there is no conflict between the two functions.

AN OFFICIAL INTERPRETATION OF THE PRSA CODE OF PROFESSIONAL STANDARDS FOR THE PRACTICE OF PUBLIC RELATIONS AS IT APPLIES TO FINANCIAL PUBLIC RELATIONS

This interpretation of the Society Code as it applies to financial public relations practice was originally adopted in 1963 and amended in 1972 by action of the PRSA Board of Directors. "Financial public relations" is defined as "that area of public relations which relates to the dissemination of information that affects the understanding of stockholders and investors generally concerning the financial position and prospects of a company, and includes among its objectives the improvement of relations between corporations and their stockholders.'' The interpretation was prepared by the Society's Financial Relations Committee working with the Securities and Exchange Commission and with the advice of the Society's Legal Counsel. It is rooted directly in the Code with the full force of the Code behind it and a violation of any of the following points is subject to the same procedures and penalties as violation of the Code.

1. It is the responsibility of the PRSA member who practices financial public relations to be thoroughly familiar with and understand the rules and regulations of the SEC and the laws which it administers, as well as the other laws, rules and regulations affecting financial public relations — and to act in accordance with their letter and spirit. In carrying out this responsibility, the member shall also seek legal counsel, when appropriate, on matters concerning financial public relations.

2. The member shall adhere to the general policy of making full and timely disclosure of corporate information on behalf of his client or employer. The information disclosed shall be accurate, clear and understandable. The purpose of such disclosure is to provide the investing public with all material information affecting security values or influencing investment decisions. In complying with the duty of full and timely disclosure, the member shall present all material facts, including those adverse to the company. He shall exercise care to ascertain the facts and to disseminate only information which he believes to be accurate. He shall not knowingly omit information, the omission of which might make a release false or misleading. Under no circumstances shall the member participate in any activity designed to mislead, or manipulate the price of a company's securities.

3. The member shall publicly disclose or release information promptly so as to avoid the possibility of any use of the information by any insider or third party. To that end, the member shall make every effort to comply with the spirit and intent of the timely disclosure policies of the stock exchanges, NASD, and the Securities and Exchange Commission. Material information shall be made available to all on an equal basis.

4. The member shall not disclose confidential information the disclosure of which might be adverse to a valid corporate purpose or interest and whose disclosure is not required by the timely disclosure provisions of the law. During any such period of nondisclosure the member shall not directly or indirectly (a) communicate the confidential information to any other person or (b) buy or sell or in any other way deal in the company's securities where the confidential information may materially affect the market for the security when disclosed. Material information shall be disclosed publicly as soon as its confidential status has terminated or the requirement of timely disclosure take effect.

5. During the registration period a member shall not engage in

practices designed to precondition the market for such securities. During registration the issuance of forecasts, projections, predictions about sales and earnings, or opinions concerning security values or other aspects of the future performance of the company, shall be in accordance with current SEC regulations and statements of policy. In the case of companies whose securities are publicly held, the normal flow of factual information to shareholders and the investing public shall continue during the registration period.

6. Where the member has any reason to doubt that projections have an adequate basis in fact, he shall satisfy himself as to the adequacy of the projections prior to disseminating them.

7. Acting in concert with client or employer, the member shall act promptly to correct false or misleading information or rumors concerning his client's or employer's securities or business whenever he has reason to believe such information or rumors are materially affecting investor attitudes.

8. The member shall not issue descriptive materials designed or written in such a fashion as to appear to be, contrary to fact, an independent third party endorsement or recommendation of a company or a security. Whenever the member issues material for a client or employer either in his own name or in the name of someone other than his client or employer, he shall disclose in large type and in a prominent position on the face of the material the source of such material and the existence of the issuer's client or employer relationship.

9. The member shall not use inside information for personal gain. However, this is not intended to prohibit the member from making bona fide investments in his company's or client's securities insofar as he can make such investments without the benefit of material inside information.

10. The member shall not accept compensation which would place him in a position of conflict with his duty to his client, employer or the investing public. Specifically, the member shall not accept a contingent fee nor shall he accept a stock option from his client or employer except as part of an overall plan for corporate employees, nor shall he accept securities as compensation at a price below market price.

11. The member shall act so as to maintain the integrity of channels of public communication. He shall not pay or permit to be paid to any publication or other communications medium any consideration in exchange for publicizing a company, except through clearly recognizable paid advertising.

12. The member shall in general be guided by the PRSA Declaration of Principles and the PRSA Code of Professional Standards for the Practice of Public Relations of which this Code is an official interpretation.

AN OFFICIAL INTERPRETATION OF THE PRSA CODE OF PROFESSIONAL STANDARDS FOR THE PRACTICE OF PUBLIC RELATIONS AS IT APPLIES TO POLITICAL PUBLIC RELATIONS

Adopted by the PRSA Board of Directors
April 3, 1974

Preamble

It is understood that in the practice of political public relations, the PRSA member will have something professional and substantial to offer his employer or client quite apart from the political dynamics of the client circumstance, and that he may serve his employer or client without having attributed to him the character, reputation or beliefs of those he serves.

Definition

"Political Public Relations" is defined as those areas of public relations which relate to:

(a) the counseling of political organizations, committees, candidates or potential candidates for public office; and groups constituted for the purpose of influencing the vote on any ballot issue;

(b) the counseling of holders of public office;

(c) the management, or direction, of a political campaign for or against a candidate for political office; or for or against a ballot issue to be determined by voter approval or rejection;

(d) the practice of public relations on behalf of a client or an employer in connection with that client's or employer's relationships with any candidates or holders of public office with the purpose of influencing legislation or government regulation or treatment of a client or employer, regardless of whether the PRSA member is a recognized lobbyist;

(e) the counseling of government bodies, or segments thereof, either domestic or foreign.

Precepts

1. It is the responsibility of a PRSA member practicing political public relations, as defined above, to be conversant with the various statutes, local, state and federal, governing such activities and to adhere to them strictly. This includes, but is not limited to, the various local, state and federal laws, court decisions and official interpretations governing lobbying, political contributions, elections, libel, slander and the like. In carrying out this responsibility, the member shall seek appropriate counseling whenever necessary.

2. It is also the responsibility of a member to abide by PRSA's Code of Professional Standards and to heed especially, articles 4, 5, 6, 8, 9, 13 and 15.

3. A member shall represent his client or employer in good faith, and while partisan advocacy on behalf of a candidate or public issue may be expected, the member shall act in the public interest and exercise care in adhering to accepted standards of accuracy, truth and good taste.

4. A member shall not issue descriptive material or any advertising or publicity information or participate in the preparation or use thereof which is not signed by responsible persons or is false, misleading or unlabeled as to its source, and is obligated to use care to avoid dissemination of any such material.

5. A member has an obligation to his client to disclose what remuneration beyond his fee he expects to receive as a result of their relationship, such as commissions for media advertising, printing and the like, and should not accept such extra payment without his client's consent.

6. A member's compensation shall not be contingent on, or measured by, the achievement of specified results, nor shall the member improperly use his position to encourage additional future employment or compensation.

7. A member shall voluntarily disclose to his employer or client the identity of other employers or clients with whom he is currently associated and whose interests might be affected favorably or unfavorably by his political representation.

8. A member shall respect the confidentiality of information pertaining to his employer or client even after their relationship ceases.

INDEX